THE POLEMICS OF EXILE IN JEREMIAH 26–45

Scholars typically view Jeremiah 26–45 as a collection of episodes constructed during the Babylonian exile that attempts to prove the authenticity of Jeremiah's prophetic status. But Jeremiah's prophetic legitimacy was already widely accepted during the period of the Babylonian exile. These chapters serve a different purpose, namely, to provide a response by the Deuteronomistic scribes to the rise of the Ezekiel tradition and the Zadokite priesthood that threatened their influence among the exilic population. By subsuming their work within an existing and earlier collection of Jeremianic literature, the ideology and political agenda of the Deuteronomists were fused with the literary legacy of a widely respected prophet, giving rise to a larger literary collection that left a profound and lasting impression on Israel's intellectual and social history.

Mark Leuchter is Lecturer in Biblical Studies at the University of Sydney, Australia. His articles have been published in many journals and edited volumes, and his first book, *Josiah's Reform and Jeremiah's Scroll: Historical Calamity and Prophetic Response*, was published in 2006.

The Polemics of Exile in Jeremiah 26–45

MARK LEUCHTER

CAMBRIDGE
UNIVERSITY PRESS

CAMBRIDGE UNIVERSITY PRESS
Cambridge, New York, Melbourne, Madrid, Cape Town, Singapore, São Paulo, Delhi

Cambridge University Press
32 Avenue of the Americas, New York, NY 10013-2473, USA

www.cambridge.org
Information on this title: www.cambridge.org/9780521879910

First published 2008

Printed in the United States of America

A catalog record for this publication is available from the British Library.

Library of Congress Cataloging in Publication Data

Leuchter, Mark.
The polemics of exile in Jeremiah 26–45 / Mark Leuchter.
p. cm.
Includes bibliographical references and index.
ISBN 978-0-521-87991-0 (hardback)
1. Bible. O.T. Jeremiah XXVI–XLV – Criticism, interpretation, etc. 2. Deuteronomistic history (Biblical criticism) 3. Jeremiah (Biblical prophet) I. Title
BS1525.52.L47 2007
224′.206–dc22 2007000304

ISBN 978-0-521-87991-0 hardback

Contents

Acknowledgments

THIS BOOK BEGAN AS A PAPER PRESENTED AT THE PROPHETIC LITERATURE session of the 2004 International Meeting for the Society of Biblical Literature in Gröningen, the Netherlands. It evolved into its current form because of the contributions of many people. Martti Nissinen, who presided at the session, offered several helpful comments on the paper, which challenged many of my presuppositions, and both Reinhard Kratz and Leo Perdue provided valuable feedback on an earlier version of the manuscript that grew out of the paper. Andy Beck at Cambridge University Press provided an ideal environment in which to develop my thoughts on the subject, and Helen Wheeler, Helen Greenberg, and Duncan Burns were instrumental in helping the book reach its current form. I am grateful to all of them for their support and sensitivity.

I must also thank Peter Machinist and Larry Stager at Harvard University, who invited me to join a seminar on the Book of Jeremiah offered by the Department of Near Eastern Languages and Civilizations. Most of the other participants in the seminar were graduate students in the department who brought fresh insights and approaches to the Jeremianic corpus in its manifold forms. The opportunity to convene regularly with such an erudite group of scholars on a weekly basis provided me with much inspiration while I conducted additional research on the present study.

While preparing the final manuscript, I benefited from the wisdom and work of many trusted colleagues: Hindy Najman, Baruch Halpern, Bernie Levinson, Mark Smith, Gary Rendsburg, Frank Polak, Ben Sommer, Joyce

Rilett Wood, Bill Schniedewind, and David Carr. I must give special thanks to my friends Jeff Geoghegan and Jacob Wright, with whom I spent many hours in conversation on matters related to the Book of Jeremiah and the literature of the seventh–sixth centuries BCE. I hope the present work does justice to their insights. I am also thankful to my loving family for their patience and appreciation of what this work meant to me as I endeavored to complete it.

Finally, I wish to thank Brian Peckham, who supervised my doctoral work at the University of Toronto from 1999 to 2003 and who remains to me a scholarly role model. Brian's unparalleled expertise in biblical studies and ancient Near Eastern civilization is matched by his warmth and congeniality. I was privileged to coedit a Festschrift in his honor and to learn how many other scholars have similarly benefited from his guidance and friendship. He has been a devoted and caring mentor, encouraging me to reexamine the ideas we explored when I was his doctoral student and to try to find new and meaningful ways to understand the text and the world that spawned it. I dedicate this book to him.

Abbreviations

Biblical Books

Gen	Genesis	Hos	Hosea
Exod	Exodus	Amos	Amos
Lev	Leviticus	Macc	Maccabees
Num	Numbers	Mic	Micah
Deut	Deuteronomy	Hag	Haggai
Josh	Joshua	Zech	Zecharia
Judg	Judges	Mal	Malachi
1 Sam	1 Samuel	Ps	Psalms
2 Sam	2 Samuel	Ruth	Ruth
1 Kgs	1 Kings	Ezra	Ezra
2 Kgs	2 Kings	Neh	Nehemiah
Isa	Isaiah	1 Chr	1 Chronicles
Jer	Jeremiah	2 Chr	2 Chronicles
Ezek	Ezekiel		

Apocryphal Books

Sir	Ecclesiasticus/Ben Sira

Rabbinic Works

B.	Babylonian Talmud

Technical Terms

DH	The Deuteronomistic History
LXX	Septuagint
MT	Masoretic Text
OAN	Oracles Against the Nations
P	Priestly tradition

Journals, Commentaries, and Series

AB	Anchor Bible Series
ABD	David Noel Freedman (ed.), *The Anchor Bible Dictionary* (New York: Doubleday, 1992)
AfO	Archiv für Orientforschung
AOAT	*Alter Orient und Altes Testament*
ASTI	*Annual of the Swedish Theological Institute*
BA	*Biblical Archaeologist*
BAR	*Biblical Archaeology Review*
BASOR	*Bulletin of the American Schools of Oriental Research*
BETL	*Bibliotheca ephemeridum theologicarum Lovaniensium*
BJS	Brown Judaic Studies
BR	*Bible Review*
BSA	British School of Archaeology in Iraq
BZ	*Biblische Zeitschrift*
BZAW	Beihefte zur Zeitschrift fur die Alttestamentliche *Wissenschaft*
CBQ	*Catholic Biblical Quarterly*
CBQM	Catholic Biblical Quarterly Monograph Series
CRBS	*Currents in Research: Biblical Studies*
EI	Eretz Israel
FOTL	Forms of Old Testament Literature Series
HAR	*Hebrew Annual Review*
HSM	*Harvard Semitic Monographs*
HTR	*Harvard Theological Review*
HUCA	*Hebrew Union College Annual*
IB	Interpreter's Bible

IDB	G.A. Buttrick (ed.), *The Interpreter's Dictionary of the Bible* (New York/Nashville: Abingdon, 1962)
ICC	International Critical Commentry
IEJ	*Israel Exploration Journal*
IOS	*Israel Oriental Studies*
IOSCS	*International Organization for Septuagint and Cognate Studies*
JAAR	*Journal of the American Academy of Religion*
JANES	*Journal of the Ancient Near Eastern Society*
JAOS	*Journal of the American Oriental Society*
JBL	*Journal of Biblical Literature*
JCS	*Journal of Cuneiform Studies*
JETS	*Journal of the Evangelical Theological Society*
JHS	*Journal of Hebrew Scriptures* (http://purl.org/jhs)
JJS	*Journal of Jewish Studies*
JNES	*Journal of Near Eastern Studies*
JNWSL	*Journal of Northwest Semitic Languages*
JSJ	*Journal for the Study of Judaism*
JSOT	*Journal for the Study of the Old Testament*
JSOTSup	*Journal for the Study of the Old Testament Supplement Series*
JSS	*Journal of Semitic Studies*
JTC	*Journal of Theology and the Church*
OBO	Orbis biblicus et orientalis
OTE	*Old Testament Essays*
OTL	*Old Testament Library*
OTS	*Oudtestamentische Studien*
OTWSA	Ou-Testamentiese Werkgemeenskap van Suid-Afrika
RB	*Revue Biblique*
SAA	*State Archives of Assyria*
SBAB	Stuttgarter biblische Aufsatzbande
SBL	Society of Biblical Literature
SBLD	SBL Dissertation Series
SBLM	SBL Monograph Series
SBLSB	SBL Sources for Biblical Study
SBT	Studies in Biblical Theology

SOFS	Symbolae Osloensis Fasc Supp
TLZ	*Theologische Literaturzeitung*
UF	*Ugarit Furschungen*
VT	*Vetus Testamentum*
VTSup	Vetus Testamentum, Supplements
ZA	*Zeitschrift fur Assyriologie*
ZAW	*Zeitschrift fur die Alttestamentliche Wissenschaft*

Note on Citations

BIBLICAL VERSES CITED IN ENGLISH ARE BASED ON THE JPS TRANSLATION, but they have been altered at the author's discretion when deemed appropriate to better reflect the sense of the Hebrew text.

Introduction

SCHOLARSHIP CONCERNING THE FORMATION OF THE BOOK OF JEREMIAH has, in recent years, undergone a type of renaissance. Whereas earlier approaches to the book and its formation were dominated by strict source-critical models, newer examinations have developed more intricate and advanced methods that in turn yield richer and more detailed results. Though the old source-critical paradigms are still useful in identifying literary genres within the book, they now seem rather limited in scope in terms of understanding the function of textual units, redactional growth, authorial intention, tradition history, and historical background to the Jeremianic tradition.[1] While modern literary criticism has opened new avenues of analysis,[2] interest in compositional and redactional analysis of the book of Jeremiah remains a staple of modern research. Most scholars have viewed the poetry in the book as largely original to the prophet, with the parenetic prose and narrative material constituting redactional additions to a once-independent collection of oracles.[3] Little consensus, though, has arisen concerning the degree to which this redaction preserves the sentiments of the prophet himself.[4] Still, there is general agreement that the book of Jeremiah has much in common with the Deuteronomistic tradition, especially when one considers the similarities in style and tone between Deuteronomy and the Deuteronomistic History (DH) and the parenetic prose and prose narratives in the Jeremianic corpus.[5]

Many have therefore postulated that the book of Jeremiah is the product of a Deuteronomistic redaction, a position most famously championed by W. Thiel.[6] Thiel's work highlights the degree to which the Jeremianic material has been subject to systematic redactions, and has been widely accepted, especially by European scholars, many of whom have offered adjustments to his analysis. T. C. Römer, for example, identifies formalistic elements within the Jeremianic material, including the repetition of stereotyped phrases at strategic points that lead him to conclude that the book went through two stages of redaction, both Deuteronomistic: an early stage that encompassed Jeremiah 7–35 and a subsequent expansion resulting in Jeremiah 1–45.[7] B. Gosse has developed Römer's theory and posited a three-stage redaction of the book.[8] Both Gosse and Römer, however, retain the perspective that the poetic materials derived largely from preexilic tradition associated with the prophet himself. In this sense, both Gosse and Römer maintain the same basic position as Thiel. R. Albertz has recently adjusted this perspective, proposing a far more intricate succession of redactions influenced by a Deuteronomistic movement that arose during the exilic period and persisted into the fifth century BCE under Persia.[9] For Albertz, even major poetic passages reflect the hand of a redactor, influenced largely by the diaspora–homeland tensions that occured first during the exile and later during the period of the Restoration. In this sense, no definitive Jeremianic corpus existed before a sustained, multitiered redactional process systematized and dramatically augmented whatever early and independent traditions had been associated with the prophet Jeremiah. As such, the materials in the book of Jeremiah carry only faint memories of the events of the late seventh and early sixth centuries, reflecting the needs of later communities.

The aforementioned views are helpful in demonstrating the potential for viewing a diversity of literary units within the book but create difficulties in light of observations that already bind Jeremiah to Deuteronomistic tradition in his early oracles. For example, Thiel's conclusions about separate authorship in the prose and poetry in Jeremiah 1–25 do not take into account the heavy reliance upon Deuteronomy already evident in the poetry, nor does he consider the function of early material in the call narrative (Jeremiah 1),[10] the unique features of the Temple

Sermon (Jer 7:1–15), or the colophonic nature of Jeremiah 11.[11] All of these prose passages interact very strongly with the poetry not simply as exegetical accretions but also as organic parts of an original and developmental compositional period, and possess elements that speak more to Jeremiah's authorship than to a later Deuteronomist attempting to bring an unrelated collection of poetry into the Deuteronomistic fold.

The more recent redaction critical analyses just cited also possess difficulties. Römer's model of Jeremiah 1–6 being secondarily added to an initial collection spanning Jeremiah 7–35 does not take into account the reliance of the Temple Sermon on material already found throughout Jeremiah 1–6; the same can be said about Jeremiah 11, which deliberately points back to these early chapters, thereby indicating their extant position as part of the same corpus.[12] By the same token, many of the texts that Albertz views as deriving from postexilic authorship are already used as sources for units that almost all commentators agree upon as exilic in origin, thereby demonstrating that they most likely possess preexilic provenance. As W. M. Schniedewind has recently noted, the similarities between the Masoretic Text (MT) and Septuagint (LXX) versions of Jeremiah 1–25 confirm that these chapters obtained a recognizable form by the beginning of the exile (the point of departure between the communities sustaining these texts), pointing to an extant collection that existed by the beginning of the exile.[13]

Further problems arise with the attempt to view some Jeremianic materials as deriving from the late sixth through fifth centuries BCE. B. D. Sommer's studies of Deutero-Isaiah's relationship to Jeremiah demonstrate conclusively that much of Jeremiah's material already existed in a form that, by the late exilic period, was considered authoritative.[14] This includes passages that are often viewed as part of a Deuteronomistic redaction, as well as poetic units that some redaction critics consider to be late as well. Sommer's observations call into question Albertz's proposed sixth- through fifth-century redactional accretions, which do not account for Deutero-Isaiah's use of much of this material already by ca. 540.[15] B. Halpern has also pointed to the role of certain Jeremianic texts, often viewed by redaction critics as later Deuteronomistic accretions, as influencing important theological concepts in the DH during the exile.[16] For Halpern, the tradition of blaming Manasseh for the failure of the Deuteronomic reform originates in the Jeremianic corpus before the exilic updates to the DH were made.[17] This is a serious problem for any scholar wishing to advocate the view that an independent Jeremianic corpus was simply brought in line with a prevailing Deuteronomistic theology by means of a broad redaction (in one stage or many) emanating from one direction. Finally, D. M. Carr's recent proposal of a Deuteronomistic standard of education-enculturation in the late seventh century can account for similarities between much of the parenetic prose in Jeremiah and that of Deuteronomy and the DH.[18] The historical Jeremiah would have certainly been trained in this method of discourse and would have readily incorporated it into his collection of oracles for rhetorical purposes, merging older modes of prophetic poetry and the contemporaneous methods of parenetic instruction into one comprehensive, multidimensional exhortation.[19]

Despite these difficulties, the aforementioned redaction critics are undoubtedly correct to note that the connection between Jeremiah 1–25 and the chapters that follow is principally the result of exilic shaping and bears witness to ensuing postexilic additions. Such is the well-known position of W. M. McKane, who views the development of the Jeremianic corpus as an ad hoc accumulation of exegetical reflexes.[20] A more recent study by G. Parke-Taylor follows a similar line of thought but looks to the doublets and recurring terms throughout the book as evidence of secondary scribal development.[21] For Parke-Taylor, later scribes expanded their received tradition as needed by relying on terms and phrases already within the corpus. In this way, newer accretions are informed and legitimized through their connection with older material. By the same token, older passages become applicable to new circumstances arising among the audience of the text, creating a more comprehensive tradition. Thus, Parke-Taylor's study adjusts McKane's proposal by suggesting that the rolling corpus theory reflects a more conscious effort on the part of later writers/redactors of the received text but still advocates that many accretions were triggered by extant texts (the issue of identifying and dating these possible accretions will be discussed later).[22] These redactional models highlight apparent tensions within the book as it grew over a centuries-long period of time, with disparate and conflicting political and religious perspectives voiced through the manipulation of terms and ideas in the received tradition.

THE THEORY OF HOMELAND VERSUS *GOLAH* REDACTIONS

The pivotal question in all this is why these scholars perceive such a flurry of activity that is generally characterized as contradictory in nature. As Albertz points out, the primary concern of the exile was the rift that had developed between the *golah* community in Babylon (beginning with the deportees of 597 and later encompassing those taken captive in 587) and those who did not settle in Mesopotamia following the destruction of Jerusalem. Much recent scholarship has been devoted to this matter concerning texts both within Jeremiah 1–25 and in subsequent chapters. C. J. Sharp has recently argued that many important texts throughout the Jeremianic corpus bear witness to two basic arguments: a "pro-*golah*" position reflecting the ideologues of the Babylonian community and a "pro-land" position preserving the voice of those who remained behind.[23] F. Pohlmann and C. R. Seitz both see similar redactional reworking of earlier material within Jeremiah 37–44 reflecting the *golah*-oriented perspective, which for Seitz arises from members of the exilic community in Babylon adjusting traditions in extant texts to represent their interests.[24] These scholars point to tensions within short units of text, highlighting contradictions as evidence of redaction and polemical argumentation as the various Jewish communities sought to identify themselves as the normative community of faith over against the competition. The position they advocate finds support in R. P. Carroll's view that the image of a vacant land in Judah during the exilic period is itself a misleading polemical construct that has wrongly informed scholarly perspectives on the history of the period for too long.[25]

It is impossible to imagine that the experience of the exile did not create rifts between major Jewish communities in the sixth century BCE; the literature of subsequent eras testifies to the distinctiveness of those with an exilic heritage over against those who did not endure deportation to Mesopotamia.[26] This tension would have been resolved only during the days of Ezra and, eventually, the Chronicler, who went to some length to reincorporate potentially marginalized groups back into the sacred community.[27] We must pause, though, before uniformly accepting the passages and fragments identified by Albertz, Sharp, Pohlmann, and Seitz as evidence of this tension *within* the book of Jeremiah. Some cases of apparent contradiction may instead reveal careful successive lemmatic transformation or parametric readjustment akin to the hermeneutical methods of the Deuteronomic scribes.[28] In some cases, texts identified as evidencing an exilic pro-*golah* perspective are better understood as emerging from the prophet's own hand in relation to well-known ancient documents, conceived to set contemporaneous events in a proper historical and political context.[29]

Other apparent cases of contradiction may in fact contribute to the larger rhetoric of the narrative units in the book of Jeremiah.[30] As A. R. P. Diamond has shown, the alternating nature of the relationship between Zedekiah and Jeremiah in Jeremiah 37–38 reflects a tactic of intimidation and persuasion employed by the king, and one that fits the image of a ruler who, on the one hand, emulated Deuteronomic law (and its itinerant regard for prophets) and, on the other, reduced it to an empty and self-serving ritual (Jer 34:8–22). In both cases, Zedekiah's behavior is consistent with problems addressed by the prophet earlier in his career with respect to hypostatization of ideas, rituals, texts, or institutions.[31] This is not to suggest that the characterization of the king in the current form of the text did not arise from disparate traditions. H. J. Stipp and J. Pakkala both present cogent arguments that the Jeremianic text preserves traditions that viewed Zedekiah as legitimate, and Pakkala suggests that this relates to debates about the legitimacy of dynastic succession among the descendants of Josiah.[32] Nevertheless, a close reading of these passages points to a purpose behind their inclusion in the Jeremianic text that goes beyond the preservation of opposing viewpoints. In all likelihood, the favorable traditions concerning Zedekiah that Stipp and Pakkala note did indeed exist, and the Jeremianic material contains echoes of these traditions. Still, the echoes appear in narratives constructed as a counter-argument to these political perspectives. As the present examination will demonstrate, passages that seem more forgiving to Zedekiah that ostensibly arise from some earlier traditions are, in fact, replete with sarcasm and foreboding elements that would not have been lost on an exilic audience and that are rhetorically connected to decidedly negative evaluations of the monarchy as an institution.

In essence, Zedekiah's rebellion against Babylon and his attempts to coerce Jeremiah into supporting an independent Judean community in the homeland stand in diametric opposition to the final tone and message of the Jeremianic text on this matter. While it is certainly likely that a pro-land party between 597 and 587 may have produced propaganda legitimizing their position, it is unlikely that such a party remained in Judah during the Babylonian period and set themselves the task of a careful redaction of Jeremianic texts. While a significant number of people certainly remained in the land, there is little to suggest that they would have been highly literate and capable of skillfully producing a detailed and compelling history involving the person of Jeremiah in what are now the narratives in the Jeremianic corpus.[33] The literati of Judah (notably the priesthood and royal scribes) who could have written these texts would have been among those deported to Babylon in 597 and again in 587, not divided between Babylon and the homeland following Jerusalem's destruction.[34] Despite assertions to the contrary, the devastation brought on by Babylon was severe. Those who remained in the land during the period of Babylonian hegemony may not have been as destitute as the biblical text depicts, but they would have indeed been among the subelite.[35] As O. Lipschits notes, the Babylonian captivity created a rift between Judeans along socioeconomic lines, with the cultural, religious, and political urban elites taken into exile and a large rural class left behind.[36]

It is, to be sure, very possible that narrative and liturgical traditions developed within this community. J. Middlemas's recent study of Lamentations and selected psalms reinforces the perspective that the works reflect a distinctively Judean response to the loss of the Temple (and, quite likely, the hardship of refugee conditions as well) in the years following 587 BCE.[37] However, during this time, and indeed even during the period of 597–587, it is difficult to imagine that *any* remnant group in Judah or eventually Egypt would have chosen Jeremiah as a mouthpiece for its interests. The prophet had already cast his allegiance with the community that settled in Babylon as early as 597, the oracles throughout Jeremiah 1–25 repeatedly look to the rise of Babylon as inevitable and justified, and the brief accretions identified by some scholars as evidence of a pro-land perspective do not eclipse the general criticism in these chapters of the post-597 homeland community.[38] At least with respect to Jeremiah 1–25, which had already obtained a discernible form by 587, it is unlikely that the Jeremianic literature received much redaction from a community in Judah following the destruction of Jerusalem.[39] Indeed, the only community that would have possessed figures capable of such literary activity was the small group associated with Gedaliah b. Ahikam, but Gedaliah's tenure was too short and tenuous to allow for dramatic reworking of the prophet's earlier oracles, and would hardly have produced a pro-land propagandistic collection that stood against the *golah*-group.[40] Politically speaking, a pro-Babylonian group led by Gedaliah would not have engaged in such an enterprise, as Jeremiah's extant oracles would have served only to legitimize the political status quo following the Babylonian destruction of Jerusalem. And though it is likely that the later community under Babylonian administration in Judah did possess literate officials,[41] there is no indication that they would have been members of the Shaphanide circle, contributors to the Deuteronomistic literary tradition, or adherents to its ideology.[42]

A central question here concerns the Deuteronomistic tones within the book that so often characterize redactional seams and flourishes: for how long can we postulate a Deuteronomistic school or movement beyond the life of the prophet? And if we view a variety of redactional hands with opposing viewpoints at work in the redaction of the book, how may we define them as part of a coherent Deuteronomistic tradition?[43]

JEREMIAH THE PROPHET AND THE DEUTERONOMISTIC TRADITION

In a previous study, I supported the views of other scholars such as R. E. Friedman, M. A. Sweeney, J. A. Dearman, and J. R. Lundbom, who see a strong connection between the historical Jeremiah and the Deuteronomistic tradition circle.[44] In that study, I argued that Jeremiah was selected to be a prophet because in part of his own training as a Deuteronomistic scribe, and his allegiance with the Shaphanide scribal circle (the likely authors of the Deuteronomistic literature) characterized his early activity and persisted throughout his career.[45] The detailed rhetorical studies of Lundbom in particular demonstrate that stylistic/rhetorical commonalities typical of the Deuteronomistic literature permeate the various genres of text one encounters in the book of Jeremiah, arguing for common authorship in many cases in the poetic and prose oracles.[46] While some of the prose may well arise from a redaction of earlier texts, this redaction is often better viewed as arising from the prophet himself than from an unrelated subsequent scribe, and the redactional material is often thematically and lexically consistent with the older texts.[47] In both cases, great similarities obtain between Deuteronomistic and Jeremianic compositions.

What reinforces the genetic connection between the Jeremiah and Deuteronomistic collections is that when we consider the polemics of contemporaneous circles of literati who stood against the prophet and his Shaphanide scribal peers, we encounter vastly different lexical, theological, and rhetorical modes of discourse.[48] If the stylistic differences during this period are any indication, then distinctively Deuteronomistic language would not have been used by groups who stood against Jeremiah or the Shaphanides; they would have drawn from a countertradition of lexemes and ideas.[49] Since stylistic continuity characterizes subsequent Deuteronomistic redactional activity that many scholars view as exilic in provenance, this further questions the viability of the homeland/*golah* model of redaction discussed earlier, as the accretions that advocates of that model view as contradictory in nature are generally expressed within a stylistic continuum.

What, then, of those scholars who are skeptical of ascribing Deuteronomistic literature to writers living during Josiah's reign and continuing during the exile? Following Albertz, many scholars have viewed the Deuteronomistic style of composition as characteristic of a single group, but one that persisted for generations well into the Persian period.[50] As such, there has developed a reticence to view the narratives of 2 Kings 22–23 or the parenetic prose in Jeremiah as viable sources for historical information or evidence of thought current in the late seventh through early sixth centuries BCE.[51] Here, linguistic considerations are of enormous help. The pioneering work of F. H. Polak has revealed objective criteria for dating biblical narratives. In a number of detailed examinations, Polak demonstrates that the style of composition evolves from the "lean" or "rhythmic-verbal" style of earlier narratives to the "dense" or "complex-nominal" style of narratives that date from the late eighth century on.[52] The first category (lean) generally involves short clauses with limited noun groups and emulates the tradition of oral literature characteristic of a preliterate society. They may be found throughout much of the Pentateuchal patriarchal narratives as well as the narratives in the books of Samuel and Kings that are generally regarded as pre-Deuteronomistic sources dating from before the mid-eighth century BCE.[53]

Polak's second category (dense) involves material conceived in a milieu strongly influenced by the neo-Assyrian, Babylonian, and Persian scribal chancery and involves long, ornate clauses, a higher frequency of subordinate or embedded clauses (complex hypotaxis), and longer noun groups.[54] These narratives are also characterized by certain sociolinguistic features such as a presupposition of increased literacy, education, written law codes, and other authoritative written texts that go largely unmentioned in the lean texts of the earlier period.[55] Though these features are common to texts from the late seventh through mid-fourth centuries BCE, Polak identifies an increase in complex hypotaxis and length in noun groups in documents set in the Persian period, reflecting the degree to which the Persian administrative infrastructure had come to dominate the compositional consciousness of the biblical writers.[56] Finally, the stylistic differences in Persian-period texts and those set in the neo-Assyrian and Babylonian periods is not a matter of personal preference on the part of the writer: Persian-period writers rarely reengage the less complex style of texts from the neo-Assyrian or Babylonian periods, just as the writers of those periods do not reengage the style of the earlier, lean compositions that emulates oral modes of composition.[57]

All of this is highly significant for our present inquiry. The narratives of 2 Kings 22–23 and other distinctively Deuteronomistic texts should not, on linguistic grounds, be dated later than the period of the exile in their final form; the linguistic style is characteristic of the late seventh to mid-sixth centuries BCE and shows the influence of Assyrian and Babylonian scribal norms. We must be cautious in viewing these materials as historically accurate at face value, but their temporal proximity to the events they overtly depict (or, in the case of Deuteronomy, to which they allude) means that they can be mined for historically relevant information concerning the ideological trends of the time. Consequently, the stylistic/thematic connection between this literature and the oracles of Jeremiah greatly increases the likelihood that Jeremiah 1–25, in large part, is also a product of the same general period. We are therefore justified in viewing the Deuteronomistic valences in the book of Jeremiah as arising from the prophet's own engagement of that tradition, his closeness to those who generated the DH in its preexilic form, and the ongoing development of the prophet's literary legacy by those strongly connected to both.

JEREMIAH 26–45: AN EXILIC "SUPPLEMENT" TO THE JEREMIANIC CORPUS

If Jeremiah 1–25 constituted a recognizable form of Jeremianic literature by the beginning of the exile, and if it contained few (if any) redactional accretions from a homeland group, how does this affect our understanding of the next major unit of tradition within the Jeremianic corpus, namely,

Jeremiah 26–45 (henceforth, the "Supplement")? As discussed previously, many scholars see various dimensions of authorship within these chapters, and it is clear that the Supplement evidences much redactional activity. Several passages are based on archival and annalistic material, as well as oracles and epistles that were once part of earlier and independent collections or archives.[58] As per our observations regarding chs. 1–25, however, we should not view a significant amount of material in the Supplement as arising from a homeland group that was only secondarily redacted by Judean scribes in Babylon. The Mizpah community under Gedaliah may have possessed the abilities, experience, and motivation to compile certain literary materials, but as discussed previously, authorship of the Supplement en masse cannot have come from this community.[59] Indeed, the narratives in the Supplement go on to discuss the dissolution of this community and the retreat of its survivors into Egypt (Jeremiah 41–44). The thematic tensions some scholars see within these narratives that are sometimes cited as evidence of homeland versus *golah* redactions are actually well integrated into the overriding theme and purpose of the Supplement and reflect a careful, coherent design.[60]

The question of authorship and purpose in the Supplement is therefore somewhat addressed, as it seems doubtful that the material therein reflects the interests of a homeland group vying for legitimacy over against those Judeans led away to Babylon. This makes it far more likely that the Supplement was shaped by members of the literati living in Babylon, or at least by someone with strong ideological sympathies to that group. Certainly, the literary style of the narrative material is extremely close to that of the DH, which had obtained its penultimate form during Josiah's reign and had been written/redacted by the Shaphanide scribal group that was later deported to Babylon in 597 BCE.[61] At the same time, the Supplement concerns itself almost exclusively with the homeland community in the twilight of the Judean monarchy and ultimately with the Egyptian fate of that group. The only real mention of life in Babylon is restricted to texts addressed to the small group of captives taken in the deportation of 597 (Jeremiah 27–29), and these texts had been composed at an earlier time, in no small part by Jeremiah himself.[62] With such an emphasis on the Judean remnant that eventually fled to Egypt, could the Supplement have been drafted by an individual or a group closely tied to the Shaphanide scribes in Babylon who never endured these specific experiences?

DATING THE CONSTRUCTION OF THE SUPPLEMENT

R. C. Steiner has followed Friedman's position that the circle of authorship involving both the DH and Jeremiah remained fairly small and, indeed, nepotistic.[63] Steiner suggests that Baruch b. Neriah may be identified as the author of the Supplement and the scribe who introduced it to the Jeremianic tradition, yielding the LXX sequence, with his brother Seraiah inheriting this earlier work and rearranging/updating it to form the early version of the MT.[64] Developing Lundbom's study of colophons in the book of Jeremiah, Steiner suggests that the colophonic formulae associated with Baruch (Jeremiah 45) and Seraiah (Jer 51:59–64) indicate each scribe's authorship or editorship.[65] These colophons certainly demand our attention, as they would have resonated at a powerful symbolic frequency to an ancient reader familiar with scribal convention. They also carry forward a hermeneutical impulse already found in texts attributable directly to Jeremiah, as the *Urrolle* was initially concluded with the prophet's own colophonic signature (Jeremiah 11).[66] As will be demonstrated in the present study, the function of the colophons associated respectively with Baruch and Seraiah should not be associated with the production of the "editions" of Jeremiah represented by the LXX and MT traditions. Still, the persistent presence and use of colophons in the book of Jeremiah suggest common strategies for the various writers who stand behind them and not an ad hoc accumulation of text with little deliberate orchestration.

A linguistic analysis is also significant in proposing a period of authorship and, provisionally, a circle of authorship. As has been noted briefly, Albertz and Pohlmann argue that many narrative passages in the Supplement reflect Persian-era composition, a period that other scholars view as a likely historical background.[67] The linguistic features of these narratives, however, suggest that this is unlikely. Polak's analyses group the narratives in the Supplement in the same category as those in the Deuteronomistic literature from stylistic, syntactical, and sociolinguistic perspectives.[68] In contrast to models that posit a centuries-long period of composition, on the one hand, or a single but late period of composition, on the other, Polak's findings point to a specific and limited period of composition behind the Supplement's narratives, composed by the middle of the sixth century BCE and (agreeing with Friedman, Dearman, Lundbom, and others) by a limited group of writers.

Relevant here is the observation of A. Van Selms that the Jeremianic materials evidence a stylistic device he terms "telescoped discussion."[69] According to Van Selms, several parenetic passages concentrate and project a sequence of dialogical events into a single oracle placed in the prophet's mouth. To be sure, this reflects a subsequent shaping of the prophet's oracles, a position advocated by many scholars. Yet, according to Van Selms, two important elements must be recognized: first, that the material telescoped into the prophet's own discourse presupposes that the telescoped sentiments are completely consistent with those of Jeremiah himself, and second, that the literary device of telescoped discussion *occurs nowhere else in any other prophetic oracles but is unique to the Jeremianic material.*[70] As the present study will demonstrate, the features of telescoped discussion may be found in Supplemental passages not analyzed by Van Selms and further point to a limited circle of authorship behind these texts.

A potential argument against this position can be found in the recent and very thorough study by Lipschits on the history and historiography concerning the fall of Jerusalem. Lipschits devotes considerable attention to the redaction of what he terms the "biography" of the prophet in Jeremiah 37–44 and identifies a variety of sources that were eventually worked into the macrostructure of the narrative.[71] Within this narrative, Lipschits categorizes a variety of passages as emerging over two generations living in exile in Babylon, and views the apparent factual contradictions and thematic variances as evidence of different source traditions finding their way into the developing Jeremianic corpus over time.[72] For Lipschits, a significant indication of disparate redactional units is the shift in location and characterization. A similar position is advocated by M. Roncace, who sees a unit spanning Jer 37:1–40:6 distinct from Jer 40:7–41:18 based on the shift from Jeremiah to Gedaliah as the main character of the narrative.[73]

The positions of Lipschits and Roncace demonstrate the many important emphases of the narrative of Jeremiah 37–44 and certain shifts in the focus of the material; in the case of Lipschits, the argument that these shifts arise from different narrative traditions provides a logical explanation of their presence in the text. But this does not necessarily point to successive waves of redaction during subsequent exilic generations, as Lipschits suggests. The variety of sources in the Supplement function similarly to those in the preexilic DH, with the redactors positioning themselves as mediators of disparate traditions.[74] The result is a narrative that addresses a variety of audiences through the rhetoric of inclusion, and it is notable that this same rhetorical strategy may be found elsewhere in the Supplement beyond the narratives of Jeremiah 37–44.[75] The author of the Supplement was concerned with two different audiences living in Babylon: those taken captive in 597 BCE and those brought into the region in successive captivities (587, 582).[76] It is natural that some of these communities would have developed and preserved different versions of tales regarding Jeremiah's activity in the final years of the monarchy; the lexical similarities identified by Lipschits reveal the desire to redact these differing viewpoints into a single comprehensive narrative that spoke to a broader and more diverse audience living in exile.[77] Indeed, the placement of Jeremiah 36 and 37 in series establishes hermeneutical connections between the contents of the two chapters that would strengthen the relationship between the audiences that went into captivity at different times and as a consequence of the policies of both Jehoiakim and Zedekiah.[78]

With regard to the shift in narrative emphasis from Jeremiah to Gedaliah, the positions of Lipschits and Roncace are legitimate but in need of adjustment. It is true that following Jer 40:6, the prophet takes a back seat to Gedaliah and resurfaces only after the latter is assassinated. This may well speak to the emphases of the different original and independent traditions that were worked into the Supplement, but again, it does not require an identification of separate redactional strata. Similar shifts occur in both Jeremiah 26 and 36. In the latter, the prophet fades from view for most of the narrative, appearing only at the beginning and end of the chapter. In the former, the second half of the narrative focuses on the elders and the citation of Micah (vv. 17–19) and then on the episode involving Uriah b. Shemaiah (vv. 20–23), with little direct emphasis on Jeremiah. Despite these shifts, these chapters are very carefully structured and possess specific rhetorical mandates that unify these passages. As will be discussed in Chapters 4 and 5 of this study, a similar mandate underlies the shift in emphasis from Jeremiah to Gedaliah and then the return to Jeremiah within the narrative of Jeremiah 37–44, with the development of an idea that seeks to establish a particular connection between the prophet and the Shaphanide administrator selected by the Babylonians to lead the community in the land.

A persistent thematic design binds Jeremiah chs. 26–36 to chs. 37–44 and, indeed, ch. 45. The framing function of Jeremiah 36–45 identified by Roncace is also in operation with respect to Jeremiah 26–36: the intervening material in both groups is qualified by these framing chapters in similar ways and repeatedly addresses similar specific issues regarding scribal authority and these same scribes as legitimate bearers of Jeremiah's prophetic legacy. Moreover, Jeremiah 26 and 44 both make clear allusions to Jeremiah 7, creating a rhetorical and intertextual envelope around the narrative complex spanning the intervening chapters.[79] Finally, Jeremiah 26, 36, and 45 all deal with the matter of foreign nations (cf. Jer 26:6; 36:2; 45:1, 5),[80] not only addressing the eventual dominance of Babylon but also connecting the materials in the Supplement to the Oracles Against the Nations (OAN). Despite surface discrepancies, Jeremiah 26–45 emerges as a single block of material with well-integrated component parts and a consistent ideological trajectory.

The convergence of Deuteronomistic themes, rhetoric, linguistic style, and unique literary devices strongly suggests that a limited group of scribes is responsible for the Supplement's narratives (for the sake of convenience, we will simply use the term "author" in reference to this group).[81] This author recognized the inherently Deuteronomistic character of Jeremiah 1–25 and was for some reason moved to construct the Supplement as an addendum to that work. It is therefore not surprising that the narratives of the Supplement emulate the style of the preexilic DH[82] and that the Supplement's redactional reflexes have much in common with the methods of the Jerusalem scribes responsible for the Deuteronomistic literature.[83] Citation, lemmatic transformation, and hermeneutical literary sequencing are all employed to a dramatic extent throughout the Supplement.[84] The author of the Supplement thus reveals himself to be both a scribe of Deuteronomistic pedigree akin to the Shaphanides and a follower of Jeremiah with access to an archive of material relating to Jeremiah's activity that served as the major source for the Supplement's composition.[85] Subsequent accretions within and beyond the Supplement are sparse and are based upon it as a prototypical work.[86] With a limited circle of authorship, the Supplement's composition can be dated to a limited period of time; Y. Hoffman has presented a strong argument for a date around the year 570 BCE, and the ensuing discussion in the present study will support this basic position.[87]

THE SUPPLEMENT IN THE TEXTUAL VARIANTS OF JEREMIAH AND IN HISTORICAL CONTEXT

If we may be confident about assigning the basic form of the Supplement to singular authorship (be it an individual or a small group) and the affiliation of that authorship to an extant Jeremianic-Deuteronomistic tradition, we are still faced with two very pressing questions. The first deals with the place of the Supplement within the two major versions of the book of Jeremiah (the MT and LXX). Research on the relationship between these two traditions has been one of the most lively avenues of Jeremiah scholarship in recent decades, especially in relation to the variant versions of Jeremiah discovered at Qumran. The basic position of most scholars is that the LXX represents an older and more authentic edition of the book of Jeremiah, one that was subsequently expanded to form the MT.[88] The most vocal proponent of this view has been E. Tov, whose programmatic 1981 study of the two traditions revealed accretions both minute and expansive in the MT that are absent from the LXX (which is a full one-seventh shorter than the MT).[89] Tov's position that the MT texts under consideration represent subsequent additions is in all likelihood correct. Lundbom's recent Anchor Bible commentaries on Jeremiah point to haplography as the main reason why many of these passages are missing from the LXX, while others have suggested that they were deliberately left out. While this may account for some discrepancies, the majority of instances are better explained as secondary additions to an older *Vorlage* or, possibly, to a similar but alternate collection of texts.[90]

A different perspective is offered by A. Rofé, who argues for the priority of the MT based on the place of the OAN in his structural analysis.[91] Rofé notes that the *inclusio* or "ring" structure of the MT is inspired by the rhetorical trends of the seventh–sixth centuries BCE and identifies distinct units marked by *inclusios* in the MT that are disrupted by the LXX sequence. While Rofé is correct to note the pervasive nature of this rhetorical device (something that Lundbom has also noted) and its dominance in the MT, counterpoints involving the same rhetorical devices challenge the force of his argument. For example, Rofé views Jeremiah 25 as part of a structural unit independent of Jeremiah 1–24 based on its dated superscription, which, he argues, places it within the same structural unit as Jeremiah 26, 27, and so on (all of which employ dated superscriptions).[92] He does not, however, consider the similarities between Jer 25:1–3 and Jer 1:2, in part because he does not consider Jer 1:2 as original to the opening chapter and thus forming an *inclusio* with Jer 25:1–3. Jer 1:2 may in fact be seen as an early text and indeed as part of the *Urrolle* of 605–604.[93] If this is so, then an *inclusio* is formed with Jer 1:2–25:1–3, disrupting Rofé's proposed arrangement. Rofé also views Jeremiah 27–29 as Deuteronomistic in origin, but as mentioned earlier, these chapters are largely attributable to the prophet and to his immediate tradition circle and date from 597–593.[94] Furthermore, Rofé's proposed fifth-century dating for the compilation of the book is compromised by Sommer's analyses, which demonstrate reliance upon key passages already in the mid-sixth century.[95] Thus, while there is much merit in Rofé's conclusions concerning the nature of the MT sequence, his methodology in identifying structural units within the book should be reevaluated.

Sharp has offered a different conclusion based on her study of the OAN collections in the MT versus LXX: the expansions may be secondary in the MT, but the MT may also have arisen from a text source different from that which became the LXX.[96] Sharp's study raises an important question: at what point in the growth of the book of Jeremiah do we find major *compositional* (not just editorial) variants? The sociopolitical circumstances of the prophet's lifetime, coupled with the nature of the scribal process, make it entirely likely that the major compositional variants obtained at an early point in time. The dispersion of communities into Mesopotamia, Egypt, and Ammon at different times and the generation of new literary collections based on older prototypes would provide an environment where different authentic Jeremianic collections would have been preserved.[97] Influence on the growth of these different collections would certainly have arisen from cultural interchange during the sixth century BCE, with certain traditions emerging as more influential than others in subsequent periods.[98] The terminological similarities, on the one hand, and significant variants between these traditions, on the other, would no doubt be facilitated by the recounting and rewriting of certain texts from memory, a common practice among ancient scribes, as demonstrated by Carr.[99] It is thus impossible to identify an original *Vorlage* for the book of Jeremiah en masse; it is better to look to the extant versions currently in our position as repositories of different collections and try to determine the forces that led to the variants we find within them.

The greatest of these variants is obviously the position of the Supplement in either tradition. In the MT, the Supplement intervenes between Jeremiah 25 and the OAN; in the LXX, it commences after the OAN come to a close. The MT of Jeremiah 25 clearly has undergone a major redactional expansion, insofar as the verses subsequent to Jer 25:13a (which anticipates the OAN) do not occur in the LXX version of that chapter. Many therefore adopt the position that the larger MT sequence is secondary and that the Supplement found its initial place in the LXX tradition; such are the implications of Steiner's and Lundbom's analyses.[100] Yet, there is a large amount of evidence within the Supplement to suggest that the MT sequence provides a better background for its initial inclusion. Seitz, for example, has already suggested this with respect to the redactional purpose of Jeremiah 45 as a bridge to the OAN,[101] and the ensuing examination herein will address this matter beyond strictly redactional considerations.[102] To state the question simply: which version, the MT or the LXX, represents the original *Sitz* of the Supplement once its author bound it to his received Jeremianic corpus?

The second question, perhaps even more pressing than the position of the Supplement in the MT or the LXX, is, why was the Supplement even written? Many scholars have suggested that the Supplement attempts to prove that Jeremiah was a true prophet,[103] but we must ask if there was any pressing need to do so. Whereas the exilic edition of the DH updates a collection of Josianic literature that did not anticipate and could not account for the destruction of Jerusalem and the deportation of its population, Jeremiah's preexilic oracles very clearly anticipate the dominance of Babylon and indeed predict the destruction of Jerusalem.[104] With the fall of Jerusalem and the exile of its citizens, Jeremiah's persistent preexilic message was completely vindicated. The prophetic voices against which Jeremiah contended before 587 BCE would have lost their audience as history proved their perspective to be obsolete, and Jeremiah's oracles would have been intensely studied, debated, and applied in the years following 587. Why did the author of the Supplement therefore feel the need to construct an entire second part to the Jeremianic corpus of his day, replete with authentic Jeremianic oracles, if there was no need to champion or defend Jeremiah's prophetic validity?

Here, the previously discussed position concerning the date of the Supplement's composition to ca. 570 BCE is crucial. There is to be no doubt that the text of the Jeremianic corpus contains an abundance of literary features and ideas that need not be anchored to a specific period or circle of authorship, and many important investigations of the text-as-literature have demonstrated the value of such an approach. Nevertheless, the Jeremianic tradition is a rich source of historical information that may be used to gain insight into critical moments in the evolution of biblical literature and Israelite concepts of communal identity and even shifting understandings of ethnicity.[105] If we wish to determine the motivation for the authorship of the Supplement, it is essential to place the author within a sequence of historical events and identify responses in his composition to the historical circumstances surrounding him. The foregoing discussion concerning linguistic, rhetorical, and stylistic features attempts to clarify certain fundamental understandings of the social and political worlds in which the author of the Supplement operated. In order to answer the aforementioned question concerning *why* he wrote the Supplement, historical considerations cannot be divorced from literary examinations.

The point of departure for the present study, as previously suggested, is the basic historicity of Josiah's reform and its sociopolitical echoes, however much the narrative of 2 Kings 22–23 may be informed by an ideological bent. Just as there is sufficient reason for many scholars to question the accuracy of this narrative,[106] there is similar reason to question the accuracy of the narratives in the Jeremianic Supplement. All ancient historiography, however, bears the mark of bias and agenda, and an immediate dismissal of its historical worth precludes any potentially useful investigation. The same impulses that drive scholars to examine these historical sources should legitimize our efforts to place the Supplement within an historical context. Z. Kallai summarizes the issue succinctly:

> Whereas the details of a historiographical description may be a literary elaboration, based on a general historical notion or motif, and not necessarily on concrete historical data, a general historical concept, and particularly one that creates a historigraphical pattern, is most likely to be based on an experienced history. There is, therefore, a certain gradation of historical veracity in historiographical compositions that accords patterns a marked degree of historicity. The rationale which I have repeatedly invoked was that any description in that category depicting specific circumstances must reflect a known situation that engendered it, serving as its model.[107]

Kallai's remarks are made in relation to geographic patterns and territorial descriptions within a variety of texts from disparate periods, but they apply in equal measure to the mode of discourse in the narratives associated with Josiah's court and the Supplement currently under consideration. In both cases, the literary events shaped by the biases of the respective authors convey information about the experience of those same authors. The foregoing discussion suggests that in the case of the Supplement, the narratives reflect events proximate to the author's own compositional activity. If this is accepted, then we are in a privileged position to discern the relationship between what M. Fishbane calls the *Traditum* and *Traditio*, the content inherited by the author and the manner in which he transmitted that content, adding his own historical and ideological biases.[108] Pursuant to Kallai's observations, and against those scholars who view secondary agendas as a corrupting force in the recovery of history within the book of Jeremiah, both the inherited content *and* the manner of biased transmission may shed light on the real-world forces that moved the author to compose the Supplement.

The present study evaluates the aforementioned concerns as refracted through the literary topography of the Supplement. Chapter 1 provides an analysis of Jeremiah 26, which is often viewed either as the historical context for the Temple Sermon in Jer 7:1–15 or as a redactional parallel to that passage.[109] There is good reason to adopt both perspectives to a certain degree, but we will see that Jeremiah 26 concentrates a good deal of history and text beyond that represented by the Temple Sermon and does much more than offer an historical context for the prophet's delivery of that exhortation. Chapter 2 discusses the composition of Jeremiah 27–29 and the manner in which the author worked this older literary collection into the Supplement alongside Jeremiah 30–31. Both of these units were shaped by Jeremiah himself but were addressed to the 597 BCE community.[110] The author of the Supplement groups them together to reflect this, but appends the episode of Jer 32:6–15 (which takes place in 587) to allow these earlier materials to speak to later audiences and to convey a message regarding the scribe's role in facilitating this exchange.[111] (The remainder of Jeremiah

32 and all of Jeremiah 33 are viewed in the present study as arising from subsequent additions to the Supplement and are discussed in an excursus and in the concluding chapter.)

Chapter 3 addresses Jeremiah 34–36. These chapters are not often grouped together, but they constitute an important literary unit that provides a transition from the relative benevolence of Jer 27–32:15 to the condemnatory themes of Jeremiah 37–44.[112] These chapters once again point to the importance of the scribes in facilitating prophecy (both in terms of the arrangement of Jeremiah 34–36 and the narrative contents of Jeremiah 36 specifically). Chapter 4 provides an evaluation of Jeremiah 37–44, which reflect the author's desire to provide the final word on those who refused to submit not only to Babylon but also to Jeremiah and the Shaphanide scribes chosen to be Babylon's Judean representatives. The chapter also considers the significance of Jeremiah 45 as both a statement on the sacral role of scribes and a redactional feature marking the end of the Supplement. Chapter 5 proposes an historical and sociological background to the composition of the Supplement and discusses what the author hoped to accomplish by attaching it to the extant Jeremianic corpus of his day; it also suggests a new way to evaluate the relationship between the MT and LXX versions of Jeremiah. Chapter 6 proposes some ways that we may view the Supplement as a window into the role of Levites during the exile and the manner in which the author appealed to this group. The Conclusion provides some insights into the scope and development of the Deuteronomistic tradition and proposes how the Supplement influenced subsequent scribal accretions and ultimately established the methodological paradigm for early Jewish exegesis.

Throughout this study, the author of the Supplement will be periodically referred to as the author of a particular chapter, unit, or verse for purposes of contextual clarity. The normative collection of Jeremianic oracles at any particular point of development will be frequently referred to as the "active corpus" in distinction from the archive (or archives) of traditions wherein certain texts were deposited, later to be included or developed further. The names "Nebuchadnezzar" and "Nebuchadrezzar" will be used interchangeably, depending on the biblical text under consideration where either name appears. The OAN will not be engaged in detail throughout this study, nor will extensive analysis be applied to the majority of materials in Jeremiah 1–25. Discussion will be limited to the Supplement itself, with external texts (Jeremianic and otherwise) brought in for purposes of comparison.

CHAPTER 1

The Hermeneutics of Citation: Jeremiah 26

JEREMIAH 26 IS MOST COMMONLY VIEWED AS A NARRATIVE PARALLEL TO the Temple Sermon (Jer 7:1–15), providing a plausible historical background to the prophet's delivery of the famous critique of the Temple cult.[1] The connection between the Temple Sermon and Jeremiah 26 is rather overt: the language and ideas of the former surface at the outset of the latter as a citation (Jer 26:4–6), demonstrating the author's belief in the centrality of the Temple Sermon to the prophet's career and message. Yet, a mere summary would have been redundant: the author's reliance on the Temple Sermon tells us that it was already well known to his exilic audience and (given its contents) central to exilic consciousness. In this respect, we must reconsider the context of the citation and the function of the chapter. Broadly speaking, Jeremiah 26 appears less concerned with the prophet himself than with the forces surrounding him. The people who hear his words seize him (vv. 8–9), the priests/prophets of the Temple prosecute him (v. 11), the royal officials decide his fate (v. 16), a representative of the scribal class saves him from reprisal (v. 24), and the chapter opens and closes with references to King Jehoiakim (vv. 1, 20–23). In short, the chapter is not about the prophet, but about the society of Jerusalem in the twilight years of the Judean monarchy. We must therefore determine if the author's citation of the Temple Sermon has been geared to advance a new theological concept that differentiated between the preexilic audience of the Temple Sermon and the exilic audience of Jeremiah 26.[2]

THE CITATION OF THE TEMPLE SERMON (JEREMIAH 26:4–6)

Instructive in this regard is a consideration of the actual citation found in Jer 26:4–6:

> And you shall say to them "Thus says YHWH: If you do not listen to me and walk in my Torah that I have set before you, to listen to the words of my servants the prophets who I send you, having sent them from early on, but you have not listened . . . then I will make this house like Shiloh, and this city a curse to all the nations of the Earth."

It is immediately apparent that much has changed from the Temple Sermon to its citation in vv. 4–6. Certain terms and ideas are retained, but they have been altered (e.g., YHWH has sent the *prophets* "from early on"; cf. Jer 7:13, where YHWH has *spoken* "from early on"). [3] Other features have either been newly added (such as the reference to "this city," i.e., Jerusalem, or the overt reference to a Torah) or completely muted (the conditional elements of Jer 7:3–7 and the שכן terminology found therein).[4] Beyond the most general purpose and tone of the passage, the reference to Shiloh and its association with the Temple appear to be all that remains from the original Sermon. This is a rather dramatic shift given the introduction to the citation that we encounter in Jer 26:2:

> Thus says YHWH: Stand in the court (חצר) of YHWH's house, and speak (ודברת) to all the cities of Judah which come to worship in YHWH's house all the words (כל הדברים) that I command thee to speak unto them; diminish not a word (אל תגרע דבר).

This contrasts sharply with the introduction to the Temple Sermon we find in Jer 7:2:

> Stand in the gate (שער) of YHWH's house, and proclaim (וקראת) there this word (הדבר הזה), and say: Hear the word (דבר) of YHWH, all you of Judah that enter in at these gates to worship the YHWH.[5]

The author of Jeremiah 26 has crafted his introduction after that of Jer 7:2 but has deliberately changed several key words and phrases. Jeremiah no longer stands in the gate of YHWH's house but rather in the court;

he is not to speak simply to those in earshot in the Temple but to the larger population served by that Temple. More significantly, the author has placed an increased emphasis on the דבר terminology, changing Jeremiah's proclamation of YHWH's message (וקראת in Jer 7:2) into a דבר-centric method of communication (ודברת in Jer 26:2).

This particular lexical shift warrants close attention, for the replacement of וקראת with ודברת alters Jeremiah's message within Jer 26:2 from *logos* to *mythos*. The term דבר is less defined than קרא. The latter represents a fixed, finite unit of speech, that is, the specific content of the Temple Sermon that ensues in Jer 7:3–15. By contrast, דבר reflects the *potential* for specific speech, an unformed word waiting to take shape.[6] It opens the door to the idea that the prophet communicated a sentiment, but that sentiment has yet to take specific shape within the chapter. This provides an opportunity for new formulations of the prophetic word to emerge, legitimizing the author's own version of what the prophet communicates. In short, the shift from קרא to דבר allows the author's exegesis to possess the authority of Jeremiah's own words; hermeneutically, they *become* Jeremiah's words.[7] The author of Jeremiah 26 is thus able to rework his source material without compromising its theological force. The scope of Jeremiah's message is altered, making the singular דבר/דבר ה׳ of Jer 7:2 into the plural כל הדברים of Jer 26:2.

The author of Jeremiah 26, moreover, adds a crucial element to his citation that does not appear in the Temple Sermon or, for that matter, anywhere else in Jer 1–25: the prophet is commanded not to diminish even a single word (אל תגרע דבר). And yet, the actual citation of the Sermon that follows seems to do just that, omitting large portions of the original decree and reworking/augmenting those that are retained into something rather different. The author's citation of the Temple Sermon in vv. 4–6 constitutes an apparent and flagrant disregard for his own addition to v. 2 (אל תגרע דבר).[8] Because of the shift from קרא to דבר in Jer 26:2, however, the charge to not diminish a word is not contradicted by the license taken by the author in his citation of the Temple Sermon (vv. 4–6). Rather, the citation reinforces the idea that his role as an exegete serves the same function as Jeremiah's role as a prophetic spokesperson for YHWH. Had the term קרא been retained from the author's source in Jer 7:2, his changes might indeed be viewed as an alteration of Jeremiah's message. The change in content and expression does not "cut off" the essence of the prophet's message but clarifies it through the author's own composition.

The citation in Jer 26:4–6, therefore, is not a summary of the original Temple Sermon or a loose recitation of the earlier tradition. The author has deliberately crafted a short piece to recall the Temple Sermon but also to use it as the platform for other important matters he wishes to address. These matters are quite conspicuous, spelled out by the author as we read through his citation:

1. YHWH's Torah (v. 4)
2. The prophetic tradition (v. 5)
3. The destruction of Shiloh (v. 6)
4. The destruction of Jerusalem (v. 6)

Of these four, only the last two receive coverage in the Temple Sermon, though in a manner distinct from that of Jer 26:6. The original Temple Sermon emphasizes the מקום terminology in its reference to both Shiloh and Jerusalem (Jer 7:3, 7, 12, 14), something that is lacking in the citation.[9] Furthermore, the destruction predicted for Jerusalem in the Temple Sermon makes no mention of its relationship to foreign nations, a concern that surfaces in the citation (לכל גוי הארץ in v. 6), thus revealing its exilic context. To these we shall return later; for the moment, we must consider the rather weighty additions of items 1 and 2. While the Temple Sermon makes implicit Deuteronomy (Jer 7:5–6, 9), it receives no explicit mention as YHWH's Torah. Likewise, while the Temple Sermon places Jeremiah in a well-entrenched prophetic tradition of figures who declare divine will, it does not make any overt mention of these prophets in its verses.[10] Why has the author of vv. 4–6 expressly incorporated both of these elements into his citation?

A clue may be found in the plural phrase כל דברי in Jer 26:2. It is obvious that the author of the citation is using it as a doorway to issues beyond his ostensible source (Jer 7:1–15), which identifies itself as a singular דבר (Jer 7:1–2). The infusion of new terms and concepts into the citation may speak to related passages in Jeremiah 1–25 that the author has also used as sources. Indeed, we need not look far. Jer 7:25, part of the supplement to the Temple Sermon, invokes the prophets with lexemes almost identical to those of Jer 26:5:[11]

> ... though I have sent unto you all My servants the prophets (כל עבדי הנבאים), sending them daily early and often (יום השכם ושלח) (Jer 7:25)

> ... my servants the prophets (עבדי הנבאים), whom I sent unto you, even sending them early and often (והשכם ושלח) (Jer 26:5)

The invocation of the prophets indeed punctuates the entirety of Jeremiah 1–25. Jer 1:6 and 15:1 implicitly and overtly (respectively) identify Jeremiah with Moses and Samuel,[12] Jer 6:17 identifies the prophets as watchmen (צופים) that the nation has repeatedly ignored, and Jer 25:4 does the same with more Deuteronomistically inflected language (עבדיו הנבאים).[13]

Similar concerns with the term *torah* also surface throughout Jeremiah 1–25 in a variety of contexts:

> Jer 2:8 – ותפשי התורה לא ידעני

> Jer 6:19 – ותורתי וימאסו בה

> Jer 8:8 – איכה תאמרו חכמים אנחנו ותורת ה׳ אתנו[14]

> Jer 9:12 – אל אזבם את תורתי

> Jer 16:11 – ואת תורתי לא שמרו

The matter of the Torah's status informs the larger units in which these passages appear and reveals the degree to which the idea of Torah is central to Jeremiah's thought throughout Jeremiah 1–25. In some cases, the text appears to reflect a debate against cultic figures (Jer 2:8) or the sages (Jer 8:8; 9:12); in others, the charge of transgressing or forgetting the Torah relates to illegitimate and competing theologies (Jer 9:12; 16:11) or the history of national apostasy (Jer 6:19). While these texts may have arisen during various periods of the prophet's career, the author of Jeremiah 26 understood them to be part of a *single* prophetic message, consistent with each other, with the Temple Sermon, and with his own scribal agenda. By hermeneutically broadening the scope of what he cites (via the shift from קרא to דבר in Jer 26:2), the author fuses all of these elements into his citation. In contradistinction to the introduction to the Temple Sermon in Jer 7:1, the entire collection of the prophet's preexilic oracles in Jeremiah 1–25 has, for the author, become "this matter" (הדבר הזה) introduced in Jer 26:1.[15]

The citation of the Temple Sermon in a narrative that so closely resembles those in the DH allows the author to tie the prophet's oracles to the broader prophetic narratives therein, but in doing so, he introduces a new concept. In the Deuteronomistic material, the people did not listen to YHWH's servants, the prophets (2 Kgs 17:13, 23). In Jer 26:5, the people did not listen to the *words* of YHWH's servants, the prophets.[16] The author has amalgamated his own דבר-centric phraseology with the Deuteronomistic phraseology, suggesting a paradigm shift in the understanding and communication of the prophetic message. The nature of this shift becomes more fully expressed in the second citation in the chapter, that of Micah's threat against Jerusalem from Mic 3:12, to which we will now turn our attention.

THE CITATION OF MICAH 3:12 (JEREMIAH 26:18)

Jer 26:18 presents the sole example of a prophetic text overtly quoting another prophetic text, Mic 3:12. The citation is offered in the context of Jeremiah's trial following the delivery of the Temple Sermon cited in vv. 4–6. The text, as typically translated, reads as follows:

> Micah the Moreshite prophesied in the days of Hezekiah king of Judah and spoke to the whole nation of Judah, saying "thus says YHWH of Hosts (לכן כה אמר ה׳ צבאות): Zion will be plowed like a field and Jerusalem will be a heap of ruins, and the mount of the house [will be like] wooded heights (במות יער)."

The clarity, specificity, and force of the citation and the episode in which it occurs have occasioned a long history of scholarly speculation. Some have maintained that the trial of Jeremiah preceding the citation is rooted in historical fact and that the elders' recitation of Micah's famous threat in vv. 17–19 reflects the real consideration of the spectators who evaluated

Jeremiah's own words in comparison.[17] Others have viewed vv. 17–19 as an addition to an earlier narrative, reflecting a redactor's desire to associate Jeremiah's oracles with an extant authoritative prophetic collection that included the prophecies of Micah.[18] Still others have adopted the position that vv. 17–19 are an original part of the larger chapter but contribute to the critical presentation of Jehoiakim (in comparison to Hezekiah) that obtains elsewhere in the Jeremianic corpus and thus do not reflect a strictly historical event.[19] There is good reason to support this third point of view (without necessarily completely eschewing any historical events underlying the chapter),[20] but there is even deeper significance to the deployment of the Micah citation as an integral part of the chapter. The author responsible for introducing the Micah citation into the chapter does so for two reasons: first, to invoke the Deuteronomic standards and processes regarding prophetic legitimization, and second, to consciously qualify and develop the implications of the Temple Sermon citation from earlier in the chapter.

Parallels between Jeremiah and Deuteronomy are often overt (e.g., Jer 1:9 and Deut 18:18) and periodically more subtle (such as the influence of Deut 13:7–10 on the prophet's call to vengeance against his own kin in Jer 11:18–23).[21] The citation of Micah in Jer 26:18 falls into the latter category, for it implicitly recalls the dynamic of Deut 18:15–22. In the Deuteronomic passage, we are informed that YHWH will raise up a succession of prophets like Moses for Israel (vv. 15–18),[22] that the nation will be compelled to heed the words of these prophets (v. 19), and that false prophets will die (v. 20). The text then goes on in vv. 21–22 to address the matter of distinguishing a true prophet from a false one:

> And if you say in your heart: "How shall we know the word which YHWH has not spoken?" When a prophet speaks in the name of YHWH, if the matter does not follow and does not come to pass, that is the thing which YHWH has not spoken; the prophet has spoken it presumptuously, and you shall not fear him.

Here we encounter what appears to be a paradox. Verses 19–20 make it clear that the Israelite must heed the words of the Mosaic prophet, but vv. 21–22 specify that one can know these words to be true only once enough time has passed for their authenticity to have been proved.[23] The evaluation is retrospective, and one may therefore know a true Mosaic prophet only by evaluating the manner in which history unfolds. The end result is that one is unable to evaluate the prophet speaking in the present, for one must wait to see if he or she is legitimate. How, then, can one heed the words of the true Mosaic prophet speaking in the moment?

The answer is provided within the Deuteronomic legislation itself: the word spoken by the true prophet is not his or her own but one that comes from YHWH, and one may therefore anticipate certain standards of consistency arising from the current prophet's message if he or she is to be counted among the ranks of YHWH's legitimate messengers. As such, the audience of Deut 18:15–22 is directed to consider the record of these earlier messengers by consulting two sources: the DH and the extant prophetic corpus. Both collections had been redacted to reflect the interests of Josiah's court and therefore contain episodes where the words of earlier prophets, whose messages were confirmed by history, resonated at similar terminological and thematic frequencies.[24] In this sense, YHWH's דבר was quite literally put in the mouths of these prophets – the scribes who redacted their sources designed a comprehensive literary system that offered examples to the readers of Deuteronomy of what happened when true prophets were ignored.[25]

This Deuteronomic dynamic is carried forward by the author of Jeremiah 26 through his use of the Micah citation.[26] Jeremiah's Temple Sermon is presented as consistent with the words of Micah, an earlier and recognized prophet of YHWH. This supports the perspective that vv. 17–19 are not secondary accretions but original to the chapter's composition, and therefore derive from the same author who composed the citation in vv. 4–6. The question we must ask, however, is, what purpose do these citations truly serve? We have already seen that by the exilic period, those familiar with the Deuteronomic standards for evaluating a prophet would not need further convincing of Jeremiah's legitimacy or that of Micah. The destruction of Jerusalem certainly would have vindicated Jeremiah's Temple Sermon and Micah's earlier threat that the Temple would be reduced to rubble. To what end, then, does the author of Jeremiah 26 cite both prophets and thereby invoke the authority of the Deuteronomic law?

We have seen that the citation of the Temple Sermon in vv. 4–6 is more a composition of the author than a quotation of the prophet. A small but significant change in the Micah citation in Jer 26:18 demonstrates that the author here, too, leaves his mark. Whereas the original oracle in Mic 3:12 begins with "therefore" (לכן), the citation eliminates this term and replaces it with the prophetic messenger formula כה אמר ה׳, which does not appear anywhere in the original oracle.[27] This change is not unwarranted, as the context of the Micah citation lends a *new meaning* to the original oracle. The new introductory note to the Micah citation heralds an entirely new message, and one created and declared by the author of the chapter. The citation, as we have seen, is invoked to complete the Deuteronomic model of prophetic legitimization at work within Jeremiah 26. But within the narrative of Jeremiah 26, the Micah citation legitimizes the author's own exegetical authority by stating that the author's own composition in vv. 4–6 is consistent with the words of Micah now cited in v. 18.

By demonstrating that his own words in vv. 4–6 are like those of Micah, the author of Jeremiah 26 identifies his own scribal voice as possessing proper authority according to the Deuteronomic model of prophecy, *now applied to the scribal office*. It is for this reason that the telescoping of discourse found in oracles directly attributed to the prophet in other contexts is found in the author's citations.[28] It is also for this reason that the prophetic messenger formula is used in introducing the Micah citation. The author's adjustment of קרא to דבר in Jer 26:2 opens the door to his adjustment of Micah's words in v. 18, suggesting that the prophetic word itself transcends literary strictures, temporal periods, and even typological classification. The author who has transposed Micah's words into his own composition is not only a curator and preserver of the divine word, but also an authoritative facilitator.

THE PROPHETIC WORD AND THE SCRIBAL WORD

The events of Jeremiah 36 shed light on the manipulation of the prophetic word in Jeremiah 26.[29] Jeremiah 36 pays more attention to the role of scribes than to Jeremiah, and to the scribes' interaction with the prophetic word.[30]

Upon hearing "all the words" (כל הדברים) of Jeremiah's *Urrolle* as read by Baruch (v. 16), the scribes in Gemaraiah's chamber immediately go to the king and tell him "all the words" (again, כל הדברים) that they have heard (v. 20). Though strategies involving memorization factored into scribal practice in late-seventh-century BCE Judah,[31] it is unlikely that the group of scribes memorized each word read aloud by Baruch: they were exposed to the scroll for the first time that same day, and the scroll would have hardly been a short, easily digested composition.[32] The narrative does not specify that the scroll was studied extensively, and indeed, the scroll itself is later brought to the king's chambers for closer examination (v. 21), suggesting that the specific contents were not recited from memory. The implication is that "all the words" of the scroll could be communicated via the scribes' own authority to summarize, alter, or interpret the actual written language of the scroll.[33] During the course of Baruch's consultation with his peers in Gemaraiah's chamber, we are informed in explicit terms that there is no difference whatsoever between scribal and prophetic proximity to the divine word (vv. 17–18):

> And they asked Baruch, saying: "Please tell us, how did you write all these words (דברים) from his mouth (מפיו)?" And Baruch answered them: "from his mouth (מפיו) he proclaimed all these words (דברים) to me, and I wrote them with ink in the scroll."

Scholars typically view this exchange as a simple statement that Baruch wrote the scroll "at Jeremiah's dictation,"[34] but this common translation misses an important nuance of the text. The AB/B'A' structure of these verses involving the words דברים and מפיו serves as a red flag to the reader to pay careful attention to their meaning. Indeed, we see here an overt allusion to the prophetic phenomenology found in Deuteronomy and again in Jeremiah's call narrative:

> . . . and I will put my words (דברי) in his mouth (בפיו) (Deut 18:18)

> . . . behold, I have put my words (דברי) in your mouth (בפיך) (Jer 1:9)

The essential purpose of Jer 36:17–18 is to demonstrate that the prophet and scribe share the same word placed in the prophet's mouth by YHWH.[35] One communicates it through proclamation, the other through writing it in ink, but both are charged with fostering and articulating it. This idea is not without precedent in some form, as both the Deuteronomic legislation and other Jeremianic texts attest to the central role of the scribe in facilitating the process of prophetic revelation and law.[36] But it is in Jer 36:17–18 that we are given a glimpse into the actual phenomenology and theology of the prophet–scribe relationship. There is no degeneration in any sense between the prophetic word and the scribal preservation/communication of that word; it is a digital transfer. This is what empowers the scribes to summarize and interpret the *Urrolle* for Jehoiakim in Jer 36:20, and this same idea permeates the author's citations of earlier prophecy in Jeremiah 26.[37]

The purpose of Jeremiah 26, then, appears to initiate a message culminating in Jeremiah 36: the authority of scribes as the principal mediators of religious tradition during the exile, with the freedom and authority to interpret and adjust preexilic tradition. Again and again, the texts spanning this unit of literature call attention to the role of the scribe in both subtle and overt terms.[38] The persistent scribal emphasis of these chapters points to a social or religious/political climate motivating their composition. In order to understand the nature of this climate, we must turn to the final citation in Jeremiah 26, which qualifies and unifies both the citation of the Temple Sermon in vv. 4–6 and the citation of Micah in v. 18.

THE CITATION OF THE URIAH EPISODE (JEREMIAH 26:20–23)

The conclusion to Mic 3:12, both in its original context and as cited in Jeremiah 26, contains the phrase במות יער. On a cursory level, the phrase translates as "wooded heights" or "forested hills," that is, an unpopulated mound overgrown with vegetation suggesting the tentative devastation that Jerusalem faced in 701 BCE at the hands of the Assyrians.[39] In its original Mican context, however, the phrase also constitutes a double entendre: the phrase במות יער alludes to the cultic center at Kiriath Yearim that had once served as the home of the Ark before its installation in Jerusalem (I Sam 6:20–7:1).[40] The reference to this Judean city follows Micah's predilection for depicting the Assyrian conquest of Judean cities via similar double entendres (see Mic 1:10–16) and provides a suitable closure to a collection of oracles delivered on the eve of Sennacherib's invasion.[41] If the oracle was delivered with Sennacherib's army already en route to Jerusalem, the force of Micah's rhetoric would have been difficult to ignore: the Davidic heritage of the Jerusalem cult and its ritual iconography would not save the city. In a short time, it would resemble the במות יער, the devastated remains of the cult center that had thrived for centuries at Kiriath Yearim until Hezekiah's revolt against Assyria and his consequent depopulation of the countryside.[42]

That Micah's double entendre was thusly understood in the exilic period by both the author of Jeremiah 26 and his audience is suggested by Jer 26:20–23, which narrates the sad fate of Uriah b. Shemaiah, the prophet whose hometown was none other than Kiriath Yearim (v. 20). Though many scholars have considered vv. 20–23(24) to be secondary additions to Jeremiah 26,[43] these verses are central to the message of the chapter. The citation of the Uriah episode reinforces the במות יער double entendre of Mic 3:12/Jer 26:18 and establishes a parallel to Jer 26:6: both address former cult sites that had been demolished and had been utilized as prototypes for Jerusalem's fate in prophetic oracles. Again, we encounter the author's interest in the hermeneutical dimensions of the prophetic דבר: Uriah is said to have spoken "all the words" spoken by Jeremiah as well (ככל דברי ירמיהו). The citation of the Uriah episode in this manner constructs a singular prophetic word spoken by Jeremiah, Micah, and Uriah. All three prophets addressed the fall of Jerusalem as filtered through their own experiences and backgrounds. The resulting message, effectively constructed by the author of the chapter himself, is that the prophetic tradition converges on the issue of Jerusalem's special sanctity and uniformly denies its legitimacy.

The foregoing raises several important points. First, Jeremiah 26 should be viewed as a unified composition in its entirety. Neither vv. 17–19 nor vv. 20–24 should be viewed as secondary accretions, as they offer semantic balance and semiotic depth to the earlier passages in the chapter and resonate at uniform theological frequencies.[44] In addition, the author takes bold steps to make explicit the authority of scribes to shape and transform prophetic and legal traditions. This authority already characterized scribal activity in the Josianic period with the production of Deuteronomy, which adapted older traditions but did so under the name of Moses.[45] Not so with the author of Jeremiah 26: he announces new messages on par with those of the prophets and in the same breath overtly draws the reader's attention to his adjustments.

There is no allusion to Kiriath Yearim in any of Jeremiah's preexilic oracles in chs. 1–25; that the author of Jeremiah 26 makes mention of the במות יער from Micah, however, suggests that during this same period a figure from Kiriath Yearim did indeed make some sort of impact or even set a type of precedent for Jeremiah to voice his own Temple Sermon. If this is the case, then the author of Jeremiah 26 categorizes Uriah alongside Jeremiah via the Micah quote, thereby establishing continuity between both prophets. Such a sense of continuity is made explicit in Jer 26:20, where Uriah is described as having spoken all the words spoken by Jeremiah as well.

Jeremiah 26 presents the image of a nation torn between competing forces: "all the nation" (כל העם) congregates to bring Jeremiah to trial in vv. 8–9, but that congregation is divided by the end of the chapter into those who want to harm the prophet (העם, minus the modifier כל in v. 24) and, presumably, those who do not.[46] The prophet's adversaries are repeatedly presented as the cultic establishment in the Temple (vv. 7–9, 16), whereas the officials (v. 16) declare him to be innocent; that these officials are scribes is suggested in v. 24, as Ahikam (a member of the Shaphanide scribal family) saves the prophet from the threatening mob. A significant part of the nation is corrupted by the priests/prophets of the Temple, a group presumably obsessed with the inviolability of Jerusalem and the Davidic covenant. It is no surprise, therefore, that Jehoiakim is identified as a despot in the Uriah episode, as he too later reveals his misguided faith in the Davidic promise and Jerusalem's special status to the violent exclusion of the prophetic word (Jer 26:23; see also Jer 36:23–24).

Jer 26:10 implies a genetic connection between the royal house and the Temple as a closed unit: the officials who appear on the scene "went up from the house of the king [to] the house of YHWH (i.e., the Temple)" (ויעלו מבית המלך בית ה'). Missing in the original Hebrew is the preposition "to" (אל). The omission, however, is subtle and effective and suggests another reading: "they went up from the house of the king, the Temple." This emphasizes the connection between institutions that, by the author's time, had both been bested by Babylon. While the Jeremianic tradition does not categorically denounce the Temple, the city of Jerusalem, or even the Davidic line, it consistently inveighs against anyone who idolizes those elements to the exclusion of YHWH's words continually spoken by the prophets.[47] By the time of the author of Jeremiah 26, these words were no longer being delivered orally. They were enshrined in the texts preserved and interpreted by the scribes.

Jeremiah 26 appears to be a unified composition. It does not possess multiple layers of composition, as some scholars have suggested, nor are its events thematically or structurally discordant. At every level, the chapter takes up Deuteronomistic matters from a consistent perspective, and the author employs the device of citation with equal consistency. It is also worth noting that by citing Micah as the prophet who caught Hezekiah's attention, the author builds and comments upon the preexilic version of the book of Kings. In that work, Hezekiah submits not to Micah's word, but to the counsel of Isaiah (cf. 2 Kings 19–20). By suggesting that Hezekiah submitted to Micah as well, this implies the consistency of their respective prophetic words, just as the author suggests consistency between Uriah and Jeremiah. The prophetic tradition is presented as a unified front, and this is accomplished strictly through the author's scribal/exegetical prerogatives. Jeremiah 26 affirms these prerogatives in terms of both form and content, setting up the issues that will be taken up throughout the rest of the Supplement.

CHAPTER 2

The Identification of Legitimate Israel: Jeremiah 27–32:15

JEREMIAH 26 ESTABLISHES THE BASIC THEMES OF THE SUPPLEMENT, containing all the fundamental issues that the author felt required the exilic reader's attention and presenting a well-known episode in the prophet's career as the prologue to the reformation of Jerusalem-based worldviews. Having identified the parameters of discourse, the Supplement's author engaged in the repositioning of the prophet's earlier work within his own subsequent and larger literary work. The complex of literature immediately following Jeremiah 26 represents the gamut of scribal activity: the Supplement's author draws from older materials, revises them, provides new historical and literary contexts for them, and relies upon their themes in formulating new textual appendages. The author's primary sources are texts and the record of events originating with the prophet Jeremiah himself from various episodes in his preexilic career: Jeremiah 27–29, which date from 594/593 BCE, and Jeremiah 30–31, which originated during the Josianic period.[1] The redaction of these traditions into the Supplement lends them significantly new meanings.

The position of Jeremiah 27–29 within the Supplement suggests that they were not included as standard entries in the earlier collections of Jeremiah's oracles, a form of Jeremiah 1–25+OAN.[2] The same may be said of Jeremiah 30–31, with the concession that they originated far earlier than Jeremiah 27–29 and were relegated to an archival or inactive position until such time as they could be reapplied.[3] The author of the Supplement did, however, have access to disparate collections of Jeremianic materials that would have included copies of these texts in their original forms; his inclusion of these materials in the Supplement shows his belief that they were authoritative despite their absence from the extant active corpus.

REDACTIONAL CONSISTENCY AND PROPHETIC POLEMICS: JEREMIAH 27 AND ITS RELATIONSHIP TO JEREMIAH 26

Jeremiah 27–29 stand out immediately as unique from a source-critical perspective because of obvious differences, most notably the use of the name "Nebuchadnezzar," rather than "Nebuchadrezzar" as it appears elsewhere in the book, and the alternate spelling of Jeremiah's name (ירמיה) in all three chapters. Moreover, the report of a false prophet's speech (that of Hananiah in Jeremiah 28) and the overt nature of the letter addressed directly to the Judean deportees of 597 BCE in Jer 29:1–23 distinguish themselves from the formal, metered poetry or one-sided parenetic prose of Jeremiah's debates with prophetic opponents elsewhere. That these chapters have been carefully redacted to fit into the Supplement, though, is evident in several ways. First, the wording of Jer 27:1 and Jer 26:1 is almost identical:

> In the beginning of the reign of Jehoiakim son of Josiah king of Judah came this word from YHWH, saying (Jer 26:1)

> In the beginning of the reign of Jehoiakim son of Josiah king of Judah came this word *unto Jeremiah* (אל ירמיה) from YHWH, saying (Jer 27:1)

As discussed in the Introduction to the present study, the wording of Jer 27:1 has led some scholars to believe that the text was somehow corrupted to read "the beginning of Jehoiakim's reign" despite the fact that the chapter deals with Zedekian matters; other scholars suggest that the entire verse is simply borrowed from Jeremiah 26 and should therefore be deleted.[4] These positions should be reevaluated; we have already seen the hermeneutical merit of employing the "reign of Jehoiakim" terminology in Jer 27:1, suggesting that Zedekiah (the king of note in the rest of that chapter) shares in the inadequacies and sins of his predecessor.[5] This would be wholly appropriate in a complex of literature directed to the deportees of 597 BCE, many of whom thought that Babylon's hegemony might be shaken and that they might soon return to their homeland with Zedekiah still on the throne. Associating Zedekiah with Jehoiakim, the king these deportees had already encountered and whose actions had led them into captivity, would have been a very effective way of curbing support for Zedekiah and promoting submission to their Babylonian captors.

Furthermore, if Jer 27:1 had been lifted from the wording of Jer 26:1, and if the "unto Jeremiah" (אל ירמיה) was simply the result of a later editorial insertion, we would expect the prophet's name to be spelled ירמיהו, akin to all other spellings of his name beyond Jeremiah 27–29. In addition, the ascription of a word regarding later circumstances to a moment in an earlier king's reign had already obtained in Jeremiah's literature from several decades earlier: Jer 3:6–11, arising during the composition of the *Urrolle* in 605 BCE and directed to Jehoiakim, is presented as emanating from an insight Jeremiah obtained during Josiah's reign years earlier. The precedent for a hermeneutical reading of seemingly anachronistic datelines was therefore already established by the time Jeremiah 27 was composed, and we are justified in viewing Jer 27:1 as an original and integral part of the chapter without any need for emendation.[6]

If Jer 27:1 in its current form is to be viewed as an original part of the chapter, then we must look to Jer 26:1 for evidence of redactional considerations as the author included Jeremiah 27–29 in the Supplement. In Jer 26:1, we find virtually identical terminology, minus one conspicuous trait: 26:1 does not claim to be a word given "unto Jeremiah" (אל ירמיה). Two reasons lie behind these absent lexemes. The first reason is that ch. 26 is a third-person narrative, wherein Jeremiah appears as a character. Though Jer 32:6–15 functions as a quasi-narrative, it is told primarily in the first person and thus affords Jeremiah the character a chance to qualify the event as a divine word.[7] Qualifying the narrative of Jeremiah 26 itself in similar terms, however, would undermine the narrative logic of the chapter, since it is clearly a work about Jeremiah written by someone else. The second reason goes beyond matters of formal logic and reveals something about the author's self-understanding: Jeremiah 26 begins the

Supplement, a work that was supposed to be an extension of the prophet's corpus and that could therefore be qualified as a divine word. However, the author of the Supplement did not simply wish his work to be attributed pseudepigraphically to Jeremiah. The wording of Jer 26:1 resonates clearly with the purpose of the citations in Jeremiah 26: it reveals that the chapter is not a word intuited by Jeremiah the prophet but a word derived from the Jeremiah tradition by a later scribe.[8]

The lexical affinities shared by Jer 26:1 and 27:1 may be attributed to the author's conscious borrowing of extant terminology from 27:1, and attempts to show that this scribal enterprise was consistent with the prophet's message and was capable of carrying forward the same revelatory impulses through the scribe's own authority as a faithful representative of Jeremiah's mission. This is also facilitated by the placement of Jeremiah 27–29 *subsequent* to Jeremiah 26, which suggests through the symbolic dimensions of the literary sequence that the prophet's original message in chs. 27–29 achieves a new meaning within the newer literary enterprise (the Supplement), explicating and developing the ideas introduced in the previous chapter.[9]

We must therefore return to the message of Jeremiah 27 that the author of the Supplement wished to assimilate into his own work. Jer 27:2–11 focuses upon the divine role of Nebuchadnezzar, pointing to a Babylon-centered audience. While the initial audience would have been the deportees of 597 BCE, the new literary context provided by the author of the Supplement extends the message to post-587 audience members as well. Indeed, the current context of Jeremiah 27 lends further support to the closing theme of Jeremiah 26 that the Davidic kings no longer offer any hope for salvation; the mention of Zedekiah (v. 3) extends this derision to the remaining Davidic line in Jerusalem beyond Jehoiakim. The ascription of divine favor to Nebuchadnezzar[10] is also consistent with the theology of Jeremiah's post-604 materials and diminishes Davidic ideology in the eyes of the reader while tying Jeremiah 27 thematically to the significant passages currently found within Jeremiah 1–25.[11] (This would be a particularly effective method of complementing the derisive polemic against Jehoiakim in Jer 23:13–23 and the rejection of Zedekiah and those in his charge in Jeremiah 24.) In these verses, though, an additional point is made: it is not only the rejection of Jeremiah's word but the rejection of Nebuchadnezzar's authority that will result in punishment from YHWH (v. 8).[12]

This last point applies not only to Judah but to all nations, evidencing the scope of Jeremiah's international theology:[13] YHWH is the master of the universe, who does what he will by virtue of his "great power and outstretched arm" (v. 5). This terminology and imagery recall the language of the Deuteronomic memory of the Exodus in Deut 26:8. The language of Jer 27:5 differs, though, insofar as the prophet's wording ("in my great power" [בכחי גדול]) differs from the Deuteronomic wording ("with a great hand" [ביד חזקה]). While this difference might further suggest the independence of this textual unit from the larger Jeremianic corpus at one point, it may simply represent the shift in circumstance.[14] The Exodus represents YHWH's direct intervention in world affairs by his own hand; YHWH's will in the days of Jehoiakim has changed, and it is now literally Nebuchadnezzar's hand (Jer 27:6, 8) that will carry out the divine plan. Nebuchadnezzar's great power over Judah and the surrounding nations is but a reflection of YHWH's own great power, and true faith in ethereal authority demands submission to its terrestrial counterpart. This wording also ties the presence of Nebuchadnezzar to similar "great power" terminology in Deut 9:29 (בכחך גדול ובזרע הנטויה), suggesting that Moses' intercession on behalf of the nation in assuaging YHWH's wrath in Deut 9:25–29 is here preserved by Jeremiah's deference to Nebuchadnezzar. Submitting to Babylon represents the aversion of total destruction.

The naming of Nebuchadnezzar as the agent of YHWH creates an inversion of traditional modes of piety, particularly with regard to Hezekiah's steadfastness in the face of the Rabshakeh's taunts (2 Kgs 18:19–36), and such a comparison cannot be avoided if Jeremiah 27 is read in sequence, after the reference to Hezekiah in Jer 26:18–19.[15] Hezekiah's great merit in the DH was his rejection of Sennacherib's suzerainty, as the Rabshakeh's assertion that Sennacherib was the agent of YHWH was, at the time, bogus.[16] The proper attitude toward foreign kingship is one of resistance in the Hezekiah narrative. In Jeremiah 27, though, resistant attitudes toward Nebuchadnezzar are blasphemous. Such ideology would have been unheard of in a world before the death of Josiah, yet the basic principles of Deuteronomic law are retained by Jeremiah's analysis of history as the proving ground of divine will: the Deuteronomic law was still applicable even with Babylon as the primary force dominating the political landscape.[17] Jeremiah here dislodges Deuteronomic law and ideology from geographic boundaries in order for it to continue to guide the lives of the people who can no longer participate in a religion hard-wired to Jerusalem.[18]

Consequently, the prophets of Jeremiah 26 who condemned Jeremiah to death are paralleled by the prophets in Jeremiah 27 whose advice would condemn those who might adhere to to it. Here, the literary sequence of chs. 26–27 allows the author of the Supplement to establish strong typological links between prophets from different times (Jehoiakim's reign and Zedekiah's reign) and in different places (Judah and Babylon) who nonetheless cultivate identical delusions concerning the centrality of Jerusalem and its cult. They deny the will of their own patron deity by denying the deity's chosen earthly agent, Nebuchadnezzar (ergo, the שקר accusation in Jer 27:10). While Zedekiah and the priests are implicated in Jeremiah 27 (v. 12), it is ultimately prophecy that comes under fire for stirring up false hopes in the security of the Temple (vv. 16–22). The true prophet is dissociated from the Jerusalem court and Temple in full recognition of YHWH's international intentions.

PROPHETS BY NAME: JEREMIAH 28–29

The theme of false prophecy is continued in Jeremiah 28 with the famous debate between Jeremiah and Hananiah and in Jeremiah 29 with the letter to the exiles of 597 BCE and the subsequent responses thereto. In both of these chapters, Jeremiah faces off against competing prophetic perspectives, and the competing prophets are mentioned by name with great specificity in contrast to the generic "prophets" of Jeremiah 26 and 27. The Hananiah episode appears to be anticipated by the charge in Jer 27:16–22 that the Temple vessels will find no safe haven from Nebuchadnezzar,[19] but the chasm of difference between this position and that of the other prophets is qualified; Hananiah is presented in terms very close to the presentation of Jeremiah, differing only in the particulars of his message.[20] The issue is thus not one of prophetic method or form but rather recognition of YHWH's work in history,[21] with Jeremiah having properly analyzed the situation and Hananiah still clinging to outdated prophetic theology, which has clouded his perceptions.[22] The narrative of this chapter is similar in form to those of Jeremiah 26, 36, and 37–44 in terms of emulating Deuteronomistic narrative styles, but unlike those chapters, it bears signs of a composition dating from before the devastation of 587.[23] While the author of Jeremiah 26 relies on references to the fall of Jerusalem, Hananiah's death provides legitimization of Jeremiah's words in Jeremiah 28 (vv. 16–17); the fall of Jerusalem would have provided a far greater vindication than the death of a single prophet.

The showdown between Jeremiah and Hananiah is reminiscent of the showdown between Elijah and the prophets of Baal (1 Kgs 18:18–40). In both of these narratives, the actions of the opposing parties are described in detail in the presence of an ambivalent audience clearly torn between two competing theological views. It is also significant that Hananiah is the son of a prophet ("Azur" in Jer 28:1), and thus likely is part of a prophetic guild rather than an authentic prophet of YHWH compelled by divine initiative to take up his office. It is Jeremiah who stands in line with the older tradition of prophetic spokespersons like Amos, who stood against professional or official guilds of prophets tied to the local shrines (Amos 7:10–15).[24] Hananiah, by default, is thus cast as a prophet akin to those at the reviled Bethel shrine and the prophets of Baal from the Elijah narrative. This too indicates a pre-587 date for the chapter's composition, as the northern setting for the Amos and Elijah narratives would have resonated more clearly with an audience more closely connected in time to the Josianic DH that fostered such antinorthern cultic sentiments.

We may also sense a rhetorical accumulation implied in Jeremiah 27–28: in ch. 27, the change in political circumstances creates associations between the competing prophetic voices and the Rabshakeh in the Hezekiah narrative. In ch. 28, the competing prophetic voice (Hananiah) is associated with modes of prophecy deemed illegitimate in the DH (via the connection to Baalism, on the one hand, and the Bethel shrine, on the other).[25] In one fell swoop, Jeremiah is made a true prophet of Deuteronomic proportions[26] and the Jerusalem cult is serious demoted: the presentation of Hananiah as a cultic prophet akin to those at Amos's Bethel and Elijah's Baal adversaries implies that the Jerusalem cult – which Hananiah champions – is as illegitimate as the Bethel sanctuary and the Baal cult of the Canaanites. Both institutions received severe condemnation in the Josianic DH; Jeremiah 28 preserves this Deuteronomistic impulse with respect to proper worship of YHWH while eschewing inappropriate emulations of Jerusalem.[27]

The incorporation of ch. 28 into the literary unit of Jeremiah 27–29 may represent the same compositional and editorial strategies behind the current form and placement of the Elijah narrative. Both were written for one purpose at an earlier period and reused for a different purpose later in the service of a more comprehensive theological message and literary corpus.[28] The setting of Jeremiah 28 is the Temple among the community remaining behind after the exile of 597 BCE, specifically "among the presence of the priests and all the people" (v. 1).[29] Though the chapter depicts events directed to the audience still in Jerusalem, it sets up a parallel to the exiled addressees of the letter in Jer 29:1–23, who are also identified as "all the people" and as "priests," though included in their ranks are the elders, the royal retinue of Jehoiachin ("Jeconiah"), and "the prophets" (Jer 29:1–2). For the exiled community Jeremiah has a similar message: do not listen to the words of the prophets in Jeremiah 29 (mentioned by name in 29:21–22) who speak similarly to Hananiah in Jeremiah 28, and who are presented as false and immoral (29:23).

A castigation similar to that of Hananiah is lodged against Shemaiah the Nehelamite in Jeremiah 29 for false prophecy and, apparently, for attempting to sway the religious hierarchy in Jerusalem from Jeremiah's influence (vv. 26–28). Shemaiah functions in ch. 29 as Hananiah functions in ch. 28:

he is a Jeremianic anti-type, who appeals to the priesthood in Jerusalem to rebuke opposing prophetic messages and does so in the same manner as Jeremiah (both write letters now preserved in Jeremiah 29).[30] It is clear, though, that Shemaiah suffers from the same delusions concerning the imminent restoration of the exiles to Jerusalem, and is even referred to by Jeremiah in the same derisive terms as Hananiah ("because he has spoken perversion against YHWH" applies to both of them [Jer 28:16; 29:32]). Both Hananiah and Shemaiah place their faith in the sanctity of Jerusalem, thereby ignoring Nebuchadnezzar's position as YHWH's agent on the world stage.[31] Jeremiah's recognition of this leads him to advise the exiles to settle into their new homes, where they will find "peace" (שלום). For Jeremiah, submission to Nebuchadnezzar (Jer 29:7) fulfills the שלום sought by the people in his earlier prophecies, and thus Babylon becomes the new ארץ שלום (see Jer 12:5) for those who have submitted to YHWH's will. Indeed, obeying Jeremiah's word in this regard constitutes obeying the Deuteronomic law and sustaining the covenant it represents;[32] the שלום of Nebuchadnezzar's Babylon will fulfill the failed promise of שלום from the Josianic period.

JEREMIAH'S 70-YEAR PROPHECY

Jeremiah did not necessarily give up on Judah's future – the reference to Babylon's "70 years" (Jer 29:10) speaks to a finite period of dominance in concert with the generational references in Jer 27:7. The 70-year reference does not constitute a subsequent addition to this material dating from after the exile, as many scholars have maintained, nor does it even reflect a stereotyped temporal trope utilized by the prophet.[33] Rather, it is a deliberate reference to the Black Stone Inscription of the Assyrian king Esarhaddon, an important text from 678 BCE that celebrates that king's rebuilding of Babylon as a reflex of Marduk's divine will.[34] Jeremiah's reference to this inscription, which would have been well known to his audience (comprised largely of the Judean literati), represents an attempt to invoke history as a witness to their current circumstances.[35] It is not Marduk but YHWH, however, who is behind Babylon's rehabilitation (Jer 29:10), one that was so clearly successful given the Babylonian dominance of the day.

This 70-year reference is bound to the oracle against Babylon currently located in Jeremiah 50–51 via the לב קמי and ששך *atbash* codes found in that chapter, both of which approximate via the Hebrew alphabetical system the inversion of the cuneiform symbol in the Esarhaddon inscription that allowed Babylon's reconstruction.[36] Both Jeremiah 29 and an early form of Jeremiah 50–51 were part of an earlier collection mined by the author of the Supplement for his own purposes, but it is likely that Jeremiah 29 was composed well before the relevant passages in chs. 50–51.[37] For the author of the Supplement and for Jeremiah himself, Babylon was the instrument of YHWH's historical intervention, and it had to be heeded. Those who accepted Babylonian hegemony were still in YHWH's favor, while those in Jerusalem longing for independence were not.

THE SEQUENCE OF COMPOSITION IN JEREMIAH 28–29

It is therefore likely that Jeremiah 28 postdates the interprophetic debates of Jer 29:1–23 as a part of the Jeremiah 27–29 collection. The problematic prophets of ch. 29 mentioned by name are mentioned only summarily, suggesting the audience's familiarity with the active debate.[38] Hananiah, by contrast, is described in great detail and even likened to Jeremiah in terms of title, indicating the type of official position he claimed to hold and the nature of the competition for that prophetic office. The 597 BCE community knew Ahab b. Kolaiah and Zedekiah b. Maaseiah (Jer 29:21–23) as well as Shemaiah the Nehelamite (Jer 29:24–32), but were not familiar with the Hananiah episode until it was put into a narrative context and reached them; the spelling of Jeremiah's name in this chapter is consistent with the spelling of his name throughout chs. 27–29, and suggests that the narrative reached them early on and was incorporated into the collection of materials preserved by the community in Babylon before the second exile in 587.

One gets the impression from Jeremiah 24 that the 597 BCE community in Babylon accepted Jeremiah's position, quite possibly through the example of Hananiah. The current textual position of Jeremiah 28, though, reflects a *post*-587 consciousness and speaks to a wider audience than that addressed in the earlier material of chs. 27 and 29.[39] The names of Ahab and Zedekiah in Jer 29:21–23 and Shemaiah in 29:24–32 would have required additional details for an audience that had only recently reached Babylon and had therefore not witnessed their activity first-hand.[40] Jeremiah 28 is inserted between chs. 27 and 29 to create a contextual bridge between the message of the former and the named figures of the latter,[41] demonstrating that the figure of Hananiah represents the proper way to understand who these other figures were and why they were eventually ignored. This scenario would also seem to be the appropriate point at which Jer 29:24–32 was secondarily appended to the chapter, which further facilitated the connection with Jeremiah 28 and the contextual continuity of the larger unit.[42]

As the finale to the literary unit of chs. 27–29, Jeremiah 29 is strongly tied to the prophet's poetry and narratives in his active corpus developing under his own direction in Jerusalem. Those who have settled in Babylon are tied in this chapter to the building and planting of Jer 1:10,[43] while those who cling to the sanctity of Jerusalem are "bad figs that cannot be eaten" (Jer 29:17) and are thus tied to Jer 24:8.[44] Jeremiah 27–29 would then have functioned as a separate message to what constituted for Jeremiah a separate community, and one in which there was hope for the future and covenantal fulfillment. The exiles addressed in chs. 27–29 became the prototype for the exiles from the final deportation of 587 BCE, and the Supplement's reworking of the older texts concerning the deportees of 597 went to support their ongoing applicability to this newer and larger community.[45] More importantly, they provided the Supplement's author with authentic Jeremianic corroboration for his own narrative derision of the circles in Jerusalem still mired in the miasma of Davidic pretensions in Jeremiah 26. Old covenants and ways of life rooted in the hills of Judah were not only illusory but an affront to divine will. YHWH's plan for Judah was to be found by the rivers of Babylon.

RESTORING THE ORACLES OF RESTORATION: JEREMIAH 30–31

The current form of chs. 30–31 is built around the original texts written by Jeremiah in his earliest mission to the Shilonites and northerners under Josiah; their absence from the *Urrolle* represents the inappropriate tone of these texts for a work that declared judgment, and they were thus sidelined for later use.[46] Like Jeremiah 27–29, the current position of Jeremiah 30–31 results from the author of the Supplement, but they were not drawn from an inactive archival state: these oracles were already reworked and in circulation by the time they were included in the Supplement's editorial schemata. Many scholars view the redaction of these oracles as inspired by similar language found in Ezekiel 18,[47] though a number of considerations weigh in favor of the influence running in the other direction and seeing the redactional accretions as deriving from Jeremiah himself. The first consideration is that while both passages refer to the popular sour grapes aphorism and speak of individual liability as opposed to corporate guilt, the Jeremiah passage is considerably shorter than its counterpart in Ezekiel. Though it is possible that this represents a truncation of the Ezekiel material, it is more likely that the Ezekiel passage further develops a base tradition originating in the Jeremiah oracle. This conclusion is supported on stylistic grounds, as Ezekiel elsewhere provides significant commentary on older and briefer traditions (many of them Deuteronomic in origin) as he develops their themes to conform to his worldview.[48]

The language found in each passage also suggests that the direction of influence runs from Jeremiah to Ezekiel: the Jeremiah passage takes up exclusively Deuteronomic language and themes, engaging in lemmatic transformation in the manner of the Deuteronomic Torah itself.[49] By contrast, the Ezekiel passage subordinates the Deuteronomic language it possesses to Zadokite modes of expression regarding the qualifications of righteousness, purity, holiness, and religious authority.[50] The Jeremianic corpus elsewhere invokes the traditions of the Zadokite literature, and indeed, the original layers of Jeremiah 30–31 deploy P terminology and imagery.[51] Had the Ezekiel text served as the source for the Jeremiah passage (i.e., had a subsequent redactor viewed such a Zadokite source as appropriate for interpolation into the Jeremiah tradition), we should expect the preponderance of Zadokite language to have filtered into Jer 31:27–34, yet no such lexemes are to be found therein. Finally, whereas Ezekiel 18 may apply broad standards of ethics to its audience, it does not possess a democratizing impulse. Rather, the repeated emphasis on matters of purity, the use of ritual language, and the persistent invocation of the root צדק in variegated forms implies that proper ethical conduct is somehow still mediated through the Zadokite priesthood and the ideology reflected by and emerging from its once-active Temple cult.[52] The Jeremiah passage, on the other hand, makes no mention of any ritual tradition, focusing instead on the individual's ability to engage YHWH's Torah, with intercessory figures such as Zadokite priests taken out of the equation altogether.[53]

Most scholars view Jer 30:3/31:27–34 as deriving from a post-587 BCE context, with a variety of opinions as to when, specifically, these oracles would have been composed.[54] It is doubtless the case that these oracles, and indeed the larger complex of oracles throughout chs. 30–31, took on a central position in the thought and theology of the exilic community; the current position of these chapters within the Supplement certainly speaks to their importance in this regard. Yet another context presents itself as a likely background to the composition of Jer 30:3/31:27–34 and other redactional accretions in these chapters, and that is the deportation of 597. It is precisely the fragmentation of the Judean community into a group taken captive (that earned the prophet's favor) and a group remaining in the land (that incurred the prophet's derision) that the theme of Jer 30:3/31:27–34 would address, especially with respect to curtailing broad condemnation of the entire Judean people. Jeremiah 30–31 were redacted by the prophet to address the 597 community in Babylon as a corollary to the materials now found in Jeremiah 27–29. In light of the linguistic connections between Jer 29:14 (ושבתי את שבותכם) and Jer 30:3 (ושבתי את שבות עמי ישראל ויהודה), we may surmise that Jeremiah lifted the original oracles in Jeremiah 30–31 from an archival state in the wake of the deportation of 597 and developed them into a form that would match the materials already in circulation among the deportees in Babylon circa 593.[55] The theme common to both the Josianic stratum and the prophet's redactional additions composed for the 597 deportees is a belief that judgment has already occurred and the opportunity for redemption is now available; this is witnessed in Jeremiah 24, where the deportees are identified as "good figs," in contrast to the homeland community under Zedekiah.[56] As such, the 597 community in Babylon emerges as a prime candidate for the original audience of these redacted oracles, as they were the first to have endured judgment and to be fit for eventual redemption in the prophet's purview.

A number of syntactical and linguistic elements delineate which texts belong to the earlier or updated material, though historical events and shifts in Jeremiah's position on key issues also determine which verses may be attributed to the various levels of composition. While Jer 30:3 directs the older material to a Judean audience, the message is set in a future period rather than the present via the phrase "for behold, days are coming (הנה ימים באים) – an utterance of YHWH – that I will [re]turn the captivity of my nation Israel and Judah, says YHWH, and return them to the land that I have promised to their fathers as an inheritance" (v. 3). Whereas the original text speaks to the inclusion of isolated northern regions in a Davidic kingdom, this text addresses a community that is in exile in a land beyond Davidic reach: the issue is one of a land given to the fathers, not to a scion of David. There is no imperialistic pretension or agenda, though it is significant that the message does speak of a return from exile.[57] The land of Judah, Jeremiah intimates, is still a tenable locus for Judean life at the time he composed the update, though it will belong only to those who have submitted to divine will and have already endured the exile of 597 BCE; those now living in the land under Zedekiah are not Jeremiah's current audience.[58] Moreover, the restoration to Judah is set in the future, in contradistinction to the imminence of the original Josianic message, addressing the lack of viability for restoration under the current circumstances and supporting the idea in chs. 27–29 that the exile will last for a long time (Jer 27:7; 29:10). The implication is that the days of promise are coming, and the continuity of life in exile will sustain the covenant for that promise to be realized, but only for a different generation.

In light of the ideology of Jer 27:7 and 29:10, the appeal to the "fathers" here must be seen as a further subversion of the original Josianic-era stratum. The reference relates to the similar terminology introduced by the Temple Sermon in Jer 7:7, where the land is also promised to the fathers and the people will be able to live there if they heed Jeremiah's words.[59] Jer 30:3 develops the concept behind the wording in Jer 7:3, where YHWH will cause his *people* to dwell where he chooses. In light of Jeremiah 27–29, this place is clearly Babylon. The restoration of Jer 30:3 is thus based on the ideology of the Temple Sermon but is channeled into a post–597 BCE reality, where life in Jerusalem under the tainted Davidic line is no longer viable, though the promise of the land to the fathers is still a possibility for those who heed Jeremiah's words.

The next appearance of the phrase הנה ימים באים is found in a unit of text (Jer 31:27–30) that picks up where Jer 30:3 leaves off, and explains in no uncertain terms how the Temple Sermon's promise to the fathers is to be realized under the rubric of Jeremiah's new prophetic word:

> Behold, the days come, says YHWH, that I will sew the house of Israel and the house of Judah with the seed of man, and with the seed of beast. And it shall come to pass, that like as I have watched over them to pluck up and to break down, and to overthrow and to destroy, and to afflict (שקדתי עליהם לנתוש לנתוץ ולהרס ולהאביד); so will I watch over them to build and to plant (לבנות ולנטע), says YHWH. In those days they shall say no more: "The fathers have eaten sour grapes, and the children's teeth have become numb."[60] But every one shall die for his own iniquity; every man that eateth the sour grapes, his teeth shall become numb.

A number of elements here support the dating of this passage to a post-597/pre–587 BCE period and the identification of its audience as the exiles of 597 in Babylon. Jer 31:27 speaks of uniting the houses of Israel and Judah, providing a transition from the themes of the earlier layers of Jeremiah 30–31 to that of the present composition. Verse 28, in turn, invokes the manifold terminology of the call narrative (Jer 1:10–12). The invocation of the שקד terminology constitutes a promise, for this new word communicated by Jeremiah thus falls under the category of דברים that YHWH will confirm through actualization (Jer 31:27; 1:12).[61] No oracles in the book of Jeremiah directed at the community under Jehoiakim or Zedekiah suggest forgiveness or restoration, though Jer 29:5–7 does leave open this possibility for those already taken to Babylon in 597 via the ongoing applicability of Deuteronomic law.[62] While the 597 community has already been told to build and plant in Babylon (Jer 29:5–7), this verse addresses restoration to Judah via the הנה ימים באים connection with Jer 30:3, thus suggesting that the land was not yet annihilated by Nebuchadnezzar's army.[63]

The following verse (Jer 31:29) further ties this oracle to the 597 BCE deportees via the reference to future generations being absolved of the sins of their forebears. The verse looks forward to this future time by citing the sour grapes aphorism, stating that its theme of generational liability will no longer apply when restoration occurs. The people of that time will be innocent, recalling the innocence of the wilderness generation (Jer 2:2–3). Like those who wandered in the wilderness under Moses, the passing of this generation outside of the homeland clears the way for a future generation to resettle the land of their fathers. This anticipates a circumstance similar to that depicted in Deut 5:1–5, addressed to the new wilderness generation untainted by the experience of slavery in Egypt. But like the covenant on the plains of Moab in Deut 5:1–5, it also anticipates a new covenant, possessing Sinaitic authority (see later). The fulfillment of the promise to the fathers, that is, life in the land, is contingent upon the adherence to Mosaic authority in the Deuteronomic passage; likewise, the restoration to the land of the fathers requires adherence to Jeremiah's authority in Jeremiah 31.

That the exiles of 597 BCE were receptive to Jeremiah's words in Jeremiah 27–29 – as opposed to the bad figs of Jeremiah 24 who had rejected him – is made explicit in the following verse (31:30), where liability becomes an individual rather than a corporate matter. Verse 30 is voiced along the lines of Deut 24:16. The purpose of Deuteronomic passage was to dismantle the clan-based systems of justice and retribution and subordinate everyone to the central authority in Jerusalem, but it is here adapted to liberate the individual from a Jerusalem authority and make each individual accountable to the Torah itself. Jer 31:30 thus seems to be adapting the Deuteronomic law in the same manner as Jer 29:5–7 and likewise maintains the force of the Deuteronomic Torah in the exilic circumstance.[64] This was not merely a matter of theology but served a utilitarian political purpose by separating the already-punished community in Babylon from the one in Jerusalem still plotting rebellion against Nebuchadrezzar. To counter the illusion of a Davidic king as a viable representative of the people, blessings for the future had to be contingent upon individual behavior rather than an obsolete sense of nationalism. The promise of restoration in the (older) surrounding poetry of Jeremiah 30–31 thereby becomes contingent upon principles no longer strictly rooted in the Jerusalem-centric ideas that permeate the older compositional layer.[65] In this way, the community deported in 597 becomes covenantally sound without having to put faith in Jerusalem as a sacred locale or its royal establishment as a sacred entity.[66] The standards of proper Israelite identity are hereby adjusted, as one obtains good standing in the eyes of YHWH by individual adherence to the law and its prophetic innovations (i.e., Jeremiah's ongoing oracles), not by allegiance to an Israelite king or to the exclusive authority of the cult he sponsors.

THE NEW COVENANT (JEREMIAH 31:31–34)

With the elimination of corporate connections under the flailing Davidic king, Jer 31:31–34 provides the program whereby the covenant can be sustained in the future when national identity will be contingent upon individual imperatives. This passage is again tied syntactically to the introduction in Jer 30:3, as well as the promise of restoration in Jer 31:27–30, by the recurrence of the phrase הנה ימים באים, and serves as the culmination of the expanded oracle with the introduction of the "new covenant" (ברית חדשה). Jer 31:31 applies this covenant of individual responsibility to both Israel and Judah, thereby creating literary continuity with the older Josianic stratum in chs. 30–31 but also lifting the corporate culpability of (northern) Israel despite the earlier condemnations in chs. 2–4.[67] The new covenant does not reverse those words of judgment, but it releases the committed individual from their threats that the prophet must have viewed as still applicable to nationalists in Judah. The separation between the deportees of 597 BCE and those still living under Zedekiah's rule in the homeland is amplified in v. 31, which plays upon the contents of the letter to the exiles in Jer 29:5:

> Behold the days are coming, says YHWH, that I will make with the house (בית) of Israel and the house (בית) of Judah a new covenant. (Jer 31:31)

> Build houses (בתים) and dwell in them . . . (Jer 29:5)

The reference to both Israel and Judah in Jer 31:31 creates continuity with the Israel-centric focus of the earlier compositional stratum in Jeremiah 30–31; the use of the בית terminology does the same with the prophet's earlier message to the exiles of 597 BCE. The new covenant is made viable through the establishment of *new* houses, which implies a continued polemic against the old Davidic "houses," that is, the Temple and the royal line in Jerusalem.[68] The covenant of blessing and restoration is as distant from these older Judean institutions as the community to whom the present oracle is addressed. The announcement of the new covenant, then, aims to retain a traditional sacral community but, in line with vv. 27–30, divorces it from earlier notions of responsibility and allegiance. This precisely parallels the difficult position facing the 597 community in Babylon, torn as they may have been between the clear evidence of YHWH's judgment (and the validity of Jeremiah's message) and the threat to their identity as Judeans should they break away from the homeland community and divest themselves of allegiance to the Davidic line and Jerusalem. A new covenant from YHWH transforms the parameters and qualifications of communal identity.

The stipulations of the new covenant are brought into clearer focus in v. 32. It is

> not according to the covenant that I made with their fathers in the day that I took them by the hand to bring them out of the land of Egypt; for they obviated my covenant and I became to them a Baal (ואנכי בעלתי בם)[69] says YHWH.

Deuteronomistic references to the fathers generally present them as a corporate entity. Verse 32 takes issue with this and develops the theme of individual accountability expressed in vv. 29–30.[70] The new covenant is presented as different from that which originated with the Exodus (להוציאם מארץ מצרים), which perhaps reflects the political tension of the era concerning Zedekiah's wavering between allegiance to Egypt or Babylon. Jeremiah isolates the new covenant from the residents of Jerusalem and the royal circles; the phrase "for they obviated my covenant" may therefore refer not only to the repeated instances of the nation rebuking the prophets but also to Zedekiah's reliance upon Egypt, a reliance that echoes the sins of Jehoiakim.[71] The Exodus covenant with the fathers meant independence from Egyptian dominance and submission to YHWH, something negated by Jehoiakim's devotion to Necho and Zedekiah's apparent faith in Hophra. The statement "and I became to them a Baal" (ואנכי בעלתי בם) also carries an idea consistent with the theme found in the prophet's earlier oracles, namely, that YHWH had also been reduced to little more than a *baal* to these people, a fetishized idol rather than a living deity shaping history (see Jer 2:13; 7:1–15; 10:1–16; see also Chapter 3 regarding Jer 34:8–22).[72] Jer 31:32 binds the current political travail to this persistent misconception.

Jer 31:33, however, provides the solution:

> But this is the covenant that I will make with the house of Israel after those days, says YHWH, I will put My law (תורתי) in their inward parts, and on their hearts I will write it (אכתבנהו אל לבם); and I will be their God, and they shall be My people.

The Torah will be placed in their midst but inscribed upon their hearts (אכתבנהו אל לבם), which in turn will reestablish the covenantal dynamic that was forged during the Exodus but lost through the nation's corporate apostasy. We encounter Deuteronomic-type terms and concepts here, especially with the overt reference to a written Torah and to the "hearts" of the people. This is reminiscent of but not identical to the Deuteronomic program regarding allegiance to YHWH (Deut 6:5 and generally throughout Deut 5–11).[73] Whereas the Deuteronomic Torah commands the people to love YHWH with their hearts (an extrinsic instruction), it is now the Torah itself that becomes the matter of the heart (an intrinsic element).

That this Torah will be written *on their hearts*, however, demands special consideration. Most scholars correctly view the text as referring to a renewed concept of a Torah now more closely bound to individual commitment rather than institutional policy,[74] and they contrast the diction of the present passage with that of Jer 17:1, where sin is written on the human heart.[75] An additional consideration, however, is that the language used here to redefine what the Torah is and where it is to be found is decidedly scribal in nature. Throughout ancient Near Eastern culture, written texts were generated for the purpose of a scribe's memorization, and the phrase commonly used for the scribe's memorization of this material was that it should be "on his heart."[76] The heart was the consciousness of the scribe, and the standard dynamic involved the scribal engagement with and internalization of an external curriculum.[77] In earlier periods in ancient Israel, this curriculum would have been referred to as תורה, instruction, in both the Deuteronomic and pre-Deuteronomic sense of the term.[78] In our passage, however, the dynamic has been completely altered. The curriculum that the scribe must engage and cultivate is now in his own heart, and upon considering the interpretive and exegetical nature of Israelite scribalism in the late seventh–early sixth centuries BCE,[79] this suggests that the exegetical impulse itself constitutes תורה.[80] This is certainly no alien concept to the Jeremiah tradition, as the prophet's own exegesis was presented as inherently Deuteronomic in nature,[81] and as we have seen, Jer 29:5–7 exegetically creates a tenable covenantal circumstance by developing the original Deuteronomic legislation.[82] In Jer 31:33, this same methodology is declared to be the basis of the new covenant, simultaneously disqualifying the older hierarchies of the Jerusalem cult while legitimizing the scribal tradition of the Deuteronomistic variety now rendered independent.[83]

The shift from external to internal symbols for covenantal dialogue with YHWH such as an emphasis on scribal exegesis provides another indication that this material was conceived for the deportees of 597 BCE.[84] Scribal exegesis is perfectly suited here as a substitute for the tangible symbols of the

Yahwistic cult associated with the Temple and the royal house, symbols that the prophet already demotes in chs. 27–29. Scribal exegesis, on the other hand, is by nature intangible, and is geared for education-enculturation.[85] As the Deuteronomic tradition had already established, such methods of enculturation were mandated for individual commitment; Deuteronomy repeatedly calls the individual to account and places the individual's commitment to the law above all other systems of allegiance. Additional exegesis to the Deuteronomic tradition advocated in Jer 31:31–34 thus follows in a trajectory of ideas that subordinate the royal and Temple institutions of Jerusalem to the individual internalization of law (Deut 17:14–20; 1 Kgs 6:11–13), replete with the scribal administration, preservation, teaching, and development of its terms (Deut 16:18–20).

For a community that the prophet had already addressed in Deuteronomic terms now separated from the doomed homeland, scribal leadership rooted in the prophet's own covenantal understandings would serve as an appropriate medium point between breaking with and maintaining tradition. Torah is distanced from the Zadokite priesthood (cf. Jer 18:18) and declared to be completely a scribal concern, thereby open to exegetical interpretation.[86] In this way, the audience could retain its Israelite identity while rejecting the corporate nature of Israelite nationhood under the king and the priests in Jerusalem.

The corporate nature of religious authority is further marginalized in v. 34:

> And they shall teach no more every man his neighbor, and every man his brother, saying: "Know YHWH; for they shall all know me, from the least of them unto the greatest of them, says YHWH; for I will forgive their iniquity, and their sin will I remember no more."

The passage specifies that covenantal knowledge of YHWH will not come from official policy, religious hierarchy, or even philosophical postulation, but, rather from individual commitment to and faith in the precepts of the Torah. The hyperbole of Jer 7:8–11 will be precluded by the new covenant; salvation comes from within and the choice one makes to adjust and apply divine (i.e., scribal) instruction. Jeremiah therefore represents the last Mosaic prophet, proclaiming the final דבר ה׳ to the community of faith mediated by prophetic intercession. The new covenant obviates the need for intercession or the prophetic proclamation of divine דברים, for the Torah-directed life among the people will itself reflect the דבר ה׳, as intended long ago at Sinai. This will lead to YHWH forgiving the people, forgetting their sin,[87] and realizing the Josianic-era words of restoration and covenant that close the earlier version of Jeremiah 31 (vv. 35–37). Restoration is not contingent upon a covenant with kings but rather with their subjects, and speaks to community rather than kingdom and a congregation rather than a Temple.[88] Such a message was entirely applicable to a Judean community cut off from the homeland in which both monarchic and Temple institutions still operated. The institutional emphasis in Jer 31:31–34 is further suggestive of the composition of the audience for which it was composed: the rhetoric addresses the concerns of elites bound to such institutions (scribes, officers, priests, etc.), especially if these institutions were still standing. There is no indication in these verses that Jerusalem or its cult has been destroyed. The oracle is most at home, then, in a pre-587 context and would most directly address the elite exiles of 597.

EXPANDING THE PROMISE: JEREMIAH 31:38–40 AND 32:1–15[89]

It is certain that with the arrival of new Judeans, questions would arise about whether they, too, could share in the blessing of Jeremiah 30–31 promised to their brethren who had arrived in 597 BCE. To broaden its applicability in the post-587 world, the author of the Supplement engaged in two additional redactional maneuvers, adding vv. 38–40 to Jeremiah 31 and appending to it the additional unit of text found in Jer 32:1–15, which was based upon an independent tradition.[90] Jer 31:38–40 represents a brief but effective closure to the oracles in Jeremiah 30–31, deploying the formula הנה ימים באים found throughout the earlier redactional layers of these chapters to facilitate the inclusion of the promise of the eventual rebuilding of

Jerusalem. The content of these verses constitutes the only overt mention of Jerusalem's devastation, identifying the accretion as temporally distinct from the preceding material.[91] The brief accretion extends the oracles of restoration to a new community that had witnessed the city's destruction and establishes an historical context for the following episode in Jer 32:1–15.

The ideas established by Jeremiah concerning the relationship between Torah and existence (introduced by the new covenant of 31:31–34) are elucidated in 32:1–15 in a largely first-person narrative form and geared for the post–587 BCE audience, indicated by Jer 32:1, which is dated to the year of the second Babylonian campaign against Jerusalem. Furthermore, Jer 32:1–15 develops Jeremiah's earlier message in chs. 30–31 to the 597 community for a community that is now larger and later.[92] In contradistinction to the form of Jeremiah 30–31 (which relies upon distinctions between the poetry and prose for rhetorical effect),[93] Jer 32:1–15 possess qualities that blur the lines of communication. A number of important features immediately stand out upon reading the passage, most significantly the faint lines between Jeremiah's reported words and Baruch's contextual additions. Verses 6–15, which detail the purchase of land in Anatoth, are attributed directly to Jeremiah, while vv. 1–5 constitute the author's depiction of the background to the event:[94]

> The word that came to Jeremiah from YHWH in the tenth year of Zedekiah king of Judah, which was the eighteenth year of Nebuchadrezzar. Now at that time the king of Babylon's army was besieging Jerusalem; and Jeremiah the prophet was shut up in the court of the guard, which was in the king of Judah's house. For Zedekiah king of Judah had shut him up, saying: "Why do you prophesy, and say: Thus says YHWH: Behold, I will give this city into the hand of the king of Babylon, and he shall take it; and Zedekiah king of Judah shall not escape out of the hand of the Chaldeans, but shall surely be delivered into the hand of the king of Babylon, and shall speak with him mouth to mouth, and his eyes shall behold his eyes; and he shall lead Zedekiah to Babylon, and there shall he be until I remember him, says YHWH; though ye fight with the Chaldeans, ye shall not prosper?" (Jer 32:1–5)

The introduction in vv. 1–5 is not straight narration but relies instead upon a complex network of quotations to establish the generating circumstances. The author quotes Zedekiah, who in turn is quoting Jeremiah, who in turn is quoting YHWH. While this literary device seems confusing, it does clarify a few issues that would otherwise arise if Jeremiah 30–31 had once been intended to be the prophet's last word to the Judean exiles to Babylon in 597 BCE. First of all, it redirects the futuristic elements of Jeremiah 30–31 to a concrete historical moment that would have remained fresh in the post-587 audience's memory, especially via the mention of Zedekiah and Nebuchadrezzar by name.[95] This device shifts the themes of the preceding oracles from the theoretical to the practical; Zedekiah is disputing Jeremiah's word, the consequences of which would have been all too obvious to the post-587 reader who was paying for the king's mistakes. The example further distances the audience from the idea of old covenantal forms (such as the Davidic kingship represented by Zedekiah) and implies that adherence to the Torah, as declared by Jeremiah, will result in the sustenance of the covenant obviated by those who shared Zedekiah's misguided perspectives.[96]

The introduction in vv. 1–5 also serves another purpose, namely, to delineate the path of transmission of divine will and prophetic instruction. The root is YHWH, whose דבר comes to Jeremiah, who in turn speaks it. Zedekiah has clearly ignored it, thus yielding the 587 BCE calamity, but the author faithfully reports it for the purposes of coming to terms with what has happened. The scribe's role in reporting these verses is pivotal to the preservation and contextualization of prophecy. It implies that it is in the dynamic between the *scribe* and his audience that the prophetic message will take root, not with the king;[97] this reflects a major theme of Jeremiah 26 and accounts for the author's inclusion of Jer 32:1–5 in the Supplement.[98] We find here another example of a telescoped discourse qualified as the citation of a Jeremianic word (32:1) made by the author of the passage, similar to the telescopic features of Jeremiah 26. Here, the telescoped discourse places in Zedekiah's mouth the same basic lexical formula voiced by the angered crowd in Jer 26:9 led by the priests/prophets of the Jerusalem cult:

> Why have you prophesied (מדוע נבאת) in the name of YHWH, saying (לאמר) . . . (Jer 26:9)
>
> Why have you prophesied, saying (מדוע אתה נבא לאמר) . . . (Jer 32:3)

Despite the diverse historical scenarios behind these episodes, the stylistic and lexical commonalities suggest a continuity of adversity. On the one hand, this speaks to common authorship in the shaping of both texts, but on the other, it highlights the persistence of a problem that transcends circumstances, namely, that the prophet's adversaries know and recognize Jeremiah's words, but subordinate them to misguided presuppositions and worldviews (a theme that continually resurfaces throughout the Supplement, as we shall see).

Another element shared by Jeremiah 26 and Jer 32:1–15 is that both texts ultimately return to the central role of the scribe in an overt manner. Whereas the citation of prophecy and the transmission of dialogue in each respective text imply the importance of the scribe, it is a Shaphanide who saves the prophet in Jer 26:24, and it is Baruch who is ultimately the vehicle for prophecy in Jer 32:6–15, the central unit of the entire chapter and one that takes on the form of a scribal colophon.[99] We will see that the form of this unit is placed on par with the content, wherein Jeremiah is quoted as reporting the דבר ה' in vv. 6–7 that his cousin will come to him and ask Jeremiah to purchase his land in Anathoth:

> And Jeremiah said: "The word of YHWH (דבר ה') came unto me, saying: Behold, Hanamel, the son of Shallum thine uncle, shall come unto thee, saying: Buy thee my field that is in Anathoth; for the right of redemption is thine to buy it."

Verse 8 then narrates the unfolding of the event that Jeremiah overtly recognizes as the דבר in question:

> So Hanamel mine uncle's son came to me in the court of the guard according to the word of YHWH (כדבר ה'), and said unto me: "Buy my field, I pray thee, that is in Anathoth, which is in the land of Benjamin; for the right of inheritance is thine, and the redemption is thine; buy it for thyself." Then I knew that this was the word of YHWH (דבר ה').

The structure here is deliberate, as it establishes an intrinsic connection between Jeremiah's prophetic activity and the דבר as the unfolding of history.[100] It is for this reason that כדבר ה' appears in the middle of v. 8 rather than simply having the verse end with Jeremiah's recognition of YHWH's דבר; existence unfurls according to Jeremiah's prophetic word, both intuited and proclaimed.[101] We should note, though, that the textual unit that preserves and conveys this proclamation possesses the features of both a narrative and a direct prophetic message, but is neither one nor the other. The phrase "and Jeremiah said" beginning v. 6 qualifies *all* the subsequent words and deeds in vv. 7–15 as part of the author's summary; the author, in this case, is likely Baruch, who is presented as the notary recording the deed that itself functions as a scribal colophon.[102] The message in v. 7, the event in v. 8, the details of the transaction in vv. 9–12, and even the command to Baruch in vv. 13–15 are attributed to Jeremiah, but it is Baruch, not the prophet, who writes the text.[103]

In this regard, vv. 12 and 13–15 are especially important, as Baruch identifies himself as a character in the very episode he writes, and his role is twofold. First, in v. 12, he is the caretaker of the deed to the land, but this is no menial responsibility since the deed is now a sacred text that results from the transmission of the divine word (vv. 6–8). Second, in vv. 13–15, he is the recipient of an additional proclamation, which itself consists of two parts: he is to take measures to preserve this text because YHWH has declared that the land will once again be inhabited:

> And I charged Baruch before them, saying: "Thus says YHWH of hosts, the God of Israel: Take these deeds, this deed of the purchase, both that which is sealed, and this deed which is open, and put them in an earthen vessel; that they may continue many days. For thus says YHWH of hosts, the God of Israel: Houses and fields and vineyards shall yet again be bought in this land." (Jer 32:14–15)

These last verses specify an important idea: that the דבר ה' results in text and that the text itself becomes the basis for future existence. This is contingent upon the understanding of the prophetic message as "a shaper of events,"[104] since the message has now been relegated to text and facilitated by Baruch's role as a scribe.

The meta-textual dynamics of this passage are complex, but the essential message is that a scribe in both vv. 1–5 and vv. 6–15 (Baruch) is the vehicle for the blossoming of Jeremiah's prophetic message. This passage infuses the scribal craft with the merits of Jeremiah's own prophetic authority.[105] That this episode is dated to 587 BCE (Jer 32:1) but appended to a unit that was originally directed to the 597 BCE community (chs. 27–31) demonstrates the ongoing applicability of Jeremiah's message beyond the limits of the Jeremianic corpus as it had already existed in the author's time (Jeremiah 1–25+OAN).[106] Jeremiah's earlier materials are subsumed within a more comprehensive literary context that could address a post-587 reality but retain the essential message that life in exile did not constitute an end to the covenant. Its declaration of blessing following the material in chs. 27–31 suggests that the part of the nation in Jer 26:24 that did not attack the prophet now constitutes the Babylonian community worthy of redemption. The purpose of Jer 32:6–15, then, is to highlight the central role of the scribe in articulating prophecy, which in turn legitimizes the scribal reworking of chs. 27–29 and 30–31 in the Supplement itself. But the appending of Jer 32:1–15 to these chapters (and its central location in the Supplement) points to a pressing need to address the diverse populations now living in Babylon, some of whom may have been uncertain about their place in the community, their relationship to YHWH, and the channels of leadership that could guide them to proper religious practice.[107] The nature of divided leadership becomes a dominant theme as the Supplement continues.

EXCURSUS 1

The Redaction of Jeremiah 1–25:13+OAN

JEREMIAH 30–31 WERE UPDATED AT A TIME WHEN MAJOR UNITS OF Jeremianic literature were already circulating among the exiles of 597 BCE. The oracles make reference to the independent collection of chs. 27–29 (30:3 invokes 29:14) as well as important older passages currently found outside of that collection (31:27 refers to 1:10–12; 31:33 refers to 24:7).[1] That the closing lines of chs. 30–31 make reference to passages from early in the prophet's career (1:10–12) and a relatively contemporaneous oracle (Jer 24:7) speaks to the likelihood that the prophet's "active corpus" circa 594/3 was comprised of oracles spanning Jeremiah 1–24, a conclusion supported by form-critical and rhetorical considerations as well.[2] We may surmise that the redaction of chs. 30–31 was also connected to the event narrated in the colophon of Seraiah (Jer 51:59–64), which was affixed to an early form of the oracle against Babylon (Jeremiah 50–51) that Seraiah was commanded to read and throw into the Euphrates as a symbolic act.[3] By the end of the first decade of the sixth century, Jeremiah 27–29/30–31/50–51 constituted a distinct collection directed to the favored 597 community,[4] conveying teachings specifically geared for them but presenting them in rhetorical forms that supported those teachings.[5] But this unique literary collection could not obviate the earlier collections of oracles that the prophet had composed, the force of which still applied to the corrupt Judeans living in the homeland who had yet to endure the inevitable wrath of YHWH.

As such, several elements strongly suggest that the redaction of the early form of Jeremiah 1–25+OAN took place very shortly after the time of Seraiah's mission involving the Babylonian oracle. Whereas Jeremiah 24 created a "vision" *inclusio* with Jer 1:10–12, Jer 25:1–3 reaches back even further to the opening lines of the call narrative, recalling the same dating scheme as Jer 1:1–2:

> To whom the word of YHWH came in the days of Josiah the son of Amon, king of Judah, in the thirteenth year of his reign (Jer 1:2)
>
> From the thirteenth year of Josiah the son of Amon, king of Judah, even unto this day, these three and twenty years, the word of YHWH has come unto me . . . (Jer 25:3)

Though the rhetorical device is the same as that of the vision *inclusio* of Jeremiah 1–24, the resulting *inclusio* creates a larger literary envelope, subsuming the vision *inclusio* within it. In addition, Jer 25:1–3 appears to be citing Jer 1:1–2 via the inversion of lexemes (Seidel's Law):

Jer 1:2 – אשר היה דבר ה׳ אליו בימי יאשיהו בן אמון מלך יהודה בשלש עשרה שנה למלכו

Jer 25:3 – מן שלש עשרה שנה ליאשיהו בן אמון מלך יהודה. . . היה דבר ה׳ אלי

Jer 25:3 thus looks back to Jer 1:2 and attempts to periodize the totality of the prophet's preexilic activity as an extended Josianic mission, despite the fact that Jer 25:1 dates the current discourse to 605 BCE, the same year that the *Urrolle* was constructed.[6] The weight and significance of the contents of the *Urrolle* – likely the early contents of Jeremiah 1–11, which history had proved true by 597 – are applied hermeneutically to the entirety of Jeremiah 1–25.[7] Jer 25:9 recalls the language of Jer 1:13–15 via the reference to "the families of the north" that will rise against Jerusalem (here under the leadership of Nebuchadrezzar), a sentiment in line with the recurring motif of a foe from the north found throughout the early chapters of the Jeremianic corpus (see also Jer 4:6; 6:22).[8] Jer 25:10 goes on to invoke Jer 7:34, part of a secondary elaboration on Jeremiah's famous Temple Sermon that was composed following the rejection of the prophet's *Urrolle* by Jehoiakim in

604 (an act that was understood to have secured the dominance of Babylon over Judah).[9] Jer 25:11 makes reference to the 70-year prophecy in Jer 29:10, demonstrating that the punishment visited upon the 597 community lies in store for those still in the homeland. Jer 25:12–13 anticipates the prophet's extant oracle against Babylon and paves the way for the collation of other foreign nation oracles by turning attention to the nations surrounding Judah that will receive punishment for their own iniquities.[10]

Finally, and perhaps most importantly, Jer 25:1–13 functions as a colophon, identifying it as the closing frame to an older assortment of material. Most of the normative features of ancient scribal colophons are present in the oracle:[11]

1. *The name of the authority or authorities licensing the composition*: YHWH is identified as the source of authority in 25:3.
2. *A delineation of the composition's length*: the oracles of the prophet from the beginning of Josiah's reign "until this day" are identified in 25:3. This would have applied to a definite collection of oracles to the ancient audience of Jeremiah's day. At the same time, the phrase בספר הזה in 25:13 looks back to the collection of orchestrated material leading up to Jer 25:1–13.[12]
3. *A date of composition*: 25:1 identifies the oracle as originating "in the fourth year of Jehoiakim" and "the first year of Nebuchadrezzar."
4. *The name of the scribe responsible for committing it to writing*: Jeremiah is identified as the author of the oracle in Jer 25:1–2.
5. *The purpose of the composition*: 25:9 declares that the families of the north (i.e., Babylon) will serve as the vehicle for YHWH's wrath against Judah for their refusal to listen to his prophetic servants (25:3–7).
6. *Curses and/or blessings*: 25:11 declares that "the voice of mirth and the voice of gladness, the voice of the bridegroom and the voice of the bride" will be silenced. Jer 25:12–13 declares additional curses by claiming that divine wrath will later be visited upon those chosen to punish Judah.

7. *The place of the text's preservation*: YHWH will bring "upon that land" all the words proclaimed by Jeremiah in Jer 25:13. This is a rather loose qualification, but it does identify a location wherein the written oracles of Jeremiah will be preserved and applied.[13]

The structure of Jer 25:1–13 parallels the earlier colophonic structure of the *Urrolle*'s closing unit, Jeremiah 11. Jeremiah 11 provides the methodological and hermeneutical precedent for the material in Jer 25:1–13, closing as it does a collection of earlier oracles that had been redacted into the *Urrolle*. The same purpose is served here by Jer 25:1–13 as it closes the definitive collection of the prophet's preexilic oracles. It is perhaps for this reason that Jer 25:1–3 carries forward the date of the *Urrolle*'s composition, the mention of the 13th year of Josiah that had initiated the *Urrolle*'s opening chapter and the עד היום הזה phrase that had earlier been employed in the colophon to the *Urrolle* (Jer 11:7). The chapter looks back to the oracles that had accumulated since the time of the *Urrolle*'s completion and attempts to argue that they address the same problems despite the change in kingship and political suzerainty.[14] If the year 594 BCE saw a septennial reading of Deuteronomy among an unfit community in Jerusalem, the same period would serve as an appropriate background to the generation of a new "Torah" collection from a Mosaic prophet like Jeremiah, alongside a new covenant (Jer 31:31–34) for the community now residing in Babylon.[15]

We should note the difference between the initial function of the 70-year prophecy and its related oracles in the material written for the deportees of 597 BCE and the reappearance of the 70-year prophecy in Jeremiah 25. While the 70-year reference in Jer 29:10 is balanced out by subsequent messages of redemption, no such assurances are made in Jeremiah 25. The chapter is not addressed to the deportees of 597 whom the prophet viewed as good figs. Rather, from the outset, it pertains to those who "have not listened" (Jer 25:3), that is, the Judeans still in the homeland under the rule of Zedekiah. As such, there is no reversal of misfortunes for them; they too will be subject to Babylon's 70-year dominance, but the text then goes on to address nations beyond the homeland Judeans (Jer 25:12). In fact, the Judeans subject to YHWH's wrath in Jeremiah 25 are categorized with these other nations that YHWH will also punish (Jer 25:9–12).[16] The application of the 70-year theme in this collection of verses serves to implicitly distinguish the 597 community from those in the homeland: they both may suffer Babylonian aggression, but only the 597 community will be redeemed and restored. The other Judeans will fall prey to Babylon without hope of restoration. In the rhetoric of Jer 25:1–13, they simply disappear into the miasma of foreign nations surrounding them in the wake of the impending Babylonian presence. At the same time, while Babylon would be the agent of YHWH's wrath against the homeland Judeans and the other nations, Jeremiah had already promised the 597 community that Babylon would fall (in the Babylonian oracle). Such a promise could not be ignored; as such, chs. 50–51 were worked into a collection of oracles that formed the early OAN and were appended to Jeremiah 1–25 (via Jer 25:13).[17]

The creation of an early form of Jeremiah 1–25+OAN served diverse purposes. It provided a comprehensive collection of material that communicated the prophet's final word to the homeland community with respect to their current and future circumstances. Indeed, the narratives dealing with Jeremiah's activity shortly after the construction of this collection reveal that the prophet refused to provide any new or contradictory oracles regarding the nation's security (Jeremiah 37–38), as chs. 1–25+OAN provided the last word.[18] But the creation of chs. 1–25+OAN also provided a definitive collection of materials for the 597 BCE community to consider alongside the literature specifically crafted for them; the 70-year prophecy in Jer 25:11 invites comparison with Jer 29:10, and, indeed, the entirety of Jer 25:1–13 contrasts sharply with the promise of blessing in chs. 30–31. The role of Babylon in ch. 25 and chs. 50–51 provides the clearest division between the two communities: for one group, it is a vehicle for purification and security; for the other, it is a harbinger of doom that obviates further dialogue with YHWH as the deity turns away from them and to more international concerns.[19]

That both the MT and the LXX possess forms of Jeremiah 1–25 speaks to the identification of this literary collection as the definitive shape of Jeremiah's "book" before the exile of 587 BCE. Versions were likely transmitted to the Judeans in Babylon before the destruction of Jerusalem, and were preserved among the homeland Judeans and carried into Egypt (becoming the foundation for the LXX readings).[20] That both versions contain an OAN collection reveals the communities' recognition that the prophet deliberately appended such oracles to these chapters. The MT version of the OAN that ends with the Babylon oracle probably more closely mirrors the shape of the early OAN that resulted from the prophet's redaction, predisposed as the prophet was to privilege the position of the 597 community in Babylon and proclaim the eventual fall of their captors.[21] The LXX sequence of the OAN, by contrast, does not reflect a cohesive thematic crescendo, and was most likely constructed from an alternative collection of the prophet's oracles concerning foreign nations not specifically arranged for the redaction of Jer 1–25:13+OAN. Like many of the texts in the LXX of Jeremiah 1–25, the OAN of the LXX may represent an earlier base textual model drawn from an archive of Jeremianic writings, and was brought into the version of Jeremiah 1–25 preserved by the Egyptian diaspora community pursuant to the alternative (proto-MT) collection preserved in Babylon.[22]

EXCURSUS 2

The Reengagement of the Royal Line in Jeremiah 33:14–26

ONE OF THE MOST CURIOUS PASSAGES CURRENTLY FOUND IN THE MT of Jeremiah 26–45 is Jer 33:14–26, a long oracle that not only conflicts with the Supplement's critique of Jerusalem's sacral institutions but is also wholly absent from the LXX tradition.[1] Some scholars maintain that the editors of the LXX deliberately left this passage out of their developing text or that the omission was the result of haplography.[2] The dominant position, however, is that the oracle is a later addition to earlier versions of the MT of Jeremiah and was not part of an earlier edition of the book. The pressing questions are threefold: when was this text composed, when was it redacted into the MT, and why is it not also reflected in the LXX?

Many commentators have ascribed this composition to a very late date, understanding the oracle as legitimization of the Zadokite eclipse of the Davidic line and dating the passage to a time after Ezra/Nehemiah.[3] Some have gone so far as to say that it was composed to address the rise of the Hasmoneans in the second century BCE.[4] Adopting these positions requires a similar position regarding a fairly late date for the oracle's introduction into the MT and therefore advancing the argument that the MT continued to develop through the Hellenistic period after the LXX had reached a fixed status. As such, the composition of Jer 33:14–26 is not viewed by these scholars as connected to the prophet himself in any way, reflecting instead the exegetical impulse of a much later writer.

These positions pose some difficulties. A Hasmonean background to its composition is highly unlikely, as v. 24 specifies two distinct families; there is little to indicate that the Hasmoneans viewed themselves as any sort of amalgamation of the Davidic and priestly lines, celebrating instead their exclusively priestly pedigree.[5] Similarly, this verse would hardly support a dating of the oracle to the period of Ezra and Nehemiah, as the Davidic line had completely disappeared from the political scene in Yehud by the mid-fifth century BCE.[6] By that time, only the Zadokite line dominated local politics, and the literature emerging from that time and beyond credits David solely with establishing the Jerusalem cult for the sake of the Zadokite priesthood.[7]

By contrast, the language of Jer 33:14–26 does much to address the religious and political problems of the late sixth century BCE.[8] The return to Judah and the rebuilding of Jerusalem roused hopes for the restoration both of a Davidic king and of an active Jerusalem cult through the leadership of the Davidide Sheshbazar and the priest Jehozadak (ca. 538) and, later, that of the Davidide Zerubbabel and the priest Joshua (ca. 522). Yet, the pre-exilic circumstances regarding royal and priestly leadership could not be reproduced. Gone were the days when a national sanctuary could properly be called the "king's sanctuary" (Amos 7:13) or when the royal line could be symbolically associated with the divine "house" (2 Samuel 7; 1 Kings 8). The rise of Cyrus created a dramatic paradigm shift in the concept of Israel's monarchy (witnessed by the משיח terminology applied to that king in Isa 45:1); Persia had given Israel a new lease on national identity, but this necessitated new standards of behavior for the old Israelite institutions, and the Davidic and Zadokite priestly lines were thus both accountable to the Persian overlord. Tension between these two distinct lineages invariably developed, and Jer 33:14–26 appears to have been utilized to address this dilemma.

But even if we view Jer 33:14–26 as part of the religious discourse of the Restoration era, we are still faced with unanswered questions. Was it composed at this time by an anonymous scribe drawing from Jeremianic terminology or, as some scholars maintain, was it composed earlier (possibly by Jeremiah himself)?[9] Was the oracle composed all at once, or was the manner of composition largely a redactional issue, with individual oracles woven together into the larger unit? Finally, did the inclusion of Jer 33:14–26 into the developing MT tradition occur in the late sixth century BCE as well, or did it circulate as an independent oracle and only later find a place in the MT during its period of canonization?

A closer examination of the oracle's structure and language is needed to answer these questions. Jer 33:14–26 may be divided into three major structural units – vv. 14–18, 19–22, and 23–26.[10] A consideration of the Hebrew text is important, as syntactical elements identify these units as distinct:

14 הנה ימים באים נאום ה׳ והקמתי את הדבר הטוב אשר דברתי אל בית ישראל ועל בית יהודה
15 בימים ההם ובעת ההיא ואצמיח לדוד צמח צדקה ועשה משפט וצדקה בארץ
16 בימים ההם תושע ויהודה וירושלים תשכון לבטח וזה אשר יקרא לה ה׳ צדקנו
17 כי כה אמר ה׳ לא יכרת לדוד איש ישב אל כסא בית ישראל
18 ולכהנים הלוים לא יכרת איש מלפני מעלה עולה ומקטיר מנחה ועשה זבח כל הימים

19 ויהי דבר ה׳ אל ירמיהו לאמור
20 כה אמר ה׳ אם תפרו את בריתי היום ואת בריתי הלילה ולבלתי היות יומם ולילה בעתם
21 גם בריתי תפר את דוד עבדי מהיות לו בן מלך על כסאו ואת הלוים הכהנים משרתי
22 אשר לא יספר צבא השמים ולא ימד חול הים כן ארבה ואת זרע דוד עבדי ואת הלוים
משרתי אתי

23 ויהי דבר ה׳ אל ירמיהו לאמור
24 הלוא רעית מה העם הזה דברו לאמור
שתי משפחות אשר בחר ה׳ בהם וימאסם ואת עמי ינאצון מהיות עוד גוי לפניהם
25 כה אמר ה׳ אם לא בריתי יומם ולילה חים ואדץ לא שמעחי
26 גם זרע יעקוב ודוד עבדי אמעס מקחת מזרעו מושלים
על זרע אברהם ישחק יעקוב כי אשוב את שבותם רחמתים

The phrase הנה ימים באים in v. 14 is found throughout other redactional accretions in Jeremieh 30–33,[11] and the ויהי דבר ה׳ refrains in vv. 19 and 23 identify the initiation of separate strophes within the oracle, marking the end of the preceding material and the beginning of a new and distinct syntactical subunit. Nevertheless, all three units are marked by recurring terminology and thematic unity, addressing the need for an equitable relationship between the Davidic and priestly leaders, who share a single covenant from YHWH. The covenant in question is greater than those made individually with David (2 Samuel 7) and the Zadokite priestly line or the Levites more generally (Num 25:12–13; Deut 10:8–9).[12] Though the text alludes to these covenants, they are subsumed within a larger covenant informed by the language of the priestly (P) creation account (compare vv. 20 and 25 to Gen 1:14–19) and the Patriarchal promise.[13] Together, they function as integral parts of the cosmos created by YHWH and the fate of the entire nation.[14] The oracle constitutes both an encouraging promise and a stern commandment: the royals and priests are equally valid, but they have the same hierarchical relationship with the Persian rulers. As such, both are charged with carrying out their roles, and no allowance is made for either to assert any agenda that would challenge or compromise what YHWH has so obviously set into motion through the dominance of Persia.

Jeremiah had indeed argued in his lifetime for the subordination of royal and priestly prerogatives to the forces of history directed by YHWH, but as we have already seen, his message pertained to submission to Babylon. The totality of the Babylonian conquest no doubt proved to many that Jeremiah had been right and that his words were divinely inspired. If Jer 33:14–26 was understood or presented as a genuine Jeremianic oracle, then it would have carried profound authority for an audience returning from exile, binding the Davidides and Zadokite priests to a divinely ordained standard of behavior. Appeals to the authority of the Jeremianic tradition, in fact, characterize much of the literature of the Restoration era: Deutero-Isaiah, Trito-Isaiah, Haggai, and Zechariah all rely heavily on Jeremianic material (in terms of both form and content) in shaping their own messages.[15] In the scriptural culture that emerged after the exile, a passage closely bound to recognized Jeremianic ideas and ascribed to the prophet himself would certainly have intensified the force of its message.

This brings us to the question of the diction within the oracle. The linguistic and rhetorical style of the oracle is apparently Jeremianic, but ascribing wholesale authorship to the prophet is problematic. The oracle presupposes the devastation of Jerusalem, an event witnessed by the prophet and addressed in material attributable to him. This has led a number of scholars to suggest that the passage may be original to the prophet, who elsewhere speaks of hope in the face of Babylonian doom.[16] However, the hope expressed in the oracle for the priestly and royal lines is not characteristic of the prophet's own opinions and perspectives that date to his activity during the fall of Judah. Jeremiah 27–31 advocated a shift in religious attitude away from sacral hierarchies such as the royal and cultic establishments in Jerusalem, and there is little evidence in the Supplement that Jeremiah changed his mind on this matter in the final years of the Judean remnant community.

Nevertheless, we cannot deny out of hand some degree of authorship to Jeremiah, as the prophet's critiques are not against the monarchs or priests as institutions but against delusions concerning their viability as covenantal vehicles. Moreover, some significant passages elsewhere in the Jeremianic corpus seem to support these institutions, and Jer 33:14–26 shares both themes and lexemes with these passages.[17] We must therefore ask, when during the prophet's career might Jerusalem's monarchy and priesthood have most likely met with the prophet's approval?

One phase in Jeremiah's career provides a possible answer to this question: his role as an advocate of Deuteronomic policy during Josiah's reign. The early stratum in Jeremiah 30–31 addresses the matter of northern restoration through a Davidic king, and priestly references punctuate these oracles. For example, the call for priestly aid to the royal cause is overt in Jer 30:21, and Shilonite priestly heritage is identified as the topic of discourse in Jer 31:15.[18] All of this, however, is subordinate to the P theology cultivated in Jerusalem, and Jer 31:35–36 invokes the P creation account to lend context to the call for Shilonite support:[19]

> Thus says YHWH, Who gives the sun for a light by day, and the ordinances of the moon and of the stars for a light by night, who stirs up the sea, that the waves thereof roar, the YHWH of hosts is his name: If these ordinances depart from before me, says YHWH, then the seed of Israel also shall cease from being a nation before me for ever.[20]

We find here the lexemes that appear throughout Jer 33:14–26, which also invokes the P creation account, though now with regard to the

Jerusalem-centric ideology of the Restoration era.[21] In both texts, the P lexemes are used to support the relationship between priestly and Davidic figures.

One might therefore be tempted to ascribe Jer 33:14–26 in its entirety to Jeremiah's Josianic-era career, but this is highly unlikely. The description of Jerusalem in v. 16 points to a day in the *future* when Jerusalem will be restored to a state of security (וירושלים תשכון לבטח), implying that it has recently been violated. This is hardly consistent with a Josianic-era depiction of Jerusalem, which was understood as the the sacrosanct dominion of the divine name.[22] Likewise, vv. 24–26 presuppose that the royal and priestly circles have at some point been deposed, neither of which characterizes the sense of inviolability assumed in Josiah's day. The death of Josiah and the failure of the Deuteronomic reform seriously compromised this perspective, with the prophet taking measures to place limits on the applicability of Jerusalem-centric ideology of the royal and priestly varieties.

We are thus faced with a potential paradox if we wish to ascribe Jer 33:14–26 to Jeremiah himself. The prophet seems to have spoken favorably of kings and priests only during Josiah's time,[23] but our passage bears undeniable signs of a post–587 BCE period of composition, a time when the prophet had already rejected the validity of the Davidic house and the Jerusalem priesthood.

A solution to the problem is to be found within one of the structural units of Jer 33:14–26, namely, that of vv. 19–22. First, we must revisit the language of the unit:

19 ויהי דבר ה׳ אל ירמיהו לאמור
20 כה אמר ה׳ אם תפרו את בריתי היום ואת בריתי הלילה ולבלתי היות יומם ולילה בעטם
21 גם בריתי תפר את דוד עבדי מהיות לו בן מלך על כסאו ואת הלוים הכהנים משרתי
22 אשר לא יספר צבא השמים ולא ימד חול הים כן ארבה ואת זרע דוד עבדי ואת הלוים
משרתי אתי

Like vv. 14–18 and vv. 23–26, vv. 19–22 invoke the P terminology found in Jer 31:35–36 (noted above) and include references to David and the Levites. However, this unit possesses unique features not found in the surrounding material: its independence from the surrounding text is identified syntactically via the ויהי דבר ה' formula in v. 19, the *setumah* at the end of v. 22, and the ויהי דבר ה' formula in v. 23 initiating a new unit.[24] More significantly, however, vv. 19–22 is the only unit in the oracle that contains no historically or thematically problematic language. There is no mention of the deposed priesthood and royal line that we find in vv. 24–26 and no presupposition that Jerusalem has been violated, as in v. 16. In addition, the depiction of the Levites in vv. 19–22 further differentiates itself as a unit from the surrounding material. Whereas the reference in vv. 14–18 is to the stereotyped Deuteronomic phrase "the levitical priests" and that in vv. 23–26 is only to a priestly "family," vv. 19–22 employ the curious phrase "the priestly levites" (הלוים הכהנים in v. 21), a variant of the more familiar Deuteronomic phrase הכהנים הלוים.

The phrase הלוים הכהנים is the key to understanding the redaction history of the broader passage, as it occurs *nowhere else* in the Hebrew Bible. While it is possible that this results from an error in transmission, it is more likely explained as an example of Seidel's Law, that is, the citation of an extant text by the inversion of its lexemes.[25] If the הלוים הכהנים of v. 21 constitutes one such citation, then the text being cited is one that employs the more familiar formula הכהנים הלוים.[26] While one could argue that the source in question might be Isa 66:21 (another passage generally associated with the political tensions of late-sixth-century BCE Yehud), the similarities are only superficial. The grammar of Isa 66:21 separates the priests and Levites as individual subjects, whereas Jer 33:21 creates a construct chain that results in a compound term, with the term הכהנים functioning as an adjective. One might also look to the phrase הכהנים הלוים בני צדוק in Ezekiel as a source (Ezek 43:19; 44:15), part of a unit that anticipates the restoration to Jerusalem. This, however, is itself strongly influenced by Deuteronomic terminology. The likely source is therefore the Deuteronomic legislation of Josiah's time that had rendered all priests in Jerusalem "levitical priests" (הכהנים הלוים).

In addition to the citation of priestly norms in Deuteronomy, vv. 19–22 contain the repeated claim that the Levites are to "minister" to YHWH (משרתי and משרתי אתי in vv. 21 and 22, respectively); the emphasis here is on Levites specifically, not on Levitical *priests*. This, too, resonates with the Deuteronomic literature: Levites divested of cultic activity still minister to YHWH on the regional level by engaging in administrative/juridical activity (see, for example, Deut 21:5, which takes place beyond the central sanctuary).[27] This should be viewed in contrast to the dynamics of the Restoration era. An oracle from this period might employ the stereotyped trope הכהנים הלוים to identify the Zadokite line à la Ezekiel, but it would hardly specify Levites on their own as part of the Restoration enterprise, both for paucity of number and ideological tension.[28] Rather, the Deuteronomic language and citation in vv. 21–22 reveal an engagement of Levitical concerns in the Josianic period, where it is in the interest of the nation and a matter of cosmic significance to adopt a Deuteronomic sensibility associated with the Davidic monarch Josiah in Jerusalem.[29]

Several elements therefore converge with respect to dating Jer 33:19–22 in distinction from the surrounding units: the syntactical markers, the lack of historically difficult language, the common P terminology shared with Jer 31:35–36, the citation of the Deuteronomic lexemes (via Seidel's Law), and finally, the allusion to the distinctively Deuteronomic concept of Levitical figurehood. We may thus view Jer 33:19–22 as deriving from the same period of composition as the early layer of Jeremiah 30–31. The strong similarities to those oracles suggest that Jer 33:19–22 was once connected to them in some way. Though Jeremiah 30–31 were worked into the Supplement during the exile, their allusions to the Davidic king are not overt; but Jer 33:19–22 does not veil its rhetoric and may have served as the finale of these oracles. Because its pro-monarchic sentiments are voiced in the open, these verses were separated from the larger collection of oracles in Jeremiah 30–31 redacted into the Supplement, which criticizes monarchic imperatives (especially in chs. 34–38). Jer 33:19–22 would therefore have been excluded from the growing Jeremianic book during the exile, only to be reengaged during the Persian period, when Jerusalem's royal and cultic restoration was a real possibility and in need of prophetic address.

The postexilic circumstance aroused the need on the part of the Jeremianic tradents to adjust their corpus to correspond to the pressing interests of the day. Jer 33:19–22 was rehabilitated for this purpose: its authenticity as an original Jeremianic oracle commanded attention and would permit the prophet to speak again, but it lacked the specificity needed to communicate a clear position on the matter of the Davidic and Zadokite roles in Persian Yehud. At this point, the author/compiler constructed a frame around the once-archival unit of vv. 19–22 using language found in that unit, in the oracles of Restoration to which it once belonged (Jeremiah 30–31), and in the larger Jeremianic corpus. Verse 14 deploys the הנה ימים באים formula that the prophet himself had incorporated into Jeremiah 30–31,[30] vv. 15–16 adjust the lexemes of Jer 23:6,[31] and vv. 17–18 anticipate the Davidic and Levitical language of vv. 19–22, going into greater detail and addressing the specific royal and priestly features of the Jerusalem leadership and the apparent difficulties that arose between these two groups.

This difficulty is addressed in the closing frame of the oracle, vv. 23–26. Here attention is specifically drawn to the restored sacrificial cult *on par* with the executive role of the Davidic governor. The terminology of v. 24 levels the playing field for both the Davidic and Zadokite lines: both are "families" that possess the same covenantal promise from YHWH. Verse 25 draws from the P terminology in v. 20, binding the Davidic/Zadokite paradigm not only to national existence but also to the cosmic order; this same idea was already observed in the opening frame, reinforcing the likelihood that vv. 14–18 and 23–26 derive from a single compositional layer.[32] The final verse in this closing frame ends with an allusion to both the Deuteronomistic tradition via the stereotyped phrase דוד עבדי and the Pentateuchal narratives via the reference to the Patriarchs (v. 26).[33] We should note that the reference to both the Pentateuchal and Deuteronomistic language in the same rhetorical breath suggests that the author/compiler of Jer 33:14–26 was working at a time when a narrative spanning Genesis–2 Kings had obtained an authoritative position in Israel's developing canon but before the time when the Pentateuch had been separated into a distinct, self-contained work.[34] This points to the late sixth century through the early fifth century BCE but does not favor a time closer to that of Ezra, when greater divisions between the Pentateuch and the Joshua–2 Kings narrative were established.

What is especially significant, though, is that this important Restoration-era oracle was redacted into the proto-MT *Vorlage* and not the proto-LXX. The Conclusion to the present study will provide additional evidence as to why the postexilic redactors opted for including the oracle in the MT and, consequently, why the oracle was never included in the LXX. Its absence from the latter is closely related to the emergence of different prototextual versions during the exile, the reasons for which emerge as we turn our attention back to the chapters of the Supplement itself.

CHAPTER 3

The Standards of Faith and Intermediation: Jeremiah 34–36

JEREMIAH 34–36 ARE GENERALLY NOT CATEGORIZED TOGETHER AS A unit; the larger unit is typically formed via the connections already observed in chs. 26 and 36.[1] It is clear from the shape of Jeremiah 27–32:15 (and even from the subsequent material added in Jeremiah 33),[2] however, that a new category begins in Jeremiah 34, as the tone shifts dramatically from the promise of redemption to harsh castigation. That critical tone appears to stop in Jeremiah 35 and then resurfaces in Jeremiah 36.[3] However, the purpose of Jeremiah 35 contributes to the overall criticism in Jeremiah 34–36, and as we shall see, there is a reason why Jeremiah 35 appears between these two chapters, both of which have more in common than commentators have generally noticed.

THE ANTICIPATION OF THINGS TO COME: JEREMIAH 34:1–7

Jeremiah 34 turns attention from the possibilities of covenantal life in exile to the vapidity of life in Judah. Unlike the community of Babylon, which now holds the promise of redemption, the reader is reminded of the alternative embodied by the desperate and dire circumstances of what is left of Judah. The introduction to the chapter is presented in a tripartite form:

> The word which came unto Jeremiah from YHWH, when Nebuchadrezzar king of Babylon, and all his army, and all the kingdoms of the land of his dominion, and all the peoples, fought against Jerusalem, and against all the cities thereof, saying:

> Thus says YHWH, the God of Israel: Go, and speak to Zedekiah king of Judah, and tell him: Thus says YHWH: Behold, I will give this city into the hand of the king of Babylon, and he shall burn it with fire; and you shall not escape out of his hand, but shall surely be taken, and delivered into his hand; and your eyes shall behold the eyes of the king of Babylon, and he shall speak with you mouth to mouth, and thou shall go to Babylon. Yet hear the word of YHWH, O Zedekiah king of Judah: Thus says YHWH concerning you: you shall not die by the sword; you shall die in peace (בשלום); and with the burnings of your fathers, the former kings that were before you, so shall they make a burning for you; and they shall lament you: "Ah lord!" for I have spoken the word, says YHWH.
>
> Then Jeremiah the prophet spoke all these words unto Zedekiah king of Judah in Jerusalem, when the king of Babylon's army fought against Jerusalem, and against all the cities of Judah that were left, against Lachish and against Azekah; for these alone remained of the cities of Judah as fortified cities.

If our view that Jeremiah 33 in its entirety was not original to the Supplement is correct, then the Zedekiah passage in Jer 32:1–15 would have led directly to the oracle of judgment to Zedekiah in Jeremiah 34 (vv. 2–5),[4] creating a redactional bridge between the disparate units in which they both appear. The oracle against Zedekiah in Jeremiah 34 is set within an historical context, the final battle against the Babylonians (vv. 1, 6–7),[5] and the oracle itself possesses genuine historical valences.[6] In the oracle, Zedekiah is condemned and punishment is declared upon him: he will not escape Nebuchadrezzar, but will see him "eye to eye" (v. 3), an eerie anticipation of Zedekiah's fate in Jeremiah 39. Yet, despite this frightening allusion and the disturbing notion that Jerusalem will inevitably fall, Zedekiah will die "in peace" (בשלום in v. 5).

Upon a reading of the later narratives, Zedekiah's gruesome fate would hardly constitute a peaceful death, which has led scholars to view Jer 34:5 and the events of Jeremiah 39 as problematic or contradictory.[7] Others have suggested that it reflects an earlier tradition before the Zedekiah polemic became more pronounced.[8] The discrepancy between the prediction in v. 5 and the events of Jeremiah 39 is nullified, though, if בשלום here refers to the idiom for Babylon expressed earlier in Jer 29:7. That is, בשלום constitutes a reference not to the *manner* of his death but to the *location* of his death, that is, to Babylon, the city whose welfare Jeremiah instructed his audience to support. This hint of Zedekiah's fate (as well as that of Jerusalem) is reinforced by the mention of the funeral pyres in v. 5, foreshadowing the flames that will eventually engulf Jerusalem.[9]

All of this suggests that the oracle in Jer 34:1–7, while consistent with Jeremiah's own thought and perhaps stemming from an original decree by the prophet, has been shaped by the author of the Supplement to provide ideological consistency with the prophet's earlier material worked into the preceding chapters and to anticipate what is to come in Jeremiah 39.[10] It also contains an ironic twist that would not have been lost on an exilic audience: Zedekiah's own father, Josiah, had earlier been granted a promise that he would die "in peace" (בשלום, 2 Kgs 22:20). That king's unexpected death on the battlefield of Megiddo constituted anything but a peaceful demise. Though the DH attempts to mute the calamity associated with Josiah's death, the audience of the Supplement would surely have remembered the more gruesome reality underlying the text.[11] In this sense, the proclamation that Zedekiah would die בשלום would be a death sentence of the most violent order.[12]

THE CRITIQUE OF EMPTY RITUAL: JEREMIAH 34:8–22

The connection implied between Zedekiah and Josiah through the שלום proclamations prepares the reader for what is to come as the chapter continues with the oracle in vv. 8–22. Though many scholars consider this episode to be based on an historical event, several have viewed the prophet's oracle as strictly secondary or solely the result of a Deuteronomistic redaction.[13] There is, however, good reason to view much of the material in vv. 12–22 as originating with Jeremiah. While the content is expressed in a Deuteronomistic manner (which, in any case, is characteristic of many parenetic passages that may be attributed to Jeremiah directly), the oracles possess unique linguistic features that are decidedly Jeremianic.[14] In addition, the citation of the Deuteronomic law of manumission (Deut 15:12) – which, as we shall see, is the heart of the entire episode[15] – contains very minute differences from its source:

> If your peer (אחיך),[16] a Hebrew man or a Hebrew woman, is sold to you, he shall serve six years; and in the seventh year, you shall send him (תשלחנו) free from you. (Deut 15:12)
>
> ... you shall let go every man his peer (אחיו) that is a Hebrew, that hath been sold unto you, and has served thee six years, you shall let him go (ושלחתו) free from you ... (Jer 34:14)[17]

Though some have viewed these slight alterations as an indication of an older or alternate Deuteronomic source,[18] the text is better understood as an actual oral citation. The changes from the original Deuteronomic source reflect memorization of the original law in a general sense, on the one hand (the altered terms אחיו and ושלחתו are nearly identical to the original wording), and the minute variations inherent in recalling memorized material, on the other.[19] Finally, the tirade employs language that reflects Jeremiah's qualified view of the Temple as a place where YHWH no longer *causes* his name to dwell but is instead a place where *others* call his name:

> ... and you were now turned, and had done that which is right in my eyes, in proclaiming liberty every man to his neighbor; and you had made a covenant *before me in the house upon which my name is called* (בבית אשר נקרא שמי עליו). (Jer 34:15)
>
> Will you steal, murder, and commit adultery, and swear falsely, and offer unto Baal, and walk after other gods whom you have not known, and come and stand *before me in this house, upon which my name is called* (בבית הזה אשר נקרא שמי עליו)? (Jer 7:9–10)

In short, the type of discourse evident in these verses may confidently be set within the context of Jeremiah, a prophet well versed in Deuteronomic law, engaging in a tirade consistent with similar episodes from earlier in his career. And it is indeed to the earliest part of his career (namely, the Josianic era) that Jeremiah appeals when evaluating the current king's conduct.[20] Jeremiah reacts to Zedekiah's pretensions at making a Josiah-style covenant, in which the manumission law is followed but only on a ritualistic level; the people immediately reclaim their slaves after a perfunctory manumission (Jer 34:11). The portrayal of Judean society under Zedekiah demonstrates how far they have fallen from the time of Josiah: unlike that king's reportedly pious response to the discovery of Deuteronomy, Zedekiah does nothing to set the people right. With the introductory oracle to Zedekiah in vv. 1–7, the Supplement's author ensures that we recognize that Jeremiah's tirade in vv. 12–22 is directed, first and foremost, to the king. As such, the prophet's citation of Deuteronomic law in the presence of the king is reminiscent of the Deuteronomic charge for the king to adhere to the teachings of the Levitical priests:

> And it shall be, when he sits upon the throne of his kingdom, that he shall write a copy of this law in a book, out of that which is before the Levitical priests. And it shall be with him, and he shall read therein all the days of his life; that he may learn to fear YHWH his God, to keep all the words of this law and these statutes, to do them; that his heart be not lifted up above his brethren, and that he turn not aside from the commandment, to the right hand, or to the left; to the end that he may prolong his days in his kingdom, he and his children, in the midst of Israel. (Deut 17:18–20)

Whereas the Deuteronomic legislation regarding the reading of the law to the king is designed to ensure that he acts in the interest of the people ("that his heart be not lifted up above his brethren"), Zedekiah takes grotesque liberties with the nation's fate as his covenant reduces the law to a technical and artificial edifice. This is no different from the שקר against which Jeremiah polemicized from the time of the Temple Sermon on (we shall return to this point later).[21] It is thus no coincidence that Jer 34:14–15 and Jer 7:9–10 both allude to Solomon's Temple dedication speech in 1 Kgs 8:43, from which both verses draw their lexical inspiration:

> . . . that all the peoples of the earth may know your name, to fear you, as do your people Israel, and that they may know that *your name is called upon this house* (כי שמך נקרא על הבית הזה) which I have built.

This use of language is decidedly pre-Deuteronomistic; Deuteronomistic passages emulating the divine name always present YHWH as the proactive figure, causing his name to dwell where *he* chooses. Instead, in 1 Kgs 8:43, it is *the king* who is the proactive figure, who builds the house, and who calls YHWH's name upon it. This conformed to ancient Near Eastern patterns of royal Temple construction, but it stood against the traditional Levitical Shilonite cult from the premonarchic period that was emulated by David during his tenure as king of Jerusalem. David had preserved the traditional tent shrine when he established the Jerusalem cult; Solomon, by contrast, took the initiative to excommunicate the Shilonite priesthood from Jerusalem (1 Kgs 2:26), to build a fixed Temple of Canaanite design (1 Kgs 5:32; 7:13–14), and to serve as chief priest (1 Kgs 8:62–66). Solomon's cult was designed to replace the Shilonite cult; this eventually led Josiah's scribes, charged with mending fences with the north, to engage in a polemic against Solomon.[22] Jeremiah's Temple Sermon extends that polemic by ridiculing the very language employed by Solomon in his Temple dedication speech. That Jeremiah was citing 1 Kgs 8:43 is demonstrated by Seidel's Law of lexical inversion:[23]

1 Kgs 8:43 – כי שמך נקרא על/הבית הזה

Jer 7:10 – בבית הזה/אשר נקרא שמי עליו

Jeremiah's Temple Sermon was recited to place limits on the ideology of those who fixated on the Temple or the Davidic covenant as salvific vehicles in and of themselves. Though both the monarchy and the Temple were viable, they were subordinate to the law; from Jeremiah's perspective, the paramount positions of these royal institutions were undone at Megiddo with Josiah's death.[24] This idea informs much of the prophet's rhetoric and resurfaces in the Supplement via the author's citations and dramatic structuring of Jeremiah 26.

The appearance of language from the Temple Sermon in Jer 34:15 speaks to the persistence of what Jeremiah considered to be a delusional theology well into Zedekiah's time. But it also ties Zedekiah and the practitioners of the ceremony in Jeremiah 34 to the same sins as the corrupt prophets and priests of the central sanctuary in Jeremiah 26 (where the Supplement first invokes the Temple Sermon). Jeremiah calls the king and the Jerusalem elite on their farce of a covenant, their hypocritical observance of Deuteronomic law, and their faith in empty ritual acts. Under Zedekiah, the people have lapsed into empty practices that have turned the law code instituted by Josiah into little more than an idol. The exilic reader is therefore confronted with the unavoidable conclusion that the royal house is responsible for the exilic predicament. By contrast, the image of a Levite prophet such as Jeremiah citing the law for the king emulates the ideal chain of sacral command in accordance with Deut 17:18–20.[25] Therefore, very much in accordance with Deuteronomistic ideology, submission to the law and its interpretation/application by licensed Levitical agents such as Jeremiah is the cornerstone of national existence, with or without a Temple (or monarch) factoring into the mix as an essential ingredient (Jer 34:15).

Especially significant here is the oracle condemning Zadokite priestly ritual behavior in Jer 34:18–20:

> And I will give the men that have transgressed my covenant, that have not performed the words of the covenant which they made before me, when they cut the calf in twain and passed between the parts thereof; the princes of Judah, and the princes of Jerusalem, the officers, and the priests, and all the people of the land, that passed between the parts of the calf;[26] I will even give them into the hand of their enemies, and into the hand of them that seek their life; and their dead bodies shall be for food for the fowls of the heaven, and for the beasts of the earth.

The ritual described here is identical to that of Gen 15:7–21, a P text ascribing this covenant ceremony to the Patriarch Abraham. Here we may detect the actual position of the prophet preserved by the author of the Supplement, as the prophet had already strongly rebuked the viability of the P ideology as a covenantal vehicle shortly after the death of Josiah in 609 BCE.[27] The proximity of this critique to the preceding one reflects the common inadequacies of the different types of insufficient or misguided ritual systems at work in Judah in its last years. While the P covenant ritual depicted in these verses must reflect its currency in Jerusalem during the last years of the monarchy, and while it is consonant with Jeremiah's thought, the episode nevertheless appears distinct from vv. 8–17, as it is not covered in the opening narration (vv. 8–11). The author of the Supplement may have thus attempted to associate this episode with that preceding it to offer a comprehensive condemnation: from the perspective of the prophet, all forms of ritual mired in technicalities and conducted by unsuitable leaders fall into the same category if they deny the teachings of those (like Jeremiah) empowered to direct and adjust Deuteronomistic tradition.

Notably, the curse that closes Jer 34:20 deploys terminology identical to that in Jer 16:4:

> They shall die of grievous deaths; they shall not be lamented, neither shall they be buried, they shall be as dung upon the face of the ground; and they shall be consumed by the sword, and by famine; *and their dead bodies shall be food for the fowls of heaven, and for the beasts of the earth.* (Jer 16:4)[28]

> I will even give them into the hand of their enemies, and into the hand of them that seek their life; *and their dead bodies shall be for food for the fowls of the heaven, and for the beasts of the earth.* (Jer 34:20)

Jeremiah 16, part of the preexilic Jeremianic collection, deals overtly with covenantal abrogation and the tenuous nature of the (marital) union between Judah and YHWH. Jer 16:11 declares that calamity will follow from the failure to uphold Deuteronomic law, and Jer 16:18 expresses this via the terminology of the divorce legislation from Deut 24:4:

> Her former husband, who sent her away, may not take her again to be his wife, for she has been defiled (הטמאה); for that is abomination (תועבה) before YHWH; and you shall not cause the land (הארץ) to sin, which YHWH your God gives you for an inheritance (נחלה). (Deut 24:4)

> And first I will recompense their iniquity and their sin double; because they have defiled (חללם)[29] my land (ארצי); they have filled my inheritance (נחלתי) with the carcasses of their detestable things and their abominations (תועבותיהם). (Jer 16:18)

What is significant about these passages is that they reengage a critique Jeremiah had earlier lodged against the north for rejecting the Deuteronomic program during the Josianic period, characterizing that rejection as marital infidelity:

> And I brought you into a land of fruitful fields, to eat the fruit thereof and the good thereof; but when you entered, you defiled (ותטמאו) my land (ארצי), and made my heritage (נחלתי) an abomination (תועבה). (Jer 2:7)

The critique in Jeremiah 16 equates the population of Judah with the apostate population of the north, a population once considered ripe for reincorporation into Josiah's greater Israel but eventually lost to foreign imperial powers following Josiah's death.[30] This allusion to the earlier prophecy declares that a similar fate will befall the prophet's present audience, who delude themselves into believing that the union between them and YHWH will not be dissolved.[31]

The invocation of the curse from Jer 16:4 is an appropriate commentary on the manumission episode and the P covenant ritual in Jeremiah 34. The image of carcasses provides an ironic counterbalance to the bisected carcasses from the P ritual, and the misguided Deuteronomic covenant attempted by Zedekiah to curry divine favor instead secures the certainty of a divine divorce. We may detect here the same compositional method employed by the author in Jer 26:4–6, where various oracles from the preexilic corpus are fused into a statement appropriate to the literary/narrative context. The passage from Jer 16:4 that recurs in Jer 34:20b is syntactically independent of the first part of the verse; following his approach to the reuse of oracles in Jeremiah 26, the author has grafted the tropes of one oracle onto another in order to stress his point.[32]

THE HERMENEUTICS OF ORGANIZATION: THE AUTHOR'S QUALIFICATION OF JEREMIAH'S ORACLES

We can discern a parity of sorts within the chapter between the authentic thought of Jeremiah and the organizational strategy of the Supplement's author. Though vv. 12–17 and vv. 18–20a are derived from Jeremiah's own exhortations,[33] the distinction between the two suggests different moments at which they were delivered. The author nonetheless recognized their compatibility and constructed a frame to house them, namely, vv. 1–7 and the concluding exhortation in vv. 21–22. As discussed previously, vv. 1–7 appear to be based on Jeremiah's sentiments regarding Zedekiah, and the closing verses in the chapter follow suit. The resulting parallel creates an *inclusio*, in good keeping with broader trends of organization within the Jeremianic corpus.[34] The end result is a new exhortation that exegetically develops the compatibility between vv. 12–17/18–20, dissolving the differences between them, since both fall prey to the idea of שקר, another idea found in Jeremiah 16 (vv. 19–20). This is presupposed in principle by the tone of Jeremiah's oracles within the chapter, but the organization of these oracles into a single unit by the author fully expresses it.[35]

All of this serves only to strengthen the paradigm of Levitical prerogative from Deut 17:18–20 implied by Jeremiah's reading/citing of the Deuteronomic legislation in Zedekiah's presence (Deut 15:12). An illegitimate approach to Deuteronomic law and ritual – that is, one that sidesteps the Levitical mediators empowered to teach proper ideology and cultic behavior – is destined to secure YHWH's wrath.[36] In this regard, we must pay careful attention to the opening phrase of Jer 34:14:

> *At the end of seven years* (מקץ שבע שנים) – you shall let go every man his peer . . .

Many scholars have wrestled with the significance of this odd opening remark, with most viewing it as a grafting of the language of Deut 15:1 (which shares the identical terminology) onto the citation of Deut 15:12 that concerns most of the ensuing oracle.[37] On the surface, this is a reasonable assumption, as Deut 15:1 relates to the release of debts, and matters of debt and economic stability may well have been involved in the initial manumission of the slaves during Zedekiah's rebellion against Babylon.[38] It is problematic, though, to view Jer 34:14 as a combination of Deut 15:1 and 15:12. The Deuteronomic law of manumission relates to individual cases of servitude; that is, different slaves began their period of servitude at different times, and thus a blanket release of all slaves "at the end of the seventh year" negates the efficacy of the law itself (the seventh year of one slave could hardly be the seventh year of every other slave in Judah!). But even if we were to assume that all slaves inexplicably entered servitude at the same time, Deut 15:12 specifies that the term of servitude ends after the sixth year, not the seventh.[39] The slave must go free at the beginning of what would be his (or her) seventh year. The statement מקץ שבע שנים in Deut 15:1 is therefore incompatible with Deut 15:12, and the association of the two would constitute a legal conundrum.[40]

Such an exegetical quagmire can hardly be attributed to Jeremiah, who exhibits a sense of cleverness, precision, and clarity with his own lemmatic adjustments and allusions. Nor can we ascribe such a problematic reference to Deut 15:1 to the author of the Supplement, a learned scribe who proves himself to be a gifted writer and a deliberate, methodical redactor/editor. The problem is completely resolved, though, when we realize that *Deut 15:1 is not the source of the* מקץ שבע שנים *formula in Jer 34:14*. Another Deuteronomic source text contains the very same language and, in light of the Levitical connection to Deut 17:18–20 discussed earlier, commands our attention:

> And Moses wrote this law, and delivered it unto the priests the sons of Levi, that bore the ark of the covenant of YHWH, and unto all the elders of Israel. And Moses commanded them, saying: *at the end of every seven years* (מקץ שבע שנים), in the set time of the year of release, in the feast of tabernacles, when all Israel is come to appear before YHWH thy God in the place which He shall choose, you shall read this law before all Israel in their hearing. (Deut 31:9–11)

This passage, and Deut 31:10 in particular, serves as the source for the מקץ שבע שנים formula in Jer 34:14. Jer 34:8–22 touches on many important features in the preceding verses: Jeremiah cites the law in the presence of the people in Jerusalem, the location that Deuteronomistic tradition had identified as "the place which He (YHWH) shall choose" (Deut 31:11b). In addition, if the confrontation depicted in the chapter indeed took place in 587BCE, then an invocation of this Deuteronomic passage is quite timely, considering the fact that 587 would have been one of the septennial years set aside for the public reading of the law.[41] Jer 34:14 therefore invokes Deut 31:10 to reinforce the connection between the episode in Jeremiah 34 and the Deuteronomic passage regarding the charge to the Levites.[42] If this is the case, then the phrase מקץ שבע שנים serves to emphasize Jeremiah's Levitical status – a contributing idea in a chapter that makes clear that neither royal nor Zadokite status is effective in securing YHWH's favor. The law alone, applied by legitimate Levitical-prophetic agents represented by Jeremiah, dominates.

All evidence points to the author of the Supplement rather than Jeremiah as the individual responsible for introducing the מקץ שבע שנים formula into Jer 34:14. We have already seen that the author employs hermeneutical organizational strategies throughout the chapter, categorizing various oracles (and shaping some of them himself) into a new meta-message that suits his own agenda. This approach is highly consistent with what we find in Jer 34:14 and the various Deuteronomic sources it cites, merging two independent categories of exhortations into a new paradigm. But the very fact that as these sources are cited their meanings are altered serves as our second indication that the Supplement's author is behind the appearance of the מקץ שבע שנים formula, for this is the guiding logic we encountered in the citations of prophecy in ch. 26. There, the author cites various oracles by Jeremiah as well as Micah's oracle from Mic 3:12. All are grouped together to create new dimensions of meaning, and this too is at work in Jer 34:14.

It is the citation of Micah in Jer 26:18, in fact, that provides the strongest indication that the מקץ שבע שנים formula in Jer 34:14 derives from the author behind the Supplement. We will recall that in the former, the quotation of Mic 3:12 is introduced with the messenger formula (כה אמר ה') not found in the author's source text. The types of qualifications that resulted from the introduction of that formula occur in our current passage with the מקץ שבע שנים formula, as it too communicates a message governed by the context into which it has been interpolated.[43] This, we must note, follows the same method as the doublet from Jer 16:4 currently grafted onto Jer 34:20, which brings the themes and threats of Jeremiah 16 to bear on the recipients of the prophet's tirade in Jeremiah 34. In Jer 34:14, the author of the Supplement has added the formula to emphasize Jeremiah's own self-perception as a Levite invoking Deuteronomic law for the king (as per Deut 17:18–20), picking up on the theme of legitimate sacral agency.

But the hermeneutical implications of the introduction of the מקץ שבע שנים formula permeate further still. The overt reference to Deut 31:10 now categorizes Jeremiah's invocation as applying to the larger audience beyond the king, since that Deuteronomic verse specifies that the Levites must read the law to the entire people. Notably, this is to occur in "the place that YHWH shall choose" (Deut 31:11). To the author of the Supplement, that place was no longer Jerusalem but Babylon, in keeping with the prophet's own religio-political thought.[44] The author's choice in applying the formula thus has an additional dimension. Because of the allusion to Deut 31:9–11, the oracle once directed to Zedekiah and the population of Jerusalem now speaks to the *exilic* audience in Babylon, the place that YHWH had chosen for them. By amplifying Jeremiah's Levitical status, the author declares that a specific order of sacral authority had to be maintained in exile, with Deuteronomistic norms still applicable; indeed, the author grafts texts from both Deuteronomy and Jeremiah's preexilic oracles into the chapter, bestowing equal status upon the two.[45] The prophet is clearly Deuteronomistically sound, but as in Jeremiah 26, the author's exegesis declares his own methodological and ideological allegiances.

THE *DRAMATIS PERSONAE* OF JEREMIAH 35

Standards of faith and legitimate innovation are developed further in Jeremiah 35. The meeting between Jeremiah and the Rechabites presents the flip side to the narrative of Jeremiah versus Hananiah in Jeremiah 28. Like Jeremiah 28, Jeremiah 35 takes place in the Temple, but specifically in the chamber of the "sons" of Hanan b. Igdaliah, an איש אלהים. The terminology here is deliberately evocative of prophetic classes.[46] The particular use of the term איש אלהים, though, suggests legitimacy from the author's point of view, resonant as it is with figures in the DH who bore that same title and who qualified as YHWH's prophetic servants.[47] That the meeting with the Rechabites takes place in this environment is thus important with respect to Hananiah in Jeremiah 28, since that episode pits two claimants to the office of Mosaic prophet against each other. In Jeremiah 35, we obtain a glimpse into the affairs of one of those claimants, Jeremiah; this warrants a closer examination of the rhetorical function of the Rechabites in this chapter.

The Rechabites make their initial appearance in the DH as part of the Jehu narrative. According to 2 Kgs 10:15–28, Jehonadab b. Rechab was a particularly devout Yahwist, who accompanied Jehu on his purge of the Baal cult in northern Israel. Jehu's purge is a likely historical event, but the literature that depicts it was shaped as propaganda to justify it.[48] The stories concerning Elijah were manipulated to proleptically legitimize Jehu as the fulfiller of prophecy; the Elijah stories are an amalgam of traditions concerning Moses, Samuel, and Elisha, all of whom were well known to the intended ninth-century BCE audience of the Jehu narrative.[49] Though this qualifies the Elijah legends as part of the Jehuite propagandistic initiative, it also reveals that Elijah must have been an important historical figure also well known to the ninth-century audience in Israel. This made Elijah an important rhetorical vehicle for the Jehuite scribes. The presentation of the Rechabites may fall under a similar category: Jehu recruits Jehonadab (2 Kgs 10:15) and declares that his own zeal is the same as that of the Rechabite he has encountered. Such a declaration points to the familiarity of the ninth-century audience with the Rechabites as a hard-core Yahwistic clan, and would lend credibility to Jehu and his subsequent actions in much the same way that Elijah's prophecies legitimize Jehu's purge (2 Kgs 10:17).[50]

The Rechabite connections to the Yahwistic cult were therefore already a widely known and long-established fact by the mid-ninth century BCE. 1 Chr 2:55 ascribes to the Rechabites a Kenite background and thus a connection to Midian, and many scholars have convincingly argued that a Kenite clan was associated with the old Yahwistic cult cultivated among the Midianites as early as the days of Moses in the thirteenth century BCE.[51] The worship of YHWH among Midianite clans in the middle to late second millennium is witnessed in Bronze Age Egyptian records that refer to the Midianite region as "the territory of YHWH."[52] Further evidence supporting early YHWH worship in this geographical region is found in the earliest Yahwistic poems, where YHWH is identified as a mountain deity in the northwestern Arabian wilderness.[53] Midianite Yahwism is evidenced in Israel within the twelfth-century traditions behind Judges 4–5, where Jael, herself a Kenite, plays a key role in the Israelite resistance to Canaanite forces. Jael is also venerated in the Song of Deborah, a religious meditation on YHWH, Israel, and intertribal relations (see Judg 4:11 [especially the overt mention of the Mosaic heritage therein], 17–21; Judg 5:24–27; see also Judg 1:16). Though the Chronicler's genealogies are often informed by the sociology of the late fifth to mid-fourth centuries,[54] the Chronicler also incorporates ancient and independent sources into his work, and the convergence of evidence supports the Chronicler's association of the Rechabites with the Midianite–Kenite line.[55] This connection was certainly known to the Jehuite scribes, who were very interested in associating Elijah with Moses in order to help solidify the credibility of Jehu as the fulfiller of prophecy. The association with the Rechabites would serve as a perfect complement to the rhetorical strategy concerning Elijah if there was general recognition in the ninth century that they, too, possessed connections to authentic Mosaic tradition.[56]

This same impulse is felt in Jeremiah 35. Jeremiah, a Mosaic prophet by Deuteronomic standards, meets with Hanan's guild, the founder of which is identified as an איש אלהים. This specific prophetic title applied to Mosaic-type prophets in the pre-Deuteronomic period, and was ascribed to Moses himself beyond and within Deuteronomistic tradition (Ps 90:1; Deut 33:1). The presence of Rechabites at this meeting may be attributed to an old association between them and Mosaic tradition. Significantly, Jeremiah presides over this meeting and issues a דבר from YHWH ensuring the ongoing integrity of the Rechabite clan (vv. 18–19), a declaration intended for a public audience (v. 13). The narrative attempts to demonstrate that whatever other prophetic voices may have been heard in the last decade of Judah's existence,

Jeremiah's was decidedly Mosaic in nature and therefore trumps these other competitors. A specific standard of faith is thereby established through the recognition of Jeremiah's Mosaic pedigree (active also within Jeremiah 28),[57] which both elucidates the pretensions of Zedekiah in Jeremiah 34 and looks ahead to the dooming behavior of Jehoiakim in Jeremiah 36.

HISTORICITY AND IDEOLOGICAL AGENDA IN JEREMIAH 35

There is no reason to doubt that the chapter is based on some actual memory or event.[58] The reference to the Rechabites' religious desperation in the shift from tent dwelling to urbanization in Jerusalem carries with it a sense of historical veracity, especially in light of earlier urbanization efforts under Hezekiah under similar circumstances.[59] The meeting, then, would have transpired during the first Babylonian conquest of 597 BCE, as the Temple was left standing by Nebuchadrezzar's army, despite the confiscation of its various sacred vessels.[60] Yet, as observed earlier, the chapter is deliberately constructed and situated in its current position for a distinct purpose in relation to its neighboring chapters. While the chapter is dated to Jehoiakim's reign, the events recounted there appear to take place only after that king has died; the author's introduction to Jeremiah 35 as taking place in the "days of Jehoiakim" (v. 1) is a hermeneutical maneuver that associates the tensions of the chapter with that king's rule already evident in Jer 26:1 and 27:1. The mention of YHWH's "servants, the prophets" (v. 15) takes the event and makes it part of a wider ideological panorama in line with both the appearance of the term in the DH and its use in various Jeremianic contexts inherited by the author of the Supplement.[61] This is particularly evident when we compare Jer 35:14 with Jer 25:3:

> . . . I have spoken unto you, speaking early and often, but you have not heard me. (Jer 35:15)

> . . . I have spoken unto you, speaking early and often; but you have not heard. (Jer 25:3)

The similar language in Jer 25:3 and 35:14 has been interpreted by some scholars as evidence of a systematic redaction, but a few differences must be noted. Jeremiah 25 is presented as a parenetic exhortation; by contrast, Jeremiah 35:18–19 ultimately reveals Jeremiah 35 to be a scribe's reporting of events ("and to the house of Rechab Jeremiah said . . . "). Moreover, the "I" of Jer 25:3 is Jeremiah; the "I" of Jer 35:14 is YHWH. These distinctions diminish the argument that the commonalities of these chapters can both be attributed to a single redactional hand.[62] It is more likely that the author of Jeremiah 35 has drawn from Jer 25:3, and has developed it to equate Jeremiah's message in that verse more directly with the divine voice being quoted in Jer 35:14. That vv. 18–19 reveal that this chapter is ultimately the result of a scribe's work (the author of the Supplement) once more suggests that faithful scribes stand in the tradition of the Mosaic prophets. This is consistent with the word choice in Jer 26:1 (which presents the scribal author's word as similar to that of Jeremiah in 27:1) and is an idea that will persist in subsequent chapters.

The narrative clearly depicts the value of adherence to Jeremiah's word and the merit of sustaining tradition through adaptation in times of need (also the implication of Jer 29:5–7).[63] The Rechabites defy their traditional directive to remain nomads, but their urban dwelling arises only out of necessity; this choice does not imply a lack of conviction, which they emphatically affirm (vv. 7–10).[64] For this, they are rewarded with a blessing from the prophet (reported by the author in vv. 18–19), where YHWH promises that a Rechabite shall always live to "stand before" him. The phrase to "stand before" (לעמוד לפני) YHWH is generally priestly/sacral in nature (see, e.g., Deut 10:8; 1 Sam 6:20; 1 Sam 16:22),[65] which contrasts strongly with the perfunctory ritual practice among the Judeans in Jer 34:8–22 who receive no kind words from Jeremiah in 35:13–17. But the chapter also points to a major theme of Jeremiah 36 – the fidelity of the Rechabites to the rules of their "father" (35:6) contrasts with Jehoiakim's straying from the ways of his own father, Josiah, upon hearing the contents of the *Urrolle* (36:21–26). The Rechabites demonstrate true piety by adhering to the spirit of their father's mandates in the face of shifting tides, a test Jehoiakim will fail.[66]

An additional feature emerges when viewing Jeremiah 35 in its larger literary context. The brief mention in Jer 35:4 of the location of the meeting makes clear that the chamber of Hanan b. Igdaliah adjoined the "officers' chamber" (לשכת השרים), a compound term whose component parts factor significantly into the narrative of Jeremiah 36. The officers' chamber in Jer 35:4 appears to be the same locale as the chamber of Gemariah b. Shaphan in Jer 36:10,[67] and it is the officers themselves who are pivotal players in the drama of Jeremiah 36 (though we should not associate all of these "officers" with the Shaphanides; see later).[68] If Jeremiah 35 establishes Jeremiah's legitimacy as a Mosaic prophet by virtue of his association with Mosaic circles such as the Rechabites and Hanan's guild,[69] then the proximity of the officers' chamber to that of this Mosaic meeting suggests to the reader the proximity of the officers to the meeting but not their involvement. By 598/597 BCE, a distinction between scribes and officers had taken place, with the latter ultimately oppressing the former under the auspices of Zedekiah's court (discussed later). The chamber once belonging to scribes is now inhabited by powerful figures diametrically opposed to the political and religious sensibilities of those scribes.[70] The reference to the "officers' chamber" thus prepares the reader for their presence and purpose in the following chapter, which takes place chronologically years earlier and which witnesses the moment when the officers cast their allegiance with the royal court rather than with the words of Jeremiah conveyed through the scribes.[71]

THE *URROLLE*: ITS TRUSTEES AND ITS ADVERSARIES IN JEREMIAH 36

Jeremiah 36 stands out as the single instance in the prophetic literature where the circumstances behind the composition of a prophetic text are described: the beginning of the chapter seems to pertain to the poetry and prose delivered by Jeremiah before his certainty that Jerusalem was doomed, followed by a reference in the closing verse to these and other words (דברים) being written after Jehoiakim's rejection of the *Urrolle*.[72]

There is a paucity of information, though, concerning which texts were written for presentation to Jehoiakim and the royal officers and which texts were written thereafter. There is only the mention of "scrolls," which might simply function symbolically as a reference to the various literary collections penned by Jeremiah.[73]

Jer 36:1–8 should be viewed in some distinction (though not in separation) from the rest of the chapter in this regard, as it may be some form of the original scribal colophon from the *Urrolle*.[74] The relationship of these verses to the *Urrolle*, particularly vv. 4–8, is suggested by the distinction between the divine command in vv. 1–3 that *Jeremiah* write his prophecies in a scroll and the report in vv. 4–8 that Jeremiah commands *Baruch* to do so. The first collection of verses pertains to Jeremiah's own writings – Jeremiah had by that time indeed written the materials implied by the text[75] – and the second represents Baruch's copying of these texts and ending them with a standard colophonic signature.[76] The events that followed (Jer 36:9–32) gave rise to the larger corpus that dislodged the colophon (vv. 4–8) from its original place; the scroll is, of course, destroyed and later reformulated by the prophet and his scribe.

That the second scroll contains "all the words" (Jer 36:32) of the *Urrolle* suggests that the textual contents of the colophon would have been retained but, obviously, would no longer serve a colophonic function, as a new scroll would require a new colophon. Verses 27–31 detail a sequence of events that are quite similar to those of vv. 1–8: Jeremiah receives a commandment from YHWH to write a(nother) scroll (vv. 27–31), and Jeremiah, in turn, has Baruch do so (v. 32). These verses therefore function as a colophon as well, facilitating the inclusion of the (former) colophon of vv. 4–8 (and, by implication, the contents of the scroll to which it was appended) in the chapter's narrative and yielding a structural *inclusio* with vv. 4–8. We may detect a similarity here between chs. 34 and 36, as both deploy the *inclusio* as a way of structuring the contents of each chapter. As we shall see, this is only one of several important connections established between these chapters (with significant implications for the entire Supplement).

THE PURPOSE OF THE COMMONALITIES BETWEEN JEREMIAH 36 AND 2 KINGS 22

As observed previously, many scholars recognize that Jeremiah 36 appears to be patterned on 2 Kings 22, casting Jehoiakim as an anti-type to Josiah. There is much more significance to the commonalities typically observed between these two chapters, however, with particular repercussions for the chapter's presentation of the scribes associated with the family of Shaphan.[77] Following the Mosaic themes of the previous chapter, the *Urrolle* in the narrative of Jeremiah 36 is presented as a licensed interpretation of the Deuteronomic Torah.[78] Jeremiah is absent when his scroll is read by Shaphanide scribes just as Moses is absent during the reading of the Deuteronomic Torah of 2 Kgs 22:8–10, and both the *Urrolle* and the Deuteronomic Torah are described in identical terms (כל הדברים in Jer 36:2 and כל הדברים האלה in Jer 36:24; see Deut 5:18 and, secondarily, Deut 1:1).[79] To this end, it is worth noting that those who respond most dramatically to the scroll are "all the officers" in the Temple,[80] the same group who declare Jeremiah innocent in Jer 26:16 along with "all the nation" (כל העם). The entire nation, however, is curiously absent from most of the account of Baruch's reading of the scroll, despite the references in Jer 36:2, 6, and 8 that the scroll was to be read publicly. Verse 13 makes a brief mention of Baruch having read the scroll publicly, but the public reaction is not noted; only Micaiah b. Gemariah is said to have been moved to action. He, in turn, rouses the attention of his father, Gemariah, Elishama the scribe, Deliah b. Shemaiah, Elnathan b. Achbor, and Zedekiah b. Hananiah, who are joined by figures named in the later verses of the chapter.

It is significant that Elnathan b. Achbor is mentioned among these officers and scribes, as he is among those responsible in Jer 26:22 for the extradition of Uriah the prophet, who ultimately suffers death at the hands of Jehoiakim. It is perhaps this dramatic event that inspires the suggestion in Jer 36:19 by the officers that Baruch and Jeremiah hide based on the contents of the scroll; Elnathan has apparently changed his mind about how to deal with prophets, or at least with *this* prophet. This suggestion has a ring of historical authenticity, as it ascribes power to Jehoiakim and suggests the susceptibility of Jeremiah despite the divine claims in the call narrative and elsewhere that YHWH will protect him. Nevertheless, this too serves the author's interest in venerating the scribes. It demonstrates that Elnathan b. Achbor's genuine concern for Jeremiah's words has transformed him, and his scribal peers, into the agents of YHWH's protection, anticipated by Ahikam b. Shaphan's protection of Jeremiah in Jer 26:24. As in Jer 32:6–15, scribes safeguard prophecy.[81]

The chapter is deeply concerned with the sustenance of prophetic authority at the hands of the scribes, and this may indeed intimate little difference between the one and the other. As observed earlier, Jer 36:17–18 informs the reader that all the words that appear in Baruch's scroll were taken from Jeremiah's "mouth," committed directly to writing.[82] The scribes who bring up this matter are concerned with the phenomenology in Deut 18:18, and the narrative details how the divine word is communicated and preserved through the hand of the scribe.[83] This same issue is brought up again in v. 32, where the second scroll is written "from the mouth of Jeremiah."[84] Baruch's scrolls are authentic vehicles for the divine דבר, and thus, Baruch and scribes like him follow the prophets in disseminating the Mosaic Torah. To this end, the author's narrative, geared to an exilic audience, fulfills the hope of v. 3 that "the house of Judah" – now those in Babylon reading the account – will hear the words that are apparently ignored by the people of Judah *within* the narrative itself. The exilic reader is drawn into this text in the same manner as the preexilic reader of Deuteronomy; there, the audience addressed by Moses within the text is no different from the audience *of* the text ("us, even us, who are all alive, here, today" in Deut 5:3). This metaliterary dimension allows the Supplement to become, hermeneutically, part of the expanded *Urrolle* itself, the composition of which it narrates in this chapter (Jer 36:32). Hence, we encounter another important connection to 2 Kings 22, as both texts deal with a document that speaks to multiple audiences simultaneously. Deuteronomy addressed the Josianic populace even as it spoke to the wilderness generation about to cross over the Jordan. Now Jeremiah's *Urrolle* spoke directly to a generation that had crossed back over the Jordan into Mesopotamia, even as ch. 36 tells us it was geared to speak to the preexilic subjects of Jehoiakim.[85]

THE SIGNIFICANCE OF JEHOIAKIM'S REACTION TO THE *URROLLE*

The apex of the chapter, of course, is the reception of the scroll by Jehoiakim. Jehoiakim's burning of the scroll reveals the influential position written works had obtained.[86] While this certainly establishes Jehoiakim as an anti-type to Josiah, both kings still react very dramatically to the texts confronting them. As some scholars have noted, the spread of literacy in the late seventh century BCE made the written word far more common and brought it out of the sacral sphere.[87] Despite this fact, the reaction to the *Urrolle* presented in Jeremiah 36, like the reaction to the discovery of the law book in 2 Kgs 22:8, points to various categories of literature that still retained a numinous dimension. Jer 34:8–22, in fact, is predicated upon such an understanding, though it is taken to an inappropriate extreme: the Deuteronomic legislation is venerated by Zedekiah not as a code of conduct but as ink on parchment fetishized into some sort of idol.

Jehoiakim's reaction to the *Urrolle* may possess connections to Zedekiah's fetishistic ceremony. Jeremiah had raged against hypostatization-as-idolatry under the repeated decree of שקר, developing a theme promulgated by the Deuteronomists of Josiah's era.[88] Within the Josianic narrative, the discovery of the Torah was followed by consultation with a Mosaic prophet (Huldah), following Deuteronomic mandates (Deut 17:8–13/18:15–22).[89] The text of the Torah, though authoritative, was subject to qualification by additional prophetic proclamation.[90] By contrast, Jehoiakim's burning of the *Urrolle* may have been conceived as a parallel to Zedekiah's ceremony (an anti-Josianic episode in and of itself), that is, the desire to eliminate the *Urrolle* was an example of the same idolatrous שקר mentality. One need not worship an idol to engage in idolatry; the narrative suggests that Jehoiakim's destruction of the text was meant to eliminate the threat behind its words.[91] If Jehoiakim did indeed historically reject Jeremiah's *Urrolle* (concerned as it was with שקר as idolatry or hypostatization), then the narrative's presentation of that rejection as an act of שקר is wholly appropriate.[92] The Supplement's presentation of the event as the antithesis of 2 Kings 22 creates an historical anti-*inclusio*: that which was begun in Josiah's time draws to a horrific end under Jehoiakim, and doom is therefore certain.

THE "SERVANTS" OF JEHOIAKIM

Since Jehoiakim's destruction of the *Urrolle* associates him with the other שקר factions that Jeremiah had accused of idolatry, the distinction between the terms "officers" (שרים) and Jehoiakim's "servants" (עבדיו in v. 24) points to correlations between typological figures mentioned within the *Urrolle* itself.[93] Elnathan, Delaiah, and Gemariah are likely some of the very scribes associated with the prophet by his detractors in Jer 8:8; the detractors who are quoted in Jer 8:8 may thus be typologically grouped with the servants of Jehoiakim. The servants of Jehoiakim would thus be those royal officers who rejected the allegiance of the scribes to Jeremiah – one of YHWH's prophetic servants.[94]

Here is the moment that distinguishes between scribes and officers in narratives dealing with later events, with the latter claiming the resources of the former for less than devout purposes (Jer 35:4; see also Chapter 4 regarding Jeremiah 37–38). Some of these nefarious officers, servants of Jehoiakim, are even mentioned by name in Jer 36:26.[95] Though Elnathan, Delaiah, and Gemariah were familiar members of the royal court, they did not defer to Jehoiakim's position concerning the *Urrolle* and are characterized as urging the king to subordinate royal imperatives to the prophetic word.[96] The narrative thus highlights the political legitimacy of the scribes and suggests that they were no strangers to the goings-on of the royal court. Here again we see a connection to 2 Kings 22, since Jeremiah 36 establishes a continuum of sorts between the ideology of the earlier Josianic court preserved by these scribes and their eventual positions among the exilic population for whom the narrative was written.

THE SCRIBES AND THE TORAH

The conscious patterning of Jeremiah 36 on 2 Kings 22 carries with it an important implication, namely, that the prophet's *Urrolle* is a form of Torah strongly bound to the scroll brought to Josiah's attention in the Kings account. This is even intimated in Jeremiah 11, which may well have been the closing chapter of the original *Urrolle*. In that chapter, mention is made of "this covenant" (vv. 6, 8) in a way that refers to both Deuteronomy and the preceding Jeremianic oracles, establishing the latter as a genetic outgrowth of the former. Pursuant to that end, Jeremiah 11 is itself patterned upon Deuteronomy 27, the ceremony conducted by the Levites that ratified the relationship between the nation and the Deuteronomic Torah.[97]

If the *Urrolle* was a second Deuteronomy, then the allusion in Jeremiah 11 to the Levitical ceremony in Deuteronomy 27 may be categorized with the charge to the Levites to read/teach the Torah to the people (Deut 31:9–13) and the king (Deut 17:18–20), a responsibility that Jeremiah took upon himself as a Levite prophet.[98] Within the narrative of Jeremiah 36, however, Jeremiah is unable to do so in person, and thus his Levitical responsibilities had to be fulfilled in absentia. This was doubtless an issue that the author of Jeremiah 36 had to address, and he did so in an ingenious way: the charges to the Levites are executed by the scribes in this chapter,[99] which may not be far from the historical reality. The scribes in question were certainly connected to the Shaphanide school that had produced the Deuteronomistic literature of Josiah's day so concerned with the status of Levites,[100] and priestly castes such as the Levites were generally among the most literate levels of ancient Near Eastern society and were often connected to the royal courts.[101] Furthermore, the office of the scribes is located within the Temple itself, which is entirely fitting for a group entrusted with producing and preserving religio-political literature in Josiah's day and beyond; one might even view this scribal activity as pseudopriestly in function.[102] The author exploits these historical realities for the purpose of his narrative, which actualizes in a rather precise manner the Levitical duties specified in Deut 31:9–13 and 17:18–20.[103] Baruch reads the *Urrolle* in the presence of the people just as instructed (v. 10), and the other scribes later report "all the words" of the *Urrolle* to the king (v. 20; discussed later). Finally, the *Urrolle* itself is brought and read to the king by one scribe in particular, Jehudi b. Nethaniah b. Shelemiah b. Cushi (vv. 21–23).

Attention has been drawn to the unusual patronymic attention given to Jehudi by the author, as he is the only scribe provided with such an extensive lineage. Some scholars suggest that the unusually long list of names is an accidental conflation of two different people.[104] Yet, for the author of the Supplement, the listing of patronymics serves as an indication of a person's significance within actual history or simply within the world of the narrative.[105] Bearing this in mind, we must take notice of Jehudi's patronyms and recognize that his function within the narrative occurs at the very intense climax of the chapter: he is the one who holds and reads the actual *Urrolle* as Jehoiakim slices its columns into pieces and consigns it to the fire. It is thus Jehudi who stands in closest proximity to both the king and the scroll, a powerful symbolic statement on the polarity of forces weighing on the execution of his duties.

Nothing is said of Jehudi after this horrific moment, and his name does not appear in any other biblical text. And among the many scribal seals discovered in archaeological excavations in Jerusalem that correspond to the other named scribes in the chapter to an extraordinary degree, no seal matches his name.[106] Yet, the author of the chapter goes to great lengths via the patronymic information to emphasize the role he plays in the drama, as his name is mentioned three times in vv. 21–23, the high point of the chapter. Jehudi is intimately involved in the poignant event, and the tension is palpable as he reads the contents of the scroll, fulfilling a Deuteronomic (Levitical) duty, regardless of the hostility of the royal court to the content of the scroll.

Perhaps one of the most significant elements in the presentation of the scribes as surrogates for the Levite prophet Jeremiah is that the contents of the scroll are presented to the king twice. It is, of course, the second presentation that leads to the burning of the scroll, but we must direct our attention to the purpose of the first, that is, the initial reporting of the scroll's contents in v. 20. This constitutes a significant departure from 2 Kings 22, where the Torah scroll is brought directly to Josiah and read to him. Not so with the scribes and the scroll Baruch has brought to their attention. They listen intently and discuss it; upon bringing word to the king, the narrative suggests, they have summarized or interpreted its contents.[107] Verse 16 makes very clear that summarizing/interpreting the scroll was their intention from the outset:

> Now it came to pass, when they had heard all the words (את כל הדברים), they turned in fear one toward another, and said unto Baruch: "We will surely tell (הגיד נגיד) the king of all these words (את כל הדברים האלה)."

The emphatic הגיד נגיד directs the reader's attention to the significance of the oral dimensions of their intended report to the king. Still, we are informed that they told "all the words" (את כל הדברים) of the scroll that still lay in Elishama's chamber.[108] The implication here is that the scribes' interpretations of Jeremiah's written exhortations are intrinsically the same in merit, content, and purpose as the prophet's written materials themselves.[109] The *Urrolle* may have been a licensed outgrowth of Deuteronomy, but the scribes' interpretive/exegetical initiatives are to be understood as licensed outgrowths of Jeremiah's work. This may have a self-reflexive dimension, suggesting that the interpretive initiatives of the author of the Supplement are consistent with the words Jeremiah composed as a prophet and taught as a Levite. In fact, the theme of reading, discussing, and teaching permeates the entire chapter and appears to be an assumed dimension of these scribes' duties;[110] we may infer that this was also characteristic of Levites in the author's day (and, presumably, in the late seventh century BCE) if the chapter has these scribes assuming Levitical responsibilites.[111]

THE PURPOSE OF THE ORACLE AGAINST JEHOIAKIM (JEREMIAH 36:30)

After focusing on the scribes, the narrative returns to Jeremiah, who pronounces a curse from YHWH for having destroyed the scroll and forsaking its contents:

> . . . and his dead body shall be cast out in the day to the heat and in the night to the frost. (v. 30)

Jehoiakim's punishment for rebuking Jeremiah, the scribes, and the *Urrolle* is exactly the same as the punishment he himself inflicted upon Uriah in Jer 26:23: a death without proper burial.[112] This issue would have had special significance to the exilic audience of the Supplement. For generations, notions of the afterlife had been firmly entrenched in the belief that the nation's traditional homeland provided the entry points into the underworld.[113] Upon death, burial involved the Israelite being "gathered unto his ancestors," that is, placing the body in the family or common local tomb; it was here that the person would find a place forever in Sheol.[114] To deny someone burial was essentially to deny him or her a place in the afterlife and consign the person to an interminable pseudoexistence in the world of the living or, worse, to nullify the person's existence altogether.

This message would not have been lost on those exiles reading or hearing Jeremiah's curse to Jehoiakim in Jer 36:30, which introduces an almost Karmic element into the narrative. Jeremiah declares to Jehoiakim exactly what the king doled out to Uriah, and therefore the ultimate burning of Jerusalem may represent the due response to Jehoiakim's burning of the scroll. To the exilic reader, the message is clear that the scribes venerated in Jeremiah 36 possess the authentic prophetic traditions that the nation may either accept or reject, but the repercussions of rejection, as per the pronouncement against Jehoiakim, will be severe. Indeed, the exilic reader has already experienced the repercussions of Jehoiakim's destruction of the first scroll. The second scroll, now inclusive of the Supplement, commands greater respect from its audience.

THE LITERARY SEQUENCE OF JEREMIAH 34–36

The sequence of Jeremiah 34–36 holds the key to understanding the role of these chapters within the Supplement. Both Zedekiah and Jehoiakim are compared to Josiah, the former leading a covenant ceremony based on Deuteronomic law and the latter taking the central role in a narrative closely patterned on 2 Kings 22. In both cases, these kings are found wanting. Zedekiah reduces the Deuteronomic law to an empty ritual, and Jehoiakim maintains an obstinate stance in the face of a compelling scroll that communicates divine will. Both monarchs are guilty of the same basic theological misconception, namely, that text alone (be it Deuteronomic or Jeremianic) bears its own fetishistic power, one that can bring salvation if it is merely carried out ritualistically (Jeremiah 34)[115] or that can eliminate a threat if it is cut apart and burnt (Jeremiah 36). These episodes are in line with the prophet's career-long campaign against hypostatization, be it of a deity or a deity's word: both written texts and dogma could fall prey to the impulse toward שקר and be reduced to little more than an idol.[116]

The narratives of both kings are juxtaposed against the standard of good faith depicted in Jeremiah 35, and its position between Jeremiah 34 and 36 reflects the author's desire to highlight the similar problems in these chapters through an equivalent contrast with the record of a meeting of faithful Yahwists. Among the similarities emphasized by the author of the Supplement are the curses regarding death and burial in Jeremiah 34 and 36:

> . . . *their dead bodies* shall be for food unto the fowls of the heaven, and to the beasts of the Earth. (34:20)
>
> . . . *his dead body* shall be cast out in the day to the heat, and in the night to the frost. (36:30)

Both of these curses conform to an established Jeremianic tradition regarding the improper burial rites for the faithless or transgressors of divine will, especially those associated with royal circles (Jer 22:19).[117] It is important to note that it is not Zedekiah or his offspring who shall receive no burial; as observed earlier, several elements in Jeremiah 34 demonstrate an awareness of what is to come with respect to Zedekiah, and historical reality is brought into the service of a broader message. Yet, while Jeremiah 34 draws from authentic traditions regarding Jeremiah's criticism of Zedekiah's manumission fiasco, it is shaped by the author of the Supplement with an eye to the broader sequence of Jeremiah 34–36. The author has established parallels with Jeremiah 36 by ascribing to those who have engaged in the P-inflected covenantal ceremony the same basic projected fate as Jehoiakim. But these are not the only connections between these chapters: both kings "cut" a covenant (the ritual in Jeremiah 34; the scroll in Jeremiah 36),[118] and significantly, as both kings face a Babylonian threat, Egypt looms in the background as an unsuitable safeguard.[119] This last parallel especially looks ahead to the depiction of the post–597BCE Judean remnant in the chapters to come as well as their ultimate fate. Though ostensibly a report of events, these chapters constitute the type of teaching or interpretation of history that we might expect from the scribes as depicted in Jeremiah 36, with the juxtaposition of piety and impiety in rapid succession challenging the reader to discriminate between the two.

An additional tone may be sensed here. The promise to the Rechabites is due to their abiding faith in their parent traditions. That this promise precedes the presentation of the scribes in Jeremiah 36 cannot be coincidental. As we have seen, the blessing given to the Rechabites in Jer 35:19 possesses priestly valences, and the role of the scribes in Jeremiah 36 is decidedly priestly (Levitical) in execution. The scribes, too, are presented as faithful to the Deuteronomistic tradition as preserved and advanced by Jeremiah, a tradition that may have been shaped in the Josianic period but that presents itself as much older and that is concerned with ancient law and praxis.[120] Both groups accept alterations to their respective parent traditions as required by history; Jeremiah blesses the Rechabites for this, and the faithful duties of the scribes in the following chapter suggest that they, too, secure divine favor through their own sense of fidelity. Thus, the example of the Rechabites is used not only to disqualify those who incur divine wrath but also to identify those whose actions fulfill covenantal obligations. This, too, suggests the historicity of the Rechabite meeting,[121] though we once again see that history is used to serve the author's ideological interests.

RECKONING WITH HISTORY

The interpretation of history via the symbolic sequence of the text is not limited to the mediating position of Jeremiah 35 in the present collection of chapters. The equation of Jehoiakim's projected fate in Jer 36:30 with that of the elite of Judah in Jer 34:20 is also informed by this editorial/compositional method and addresses a problem that the author of the Supplement recognized. While the oracles in Jeremiah 34 are generally consistent with historical fact, the prophet's declaration of death to Jehoiakim in 36:30 does not match Jehoiakim's actual fate. Jehoiakim's reluctance to accept Babylonian hegemony resulted in the campaign of 598 BCE and the deportation of 597, but the king is reported to have died in Jerusalem and been buried in the royal tomb (2 Kgs 24:6).[122] *Faced with the dilemma of an apparently inaccurate oracle, the author's rhetorical parallels in Jer 34:20 and 36:30 hermeneutically allow the post-597 homeland community to bring Jeremiah's oracle against Jehoiakim to fruition.* This, too, points ahead to the events of Jeremiah 37–44, where the remnants of this same community are eventually cast out of the land, and further weighs in favor of these chapters all resulting from common authorship.[123]

But this also provides us with some insight into the historical veracity of elements within the Supplement. The author did not freely compose Jeremiah 36 in the manner of pure exegesis or *midrash*, as some commentators have suggested.[124] If he had, we would not encounter the discrepancy between Jer 36:30 and 2 Kgs 24:6; a contrived *ex eventu* oracle simply placed in Jeremiah's mouth would not raise the possibility of questioning its veracity. Rather, the author has incorporated into his account what appears to be an authentic oracle issued by the prophet in an actual historical episode, and has relied upon another historical event regarding Zedekiah to address the problem. Both chapters reflect a concern with historical authenticity (Jeremiah 35 contributes its share of historical detail as well), though neither chapter strictly recites historical events. History is *interpreted* both within and between these chapters, relying on lexical, thematic, and hermeneutical elements to convey deep dimensions of meaning that surfaced earlier in the Supplement and that would relate to the narrative events to come.[125]

CHAPTER 4

The Fall of Judah, the Descent into Egypt, and Baruch ben Neriah: Jeremiah 37–45

WHILE JEREMIAH 26–36 CONSTITUTE A COMPILATION OF DIVERSE MATErial, Jeremiah 37–44 are almost exclusively narrative in nature (though oracles have been incorporated into these narratives). This has led a number of scholars to argue that they derive from a different compositional circle or author than Jeremiah 26–36,[1] but in addition to the elements already discussed, several considerations weigh in against this conclusion. Like the earlier literary unit, this second unit provides an historical background for a number of Jeremiah's oracles (poetry and prose) contained in Jeremiah 1–25.[2] We also encounter indications throughout Jeremiah 37–44 of the fissure between the royal officers (scribes and otherwise) that surfaced in Jeremiah 26–36, with the prophet clearly identified as an ally to some and an enemy to others, contributing to the sense of political and sociological chaos in the twilight years of Judah. This not only would have lent immediacy and authenticity to the narrative for an exilic audience that had experienced a devastating break in the continuity of their own lives via the exile, but it also developed issues that were already present in Jeremiah 1–25, with the prophet's critique of the infallibility of the Davidic dynasty finding fruition in the depiction of the reign of the last king to rule from Jerusalem (this same element surfaces in Jeremiah 34–36, as observed earlier). Finally, as we will see, the characterization of the Shaphanides is consistent in both units, with allusions both explicit and implicit to the book of Deuteronomy associated with them and their scribal peers.

One of the most dramatic elements of the narrative concerning the fall of Judah to Babylon and the subsequent fleeing of the remnant community into Egypt is that there is no transition whatsoever between it and the end of the preceding chapter, Jeremiah 36. That chapter ends in the middle of Jehoiakim's reign, and Jeremiah 37 begins with the simple and rather stark note that Zedekiah reigned in the place of Jehoiachin, Jehoiakim's son (v. 1). We are given no details concerning Jehoiakim's revolt against Babylon; some sense of these events has already been communicated in Jeremiah 35, which takes place during the Babylonian siege resulting from Jehoiakim's revolt, but even then, the details are limited, with the author opting instead to focus on the fidelity of the Rechabites. While this reflects different sources pertaining to different historical moments, the skipping of details that would lead the reader from the temporal setting of Jeremiah 36 to that of Jeremiah 37 is not without precedent in Deuteronomistic tradition. 2 Kgs 19:36–37 presents the death of Sennacherib as a direct result of his campaign against Jerusalem, though Sennacherib's death occurred many years later (in relation to his desecration of Babylon).[3] In this case, the Deuteronomistic author also skips over intervening events in order to stress a point: hostility against Jerusalem spells disaster.[4] The same strategy governs the sequence of Jeremiah 36–37, suggesting that the actions of one rotten Davidide somehow directly affect those of his successor and reflecting an established rhetorical/stylistic device of the Deuteronomistic Shaphanide scribes.[5]

This stylistic device also is suggestive of a date for the orchestration of these chapters. The textual sequence of Jeremiah 36–37 presupposes that the political details of Jehoiakim's revolt and Zedekiah's placement on the throne are fairly fresh in the minds of the audience.[6] This frees the author to make a potent hermeneutical suggestion via the abrupt transition between the two chapters: the dominance of Babylon and the positioning of an ultimately doomed king on Judah's throne is the direct result of the refusal to recognize Jeremiah's written words. What is notable is that the closing statement in Jeremiah 36, that a new version of Jeremiah's written words was generated with additional material, suggests to the audience that the very narrative they now read or hear – which continues in Jeremiah 37–44 – requires a degree of attention that was denied the *Urrolle* read to Jehoiakim if similar punishment is to be avoided.

Comparisons can also be made between Jeremiah 36 and 37 via the introductory verses of the latter. The royal retinue under Zedekiah is described in the same terms as the royal officers siding with Jehoiakim (עבדיו in Jer 37:1; see Jer 36:24), and the introduction to Jeremiah 37 shares another feature with Jeremiah 36, namely, it is also influenced by 2 Kings 22.[7] A comparison of the opening verses of each chapter is revealing:

> Josiah was eight years old when he began to reign; and he reigned thirty and one years in Jerusalem; and his mother's name was Jedidah the daughter of Adaiah of Bozkath. And he did that which was right in the eyes of YHWH, and walked in all the way of David his father, and turned not aside to the right hand or to the left. (2 Kgs 22:1–2)

> And Zedekiah the son of Josiah reigned as king, instead of Coniah the son of Jehoiakim, whom Nebuchadrezzar king of Babylon made king in the land of Judah. But neither he, nor his servants, nor the people of the land, did hearken unto the words of YHWH, which He spoke by the prophet Jeremiah. (Jer 37:1)

Though the evaluation of Zedekiah is negative, the opening verses of Jeremiah 37 contain the same type of information that characterizes much of the book of Kings, including the introduction to the Josiah narrative. Jeremiah 36 and 37 should therefore be viewed with an eye to each other, as they establish that the regimes of both Jehoiakim and Zedekiah suffer from the same flaws and are the antitheses of the reign of Josiah, who clearly submits to the words of the prophets. But these are not the only elements that bind Jehoiakim and Zedekiah together as typologically interchangeable. Jehoiakim's burning of the *Urrolle* looks forward to the burning of Jerusalem in Jeremiah 39 (an event that takes place under Zedekiah's reign),[8] as does Jeremiah's decree to Zedekiah in Jer 34:3 that the king shall join in the funeral pyres of his ancestors.[9]

The reference to fire in Jer 34:3 sets the stage for Jehoiakim's reaction to the *Urrolle* in Jeremiah 36, intensifying the connection between these kings and their contribution to the fate of Jerusalem. As such, Jeremiah's decree in Jer 36:30 that Jehoiakim will not be buried among his ancestors finds a sort of fulfillment in Jer 39:7, where *Zedekiah* is led in chains out of Jerusalem to eventually die in Babylon – the earlier hermeneutical equation of the two kings facilitates this process. In this same verse, we find the fulfillment of another decree made by Jeremiah in Jer 34:3, namely, that Zedekiah's eyes will behold the king of Babylon.[10] Jer 39:7 makes abundantly clear that this is indeed the case, as Zedekiah does behold the Babylonian monarch with his own eyes, right before he is blinded. Finally, just as Jeremiah 26–36 begin and end with mention of Jehoiakim, Jeremiah 37–44 begin and end with references to Zedekiah (37:1; 44:30).[11] In essence, the two kings are typologically identical because of their role as Davidic kings in Jerusalem.[12]

These connections further support the argument that Jeremiah 37–44 are indeed part of the same literary enterprise as Jeremiah 26–36.[13] Nevertheless, Jeremiah 37–44 introduce new features. While Jehoiakim is a despot, his obstinate attitude reflects his relative strength as sovereign; the Davidic line still commands attention and retains a degree of power. This is not the case in Jeremiah 37–44; the Davidic house has lost significant credibility, so that Zedekiah fears being mocked by the people already in exile (Jer 38:19).[14] The narrative thus alludes to circumstances that had indeed developed by the time Zedekiah admits this fear, with the exiles of 597 BCE identifying Jehoiachin as their expatriate leader but also recognizing the dominance of Babylon. The language of Jeremiah 37–44 is the language of polemics, immediately advocating in Jer 37:1–2 the prophet's earlier message to the 597 community concerning the regime of Zedekiah (Jer 24:8–11). No discussion, however, is given to the actual events of the 597 deportation; it is a presupposed event, and no condemnation is made of the community taken at that time to Babylon. The Supplement thereby attempts to blur the lines between the captives of 597 and 587 and speaks directly to the commonality of experiences endured by both groups.[15]

THE PRESENTATION OF ZEDEKIAH

Chief among the author's strategies is the presentation of Zedekiah himself. Despite the connections to Jehoiakim observed earlier, some distinctions emerge. Whereas Jehoiakim is a specter in Jeremiah 26–36, surfacing only briefly in Jeremiah 26 and 36, Zedekiah receives a far greater degree of coverage in Jeremiah 37–39, serving as a major *dramatis persona* throughout these chapters.[16] This is suggestive of the greater historical proximity of the events in Jeremiah 37–44 to the author's intended audience than the narrative material in Jeremiah 26–36, and perhaps the perception of Jerusalem's destruction in comparison to earlier events and details. Zedekiah's role in these chapters is pivotal, and the author emphasizes that he is not merely a clone of Jehoiakim. In the theology of the book of Jeremiah, Jehoiakim's burning of the *Urrolle* secured Babylon's dominance,[17] but Zedekiah is personally credited with securing Jerusalem's actual destruction. And though Zedekiah appears to respect the prophetic office more than Jehoiakim, his petitions for Jeremiah to intercede with YHWH are interspersed with more menacing episodes. Jeremiah suffers charges of treason (Jer 37:11–14; 38:1–4), death threats from the royal servants and imprisonment (Jer 37:15–21), and cruel humiliation and punishment (Jer 38:6). Zedekiah's ostensible respect for the prophetic office is revealed to be little more than a game of good cop/bad cop; his sympathetic requests for intercession are buttressed by extortion tactics in the hope of obtaining a supportive oracle.[18]

Here, however, we encounter yet another implicit similarity between Jehoiakim and Zedekiah, and one already anticipated in Jer 34:8–22. Both kings fall prey to the ideology of שקר that permeates Jeremiah 1–25 by fetishizing or ritualizing the prophetic word.[19] The forcing of a supportive oracle from Jeremiah in Jeremiah 37–38 carries this reductive logic, with the king believing that the mere recitation of a positive oracle would be enough to shape the forces of history. It is entirely possible that Jeremiah 37–38 reflect a generally accurate portrayal of Zedekiah's behavior (a desperate king living in desperate times). Still, the presentation of Zedekiah carries forward too many motifs from Jeremiah 26–36 to be purely historical;

like the narratives in that earlier text, it is informed by rhetorical purpose.[20] Zedekiah's behavior as presented by the author would obviously have seemed futile to an exilic audience that had seen Jeremiah's earlier oracles of devastation come to fruition. The king's preoccupation with the sacral inviolability of Jerusalem (and his desire to subordinate prophecy to the service of that inviolability) is regarded as severely misguided and indeed as the immediate cause of the city's destruction (as per Jer 38:17–18).

THE BROADENING RIFT BETWEEN THE OFFICERS AND THE SCRIBES

The royal retinue in these chapters fares no better than their patron, Zedekiah. As observed earlier, following the events of Jer 36:24, the term "officer" denotes enemies of the prophet and, thus, enemies of the nation, maintaining the push for autonomy in the face of Babylonian domination by rejecting the written words of Jeremiah (Jer 36:24–25) or the declaration of an unwelcome oracle (Jer 38:4–6). Especially instructive in this regard is the episode of Jer 37:11–21. Here, Jeremiah is presented as making his way to his ancestral territory when various royal officials led by Irijah detain him and charge him with defection to Babylon (Jer 37:13–15). It is impossible to determine whether or not Jeremiah was indeed in the process of defecting; this would not have constituted treason or apostasy in his eyes, as the prophet had already declared Judean autonomy to be fallacious and viewed Babylon as YHWH's earthly agent.[21] What is significant in this passage is the association forged by the author between this event and the prophecy of Jer 32:6–15, a symbolic act prescribed by the written deed overseen by Baruch the scribe that the officers of Jer 37:15 prohibit Jeremiah from carrying out.[22] Again, we are presented with the same typological figures from Jer 36:24–25 who took a stand against written prophecy, emulating instead a delusional sense of nationalism. The author of the account here goes beyond mere criticism of Zedekiah and points his accusatory finger at those officers abusing the administrative and military power clearly granted them by the king

(Jer 38:5). Leadership associated with the Jerusalem court under Zedekiah is presented as contraprophetic at all levels.[23]

The split between these obstinate officers and the scribes who deferred to Jeremiah's words in Jeremiah 36 is invoked yet again in the episode of Jer 37:11–21 through the description of the prison where Jeremiah was kept under arrest by Irijah and his supporters. The prison (בית הכלא) is described as having once been the house of "Jonathan the scribe" (v. 15). We know nothing of Jonathan beyond the mention of his role as a scribe, but this fact is important. Just as the שרים terminology ascribes to Irijah and his peers a typological association now replete with symbolic meaning, the identification of Jonathan as a scribe (סופר) implies an adversity between Jonathan and Jeremiah's tormentors. The narrative informs us that "they" (Irijah and his officer peers) had turned Jonathan's house into a prison. One possible reading implied here is that Jonathan's home was forcibly claimed by Irijah and his peers, suggesting that the officers of Jerusalem stood not only against the prophetic word of Jeremiah but also against the scribes who had earlier heeded it, taking from Jonathan his own domicile according to their own whims. It may also be the case that Jonathan was among those taken to Babylon in 597 BCE or who fled to the northern frontier or the land of Benjamin after the first Babylonian siege was interrupted by the approaching Egyptians,[24] leaving his home open to Irijah and his henchmen to claim.

If this is the case, then the author of the account draws attention to the void left in the wake of the first Babylonian incursion, with the vacancy of legitimate social leadership filled by ruffians and vagabonds too fervently bound to the idea of Judean autonomy. Similar elements characterize the reference in Jer 35:4 to the "chamber of the officers" (לשכת השרים) that had been known a few years earlier as "the chamber of Gemaraiah" (לשכת גמריהו in Jer 36:10), that is, the office of a major Shaphanide scribe who had a close association with Jeremiah. The shift in title evident in Jer 35:4 reflects the deportation of the Shaphanides and their associates in 597 BCE,[25] with Zedekiah's officers taking over a space once occupied by those sympathetic to Jeremiah. Regardless of whether Irijah actually forced Jonathan out, if

Jonathan had been taken to Babylon in 597, or even if the entire event is a literary construct, the claiming of Jonathan's house in Jer 37:15 indicates that figures faithful to the prophetic word and prophetic processes such as the scribe Jonathan are now few indeed in the land. Those with any power who remained are presented as vindictive, cruel, and criminal.

GEDALIAH'S TENURE AT MIZPAH

The adversarial relationship established between the royals/officers and the scribes becomes more pronounced as the narrative continues in Jeremiah 40, which details the establishment of the postdestruction administration of Gedaliah b. Ahikam (a Shaphanide) at Mizpah under the auspices of Babylon.[26] Gedaliah's position as a regent of Babylon is consonant with Jeremiah's policy of submission, demonstrating that the scribes who had previously been associated with supporting Jeremiah's prophetic career now continue to do so by facilitating Babylonian hegemony.[27] The religious repercussions of this administrative authority are evident in Gedaliah's decree to the people in Jer 40:9–10 to continue with their ritual calendar:

> And Gedaliah the son of Ahikam the son of Shaphan swore unto them and to their men, saying: "Fear not to serve the Chaldeans; dwell in the land, and serve the king of Babylon, and it shall be well with you. As for me, behold, I will dwell at Mizpah, to stand before the Chaldeans that may come unto us; but ye, gather ye wine and summer fruits and oil, and put them in your vessels, and dwell in your cities that ye have taken."

The author reports that Gedaliah's decree was observed not only by those in Judah but also by the Judeans who had fled to neighboring vicinities (vv. 11–12); all of these people gathered at Mizpah to reconstitute the community in the wake of the destruction of Jerusalem, and Jeremiah figured prominently among them (v. 6). This episode, with its emphasis on continued life and Jeremiah's residence in the land, has led some scholars to view this as a base narrative composed by a pro-homeland party.[28] The legitimacy of life in the land, however, is not the primary purpose of this episode; a closer reading of Gedaliah's decree demonstrates strong parallels to Jeremiah's own earlier oracles in terms of both themes and lexemes:

Gedaliah's decree	*Jeremiah's oralces*
Service to the king of Babylon	Service to the king of Babylon (Jer 27:12–17)
"It will be good for you" (ייטב לכם)	Exile to Chaldea "for good" (לטובה in Jer 24:5)
	The "good word" (דברי הטוב in Jer 29:10)
Summer fruit (קיץ)	The vision of good figs (Jer 24:5–7)[29]
Dwelling in the [new] cities (ערים)	Seeking the peace of "this city" (העיר in Jer 29:7)

The oracles of Jeremiah alluded to in Gedaliah's decree contain the prophet's earlier message to the 597 BCE community in Babylon, presenting them with the potential for continued existence under the covenant.[30] Gedaliah's decree extends the same potential for ongoing dialogue with YHWH to the Judean remnant community. It is clear, however, that this opportunity has less to do with residence in the land as a special or unique condition than with recognizing the authority of a Shaphanide in a sacral capacity, serving the interests of Babylon commensurate with YHWH's will. Gedaliah specifies that he will "stand before the Chaldeans" (v. 10), deploying the לעמוד לפני terminology typical of intercession or representative subordination to a higher authority.[31] The sacral dimensions often associated with this phrase are implicit insofar as Babylon's king has replaced the Davidic kings as YHWH's earthly agent in Jeremianic discourse. To stand before the Chaldeans is, in essence, to facilitate divine will. Such is the counsel Jeremiah offered the 597 community; it is assumed here by Gedaliah, who is presented as instituting a feasible program for the application of Jeremiah's prophetic word.

An important consideration here (and one that persists throughout the subsequent chapter) is the absence of Jeremiah from the events in the narrative. Jeremiah 40:6 reports that the prophet joined the Mizpah community under Gedaliah, but the ensuing events make no mention of him, and he resurfaces only in Jeremiah 42. As mentioned briefly in the Introduction to the present study, a number of scholars view this as evidence of different extant narratives redacted into the current literary superstructure at different times. Yet, the mere absence of Jeremiah from the narrative should not be viewed as evidence of a fully developed narrative tradition only secondarily connected to those where Jeremiah is an active character. As discussed earlier, Jeremiah fades into the background during the narrative of Jeremiah 26 and especially in Jeremiah 36, where emphasis is placed on the scribes as faithful curators of the prophet's message against a hostile Davidic court. Jeremiah 40–41 take up this same strategy, with Gedaliah as a stand-in for Jeremiah who must eventually contend against a Davidic threat (Ishmael b. Netaniah; see the next discussion).

The connection between Gedaliah (representing the Shaphanide scribes) and Jeremiah (representing the Mosaic prophetic tradition) is anticipated by Jer 40:7, which initiates the account of Gedaliah's administration in Mizpah. In the MT tradition, the citizens at Mizpah are called "the poorest in the land"; this comment, however, is lacking in the LXX parallel. Some commentators therefore view its presence in the MT as a later addition that voices an exilic or postexilic polemic against the homeland community.[32] Jer 41:17–18, however, relates that this population fled into Egypt with Johanan b. Kareah. The statement that they were the poorest in the land is used as part of a polemic to anticipate the flight to Egypt and thus to denigrate the Egyptian remnant community rather than the homeland population, which is in fact not mentioned in this narrative complex. The comment on the poorest in the land may therefore be understood as original to the account; its absence from the LXX appears to be the result of haplography.[33] The likelihood of haplography is increased by a comparison of the MT of Jer 40:7aβ with the opening words of Deut 31:12, part of the Levitical charge to read the Torah to the people:

Jer 40:7aβ – כי הפקיד אתו אנשים ונשים וטף

Deut 31:12 – הקל את העם האנשים והנשים והטף

The doublet here is too precise to be accidental, especially given the context of Jeremiah 40.[34] In light of the Deuteronomic reference in Jer 40:7, the author suggests that Gedaliah's programmatic application of Jeremiah's oracles in 40:10 actualizes the directive in Deut 31:9–13 for proper administration of the teachings of Moses. The wording of the original Deuteronomic passage corresponds precisely to the events in Jeremiah 40. The people have been summoned, and the words of a Mosaic prophet (Jeremiah) have been invoked for the purpose of ongoing life under divine will. Yet this Deuteronomic passage involves an important subtlety: the people will follow the teachings of the Mosaic Torah *for as long as they live in the land* (Deut 31:13). From the exilic perspective, this condition for secure life would seem to have certainly run its course, and the reference foreshadows the tragedy that is to come in the ensuing chapters.

Taken together, the implications of Jer 40:7 and 40:10 reveal a great deal about the author's intentions in relation to his audience. They suggest strongly that Jeremiah's oracles had already been understood as consistent with the Deuteronomic Torah, that Jeremiah himself was indeed already recognized as a prophet like Moses in the author's time, and the particular allusion in Jer 40:7 to Deut 31:10–13 demonstrates that Deuteronomic discourse was current among the author's exilic audience, or at least among part of that audience.[35] What emerges in this episode, then, is the argument that Gedaliah is a proper executor of Deuteronomic tradition, interpreting it in a manner that would allow its essential ideas to remain active and that, in turn, would have sustained the Mizpah community.[36] Jeremiah's absence from most of this narrative is not, in the end, a matter of narrative dissonance or inconsistency. Rather, it is an effective rhetorical strategy meant to reinforce the role of the scribes as authoritative communal leaders and curators of authentic prophetic and legal tradition.

Upon considering the presentation of the scribes in Jeremiah 36 in relation to the present episode, we may conclude that Gedaliah and the Shaphanides in general were Levites who became associated with the Jerusalem court.[37] The Levitic concerns of the Josianic-era redactors of the DH – who are identified by many scholars as the Shaphanides – surface regularly throughout their historiography and constitute a major purpose behind both the DH and the Josianic stratum in Deuteronomy.[38] Deut 31:9 reveals that the charge to read and implement the law in vv. 10–13 is directed to the Levites,[39] and Jeremiah 40 presents Gedaliah as fulfilling this duty (by programmatizing Jeremiah's oracles). Levites are more generally understood in the Deuteronomic Torah as scribes *and* administrators (two qualifications that certainly apply to Gedaliah),[40] and as noted previously, the phrase לעמוד לפני uttered by Gedaliah in Jer 40:10 carries sacral connotations characteristic of Levitical figurehood.[41] We should recall that during Jehoiakim's reign, Gemaraiah's office was prominently located in the Temple (Jer 36:10), a fitting place for Levites engaged in the production of sacred literature who also had a role in the royal affairs of state (Jer 36:12; cf. Jer 26:10).[42] The influence Hosea's oracles exerted on Jeremiah's writings (both prophets possessed northern Levitical heritage) is widely recognized by scholars as prominent also throughout Deuteronomy,[43] and the Deuteronomistic tradition is deeply concerned with pre-monarchic sacral locations associated with Levitical activity that led to the founding of the monarchy.[44] Finally, as we have seen, the scribes in Jeremiah 36 fulfill Levitical duties in Jeremiah's stead, and given the Deuteronomistic tone of the chapter (and the entire Supplement), it is difficult to imagine that these scribes would execute such duties if they were not of Levite stock themselves (cf. 1 Kgs 12:31). It is perhaps not surprising, therefore, that Gedaliah officiated as communal leader at Mizpah: it was at Mizpah that the Levite Samuel governed the people and eventually facilitated the paradigm shift to monarchy by inaugurating Saul at the site (1 Sam 10:17–25). Now, with a new paradigm shift from monarchy to Babylonian province in effect, Gedaliah was to serve the same purpose.[45]

ISHMAEL'S MASSACRE AND THE REMNANT'S RESPONSE

Gedaliah's program is demolished, perhaps not surprisingly, by Ishmael b. Netaniah, a member of the royal house who carries out a brutal slaughter of Gedaliah and the Babylonian officials stationed at Mizpah (Jer 41:1–3). Ishmael's political motivation is understandable, as capitulation to Babylon worked against royal interests for any sort of eventual independence.

Consequently, few scholars dispute the historicity of this account, which is paralleled in a truncated form in 2 Kings 25.[46] The account that follows (the murder of the pilgrims to Jerusalem [Jer 41:5–7]) is not, however, paralleled elsewhere in the biblical record. Though quite likely based on historically analogous events involving pilgrimage to the ruins of Jerusalem,[47] the account bears the marks of a commentary by the author on the nature of the royal line and the state of affairs among the remnant community in the absence of Gedaliah's leadership. The pilgrims hail from Shechem, Samaria, and Shiloh, three major Ephraimite cities, all of which received significant attention in the literature emerging from Josiah's court decades earlier,[48] and all associated with Israel's pre-Deuteronomic cultic and political history.[49] The Josianic literature had attempted to extend Davidic hegemony into the north via the implementation of Deuteronomic policy; the pilgrims' appearance at the ruins of Jerusalem presents a long-overdue acceptance of Deuteronomic policy on the part of the northerners. This, however, is all for naught, as their fidelity to a Jerusalem-centric program and the royal line that sponsored it secures their demise. The imagery is stark and unforgiving: a massacre of pilgrims at a ruined Temple mount, carried out by a corrupt Davidide who loots bounty reserved for sacrifice and who takes hostages from his own people as he flees to Ammon (Jer 41:10). The account presents a bitter commentary on the old covenantal institutions (the Temple and the royal line as sacred): these fixtures lead to destruction and death over against the potential represented by the prophetic word as mediated programmatically through Gedaliah.[50]

The narrative following Ishmael's massacre (regardless of whether or not the slaughter of the pilgrims was an actual event) must accurately preserve the essence of the political climate among the Judean remnant before their descent into Egypt. Twice had a Davidic king rebelled against Nebuchadnezzar,[51] and twice had Nebuchadnezzar devastated Judah, the second time involving greater brutality. That the slaughter of Gedaliah and the Babylonian officials came at the hands of a Davidide such as Ishmael would have clearly raised fears of a Babylonian reprisal; fleeing to Egypt would have appeared to be a safe and logical alternative.[52] The counterargument could be made, however, that the Babylonian retaliation would not have been aimed against the remnant now headed by Johanan b. Kareah but against Ishmael and his brood, who had by then fled to Ammon. Indeed, the very fact that Johanan had already made known his antipathy to Ishmael (Jer 40:13–15) may have weighed in the community's favor in terms of Babylon's actions, and the presence of Jeremiah and Baruch – two figures whose pro-Babylonian position would have been well known to Nebuchadnezzar's agents – among the community may well have been enough to avoid incurring Babylonian wrath. This political dynamic likely stands behind the oracle in Jeremiah 42, which strongly advocates remaining in the land under Babylonian hegemony and, we may imagine, under the administration of scribal leadership (such as that of Baruch, a Shaphanide ally and Babylonian advocate).[53]

We may thus view the tradition of Jeremiah delivering an oracle in Jeremiah 42 as rooted in historical memory and based on the prophet's actual sentiments. That the reliance upon Egypt (Babylon's enemy) is an affront to YHWH presupposes the relocation of divine favor to Babylon from Jeremiah 27–29 and is therefore consistent with authentic Jeremianic tradition.[54] Nevertheless, the present oracle of Jeremiah 42 is part of the chapter's carefully constructed rhetorical strategy, one that is consonant with the extended themes initiated in Jeremiah 26.[55] Indeed, the final verses of Jeremiah 42 presuppose the events of Jeremiah 43–44 and identify the current form of the oracle as a retrospective statement rather than a direct transcription of the prophet's words.[56] We should not reject out of hand the basic veracity of the narrative, but as we shall see, the chapter is too deliberately structured and evocative of related texts to be a strict chronicle of events.

DEUTERONOMISTIC FORMS AND IDEOLOGY IN JEREMIAH 42

Jeremiah 42 is firmly founded upon patterns deriving from Deuteronomistic traditions inherited by the author. This is powerfully evident in the threat dimensions of the oracle, which draw directly from the penalties for obviating the stipulations of the covenant in Deuteronomy 28,[57] but the influence of Deuteronomistic thought runs even deeper. This is especially apparent in vv. 1–6, which present the *community* petitioning Jeremiah to act as their intercessor and pledging to adhere to his instructions (an allusion to this appears later in v. 20). The model for this episode derives from Deuteronomy's account of the Sinai theophany and the Deuteronomic model of Mosaic prophecy, where similar dynamics characterize the recitation of Israel's petitions to Moses to serve as prophetic intercessor:

> And you said: "Behold, YHWH our God has shown us his glory and his greatness, and we have heard his voice out of the midst of the fire; we have seen this day that God does speak with man, and he lives. . . . *Go thou near, and hear all that YHWH our God may say; and you shall speak unto us all that YHWH our God may speak unto you; and we will hear it and do it.*" (Deut 5:20–23)

> A prophet will YHWH thy God raise up unto you, from your midst, of your brethren, like unto me; unto him you shall hearken; *according to all that you did desire of YHWH your God in Horeb in the day of the assembly, saying: "Let me not hear again the voice of YHWH my God, neither let me see this great fire any more, that I die not." And YHWH said unto me: "They have well said that which they have spoken.* I will raise them up a prophet from among their brethren, like unto you; and I will put my words in his mouth, and he shall speak unto them all that I shall command him." (Deut 18:15–18)

Here the Deuteronomic concept of prophecy already adopted by Jeremiah earlier in his career (e.g., Jer 1:9) is cast against the role of the *people* in requesting the office. In both Jeremiah 42 and the Deuteronomic passages previously cited, the people recognize the need for the office and affirm their allegiance to whatever the prophet has to say. The reference in Jer 43:1 to the oracle in Jeremiah 42 thus carries a significant clue as to how the author wished to characterize that oracle:

> And when Jeremiah finished speaking (ויהי ככלות ירמיהו לדבר) to all the people all the words of YHWH their God, by which YHWH had sent him to them, [even] all these words (את כל הדברים האלה). (Jer 43:1)

Identical terminology characterizes the narration following Moses' completion of the writing and recitation of the Song of Moses (Deut 32:1–43):

> And when Moses finished speaking all these words to all of Israel... (ויכל משה לדבר את כל הדברים אלה אל כל ישראל). (Deut 32:45)

The lexical similarities here are no coincidence. The author has deliberately directed the reader's attention to this Deuteronomic passage, reinforcing the parallel between Jeremiah and Moses in this instance.[58] One might view this clause as a secondary redactional accretion, but even if this is the case, it simply amplifies what is already explicit in the oracle in Jeremiah 42, which draws from Deuteronomic concepts of covenant, obedience, and punishment. Yet, the author's decision to allude specifically to the Song of Moses is highly significant. The early poem was likely worked into the Deuteronomic corpus during Josiah's time as a statement on how the legal innovations of Josiah's scribes should be viewed as sharing in the poem's ancient pedigree.[59] The reference in the Supplement to the Song of Moses supports the position that by the author's time, the poem was indeed already part of the Deuteronomic corpus, but it also draws upon the poem's status as a witness against those who would reject the divine covenant mediated by Moses in the preceding Deuteronomic legislation (Deut 31:19–22). The semantic paralleling of Jeremiah's oracle in Jeremiah 42 with Moses' transcription of the Song of Moses in Deut 32:45 suggests that the stakes facing those who would reject Deuteronomy now face those who would reject Jeremiah's oracle: YHWH will "hide [his] face" from them (Deut 31:18; 32:20), denying them the right to engage in the covenantal relationship.[60]

Not only have the people invoked the Deuteronomic prophetic paradigm by asking for intercession and pledging obedience, the oracle itself draws deeply from the Deuteronomic traditions concerning a return to Egypt. While the oracle invokes standard Jeremianic language (e.g., vv. 11, 17), the ferocity of the prohibition against Egypt matches that of Deut 28:68:

> And YHWH shall bring you back into Egypt in ships, by the way whereof I said unto you: "you shall see it no more again"; and there you shall sell

> yourselves unto your enemies for bondmen and for bondwoman, and no man shall buy you.

With the devastation of Jerusalem and the reality of exile, much of Deuteronomy 28 had already come to pass. The oracle in Jeremiah 42 presents the possibility that *all* of the curses in Deuteronomy 28 will come to pass with the descent into Egypt. The allusion is unmistakable, certainly to an exilic audience that had seen many of the curses and threats of Deuteronomy come true in their own day. Nevertheless, the oracle's vehement position concerning Egypt reflects other passages concerning Egypt that occur throughout Deuteronomy (4:44–45; 5:6; 6:12; 7:8, 18; 8:14; 9:12; 9:26; 10:19, 22; 16:12; 17:16; 24:18). These passages (and others) consistently invoke the formative dimensions of the Exodus from Egypt. It is the emergence from Egypt that characterizes national identity above all other traditions of ancestry or kinship, taking precedence over the priestly or epic concepts of covenant and community. This idea obtains in traditions that predate Deuteronomy,[61] but it finds its ultimate and most forceful expression in that book.

Under Josiah, the Deuteronomic Torah was to become the foundational ideology that would establish communal boundaries and define nationhood, so much so that even the mixed population of the former northern kingdom could have been included in Josiah's "greater Israel" had his annexation of the north and application of Deuteronomic policy been successful.[62] And yet, at every turn of the Deuteronomic corpus, Israelite identity is defined through contradistinction with conditions before the Exodus from Egypt. This is most clearly articulated in the well-known liturgical statement in Deut 26:5–8:

> And you shall speak and say before YHWH your God, my father was a wandering Aramean, and he went down into Egypt, and sojourned there with a few, and became there a nation, great, mighty, and populous. . . . And YHWH brought us forth out of Egypt with a mighty hand, and with an outstretched arm, and with great terribleness, and with signs, and with wonders.

The Exodus from Egypt here transforms the individual from a generic Aramean to an Israelite, a member of a collective culture and history.[63] This is expressed by the contrast between the singular, isolating terminology of conditions before the Exodus (e.g., "my father," "a wandering Aramean," "he went down") and those following the Exodus reflecting common and public experience ("YHWH brought *us* out of Egypt"), persisting into the day of the audience/speaker of the text. The message of Deuteronomy is absolute: regardless of clan or individual ethnic origins, Israel as a nation was born in the Exodus from Egypt.[64] It is this profound belief that underlies the oracle in Jeremiah 42, resulting in a simple but severe message: returning to Egypt would constitute an annulment of Israelite status.

THE THREAT OF FOREIGN STATUS IN JEREMIAH 42–43

The author of Jeremiah 42 casts the die, leaving no options for the Judean remnant community apart from those articulated in the oracle. The terms of the oracle stand very close to the Deuteronomic choice of life or death (Deut 30:15–19); the response to the oracle in Jeremiah 43 thus leaves no room for interpretation in terms of where the audience stands with respect to Jeremiah and his supporters such as Baruch. This is clearly articulated with Johanan's accusation that Jeremiah has been unduly influenced by Baruch the scribe and the pro-Babylonian ideology he must have advocated (Jer 43:2–3).[65] The words the author ascribes to Johanan convey two related ideas. On the plain level, Johanan's accusation is a rejection of Jeremiah's oracle in Jeremiah 42, but since that oracle resonates so deeply with Deuteronomic ideology, Johanan's accusation is also a rejection of the fundamental Deuteronomic understanding of Israelite identity. Johanan's community has opted for the unthinkable, a descent into Egypt and a relapse back into a pre-Israelite state of being, cut off from the covenantal relationship with YHWH born during the Exodus and clarified through Moses' farewell speech in Deuteronomy. A careful examination of Jer 42:10 quietly anticipates this turn of events, as the author presents Jeremiah offering his audience a choice for covenantal existence, but one that they deny:

> If you will return/repent (אם שוב תשבו) in this land, then will I build you, and not pull you down, and I will plant you, and not pluck you up; for I repent me of the evil that I have done unto you.

The verse employs the standard Jeremianic build/plant language found throughout the book,[66] but the pivotal addition is the phrase שוב תשבו. The combination of the שוב terminology with the build/plant language appears elsewhere in the Jeremianic corpus only in Jer 18:7–8, and the context is noteworthy:

> At one instant I may speak concerning a nation, and concerning a kingdom, to pluck up and to break down and to destroy it; but if that nation turn from their evil (ושב הגוי ההוא), because of which I have spoken against it, I repent of the evil that I thought to do unto it.

The message in Jer 18:7–8 is directed to *foreign* nations that repent, not to the people of the covenantal community.[67] This further supports the retrospective nature of Jeremiah 42 and its relationship to Jeremiah 43. The position of Johanan and his community in the latter chapter brings them dangerously close to being a foreign nation, forsaking the Deuteronomic injunction against the return to Egypt and rejecting a prophet whom – for the exilic audience of the Supplement – history had already proved to be legitimate, another Deuteronomic qualification (Deut 18:21–22).[68]

JEREMIAH 44: THE DISOWNING OF THE EGYPTIAN REMNANT

All of this culminates in the great debate of Jeremiah 44. Shanghaied by those fleeing the wrath of Babylon, Jeremiah declares an oracle to the Judeans in Egypt, citing the horrific destruction of Jerusalem as the result of impiety and, notably, a rejection of the prophetic tradition (vv. 2–14), imploring them not to continue these abominable practices. The response to this oracle in vv. 16–19 voiced by the Judeans in Egypt is dramatic:

> As for the word that you have spoken unto us in the name of YHWH, we will not hearken unto you. But we will certainly perform every word that is gone

> forth out of our mouth, to offer unto the queen of heaven, and to pour out drink-offerings unto her, as we have done, we and our fathers, our kings and our princes, in the cities of Judah, and in the streets of Jerusalem; for then had we plenty of food, and were well, and saw no evil. But since we let off to offer to the queen of heaven, and to pour out drink-offerings unto her, we have wanted all things, and have been consumed by the sword and by the famine. And is it we that offer to the queen of heaven, and pour out drink-offerings unto her? Did we make her cakes in her image, and pour out drink-offerings unto her, without our husbands?

The community here takes steps even more dramatic than the return to Egypt or the refutation of Jeremiah. They refute the entire Deuteronomic enterprise:[69] the prophets, the legislation concerning the cult, and, implicitly, the basic element of Israelite religion (worship of YHWH alone). In all of the refutation of vv. 15–19, replete with references to cultic praxis, there is nary a mention of Israel's divine patron. Rather, the people worship the Queen of Heaven, a generic reference to the astral goddesses worshipped in the pre-Josianic period and classified as foreign by the Deuteronomic legislation (Deuteronomy 12).[70] The silence concerning YHWH's place among the people does not go unnoticed by Jeremiah, who speaks on YHWH's behalf in vv. 26–27:

> Therefore hear you the word of YHWH, all Judah that dwell in the land of Egypt: Behold, I have sworn by my great name, says YHWH, that my name shall no more be named in the mouth of any man of Judah in all the land of Egypt saying: As YHWH God lives. Behold, I watch over them (הנני שקד עליהם) for evil, and not for good; and all the men of Judah that are in the land of Egypt shall be consumed by the sword and by the famine, until there be an end of them.

The author has distilled the nature of the relationship between YHWH and the remnant now in Egypt into the starkest terms. They have chosen to eliminate YHWH from their religious world, and YHWH answers in kind, essentially disowning the community. Gone now is the conditional dimension of Jeremiah 42; inspired by the cataclysmic choice presented to Israel in Deut 30:15–19, the author clarifies in Jeremiah 44 that the remnant in Egypt have chosen evil and death, and shall therefore perish. For them, Jeremiah's prophetic career is indeed over: the recurrence of the שקד terminology in Jer 44:27 provides a closure paralleling the appearance of the term in Jer 1:12 (כי שקד אני על דברי), part of the prophet's call narrative. In short, the book of Jeremiah may continue to speak beyond Jeremiah 44, but not to the community depicted in that chapter.

The call narrative, however, is not the only Jeremianic text that is recalled in Jer 44:26–27. The passage represents the polar opposite of the covenant formula expressed to the Judeans in Babylon a decade earlier:

> . . . not according to the covenant that I made with their fathers in the day that I took them by the hand to bring them out of the land of Egypt; forasmuch as they broke my covenant, and I became to them a Baal,[71] says YHWH. But this is the covenant that I will make with the house of Israel after those days, says YHWH, I will put my law in their inward parts, and in their heart will I write it; and I will be their God, and they shall be my people. (Jer 31:32–33)

Beyond the qualification of the respective communities, the pertinent material in both passages addresses the issue of the fathers (31:32; 44:17) and their relationship to the covenant. Jer 31:32 recognizes and separates its audience from the failure of the fathers. The author of Jeremiah 44 has the remnant in Egypt *emulate* that failure and swear allegiance to it.

What is most remarkable about the refutation in Jer 44:15–19 is the specificity and detail it contains. The literature generally associated with the Deuteronomistic tradition regularly speaks of the rejection of the prophets, the transgression of law, and the veneration of illegitimate deities, but it rarely gives the opposing side a forum to voice its arguments. The two exceptions to this pattern are the refutation in Jeremiah 44 and the speech of the Rabshakeh in 2 Kings 18, and the two ultimately share a common rhetorical purpose. The Rabshakeh's speech gives voice to perspectives that the author wished to classify as foreign/alien to Israelite thought.[72] The speech likely cites examples of actual pre-Hezekian Israelite religion, but the placement of these ideas in the mouth of a servant of the Assyrian king identifies them as anti-Israelite and therefore anathema to the interests of the nation.[73]

The same strategy underlies Jeremiah 44, and it is for this reason that the refutation in vv. 15–19 is given such prominence. Like the speech of the Rabshakeh, it strictly delineates which ideology pertains to proper Israelite identity (Jeremiah's oracles) and which does not (the people's refutation). Like 2 Kings 18, Jeremiah 44 must have some historical veracity,[74] though, as in the narratives leading up to it, the author has constructed the chapter to inveigh against the remnant community in Egypt and qualify them as thoroughly corrupt. But this degree of corruption is beyond redemption or forgiveness, and its ramifications go beyond anything previously encountered in Israelite historiography.

JEREMIAH 44 AND THE OAN: POLEMICAL IMPLICATIONS VIA LITERARY CONTEXT

With the author already writing from a position that assumed Jeremiah's prophetic legitimacy, the entirety of Jeremiah 26–44 has been constructed to build up to the refutation of Jer 44:15–19 and the divine response voiced by Jeremiah that closes the chapter.[75] Jeremiah 26 introduces the notion of the scribes standing against the rest of the Jerusalem establishment and the nation divided between them. Jer 27–32:15 identify the Babylonian Judeans as a community of promise; Jeremiah 34–36 separate them quite literally from the doomed and dooming events that ensue, and Jer 34:20 in particular associates the homeland community with the sins of recalcitrant and misguided kings.[76] Jeremiah 36 returns us to the terrain of Jeremiah 26 but advances the story, demonstrating the moment when rejection of the prophetic word and the position of the scribes secure the impending dominance of Babylon.[77] The narratives spanning Jeremiah 37–43 successively tighten the noose, disqualifying nonscribal leadership and separating the group that finds itself under Johanan's command from the Babylonian community in increasingly dramatic terms.

This eventuates in the aforementioned Jeremiah 44, where we catch a final glimpse of the prophet's Egyptian audience: they identify with foreign deities, they reside in a foreign land, and they are associated with a foreign king (Hophra) who stands against Nebuchadnezzar, the servant of YHWH.[78] Scholars are certainly correct to detect disputation between the *golah* community in Babylon and the remnant community in Judah and eventually Egypt,[79] but as discussed in the Introduction to the present study, this disputation is not represented by conflict *within* the Supplement.[80] Rather, the entirety of this work represents one side of the dispute: the Babylonian side. By the end of Jeremiah 26–44, there is only one remaining Israelite community under consideration, namely, the one that resides in Babylon.[81] The Supplement has been shaped to demonstrate that those who are now in Egypt have been transformed into a foreign nation.

It can be no coincidence that the image of the remnant community as foreign presented in Jeremiah 44 is followed almost immediately by the OAN in the MT (the first of which, quite fittingly, is against Egypt).[82] As we have already observed, it is highly likely that the Babylonian Judeans possessed some form of Jeremiah's early active corpus, given the dialogue preserved in Jeremiah 29, the updated version of Jeremiah 30–31, and the word to Seraiah in Jer 51:59–64.[83] This word to Seraiah is the conclusion to the OAN that ends the primary MT tradition (Jeremiah 52 notwithstanding) and functions as a colophon attributed to Seraiah himself.[84] That the word was given in 593 BCE, the fourth year of Zedekiah's reign (Jer 51:59), means that it predates the Supplement, which, as we have seen, possesses a post-587 consciousness (though incorporating pre-587 material), and we have already suggested that an early form of the Jer 1–25:13+OAN existed around the time of Seraiah's mission that obviously did not include the Supplement.

The Supplement's many references to the pre–587 BCE texts reveals that the author sought to make his work compatible with this older corpus, and the well-known disruption in Jer 25:13/14 found between the MT and LXX versions identifies the point at which the supplemental material was inserted. The ensuing material in Jer 25:15ff. anticipates the varied material within the Supplement and points ahead to the OAN that once stood after Jer 25:13, now relocated to the end of a much larger literary corpus.[85] In shaping his material to be accepted by the Babylonian Judeans, the author legitimized their distance from the land and their total separation from the other communities claiming Judean heritage, especially that of the remnant in Egypt and their related satellites (see Jer 44:28).[86] This group, as we have seen, becomes a foreign nation, and it is for this reason that the author inserted his material at a specific strategic point: before the OAN of the earlier corpus. This resulted in a longer text that made the Supplement an integral part of the Jeremianic tradition, vilifying the Egyptian group as effectively excommunicated. The theological crescendo begins at the outset of his work (Jeremiah 26) and climaxes with Jeremiah's oracle of judgment against Johanan's community (Jeremiah 44), a perfect lead-in to the already existing OAN, leaving the Babylonian Judeans as the only true Israel. This leaves us with the task of determining the role of Jeremiah 45, which intervenes between the otherwise natural thematic flow of Jeremiah 44 and the OAN and which must therefore serve a very specific purpose.

THE REDACTIONAL AND HERMENEUTICAL PURPOSE OF JEREMIAH 45

Jeremiah 45 provides the essential functions needed to ensure the incorporation of Jeremiah 26–44 into the extant corpus. The chapter serves two purposes, one redactional and the other hermeneutical: it anticipates the ensuing OAN,[87] and its colophonic form ratifies Jeremiah 26–44 as a legitimate prophetic message communicated by a faithful scribe.[88] The superscription in Jer 45:1 identifies the chapter as a דבר directly from YHWH "from the mouth of Jeremiah": in keeping with Deut 18:18 and the phenomenology of Jer 36:17–18, the chapter is identified as part of an equally direct process of revelation, and its colophonic characteristics extend a similar quality to the entire Supplement.[89] But another essential feature of Jer 45:1 is the date it offers to the chapter: "in the fourth year of Jehoiakim."

This was, of course, 605 BCE, the year of the battle of Carchemish and the year of the compilation of the *Urrolle* that would eventually be burned by Jehoiakim. The narrative of Jeremiah 36 clarifies that the scrolls written by Baruch derive directly from Jeremiah's mouth,[90] and therefore the second scroll in Jeremiah 36 and the message of Jeremiah 45 are on par with whatever constituted the extant collection of Jeremiah's writings in the author's day. As many scholars have already noted, this equates the entire Supplement with the "many similar words" of Jer 36:32. This is important in the facilitation of Jeremiah 26–44 as a lead-in to the OAN, as Jer 36:2 had specified that the Jeremianic tradition possessed an international scope in every stage of its development:

> Take for yourself a scroll and write therein all the words that I have spoken to you against Israel, and against Judah, and *against all the nations*, from the day I spoke to you, from the days of Josiah, even *until this day* (עד היום הזה).

In addition to the overt mention of oracles "against all the nations,"[91] the author draws attention to the Josianic-era Deuteronomistic phrase "until this day" (עד היום הזה).[92] Here, cast in *distinction* from Josiah's day, it is a hermeneutical device that extends authority from the moment of authentic prophetic revelation to Jeremiah in Josiah's day to the point in time that saw the inclusion of Jeremiah 26–44 in the corpus. The author of Jeremiah 36 (and the Supplement en masse) knew full well that his work was going to be incorporated into a text that did indeed speak of foreign nations, and the temporal reference in Jer 45:1 to the composition of the scrolls in Jer 36:2/32 subsumed his new material within the broader corpus.[93]

The date given (605 BCE) in the superscription of Jeremiah 45 may attempt to present Baruch's actual sentiments in preparing the disturbing content of the *Urrolle* in that same year for presentation to Jehoiakim.[94] As a figure of significance, his political position in the royal court would no doubt suffer from his association with this material.[95] This concern, though, is turned into a meditation on faith and theological fidelity: Baruch's personal aspirations must be put aside due to the imminent realization of the divine דברים in the call narrative. The social structure to which Baruch had hitherto belonged was going to be uprooted; he is instead charged with a more significant mission: to broaden the corpus already possessed by the Judeans of Babylon that included the OAN and thereby to institute important new ideas within that religious community. This, we will recall, was one of the major purposes of Jer 25:1–13, which is dated to the same year as Jeremiah 45 (see Jer 25:1).[96] In this sense, Jeremiah 45 may have been shaped in conscious awareness of Jeremiah 25, which had earlier been redacted by Jeremiah for similar purposes (to function as a colophon that closed a definite collection [Jeremiah 1–24] and to serve as a bridge to the early OAN collection).[97] Baruch's colophon thus again advances the idea that scribal methods emulate and preserve prophecy.

BARUCH B. NERIAH AND THE AUTHORSHIP OF THE SUPPLEMENT

The author therefore presents Baruch as a dedicated servant not just of Jeremiah but also of YHWH, signified by the blessing in v. 5: "I will give your life to you as a prize of war (לשלל) in every place you go." This same blessing is bestowed upon Ebed-Melech (in a shorter form) in Jer 39:18, in consideration for his helping Jeremiah out of the pit (Jer 38:11–13),[98] suggesting that the creation of the Supplement also provides salvation, and not only to Jeremiah. Baruch's allegiance to the prophet in Jeremiah 45 merits blessing of life and survival, even in the direst circumstances, for it maintains the vitality of the prophetic word.[99] Thus, the Baruch of Jeremiah 45 is saved from woe and injury, and those who accept the message of the Supplement brought to an end by Jeremiah 45 may receive similar benefits.

The implication of the chapter, in terms of its internal colophonic form and shared themes with the preceding material, is that Baruch is the author of the Supplement. This does not necessarily equal historical fact, but the chapter should also not be strictly considered a literary construct; the reality may fall somewhere in between. Some scholars have pointed to the lack of details concerning Egypt as evidence that Baruch (who is taken there by Johanan's community) could not have been responsible for any significant portion of the Supplement.[100] If, however, this literature was constructed to characterize the Egyptian remnant community as illegitimate, then extensive details about the life and institutions of these communities would be superfluous beyond that which has currently obtained in the text. And in fact, a good deal of detail *is* provided. The names and lineages of the community leaders are specified, their political sentiments concerning Babylon are revealed, the cities in which they take up residence are enumerated, and their religious predilections (however shaped by polemical interests) are described in detail.[101]

These details could indeed come from Baruch, a scribe with firsthand knowledge of the community surrounding him, with a deeply entrenched pro-Babylonian political perspective, with affinities to the Shaphanide scribal circle and the theology they advanced, and with ready access to the catalog of older Deuteronomistic and Jeremianic materials referenced throughout the Supplement.[102] The archaeological evidence concerning the scribes mentioned in Jeremiah 36 and the events depicted throughout the narratives of the Supplement attest to their basic historicity in a general sense and Baruch's position as an influential Jerusalemite figure in specific.[103] Though the major purpose of the Supplement is to provide an interpretation of the meaning of events and the role of individuals within them, those individuals and events were real, and the presentation of Baruch as the author/compiler of the Supplement may well reflect Baruch's important position in shaping the Jeremianic literature.[104]

Here we encounter difficulty in determining the degree of Baruch's actual contribution to the Supplement. Baruch's residence in Egypt would account for the details regarding the settlement of the fleeing Judeans therein, but there is no indication that he left Egypt and settled in Babylon among the Shaphanides, and it is clear that the Supplement took shape within that community. A sense of mobility is, however, implied in Jer 45:5, which tells us that Baruch will find security "in every place" (אל כל המקמות) he goes. This may simply account for the narrative's depiction of his eventual residence in Egypt within a community that obviously does not share in the blessing that he has secured, but given the application of the term מקום to Babylon in an earlier text (Jer 51:62), it may allude to his eventual residence in Babylon.[105] It is more likely, though, that Baruch managed to send to his scribal peers in Babylon archival materials that were rewritten as what became the Supplement.[106] As we have seen, the composition of the Supplement involved the redaction of disparate sources associated with Jeremiah's career, and this may have included chronologies, lists, summaries of oracles, and other assorted notes collected by Baruch and placed in an archival state for later use.[107] In this case, the group or individual who did redact these archival sources into the Supplement felt compelled to credit Baruch's contribution via the colophon in Jeremiah 45.[108] The crediting of Baruch may well have carried propagandistic valences if he had been a well-known and respected figure to the Supplement's audience, and one who provided the Supplement's shaper(s) with significant information.[109]

Regardless of whether or not Baruch wrote the Supplement himself or was a pivotal figure in its development, what matters is that the Supplement *presents* him as the author via the position and function of the colophon in Jeremiah 45. The Baruch of Jeremiah 45 is not simply a secretary.[110] The chapter is identified as a divine word (דבר) spoken by Jeremiah, but it is "to" (אל) Baruch (v. 1). This is very close to the designation of prophetic qualification elsewhere, where the דבר is "to" the classical prophets themselves (i.e., Jer 7:1 הדבר אשר היה אל ירמיהו–; see also Mic 1:1; Hos 1:1; Zeph 1:1)[111] as well as to prophetic figures in the DH (e.g., 1 Sam 3:1b, 21; 2 Sam 7:4; 1 Kgs 12:22). This is followed by Baruch's own lament in v. 3 (conforming to the laments of Jeremiah that punctuate chs. 11–20) and the invocation of the נטע/נתש terminology found throughout the book. The closing verse echoes Jeremiah's own call in Jer 1:8, where Baruch's security, like that of Jeremiah, is assured by YHWH.[112]

Baruch is thus patterned on the prototype of Jeremiah,[113] not simply as a servant of the prophet but also as an authoritative voice in his own right. Jer 45:1 reinforces the דבר phenomenology depicted in Jer 36:17–18, contributing to the author's conscious awareness of that chapter; the author makes it abundantly clear that the scribe Baruch has inherited and preserved the prophetic word. The דבר has been directly entrusted to him, and the colophonic quality of Jeremiah 45 identifies the Supplement as an expression of that דבר. This constitutes the final instance of the connection between Jeremiah and the scribes that permeates every major unit in the Supplement, and indeed, Jeremiah 45 concludes that strategy with increased intensity, making plain what the other episodes only strongly imply.[114] The audience's acceptance of the Supplement's place in the Jeremianic corpus merits the same blessing as that given to Baruch, but doing so requires the recognition of the scribes' sacral authority.

EXCURSUS 3

The "Words of Jeremiah" and Seraiah's Colophon in the MT and LXX Traditions

THE ABSENCE OF THE "WORDS OF JEREMIAH" NOTICE IN THE LXX VERSION of Seraiah's colophon has contributed to the view that the MT position of this notice obtained only secondarily, added at a time of the MT's growth subsequent to the emergence of the LXX corpus.[1] According to this model, Seraiah's reediting of an earlier corpus involved his moving his colophon to the end of the work, along with the OAN, and then adding the words of Jeremiah notice, closing the early MT version of the book. The appearance of the words of Jeremiah in MT Jer 51:64 provides a very neat closure to the collection beginning with the identical phraseology in Jer 1:1, but it would not have been the result of Seraiah's editing of an earlier LXX corpus that already included the Supplement. Rather, it would have arisen from the development of an early version of Jeremiah 1–25+OAN that the author of the Supplement inherited.

The *inclusio* device one finds in the MT version of Jer 1:1 and 51:64 is already put to use extensively in the early layers of the Jeremianic corpus, and would have been readily deployed when the basic theme of the prophet's words had been proved true and his oracles were collected sometime after the deportation of 597 BCE.[2] The words of Jeremiah notice would have been at the end of the early OAN collection that included Seraiah's colophon.[3] An existing version of Jeremiah 1–25+OAN was preserved with minor variations by both the Egyptian and Babylonian Jewish communities of the sixth century, strongly suggesting that this collection had already emerged shortly after the destruction of Jerusalem in 587, that is, before the Supplement was constructed. The shaping of this early collection would have provided the background for the words of Jeremiah notice to be placed after Seraiah's colophon. This would have resulted in a literary work that began with Jeremiah's preexilic oracles and continued with an OAN collection, culminating in the oracle against Babylon and ending with Seraiah's colophon – a work framed at the outset and conclusion with the phrase "the words of Jeremiah."

The later redaction of a much longer work including the Supplement does not seem a likely background to the introduction of the words of Jeremiah notice. As Dearman has observed, the exilic redactors of the DH chose to leave the Jeremianic corpus as a pseudoindependent prophetic witness to the DH.[4] If the closing words of Jeremiah notice belongs to an exilic redaction of the entire Jeremianic corpus (inclusive of the Supplement), we would more likely find it at the end of Jeremiah 52, which in its current state attempts to associate the Jeremianic corpus with the DH by drawing directly from 2 Kgs 25.[5] The insertion of the notice at the end of Jeremiah 52 would have provided balance, allowing connections to the DH while subsuming all within the words of Jeremiah. The notice's current connection to Seraiah's colophon in the MT, occurring *before* Jeremiah 52, supports our view that it was already associated with the OAN collection at an earlier time and should not be viewed as arising from a subsequent redaction. When the Supplement was introduced, the OAN was shifted to the end of the book, including Seraiah's colophon and the words of Jeremiah notice that were already appended to the closing oracle against Babylon.[6]

This leaves the question of the notice's absence in the LXX and the view that it arose from an initial redaction by Baruch before it was reworked into the MT by Seraiah. If the LXX reflects the earlier structure of the book of Jeremiah, then why does the words of Jeremiah notice not appear at the end of *that* version? As Lundbom has proposed, Baruch and his brother Seraiah were schooled in the same scribal tradition, were both close supporters of Jeremiah himself, and were intimately involved with the growth of the Jeremianic literature.[7] If Seraiah had taken it upon himself to append the words of Jeremiah notice to his closing colophon, we would expect Baruch to have done the same. Yet, this is not the case; the colophon of Baruch that ends the LXX version of Jeremiah offers no rhetorical closure to the lexemes of Jer 1:1 and does not submerge that scribe's work within the prophet's exhortation.

An objection could be raised that such a notice *did* once follow Baruch's colophon. Seraiah, inheriting the proto-LXX version, could have dislodged the notice from his brother's colophon and attached it to his own, closing his newer, proto-MT collection.[8] This, however, would not account for the absence of such a notice in the current LXX version of Baruch's colophon. Had Seraiah copied and then deleted this notice from Baruch's colophon, other proto-LXX manuscripts that were never subjected to Seraiah's reworking would have still retained it, and it would have survived in the current LXX tradition. It is therefore unlikely that Seraiah simply added the words of Jeremiah notice to his colophon after inheriting some extant version of the proto-LXX corpus.

As suggested previously, then, the absence of the notice in the LXX may be attributed to its belonging to an earlier version of Jeremiah 1–25+OAN that predated the construction of the Supplement and its subsequent deletion as the Supplement and other major units were brought together to form the LXX. Upon appending the Supplement to the end of the proto-LXX version of Jeremiah 1–25+OAN, no scribe would have been at ease with a phrase such as "thus far the words of Jeremiah" attached to a text located in the center of his edition of the book.[9] In any case, the absence of the notice in the LXX and its presence at the end of Seraiah's colophon in MT Jer 51:64 is one more important piece of evidence suggesting that the principal development of the book of Jeremiah led to the early MT tradition, with the LXX taking shape in a mature form at a later time.

CHAPTER 5

The Polemics of Exile

AT EVERY TURN, THE SUPPLEMENT ADDRESSES THE JUDEAN COMMUNITY in Babylon arising from the various deportations to that city. Jeremiah himself becomes a character in the narratives within the Supplement, manipulated by the author as a symbol of the deportees' own experience. He shares in the prohibition from living in his ancestral homeland (Jer 37:11–14), he is imprisoned and given rations like Jehoiachin (Jer 37:15; cf. 2 Kgs 25:27, 30; Jer 38:32–34), and he is cast into a pit (בור), only to sink into the mud in a miserable sort of nether existence (Jer 38:6), paralleling the questions of the afterlife that would have accompanied the exile to Babylon.[1] Indeed, his experience in the pit is reflected in a dirge to Zedekiah by the women of the royal circles who are brought to Babylon, though this dirge is couched in liturgical terminology (Jer 38:22).[2] Finally, Jeremiah is forcibly taken captive to a foreign land (Jer 43:6–7), to live among a people who are not part of the covenantal community.

In every one of these instances, the perpetrators are the post–597 BCE Judeans of Jerusalem or those who settled in Egypt, who have become foreigners.[3] It is for this reason that the judgment pronounced upon them in Jeremiah 44, though exilic, does not include captivity among the list of punishment YHWH will inflict on them (in v. 13); the Judeans of Egypt are themselves the captors who have taken Jeremiah and Baruch against their will. Now excommunicated from Israel, they cannot even qualify under the rubric of captivity, a punishment experienced now only by the true Israel, the Babylonian Judeans.

RECONSIDERING THE MT AND LXX SEQUENCES

At this point, some observations may be offered concerning the development of the MT and LXX traditions and the place of the Supplement in both. As discussed in the Introduction to the present study, the majority of text-critical analyses of the book of Jeremiah rightly note that the LXX tradition lacks many of the secondary expansions currently found in parallel passages in the MT. This would indeed speak to a frequently more archaic state of the *Vorlage* to the LXX from unit to unit within each chapter.[4] These observations are of great use to scholars attempting to identify the earliest form of these units and chart their individual development. Consequently, it is common for scholars to view the LXX sequence of the book of Jeremiah (Jer 1–25/OAN/the Supplement) as the older and original sequence of the tradition.[5] As already noted, the MT text itself is thus often viewed as a subsequent reworking of the LXX text, with the word to Seraiah (Jer 51:59–64) often seen as a colophon identifying him as the editor of a work that originally ended with the Supplement and the colophon of Baruch in Jeremiah 45.[6]

The foregoing examination requires that we pause, however, before viewing the entire LXX as a witness to an earlier or original sequence of the book's primary parts. The rhetorical logic of the Supplement does not cohere well if the work was intended to follow the OAN, as it does in the LXX. Rather, the hermeneutical, thematic, and literary features elucidated in the present study suggest that the Supplement was intended from its inception to be *followed by* the OAN. In other words, the Supplement was conceived to be introduced into the *middle* of a recognized sequence that began with Jeremiah 1–25 and ended with the OAN. If this is so, then the position of the Supplement in the LXX should not be viewed as older or superior. Rather, the relationship between the Supplement and the OAN points to its introduction into the Jeremianic corpus with what would become the MT tradition.[7] By submerging the supplementary material in Jeremiah 26–45 within the "words of Jeremiah" *inclusio*, the MT sequence is closer to the preexilic Deuteronomistic theology, where the scribal authors worked anonymously in the service of prophecy.[8] The LXX sequence of Jeremiah, by contrast, presents the scribe Baruch as a successor to the prophet, with Baruch's colophon closing the corpus.[9] The MT occupies a middle ground: the activity and personality of many scribes associated with the Deuteronomistic group surface rather prominently, but all are subordinated to the name and legacy of the prophet Jeremiah that opens and closes the corpus.[10] This points not to succession but parity between prophetic and scribal processes, an idea that underlies the appearance and function of the colophons throughout the book and that is already witnessed in the preexilic oracles of Jeremiah.[11]

The Supplement's appearance at the end of the LXX tradition suggests that the curators of the LXX *Vorlage* received and canonized it only after it had become a normative, recognized part of a book of Jeremiah elsewhere, that is, among the Judeans of Babylon during the exile (to whom the Supplement is consistently addressed). It was the emissaries from this community who later became the officials of early Judaism in Yehud during the Persian period,[12] and we should therefore not be surprised that the important accretion in Jer 33:14–26 addressing the politics of Yehud under Persia appears in the MT and not in the LXX.[13] If the Judeans of Babylon had fostered a corpus that had the unique quality of possessing the Supplement over other (shorter) variants, it would have been the natural choice to receive this important passage addressing the political tensions of the Restoration era.[14] We should therefore see the birth of a discernible MT corpus not as a reworking of an extant *Vorlage* to the LXX but with the composition and initial inclusion of the Supplement, establishing a normative collection that would receive greater attention in the ensuing decades.

This means, of course, that at the time of the inclusion of the Supplement in what would become the MT corpus, there *was* no LXX corpus to speak of (in terms of a work approaching the shape of the current LXX Jeremiah), only another collection of Jeremianic writings that included earlier versions of Jeremiah 1–25, the OAN, and assorted other oracles and accounts, probably one of many such collections.[15] The Supplement itself appears to recognize that these variant texts existed and circulated among disparate groups even during the preexilic period and does not question their legitimacy in and of themselves; after all, the author of the Supplement inherited and introduced his work into a collection of Jeremianic texts quite similar to those others.[16] The major distinction between the priority and authority of text traditions would only have taken place once the MT sequence emerged, replete with the Supplement. The fusion of the earlier prophetic corpus with this large scribal literary construct was ultimately widely regarded as legitimate, since the curators of the eventual LXX tradition incorporated a form of the Supplement into its pages.[17]

It may be that the Supplement was introduced to the curators of the LXX tradition during the Persian period, when the Achaemenid rulers finally controlled the Egyptian communities where the LXX *Vorlage* developed. At that point, the LXX tradents would have incorporated the new material, placing it at the end of a literary work that they had already long possessed and did not wish to disrupt.[18] That the LXX retains the OAN in the center of the collection evidences conformity with the more mature forms of Isaiah and Ezekiel, which also find foreign nation oracles in the middle of their respective collections.[19] This further supports a later period in which the LXX obtained its own canonical shape.[20] We may go further and suggest a *terminus a quo* for the creation of the LXX sequence: in contradistinction to the MT sequence, which subsumes the Supplement within the words of Jeremiah (Jer 1:1; 51:64), the LXX sequence presents Baruch as a successor to the prophet.[21] This reflects a period when scribes had indeed become successors to prophets, that is, the Second Temple period, especially the fifth to fourth centuries BCE. It is during this time that prophecy fades and scribes emerge as the primary custodians of tradition; Ezra-Nehemiah places Ezra at the top of the religious hierarchy because of his scribal qualifications (Ezra 7:1) and presents Levites as authoritative exegetes of written material (Ezra 8:15–20; Neh 8:7–9).[22] Likewise, the Chronicler refers to Levites in prophetic terms due to their recitation and preservation of sacred texts, which constituted part of their own scribal duties during this period.[23] Finally, the letters from Elephantine (late fifth century) also support a proposed dating of the LXX sequence to this period, as they demonstrate the influence of Jerusalem's religious authority on Egyptian Jewish communities, which would have included those possessing the texts that would result in the LXX.[24]

The centrality of scribes in Jerusalem would have exerted a powerful force on the curators of the LXX tradition to shape their text in ideological conformity to the dominant modes of Judaism in their day. That the translation of the LXX *Vorlage* into Greek took place in the mid-third century BCE proves that the basic shape of its Jeremianic material was already firmly entrenched by then, indicated as well by some text-critical features of the Supplement in that tradition.[25] The LXX of Jeremiah obviously obtained a canonical status in its own right among some Egyptian communities, but as per the preceding discussion, it was not the first version of the book of Jeremiah to possess the Supplement. This calls for a reevaluation of scholarly models regarding the priority of the LXX to the MT of Jeremiah as complete collections and theories regarding various stages of redaction.[26] As indicated previously, it is clear that the LXX often preserves older versions of Jeremianic texts, though this does not necessarily mean that these texts were worked into a sequence before those that we currently find in the MT. Rather, they indicate the shape of earlier sources lifted from an archival state and worked into the larger narrative by the author of the Supplement. The case of MT Jeremiah 39 provides one very good example of how this may have occurred. As discussed in the notes to the previous chapter, MT Jer 39:4–13 – which, along with vv. 1–2, does not appear in the LXX – is based on an annalistic source or sources regarding the conquest of Jerusalem that were also used to provide details in 2 Kings 25/Jeremiah 52.[27] The author of the Supplement working in Babylon had access to this annalistic source or sources as well as a biographical source of Jeremiah being taken by the Babylonian officers to Gedaliah and ending with the oracle to Ebed-Melech that follows. The author then interpolated information from the annalistic account of Jerusalem's destruction into his biographical source (along with the introductory material in vv. 1–2), yielding the MT version of Jeremiah 39 that is thematically and literarily well integrated into the larger Supplement.[28]

Once the Supplement in its entirety became an integral part of the Jeremiah tradition (forming the early MT sequence), the scribes behind the LXX constructed their own version as closely as possible, placing their textual parallel to MT Jeremiah 39 in its proper sequential place. Their textual parallel, however, would have been the same biographical source that the author of the Supplement updated years earlier in Babylon, missing the information regarding Jerusalem's fall. One might expect that the Jewish scribes in Egypt would have updated their source with the relevant information, but if the appendix of Jeremiah 52 had already been affixed to the early MT sequence by the time it reached the LXX tradents, these scribes would have had no reason to alter their original document to include the details of Jerusalem's destruction – the details were already provided in that appendix.[29] In this way, the LXX *Vorlage* emerged as a tradition that could compete with its MT counterpart in terms of general scope while still addressing a local community more familiar with its unique component parts and traditions. In some cases, material was taken directly from the Supplement as found in the MT sequence when comparable sources had not been preserved by the LXX tradents. At other times, the LXX tradents worked from older independent sources, often the same as those underlying the MT text (such as with the biographical source for MT Jeremiah 39). In either case, the LXX tradents constructed their own fuller corpus as a response to what had already obtained in the growing MT tradition.

The initial appearance of the Supplement with the MT tradition challenges notions that the LXX represents an initial "edition" of an authoritative and comprehensive Jeremianic corpus incorporating all major structural elements only subsequently developed into an MT "edition."[30] Rather, the developing MT tradition appears to have been the text that was viewed as authoritative by the Jewish religious authorities in Babylon and eventually in Jerusalem during the Persian period. It was also the version that initiated the rise of the scribal class, as evidenced by the fifth- to fourth-century BCE literature and the eventual shape of the LXX sequence. We must therefore turn our attention again to the function of the scribes identified by name as the curators of Jeremiah's literary legacy.

THE SONS OF NERIAH IN RELATION TO THE MT AND LXX SEQUENCES

Based on the discussion in the present study, the presentation of Baruch as the author/editor of the Supplement (symbolically or otherwise) should not be associated primarily with the formation of the LXX tradition often viewed as the first edition of the book of Jeremiah. We should likewise refrain from a de facto association of Seraiah as the editor of the MT (often viewed as the second edition) based on the colophon associated with his name in relation to that of Baruch.[31] As observed earlier, the colophon of Baruch in Jeremiah 45 functions in part as a *bridge* between the Supplement and the OAN;[32] it appears only at the end of the LXX tradition because of a later introduction of the Supplement (of which it was a part) into the corpus. While a strong argument can be made for Seraiah as the trustee of an early Jeremianic collection (the colophon of Seraiah in Jer 51:59–64 does not function the same way as Jeremiah 45 but indeed closes an early comprehensive corpus),[33] this would have occurred at a stage in the development of the text (ca. 593 BCE) that predated the composition of the Supplement (post-587).[34] If the Supplement was indeed inserted into this earlier collection already bearing Seraiah's colophon, then the author of the Supplement is the editor of what would become the early MT version of the book. In short, the names of Baruch and Seraiah should not be ascribed respectively to the developing LXX and MT sequences, as the colophons associated with both pertain to the development of a single corpus directed to the Babylonian Judeans largely represented by the MT alone.[35]

The foregoing discussion has led us to conclude that the Supplement first became part of the Jeremiah tradition as a unit that intervened between Jeremiah 1–25 and the OAN. Nevertheless, the LXX presentation of Baruch as the successor to Jeremiah seems to develop a major theme in the Supplement, namely, the scribes' central role in Israel's religion. While this was certainly a feature of Israelite religion during the exilic period, we have seen that the notion of succession would surface only at a time in the postexilic period when classical prophecy had ceased and scribes truly did emerge as the bearers of their authority.[36] It is clear, however, that from the Shaphanide/Deuteronomistic perspective, this would not have been an appropriate rhetorical strategy during the exile. The model of classical prophecy so integral to Deuteronomistic ideology persisted into the early postexilic period, with figures such as Haggai and Zechariah attempting to carry on in the footsteps of their preexilic prophetic forebears.[37] The author of the Supplement wished to stake a claim for scribes as facilitators of the prophetic message, but did not present scribal authority as the successor to a still-living prophetic tradition associated with Jeremiah.

The author of the Supplement did not attempt to subordinate the Jeremianic corpus to his work; the insertion of his material between Jeremiah 1–25 and the OAN preserves the older דברי ירמיהו *inclusio* of Jer 1:1 and (what is now) 51:64,[38] and therefore Jeremiah himself still functions hermeneutically as the "author" of the entire collection.[39] But the words of Jeremiah that include the Supplement now address a different reality from the initial collection entrusted to Seraiah years earlier. It is a reality where the Egyptian remnant is a foreign entity, the Babylonian Judeans alone preserve the relationship with YHWH, and, most significantly, this relationship is mediated through the authority of the scribes entrusted with prophetic revelation. The insertion of the Supplement into the extant sequence of the Jeremianic literature constitutes an appeal to the recognized and ongoing prophetic authority of Jeremiah in promoting the message of the Supplement.

THE CIRCUMSTANCES BEHIND THE COMPOSITION OF THE SUPPLEMENT

But what, in the end, is the Supplement's message? The rabid condemnation of the Egyptian diaspora is so obvious as to be suspect. The total dominance of Babylon and the challenge of adapting to Mesopotamian culture would make unlikely the obsession with the Egyptian Judeans and the ferocity visited upon them, as evidenced in the Supplement. Indeed, we may question whether any community living in exile – be it in Egypt or Babylon – might have posed a threat to any other group enduring similar circumstances.[40] Moreover, the strong anti-Egyptian sentiments that dominated preexilic Israelite culture would lead us to believe that the exilic audience in Babylon would have *presupposed* the illegitimacy of a Judean group choosing residency in Egypt, and this presupposition surfaces in more subtle (but unmistakable) ways in contemporaneous literary works.[41] And while one might imagine that a scribe concerned with the nature of the fractured community might engage in some redactional activity within the extant version of Jeremiah 1–25, the construction of an entirely new and extensive literary unit such as the Supplement seems an excessive response to the mere existence of the Egyptian diaspora, especially since this community is not even blamed for the fall of Jerusalem or the various deportations to Babylon. Finally, animosity toward the Egyptian diaspora does not explain the persistent attention given to the role of the scribes throughout the Supplement, a role that lies beneath the preexilic Deuteronomistic literature but that is never highlighted overtly, as in the Supplement.[42] What circumstances could have arisen during this time among the Babylonian Judeans to warrant the systematic elevation of the scribal class to such a heightened status through the expansion of the Jeremianic corpus and the preservation of the prophet's own voice?

The answer is found at the beginning of the Supplement. Jeremiah 26 identifies the prophet's adversaries as the cultic establishment of Jerusalem, a reality from the prophet's own lifetime.[43] The point of departure for the chapter is the prophet's Temple Sermon (Jer 7:1–15), which most clearly articulated the perspective that delusions concerning the sanctity of the Temple and the covenants strictly bound to its precincts would lead the nation into ruin. The destruction of Jerusalem and the exile had proved this to be true, and to a great many Judeans now living in Babylon, the conditional elements of the preexilic Deuteronomistic tradition had been proved true as well. Jeremiah's writings to the 597 BCE community had attempted to preserve the essential ideology of the Deuteronomistic tradition but adapted it for their exilic circumstances; the author of the Supplement follows the prophet to a degree in this regard by adopting the standards of Deuteronomistic narrative discourse throughout his work. The audiences of their respective compositions, though, were very different. The 597 audience addressed by the prophet consisted in no small part of the Shaphanides and others who were predisposed to Deuteronomistic ideology or at least very conversant with it.[44] Other positions surfaced (Jer 29:20–28), but the community eventually gave priority to Jeremiah's arguments (Jer 24:5–7). The author of the Supplement, by contrast, addressed a post-587 community of Judeans in Babylon that was much larger, consisting of disparate groups of people uncertain of the applicability of Deuteronomistic thought.

Jer 26:7–8 hints strongly at the adverse forces dividing the exilic audience on this matter by specifying the characteristics of the people contending against Jeremiah during his trial:

> So *the priests and the prophets* and all the people heard Jeremiah speaking these words in the house of YHWH. Now it came to pass, when Jeremiah had made an end of speaking all that YHWH had commanded him to speak unto all the people, that *the priests and the prophets* and all the people laid hold on him, saying: "you shall surely die."

In this passage, "all the people" are clearly under the influence of Jerusalem's cultic functionaries, the priests and prophets. The ensuing events demonstrate that Jeremiah is successful (to a degree) in defending himself, and the people and officials to whom Jeremiah speaks view his defense as a foil to the perspective advocated by the priests and prophets:

> Then said the princes and all the people unto *the priests and to the prophets*: "This man is not worthy of death; for he has spoken to us in the name of YHWH our God."

The dynamic created here establishes that while the influential priests and prophets so set on the inviolability of Jerusalem considered Jeremiah to be blasphemous, the larger population was open to new modes of thinking ratified under the banner of a developing Deuteronomistic theology. This narrative, conceived for an exilic audience, speaks metaphorically for the vitality of the Jeremianic voice to the culture of exile and the need to sustain certain Deuteronomistic understandings while adapting and even abandoning others, namely, the centrality of the Temple establishment and the applicability of the Davidic covenant.[45] It is these outdated concepts that motivate the cultic functionaries in Jeremiah 26, and the author thereby addresses a reality of his own day. The differences between the Judeans taken captive in 597 BCE and those who arrived in Babylon a decade later were strong, as the first part of Jeremiah's corpus (chs. 1–25) had been shaped to castigate the latter. The working of Jer 32:1–15 into the Supplement constituted an attempt to appeal to this group and demonstrate that they could and should adopt the political perspectives of those taken captive in 597. Yet, while these earlier captives continued to venerate the Jeremianic and Deuteronomistic theologies that had come to critique the Jerusalem cultic traditions, other theological options were present in full force among the Judeans in Babylon. The central stanza of Psalm 137 (vv. 5–6) reveals the predominance of a Jerusalem-centered ideology still evident among the exiles:

> If I forget thee, O Jerusalem, let my right hand forget
> Let my tongue cleave to the roof of my mouth if I do not remember thee
> If I do not set Jerusalem above my highest joy

The impulse for lamenting over Jerusalem would have been widespread in the exilic community and beyond, and the repeated calls to seek Babylon's welfare throughout the Supplement must have been conceived to combat this understandable sentiment. This call for Babylonian welfare surfaced earlier in Jeremiah's own material and was directed at the dissenting prophets of the 597 BCE community (Jeremiah 27, 29) and those such as Hananiah in Jerusalem (Jeremiah 28) who felt that Babylonian dominance was soon to be reversed.[46] By the time the author of the Supplement was writing, however, the oracles of these dissenting prophets had been proved false. Though hope existed for the future, it was a distant future, and the dominance of Babylon was accepted for the present as a political reality. There is little to indicate that the post-587 community in Babylon produced any dissenting voices similar to those preserved in Jeremiah 27–29 that anticipated an imminent Babylonian collapse.

Yet, dissenting voices were very clearly heard on other matters, especially the significance of Jerusalem's cultic ideology. In this regard, the Zadokite priesthood proved to be a more enduring force. While some Judeans in Babylon must have accepted the view that a lack of proper adherence to the spirit of the law and their prophetic advocates (such as Jeremiah) had led to the exile, the Zadokite circles also deported from Judah advanced a counterargument, namely, that the Deuteronomistic enterprise itself had led the nation into ruin.[47] The Zadokites of the exilic period attempted to draw attention to the unique position of the Jerusalem cult and its ideology: the Holiness Code (Leviticus 17–26) was rehabilitated during this period as an alternative to the Deuteronomic legislation along with the preexilic P material, all systematically worked into the older Israelite narrative traditions forming the basis of what would eventually emerge as the Pentateuch.[48] This larger Zadokite narrative incorporated the redactional tropes of the preexilic Josianic DH but was applied to the exilic circumstance,[49] arguing that Zadokite theology was communicated long before Israel entered the land (though it was ultimately geared to their residency therein).[50] By extension, Israel's exilic tenure should likewise focus on the special status of the Zadokite cult, which had been compromised by the Deuteronomic experiment resulting in the exile.[51]

THE EZEKIEL TRADITION

The greatest exilic advocate of this theology was Ezekiel, *a priest and a prophet* who presented an argument quite different from the Deuteronomistic perspective. It was not the Deuteronomic theology that would sustain the people through adaptation, as Jeremiah had argued (in fact, Ezekiel begins his oracles by suggesting that the roots of the exile could be dated specifically to the Deuteronomic reform of Josiah in 622 BCE).[52] Rather, it was the proper understanding of the old Zadokite traditions concerning the divine presence of YHWH, one that was still vital and accessible through the proper channels of intermediation. According to Ezekiel, Jerusalem itself may have been demolished, but the Zadokite theology that had once been at home in that city was preserved intact, lifted beyond the Temple precincts well before the Babylonian devastation. This was revealed to Ezekiel through a succession of symbolic visions,[53] demonstrating the overwhelming complexity of the cosmos that only he, a Zadokite, could understand and internalize.[54]

Ezekiel's vision of a restored Jerusalem (Ezekiel 40–48) attempted to correct any Deuteronomistic mistakes from the earlier era and precludes a reinstitution of those practices or ideas, a concept expressed elsewhere in Ezekiel's writings (Ezek 20:25–26).[55] Deuteronomic tropes are subsumed within and dramatically subordinated to Ezekiel's worldview.[56] Indeed, the theology of Deuteronomy was legitimate only insofar as it preserved certain ideas from the pre-Josianic period: Jerusalem's priests were to be Levites, but only Levites of Zadokite heritage, and all other Levites were to be relegated to a subordinate office with a very narrow scope of responsibility (Ezek 44:10–13). The authority granted to Levites beyond Jerusalem to serve as local administrators of Deuteronomic law receives nary a mention;[57] the local sphere of the restored community is marginalized, with all attention paid to the Jerusalem cult both in terms of sacrifice and legal instruction.

Ezekiel's plan for future restoration reveals a good deal about the Zadokite perspectives on how life should be conducted in Babylon during the exile. The consistent limitations placed on Deuteronomy's norms constitute a definitive statement against those in exile who had been associated with that book's composition, that is, the Shaphanide scribes and their Levite confederates exiled to Babylon from the satellite communities surrounding Jerusalem.[58] The Deuteronomic legislation had provided these Levites with a juridical and scribal/exegetical authority[59] that would certainly have been more pronounced during the exile, with the extant law in need of development for the exilic communities operating without a central Temple and on foreign soil.[60] It is against this exilic culture that Ezekiel voices his tirade against the Levites, attempting to rebuild the need for an authoritative Zadokite leadership even with the loss of the Temple cult.

Prophecy, it seems, became an effective surrogate for cultic authority and operations.[61]

A *Kulturkampf* thus erupted among the literati of the Babylonian Judeans: two forms of religious leadership emerged, one Zadokite, the other Shaphanide. The first is reflected in Ezekiel's writings, the second by the Deuteronomistic literature and the extant Jeremianic corpus. The dates in the book of Ezekiel inform us that his prophecies spanned 20 years of exile (ca. 592–572 BCE), the time span of a priest's active cultic duties;[62] whether this is historical or a literary construct, it attests to the persistent Zadokite claim over prophetic authority represented by the Ezekiel tradition.[63] This voice consistently plays on the concerns of the lay leaders of the exilic community in Babylon via regular interaction with the elders (Ezek 4:1; 8:1; 20:1). This is often presented as the elders coming to Ezekiel himself, but the effect contributes to the securing of grass-roots support among the public for the Zadokite leadership. This is reflected not only in the presentation of Ezekiel's prophetic activity as the proper execution of priestly service, but also in the subordination of Deuteronomistic language to Ezekiel's rhetoric.[64] Ezekiel assumes the role of the prophet like Moses, contravening the preexilic typological distinction forged by Deuteronomy between the prophet Moses and priestly figures.[65]

This method of lexical appropriation also accounts for the terminological similarities between Jeremiah's oracles and those of Ezekiel. Like the author of the Supplement, Ezekiel appears to have recognized the authority of Jeremiah and takes up that prophet's own terminology and rhetoric. A salient example is Ezekiel's use of the "watchman" (צופה) terminology for his own prophetic activity, which had earlier been a staple of Ephraimite prophetic tradition put to use both typologically and lexically by Jeremiah (Jer 6:17).[66] Additional points of influence can be found in Ezekiel 16 (which draws from Jeremiah 2) and Ezekiel 23 (which is patterned on Jer 3:6–11). But Ezekiel takes Jeremiah's rhetoric and expands it dramatically.[67] This is especially the case in Ezekiel 18:1–20 (discussed in Chapter 2), which develops Jeremiah's earlier oracle in Jer 31:27–34. Ezekiel's oracle suggests that Zadokite ideology is at the heart of the proper execution of Jeremiah's directive: if a man is righteous (ואיש כי יהיה צדיק), then the quality of Zadokite righteousness, implied through a less than subtle wordplay, will be upon him (צדקת הצדיק תהיה עליו) (Ezek 18:5, 20). It is Ezekiel's Zadokite concept of law that is binding if one wishes to emulate Jeremiah's oracle, which points ahead to Ezekiel's vision for a restored community in Ezekiel 40–48, the book's major unit of instruction that serves the Zadokite agenda exclusively.[68]

THE POLITICS BEHIND EZEKIEL'S PROGRAM

A key political development during the exile served as a catalyst for the Ezekiel tradition's program in Ezekiel 40–48: a definitive position taken by the royal Judean circle in Babylon regarding the hegemony of their captors. As is well known, Jehoiachin was eventually brought out of prison in Babylon ca. 562 BCE and given a place in the royal court of Amel-Marduk.[69] The rehabilitation of Jehoiachin must have sent shock waves throughout the exilic community.[70] Those holding out for restoration to Judah and Jerusalem may well have viewed this action as a first step, while others may have viewed it as evidence of the persistence of the Davidic covenant.[71]

Yet, restoration was not, in the end, associated with Jehoiachin's rehabilitation. In the final analysis of both the Jeremianic and Deuteronomistic accounts of his release, Jehoiachin is alive and well, but in the Deuteronomistic account he becomes a lackey of the Babylonian court "all the days of his life" and, in the parallel Jeremianic account, "until the day of his death." Jehoiachin had apparently fully submitted to Babylonian hegemony, and his rehabilitation was a diplomatic gesture by Amel-Marduk. This reflects a convergence of political sentiment between the Davidide king and the Deuteronomistic point of view fostered by Jeremiah and the Shaphanides, one already witnessed by Jehoiachin's deferral to Babylon in 598/597 BCE following his father's rebellion. Jehoiachin's rehabilitation in 562 would only further reinforce Shaphanide influence among the exilic population that accepted Jehoiachin as the scion of the Davidic house.

We may reasonably assume that although Jehoiachin's official rehabilitation took place ca. 562 BCE, political sentiments among the Judean elite in Babylon who were part of his inner circle had favored deference to Babylon for many years beforehand. Certainly, the precedent was already set by Jehoiachin's surrender in 597, and Jeremiah's support of this deferential attitude is in evidence in several oracles and epistles. This political purview would likely have gained momentum in 572 with the Babylonian conquest of Tyre, which had been under siege since roughly the time of the conquest of Jerusalem in 587/586.[72] Tyre had suffered a major defeat by the Assyrians ca. 641; Isa 23:15–18, composed during a Josianic-era redaction of Isaiah's oracles, invokes the 70-year trope of Esarhaddon's Black Stone inscription to indicate that the defeat was due to YHWH's divine will, not that of a Mesopotamian deity.[73] The Babylonian defeat of Tyre (almost exactly 70 years after the Assyria campaign) must have reinforced Jeremiah's prophecies regarding Babylonian geopolitical dominance, with Babylon now quite literally inheriting the position of Assyria.[74] With the subsequent attempt to restore Hophra to the Egyptian throne under the aegis of Nebuchadrezzar (in 567),[75] Babylon's international influence would have seemed even more indomitable to the exilic audience.

The change in political climate would have inspired the additions to 2 Kings 25/Jeremiah 52 chronicling Jehoiachin's release as part of a propaganda effort to solidify support of the Babylonian status quo from the exilic point of view. But even before Jehoiachin's release, the recognition of Babylonian supremacy (with its itinerant mythic-cosmic implications) would have had major consequences for traditional Zadokite understandings of covenant, religious authority, law, and cosmology, with the old Jerusalem-centric paradigm completely disrupted. The Zadokite response to this reality is felt throughout Ezekiel 40–48, as the Davidic heir is no longer presented as a king (מלך) but, rather, as a "prince" (נשיא), a sacral demotion in the language of the ancient Near East, as kings typically headed their cults.[76] Yet, in demoting Jehoiachin, Ezekiel 40–48 also demotes the importance of the Shaphanide scribal circles closely associated with him who likely influenced his political attitudes.[77] The end result is a program for restoration that attempted to draw out the nationalistic impulses of the Judean exiles and place the Zadokites in charge both during the exile and, consequently, once the exile was to come to an end. This message must have appealed enormously to the exiles of 587 BCE, providing for them what Jeremiah's message had provided for the deportees of 597, many of whom had been involved in the Deuteronomistic movement that Ezekiel discredited so vehemently.

THE SCRIBAL COUNTERSTRATEGY

The Zadokite agenda represented by Ezekiel was a serious threat to the original message of Jeremiah (who had fervently decried the privileged status of the Jerusalem cult)[78] and the ongoing importance of the Shaphanides during the exile. The author of the Supplement takes aim at this Zadokite argument by taking up the same issues as Ezekiel from the outset of his work, albeit from the opposite perspective. In Jeremiah 26, those who deny Jeremiah's words – which for an exilic audience had already been proved true – are the priests and prophets bound to the Jerusalem cult, a categorization that would certainly have pertained to Ezekiel and those supporting his message. Moreover, the author's citations of earlier prophecy invoke history as a witness against the Zadokite perspective: YHWH had indeed overturned Jerusalem, just as he had other Israelite cult sites. Micah, Jeremiah, and Uriah, all *non*-Jerusalemites, are vindicated through the rhetoric of the chapter, as are the scribes who inherited and developed their words.[79]

In addition, while Ezekiel rails against the Deuteronomic legislation (Ezek 20:25–26), Jeremiah 26 emphasizes the Deuteronomic process involved in the ratification of Jeremiah as a Mosaic prophet and credits *the elders* with facilitating this process at his trial (v. 17).[80] Thus, Jeremiah 26 constructs a reality pertinent to the elders of the author's day that Ezekiel attempted to influence: the elders before the exile heeded Jeremiah's words, whereas others in the crowd at Jeremiah's trial apparently sided with the prophet and priests and, by implication, Jehoiakim (vv. 20–24). The hermeneutical relationship between Jeremiah 26 and 27–29 (via the literary sequence/proximity and the superscription commonalities in 26:1/27:1)[81] implies that the portion of the crowd that supported Jeremiah ultimately becomes the legitimate 597 BCE community to which Jeremiah 27–29, and subsequently 30–31, were addressed. The choice to accept Jeremiah's words had earlier secured blessing in exile (Jer 24:4–7; 30–31), a condition that the author implies could be repeated if the people heed the new message now subsumed within the words of Jeremiah (Jer 1:1; 51:64) and its advocacy of the retention and adjustment of Deuteronomistic tradition. Furthermore, the redaction of Jeremiah 27–29 into the Supplement revived the illegitimate positions of the prophets among the 597 community who had once proclaimed an imminent restoration to Jerusalem and the reconstitution of its cult; the Zadokite perspective, the author implies, suffers from the same misguided focus. The recognition of the scribes' centrality to Jeremiah's prophecy, the author posits, is the key to one day returning to the land, a promise now extended to the 587 deportees (Jer 31:38–40; 32:6–15). Those who deny the scribes' authority – regardless of priestly pedigree – are no better than the ruffians who brought about the destruction of Judah (Jeremiah 37–39) or those who shanghaied the prophet to Egypt (Jeremiah 43–44).

Through the language of metaphor and polemics, the priests and prophets of Jeremiah 26 constitute an assault on the Zadokite circle represented by Ezekiel, as both possess what the author argues to be an unhealthy fixation on Jerusalem to the detriment of divine law, the prophetic tradition, and scribal authority. This assault is only intensified in subsequent episodes, especially Jeremiah 34, which equates those who engage in P rituals with the vilification of Jehoiakim (Jer 34:20/36:30). The condemnation continues in Jeremiah 36, which champions the scribal office as sacral via Levitical characterization; in Jeremiah 41, which denies the ongoing viability of the Jerusalem Temple cult;[82] and finally, in Jeremiah 43–44, where those who deny the theology of Deuteronomy in turn deny their own Israelite identity. This is an important consideration when evaluating the polemical purpose of the Supplement. The argument against the Zadokite Ezekiel tradition initiated in Jeremiah 26 emphasizes the delusions of those fixated on the Jerusalem cult (even in the abstract, as would be the case among exilic Zadokites), but the antagonistic portion of the public depicted in that same chapter becomes the Egyptian remnant of Jeremiah 44. Whereas the Judeans in Babylon would have probably looked down upon residency in Egypt, and whereas Ezekiel himself castigates such residency, the author of the Supplement goes even further by concluding that the Egyptian remnant is no longer even part of Israel.[83]

While there must have indeed been a cadre of Judeans who did revert to pre-Deuteronomic forms of religion following Josiah's demise and the destruction of Jerusalem,[84] the author of the Supplement suggests that the Jerusalem-obsessive ideology of the Zadokites represented by Ezekiel is a link in a chain that led to the fall of Judah and, ultimately, is as alien to Israelite religion as the paganism expressed in Jer 44:15–19. Both positions reject the essential features of Israel's relationship with YHWH as established in Deuteronomy, advanced by Jeremiah, and developed by the Shaphanide scribes. That the Supplement closes with Jeremiah 45 is the ultimate testament to this line of reason: as observed previously, revelation is entrusted to a scribe, who amplifies the prophet's voice. Here we must consider the weight of the statement that Baruch should not seek "great things" (גדלות) for himself (Jer 45:5); in the context of the book of Jeremiah, the גדל terminology most often refers to prophetic authority.[85] A degree of parity had been intimated in Jeremiah 36, where the scribe himself reads aloud the prophetic word, and the implied literary parallel between Gedaliah's decree and Jeremiah's oracles (Jer 40:10)[86] addresses the fitness of scribes to execute the teachings of the prophets on an administrative level, but Jer 45:5 makes it clear that the scribe is not to become a prophet himself. The colophonic structure of Jeremiah 45 may legitimize the scribe in preserving and adapting Jeremiah's teachings, but it fixes the distinct relationship.[87] The already-recognized position of Jeremiah as a Deuteronomic prophet like Moses would have facilitated a parallel between what we encounter in

Jeremiah 45 and in earlier Deuteronomistic literature: Joshua carries on after Moses, but as a subordinate who institutes his master's words, teachings, and writings as decidedly Mosaic.[88] Similarly, Baruch is to preserve his prophetic master's words, teachings, and writings as decidedly Jeremianic. This would have curbed and countered the message of Ezekiel, who declared prophetic authority for himself and who subsumed Jeremiah's teachings within his own.

The Supplement thereby ends with an injunction not to subordinate the prophetic teachings of Jeremiah to other systems of discourse. This idea was already current in the smaller collection of text directed to the deportees of 597 BCE (now expanded for the post-587 deportees): the new covenant of Jer 31:31–34 claims that the new standards of faith will involve a direct engagement of written teachings no longer mediated by priestly figures.[89] Scribal figures, however, had long been entrusted to interpret these written teachings, prophetic or otherwise, and were already mandated by the Deuteronomic Torah of Josiah's era to supervise and adjudicate matters based on the texts in their possession.[90] By inserting the supplement *within* the extant Jeremianic corpus, the injunction safeguards the centrality of the scribes, presenting them, not the Zadokites, as an organic part of Jeremiah's tradition.

The author ultimately presents his audience with a choice reminiscent of Deut 30:15–19: the acceptance of scribal authority leads to blessing, security, and life (quite literally so in Jer 45:5).[91] Conversely, rejection leads to evil and covenantal death, with a community cut off from the living God, as expressed in Jeremiah 44 (see also Jer 42:10–16). The nature and purpose of the Supplement thereby emerge: just as the Ezekiel tradition must have spoken to the deportees of 587 BCE, so too does the Supplement, arguing that they now have the chance to share in the privileged position of the 597 community (Jeremiah 24; 27–32:15) but will become like the Egyptian diaspora and be cut off from their deity if they follow the Zadokite agenda advanced by Ezekiel.[92] If the dates in the book of Ezekiel correctly reflect his period of activity down to roughly the year 572 BCE,[93] our proposed dating of the Supplement to ca. 570 suggests that its authors did not take long to respond to the Zadokite threat he represented.[94] The first decade and a half of the exile must have been fraught with polemics at every turn between two once powerful but now compromised sacral groups, each attempting to account for the shifting tides of history and trying to secure public support for its authority.

CHAPTER 6

The Exilic Coalition between the Shaphanides and Levites

THERE IS STRONG SCHOLARLY CONSENSUS THAT THE SHAPHANIDES IN exile maintained close connections to the royal circle of Jehoiachin in Babylon and were responsible for a significant amount of redactional activity during the period of Babylonian domination.[1] As discussed in the present study, the development of the book of Jeremiah was paramount to this literary endeavor and indeed serves as a key to understanding its ongoing development. The exilic adjustments and expansions to the preexilic literary collections reflect an attempt to establish ideological continuity from one epoch to the next, despite the obvious sociological, political, and theological disruption represented by the death of Josiah, the dissolution of Judah's autonomy, and the conditions of expatriate life.[2] These adjustments are deployed to provide comprehensiveness to the literature, and thus to maintain the influence and vitality of the political ideology and scribal group standing behind it.[3]

The Shaphanides, however, would not have been the only group interested in preserving the Deuteronomistic tradition in exile. The preexilic version of this tradition attempted to appeal to a variety of Levitical groups,[4] and the narrative regarding Josiah's reform activity in Judah suggests that the Levites of Josiah's realm did conform to the Deuteronomic program.[5] The reform may have prohibited them from engaging in local cultic activity in the wake of Josiah's centralization efforts, but it provided them with regional juridical authority as executors and licensed exegetes of the written

Deuteronomic legislation, stationed in each village or city gate.[6] In this way, local legal traditions would have developed alongside the national Deuteronomic legislation. One might view the decree in Deut 31:10–13 to congregate the nation and read the law publicly every seven years as a way of broadly establishing a standardized, updated version of the national constitution that would account for these local legal traditions and additional cases of national import not covered by older editions of the Deuteronomic law code.[7] As such, local Levites contributed directly to the growth of the Deuteronomic law code and the development of Deuteronomistic ideology.

LEVITICAL ACTIVITY AND DEUTERONOMIC AUTHORITY IN EXILE

This model of Levitical authority would prove to be essential to those Levites taken into captivity alongside the citizens of the satellite communities surrounding Jerusalem and elsewhere.[8] Because they were separated from the land and the opportunity to reclaim the old rural shrines, the possibility of these Levites turning away from the Deuteronomic model was greatly diminished, as it provided the only option for maintaining ongoing influence and authority in the religious life of the exiles. In fact, these Levites were actually in a prime position to sustain their influence: already empowered by the Deuteronomic legislation to act as mediators and exegetes of legal tradition, the Levites could interpret the Deuteronomic laws regarding life in the land to apply to life in exile with respect to their communal roles.[9] This practice would have likely been supported by many of the exiles, providing a much-needed sense of cultural/social continuity in a circumstance otherwise fraught with uncertainty and anxiety.[10]

While the Shaphanides carried with them a legacy of scribal influence and viewed themselves as guardians of the Jerusalem literary traditions of the preexilic period, the literature that they had once produced was thus very likely also being developed among the Levites of other uprooted Judean towns now living in and around Babylon. Scholars who have proposed that various biblical traditions were developed through the discourse in early synagogues during the period of the exile are perhaps not far from the historical reality.[11] It is indeed anachronistic to speak of "synagogues" during the sixth century BCE (synagogues first appear only in the Hellenistic period),[12] but the antecedents to what would become the institution of the synagogue were already in place in the late seventh century. As we have seen, Deuteronomy transformed the tradition of congregating at village gates into a specifically sacral activity, with Levitical religious leaders supervising the study, application, and development of sacred law. In exile, this practice would have continued in some surrogate locale among those now separated from the homeland cities and villages. With the conditions of exile spurring intense reflection upon preexilic legal, liturgical, and narrative traditions among the captive population, the Levites would have served as mediators dealing with the profoundly difficult questions and problems that the study of these materials would generate.[13]

The Shaphanides were not, in all likelihood, inherently opposed to this development. Though disparate communities under Levitical religious leadership would have developed different views and exegetical reflexes, the Deuteronomistic tradition produced by the Shaphanides still established the parameters within which all of these Levitical exegetes operated. The interests and ideological predilections of the Shaphanides thereby became the starting point for all varieties of exilic Levitical discourse.[14] It would be the rise of the Zadokite agenda via the Ezekiel tradition, though, that would ultimately motivate the Shaphanides and Levites to more actively form a coalition, as Ezekiel's rhetoric left little room for either Shaphanide or Levitical leadership among the exilic masses whom the prophet directly addressed.[15]

THE LEVITICAL CONCERNS OF THE SUPPLEMENT

Of the Supplement's many sources, we encounter both annalistic accounts typical of royal scribal composition and echoes of folk traditions developed into a sophisticated narrative superstructure.[16] As noted in the Introduction to the present study, many of these traditions appear to contradict other accounts within the Supplement, and this represents an inclusive strategy on the part of the author also witnessed in the preexilic Deuteronomistic literature. In that literature, we have seen that repeated emphasis was placed on the history, ideology, and social location of Levites.[17] This was part of an attempt to incorporate Levitical groups into the Deuteronomic ideological fold, which in turn would help facilitate the Deuteronomic program among the Judean population.[18] Given the profound stylistic and thematic commonalities shared by the preexilic Deuteronomistic literature and the Supplement, not to mention the largely common Shaphanide authorship, we may assume that the Supplement (in part) also addresses the Levites now in exile. The development of the Jeremiah tradition may reflect an attempt by the Shaphanides to enlist the support of the Levites in appealing to the exilic masses. The author responsible for shaping the Supplement could not have selected a more appropriate tradition to house his work: not only was Jeremiah a well-known prophet whose oracles had largely come to pass, but he had strongly identified himself as a Levite throughout his preexilic career.[19] Undoubtedly, Jeremiah's self-proclaimed Levitical status would have made his oracles highly regarded among the Levites taken captive into Babylon. The accuracy of these oracles emanating from a Levite dedicated to Deuteronomistic ideology such as Jeremiah would provide increased credibility to Levites working within the Deuteronomic paradigm in the eyes of their respective exilic communities. To these Levites, Jeremiah became a paradigmatic figure.[20]

We should not be surprised, then, to see a strong Levitical concern running through the Supplement. Levitical-priestly language occurs subtly in a few notable episodes;[21] as discussed previously, the Shaphanide scribes are characterized in Levitical terms in Jeremiah 36 in accordance with the Levites' responsibility to administer the Torah to the king (Deut 17:18–19) and to the people (Deut 31:9–13).[22] We have also seen that the latter Deuteronomic passage qualifies Gedaliah's fitness as a communal leader in Jeremiah 40.[23] While this highlights the Levitical heritage of the Shaphanides, it also establishes that the exilic Levites and the Shaphanides shared common interests and goals. Furthermore, if Jeremiah was indeed a paradigmatic Levitical figure, then the interchangeability between the prophet and the Shaphanide scribes in Jeremiah 34/36/40 suggests that the Shaphanides should be role models for the exilic Levites as well.

It is here that we can sense the pivotal role played by the elusive Jehudi b. Nethaniah b. Shelemiah b. Cushi in Jeremiah 36, a chapter that many scholars see as the keystone to understanding the development of the Jeremiah tradition or the structure of the larger book of Jeremiah.[24] Jehudi is himself a keystone to the chapter: he is the one sent by the scribes to bring Baruch and the *Urrolle* to them, and he is the one also sent by the king to retrieve the scroll itself from Elishama's chamber. Long before Jehudi must read Jeremiah's words to a king who burns them, the chapter establishes that he is caught between a rock and a hard place, as his allegiance is divided between the Shaphanide scribes who supported Jeremiah and the king who stood against the prophet. It is no surprise that the author introduces him with such an extended patronym, beckoning us to pay attention to this character and consider the pressures that confront him within the chapter.[25]

That Jehudi's name is never mentioned again in the book of Jeremiah or anywhere else is curious, especially when we consider that Jeremiah 36 is extremely concerned with its own sense of historicity;[26] tying this important character to other historical episodes in the Supplement would serve that agenda, but Jehudi is nowhere to be found beyond Jeremiah 36. Considering the chapter's interest in historical authenticity, however, it is difficult to view him as an entirely literary creation despite the fact that he functions as such an important symbolic character. Moreover, the patronymic information is suggestive of his historical importance in the eyes of the author. The generational scheme associated with his extended name points to a connection to the reign of Hezekiah, an important historical period in Deuteronomistic consciousness and one also invoked at the beginning of the Supplement (Jer 26:17–19).[27] It is especially notable in this regard that Jehudi's grandfather is identified as בן כושי. It is possible that this is a genealogical notice, but it might also be a gentilic marker, that is, בן כושי = "a Cushite." We should also note that "Cushi" appears as a proper name in the superscription to the book of Zephaniah the prophet:

> The word of YHWH which came unto Zephaniah the son of *Cushi* (בן כושי) the son of Gedaliah, the son of Amariah, the son of Hezekiah (בן חזקיה), in the days of Josiah the son of Amon, king of Judah. (Zeph 1:1)

Here we can see that Zephaniah's patronymic information overtly identifies him with Hezekiah. Rather than direct ancestry, though, it may be that Zephaniah's grandfather, Amariah, was a member of Hezekiah's court, and thus the phrase בן חזקיה may instead be an official title; parallels occur in both biblical texts and various excavated bullae.[28] If, as several scholars have suggested, the roots of the Deuteronomistic movement may be traced to Hezekiah's court (or if the Josianic scribes sought to identify their roots with that court), then it would be sound rhetorical strategy to link the family of a Josianic propagandist like Zephaniah to Hezekiah's reign.[29]

Similarly to this proposed reading of בן חזקיה, the בן כושי in Zephaniah 1:1 may be a title rather than a name. More to the point, it may be a gentilic marker relating not to the Zephaniah's father but, rather, to the prophet's own lineage roots.[30] Why do we encounter two instances of the phrase "Cushite" related to figures bound to the Hezekian period?[31] A consideration of the term כושי is suggestive, as it carries a number of ethnographic implications.[32] In most cases, the word indicates Ethiopian ethnicity, as is evident in Jer 13:23,[33] but Cushi may also belie a Midianite provenance, derived from Cushan, an ancient pseudonym for Midian (Hab 3:7; cf. Num 12:1). As discussed previously, the presence of Midianite-Kenites in Israelite society is well documented, and their long-standing connection with Arad – an important royal Judean stronghold – would have facilitated interaction with Hezekiah's governmental infrastructure during that king's process of urbanization between the years 705 and 701 BCE.[34] The reign of Hezekiah saw the production of literature and the spread of an ideology deeply concerned with hallowed antiquity, coinciding with a general tendency throughout the ancient Near East of the late eighth century to appeal to the heroic past.[35] Considering the mixed population that Hezekiah's agents attempted to forge into a single community (urban Judeans, rural Judeans, northern refugees), it is not surprising that some would consciously attempt to emphasize their unique lineages while tolerating the social mandates of the state and its attempt to homogenize the citizenry. This would especially be the case among those like the Kenites, with old priestly connections to Mosaic tradition and the most ancient versions of Yahwism.[36] Like the extra patronymic item in Zephaniah's lineage list, the בן כושי following the name of Jehudi's grandfather, Shelemaiah, may be a reference to Midianite-Kenite heritage.[37]

If the faithful Jehudi possessed ties to the venerable Kenite line, this would support his important role in a narrative written for an exilic audience questioning how proper religious ideology could be preserved (and the role of the Jeremiah tradition therein). It is fortuitous that his name literally means "Judean" (יהודי). The character's centrality to Jeremiah 36 automatically pulls every exilic Judean into the narrative and suggests that they, like Jehudi, have a responsibility to become part of the drama involving the development of Jeremiah's book. Thus, while Jehudi's extended patronyms support that character's historicity, it is clear that his central role in the chapter serves the author's agenda in emphasizing the importance of Levitical interaction, fortifying an argument that sympathies to Jeremiah and those developing his literary legacy should transcend lineage roots and kinship-based ideological boundaries.[38]

The most significant Levitical element in the Supplement is its consistent attitude toward kings. For the author of the Supplement, a king's worth is a matter of his submission to the law and its prophetic qualification;[39] this obviously carries forward the Deuteronomistic criteria, but it also reaffirms long-standing Levitical views regarding the institution of the Israelite monarchy.[40] This critique is expressed both in the structured official scribal reports *and* in the more folkloristic sources.[41] That these folkloristic sources share the same basic attitude as the sources that emanated from the Shaphanide scribal chancery suggests that the former emerged from Levitical oral exegesis or teachings that accompanied the study of Jeremiah's oracles and other literature relating to the events of his lifetime.[42]

Here we may pause to reconsider the Ebed-Melech episodes in Jeremiah 38–39, and it is worth considering the fact that he is the only character among the royal officers who is depicted by title and not by name/patronym.[43] Several parallels obtain between this Ethiopian officer and Jehudi in Jeremiah 36. Both characters prominently contain "Cushi" in their respective names/titles, and as we have seen, Jehudi is characterized as much by his function as a *servant of the king* as he is by his function as a scribal (cum Levite) agent. An additional commonality with the character of Ebed-Melech may be implied here. Terminology nearly identical to that character's name (עבד מלך) is found on the seals of royal officials identified with scribes who are mentioned alongside Jehudi in the book of Jeremiah: seals belonging to both Gedaliah and Elishama identify each as "servant of the king" (עבד המלך).[44] Certainly, a connection between Ebed-Melech and the scribes is sensed with the doublet blessing given to both Baruch and the Cushite royal officer (Jer 39:18/45:5); this would be consistent with the other instances discussed earlier involving Levitical-scribal parallels.[45]

There is no reason to doubt that early-sixth-century BCE Jerusalem saw interaction with a diversity of ethnicities associated with Egypt or sub-Saharan Africans or that the Ebed-Melech episodes are rooted in historical events.[46] But if our suggestion is correct that Jeremiah 36 emphasizes Jehudi's Levitical status via the name Cushi in his patronymic list, then the confluence of terms and typological figures (the name/title Cushi, scribal figures called "servant[s] of the king," sympathies to Jeremiah, and Levitical–scribal parallels throughout the Supplement) is difficult to dismiss. These common features suggest that the Ebed-Melech episode was developed (through Levite discourse) as an example of proper conduct and allegiance to sacral figures like Jeremiah. The memory of an historical episode involving Jeremiah and an Ethiopian steward in the service of Zedekiah, developed for didactic purposes, may well have informed the rhetorical presentation of that folkloristic episode and its resonances throughout the structure of the Supplement.[47]

In addition to the folkloristic narrative sources, it may be that some of Jeremiah's oracles within the Supplement, though based upon authentic utterances, may have similarly been rewritten by the author to incorporate the perspectives of these Levites. One such example would be the prophet's tirade in Jer 34:12–22. The presentation of Jeremiah citing Deuteronomic law for the king is, as we have seen, modeled upon the duties of the Levitical priests in Deut 17:18–19, and the author's introduction into Jer 34:14 of the מקץ שבע שנים formula from Deut 31:10 intensifies the Levitical connection. A tradition of popular Levite teachings regarding Jeremiah's role in the final years of the Judean kingdom or even in relation to Zedekiah's manumission fiasco specifically would be a powerful motivation for the Shaphanide author of the Supplement to characterize the prophet with a deliberate reference to Deut 31:10.[48]

Along the same redactional/rhetorical line of logic, the reference in Jer 43:1 to Deut 32:45 calls to mind the ancient poem preceding that Deuteronomic passage, that is, the Song of Moses (Deut 32:1–43). Many scholars view this poem's current position as the result of an exilic redaction of Deuteronomy,[49] but its function as the source of the allusion in Jer 43:1 suggests that it was already part of the Deuteronomic corpus by the time the Supplement was written. The poem had at one point been part of a Levitical liturgical tradition and was very likely included in Deuteronomy as part of the general appeal to Levites throughout the Josianic period.[50] The poem took on new meaning following the destruction of Jerusalem and the deportation to Babylon, and once again functioned as a liturgical text among the Levites meditating on the meaning of the exile.[51] The allusion in Jer 43:1 therefore not only plays upon the connections between Jeremiah and Moses and the well-known status of Jeremiah as a Levite, but also suggests to the Levite reader or listener that the Shaphanide author esteems Levitical tradition as highly as the Josianic-era literature.

Finally, the Supplement's attitude toward Egypt continues the long tradition of anti-Egyptian sentiments among Levites.[52] The immediate source for the author is obviously the Deuteronomistic literature, though that literature's interest in Levitical thought opens the door to a longer history of anti-Egyptian polemics. The earliest narrative and oracular traditions regarding the Shiloh priesthood define the legitimacy of that line via the Exodus from Egypt; the Solomonic composition Psalm 78 usurps the traditional discourse of Ephraimite Levites and attempts to redefine its parameters with respect to Solomon's foreign policy toward Egypt.[53] The Mushite–Levite narrative in Exodus 32 presupposes the Exodus as a foundational moment in the development of Yahwism,[54] and Hosea's oracles are strongly informed by the idea of the Exodus, leading to his declaration that Israel's national unity rested on the departure from Egypt led by Moses.[55] The liturgical traditions of the Asaphite Levites that influenced Hosea's rhetoric also repeatedly refer back to the Exodus from Egypt as the basic feature of Israelite identity.[56] This is the traditional critique from which the Deuteronomistic perspective drew, and it is a very small step to the attitude of the Supplement on the same issue.

The Supplement, in short, functioned similarly to the preexilic Deuteronomistic works, appealing to the interests of Levites by working diverse traditions into a singular and definitive religio-political statement.[57] The end result produced a win-win situation of sorts: the exilic Levites had their perspectives "canonized" into an official version of a book bearing the legacy of a highly influential prophet (and one of well-known Levitical heritage), and the Shaphanides could rely on these Levites to promulgate their work to the exilic masses against the Ezekiel tradition and other Zadokite literary endeavors.[58] The Shaphanides thereby secured for themselves a position as founders of an ideological and literary tradition that would be taken up by the various exilic Levitical groups around them, establishing standards of discourse and inquiry that would persevere in ensuing eras alongside (and often in contestation with) the Zadokite establishment.[59]

The conflict between the Zadokites and the scribes behind the Jeremiah tradition appears to have persisted for quite some time. The return from exile in the last quarter of the sixth century BCE saw the rise of the Zadokites as the religious leaders of the Restoration community, but the literature arising immediately after this period reveals that Levites had very little place in the original Zadokite-led administration in Jerusalem.[60]

Malachi strongly castigates the Zadokites from a disadvantaged Levitical perspective,[61] and Ezra 7–8 suggests that few Levites could be found in the Zadokite-dominanted Restoration community before Ezra's mission to Jerusalem, nor were many Levites in Mesopotamia enthusiastic about joining this community.[62] Considering the scribal duties given to the Levites in the Deuteronomic legislation, the Levitical interests of the Shaphanide historiographers,[63] and the united front forged between the Shaphanides and the Levites during the exile, it may be the case that two distinct bodies of historiographic/prophetic works emerged within the two camps: a Zadokite historiography incorporating the Pentateuch (in some penultimate form) with the book of Ezekiel and a Shaphanide–Levite historiography incorporating Deuteronomy–Kings with the book of Jeremiah.[64]

It would only be later, during the early years of the Restoration, that the two historiographic works would be merged into a single narrative spanning Genesis–Kings, bringing together the great prophetic works as well.[65] This would constitute a first step toward reconciliation between the Zadokite and scribal–Levitical worldviews, methods, and literary traditions eventually sensed in the fifth- and fourth-century BCE literature. The subsequent position of Levites as teachers, scribes, and curators/editors of sacred texts must have derived substantially from the increased role they played as important religious and social figures during the exile, and indeed the Chronicler's very obvious emphasis on the Jeremiah tradition suggests that the development of the book of Jeremiah was significantly affected by these Levites on a number of levels.[66] In time, the Supplement transcended its polemical role in the Jeremiah tradition. This important collection of literature thoroughly affected methods of composition, exegesis, and hermeneutics as Israel continued to generate its texts and ideas.

Conclusion

THE DEBATE WITH THE EZEKIEL TRADITION CIRCLE BRINGS TO LIGHT A number of important considerations regarding the ideological and literary connections between the Jeremianic material and the Deuteronomistic works. Isolating Deuteronomistic language in the book of Jeremiah is not enough to suggest a broad or systematic redaction of older documents that initially had little in common with Deuteronomistic concerns.[1] As observed in the Introduction to the present study, material often ascribed to Jeremiah on a compositional level was already inherently Deuteronomistic before undergoing any redactional activity.[2] It is possible to speak of a broad, systematic Deuteronomistic redaction of the Jeremianic material only insofar as both Jeremiah and the author of the Supplement were already associated with the circles responsible for the composition and compilation of the Deuteronomistic works that emerged in the preexilic period.[3] The prophet himself was strongly inspired by the literature that emerged under Josiah and conceived his own work as an extension of and commentary on that literary enterprise during the years of Josiah's reform and following Josiah's death.

DEUTERONOMISTIC THOUGHT IN EXILE

The author of the Supplement presupposed the basic compatibility of these works and integrates them into his own, interspersing Jeremianic oracles and episodes from the prophet's life with narratives that pick up where the

Josianic DH left off. The author also shapes Jeremianic oracles with an eye to Deuteronomy, developing elements of the prophet's positions and opinions into exhortations that emulate those of Moses (i.e., Jer 42; 43:1).[4] Indeed, the very strategy of appealing to the authority of a recognized Mosaic prophet such as Jeremiah recalls the decision of the Josianic scribes behind the book of Deuteronomy to ascribe their innovative ideology and legislation to Moses and to sandwich them between established and ancient Mosaic literary traditions.[5] Both Jeremiah and the author of the Supplement therefore draw inspiration directly from the preexilic Deuteronomistic literature.

Evidence for this sequence of composition may be deduced by a comparison of the post-Josianic narratives in the DH and the narrative material in the Supplement. The Supplement contains many details regarding Jehoiakim, Jehoiachin, and Zedekiah; the DH does not. The exilic notes in the DH regarding these figures employ brief, repetitive language in evaluating their respective reigns and competencies, compacting the events that transpired on their watch into little more than two chapters.[6] Yet, these events were dramatically disruptive and generated enormous prophetic, priestly, and royalistic debate among Judeans in a variety of locations. The relative lack of discussion or detail in the DH regarding the post-Josianic period makes sense only if extensive discussion had already occurred in another closely related corpus. The exilic editors of the DH must have viewed the repository of information in the Jeremianic corpus (inclusive of the Supplement) as such a corpus and opted to employ a shorthand form of allusion to that corpus in updating their own.

Further evidence for this may be adduced by the manner in which these allusions are made. The exilic editors of the DH categorically denounce all post-Josianic kings: Jehoahaz, Jehoiakim, Jehoiachin, and Zedekiah are all said to have done "that which was evil" in YHWH's eyes, despite the fact that none are charged with the major transgression of the pre-Josianic kings, that is, allowing high-place worship.[7] This is a curious statement on its own, as Jehoahaz is not reported to have done *anything* in either the DH or the book of Jeremiah, and the latter goes to some length to legitimize Jehoiachin after his submission to Babylon.[8] There would appear at first to be no Jeremianic basis for the statements in the DH regarding these monarchs, but we must consider the general attitude toward Davidic kingship developed throughout the Jeremianic corpus (both before and after the inclusion of the Supplement). Individuals are judged according to their own merits (such is the import of Jer 31:28–29), but the monarchy as an institution is no longer a viable avenue for covenantal sustenance.[9]

The exilic editors of the DH adopt this same perspective. Since the DH narrative concerns the institution of the independent Davidic monarchy (and how that monarchy met its end), the Jeremianic view on monarchy in general is deployed in evaluating the reigns of these kings alongside those of Jehoiakim and Zedekiah. The brevity of the evaluations, however, points to the editors' presupposition that details could and should be found in the accompanying Jeremianic corpus, suggesting that by the time the exilic editors of 2 Kings were active, the book of Jeremiah (including the Supplement) was considered a normative part of the Deuteronomistic literary culture. The nearly identical nature of 2 Kings 25 and the secondary ending added to the book of Jeremiah (Jeremiah 52) further points to these later editors' understanding that the two works must be viewed in tandem, with one offering insight into the other.[10] This might also explain why the exilic editors of the DH saw no need to include Jeremiah in their account of the twilight of Judah: details concerning the prophet's activity already existed in a text now bound to the DH as a co-corpus.[11]

Influence from the Jeremiah tradition may also be sensed in 2 Kgs 24:13–14. These verses close with the "poorest of the land" trope found in both Jeremiah 52 and 2 Kings 25. In fact, the verses combine the wording of both accounts, and connections are established between Nebuchadnezzar's conquest of Jerusalem in Jehoiachin's day and Shishak's campaign depicted in 1 Kings 14:26, as both foreign kings destroy items "that Solomon king of Israel made."[12] However, nearly identical language characterizes Josiah's demolition of the high-place altars outside of Jerusalem ("that Solomon king of Israel built") in 2 Kgs 23:13, and it is significant that Nebuchadnezzar's actions are qualified as being in accordance with divine will ("according to the word of YHWH" in 2 Kgs 24:13), just as Josiah's actions follow all of YHWH's commandments (2 Kgs 23:24–25). The presentation of Nebuchadnezzar as YHWH's servant in the Jeremiah tradition finds expression in the 2 Kings 24 presentation of that king, and the note that he acted "according to the word of YHWH" may constitute an oblique reference to the oracles of Jeremiah that predicted Babylonian hegemony. While some scholars view the "poorest of the land" in v. 14 as a postexilic polemic meant to distinguish between the returning exiles and those who remained in the land,[13] the characterization of Nebuchadnezzar as a servant of YHWH echoing Josiah, coupled with an intertextual allusion to an Egyptian king (Shishak) in the preceding verse, suggests that the "poorest of the land" trope is here a shorthand reference to the Jeremiah narratives regarding the community that will eventually flee to Egypt, and one that the Jeremiah tradition already identifies via the same language (Jer 40:7).[14]

METHODOLOGICAL AND HERMENEUTICAL INFLUENCE OF THE JEREMIANIC CORPUS IN THE DH

The fusion between the Jeremianic and Deuteronomistic traditions was thus initially facilitated by the addition of the Supplement, but further influence of the Jeremianic corpus may be felt in Deuteronomy and the DH. One of the principal features of the exilic DH is the blaming of Manasseh for the ultimate demise of Josiah as well as the exile; this derives from Jeremiah's polemics against Jehoiakim, which itself was drawn from the preexilic example of Manasseh preserved in 2 Kgs 21 as a Josianic antitype.[15] The source text, however, did not incorporate the later compositional stratum found in vv. 12–15 (beginning in v. 10), which intrudes upon the otherwise continuous narrative that served as Jeremiah's inspiration.[16] The passage reads:

> And the LORD spoke by his servants the prophets, saying, Because Manasseh king of Judah has done these abominations, [and] has done wickedly above all that the Amorites did, which [were] before him, and has made Judah also to sin with his idols: *Therefore thus says YHWH God of Israel* (לכן כה אמר ה׳ אלהי ישראל), *Behold, I [am] bringing [such] evil upon Jerusalem and Judah, that*

> *whosoever hears of it, both his ears shall tingle.* And I will stretch over Jerusalem the line of Samaria, and the plummet of the house of Ahab: and I will wipe Jerusalem as [a man] wipes a dish, wiping [it], and turning [it] upside down. And I will forsake (ונטשתי) the remnant of my inheritance, and deliver them into the hand of their enemies; and they shall become a prey and a spoil to all their enemies; Because they have done [that which was] evil in my sight, and have provoked me to anger, since the day their fathers came forth out of Egypt, even unto this day (ועד היום הזה).

Unlike the rest of 2 Kings 21, vv. 12–15 overtly presuppose the exile and employ the properties of direct speech typical of prophetic utterance – the messenger formula (לכן כה אמר ה׳ אלהי ישראל) – rather than simply adopting the norms of narration, as is the case in 2 Kgs 17:7–23.[17] The use of the messenger formula in Jer 26:18 appears to have inspired the similar reflex in 2 Kgs 21:12–15, where a scribe has employed the messenger formula to announce a prophetic judgment.[18] In this instance, the source of the proclamation appears to be Jeremiah himself. These verses contain distinctively Jeremianic terminology: 2 Kgs 21:12 draws from the language of Jer 19:3 (re: tingling ears),[19] and 2 Kgs 21:14 seems to play on the נטש terminology found throughout the book of Jeremiah.[20] Finally, the passage ends with the redactional formula עד היום הזה; we have seen that this formula originated in the Josianic era and was adopted by both Jeremiah and the author of the Supplement to align their work with the Josianic literature (Jer 3:25; 7:25; 11:7; 25:3; 36:2; 44:10).[21] In 2 Kgs 21:15, the redactor now reuses the formula from the Jeremianic context,[22] creating further associations between the typology of Manasseh's reign and the ideas within the Jeremianic corpus. As such, the scribe responsible for the accretion in 2 Kings 21 has drawn upon the language of Jeremiah's oracles, the methodological precedent set by Jer 26:18, and the broad standards of discourse that now bound together the Jeremianic and Deuteronomistic works into a single meta-corpus.

The reliance upon Jeremianic diction is significant, as it alters the impact of the original Josianic account, making the "innocent blood" of Manasseh now consonant with the same sin Jeremiah charged against Jehoiakim. Jeremiah had hermeneutically transformed Jehoiakim into a second Manasseh through his dire polemics, and the Supplement makes it clear that Jehoiakim secured the tainting of the monarchic office and the dominance of Babylon. Here, however, the exilic editors of the DH once again draw inspiration from Jeremiah: they transform Manasseh into Jehoiakim by blaming the exile on the former. The addition of vv. 12–15 to 2 Kings 21 represents a new revelation about the circumstances of the exile that is drawn from an extant (and apparently authoritative) Jeremianic corpus inclusive of the Supplement. The word of Jeremiah no longer merely applies to Jehoiakim within the prophet's writings but also to the pivotal moments of Josiah's death and the exile of 587 BCE.[23]

Another text demonstrating direct influence from the Jeremianic tradition is Deut 30:11–14, an exilic passage that subordinates the implied dimensions of older Deuteronomic concepts originated during the Josianic period:[24]

> For this commandment which I command you this day, it is not too great for you (לא נפלאת היא), neither is it far off. It is not in heaven, that you should say, who shall go up for us to heaven, and bring it to us, that we may hear it and do it? Neither is it beyond the sea, that you should say, who shall go over the sea for us, and bring it to us, that we may hear it and do it? But the word is very near to you (כי קרוב אליך הדבר מאוד), in your mouth (בפיך) and in your heart, that you may do it.

Verse 11 refers to YHWH's commandment (the Deuteronomic Torah, in context) as being neither distant nor overwhelming. Jeremiah had criticized the concept of a "near" God, a ritualized illusion spoken of by his prophetic competitors who were committed to foolish notions concerning the centrality of the Temple.[25] The דבר itself, though, was omnipresent both in the text of the Deuteronomic Torah and in subsequent proclamations by Mosaic successors and transcends the strictures of the Davidic covenant. This same idea is present in v. 11 with its allusion to the Deuteronomic Torah as a grounded and accessible entity. Pivotal to this concept is the parallel use of the term פלא (לא נפלאתהיא) in the same verse, as it invokes the same term used in an earlier Deuteronomic passage, namely, Deut 17:8.

In that earlier passage, concessions were made for a דבר being too grand and overwhelming for the common individual to bear (כי יפלא ממך דבר), in which case it was to be referred to the central court; this presupposes that there were limits imposed on the exegetical authority of the regional Levite judge/scribal magistrate to curb the return to full juridical or religious autonomy. Though Deuteronomy does preserve Levitical interests, it nevertheless elevates Jerusalem and its sacral institutions above and beyond all else, and new categories of legislation had to be refracted through the prism of the central authority. Deut 30:11 countermands this fundamental concept so characteristic of the Josianic policy of centralization, as it informs the reader that no part of the Torah is beyond the individual's ability to understand. As such, there is no need for a central court. The word and the law are still matters of the heart, and thereby fall within the jurisdiction of scribes,[26] but these scribes are now liberated from the limitations set by an obsolete hierarchy. The ideology of this passage draws directly from Jeremiah's oracle to the 597 BCE community:

> Behold, the days come, says YHWH, that I will make a new covenant with the house of Israel, and with the house of Judah: Not according to the covenant that I made with their fathers in the day [that] I took them by the hand to bring them out of the land of Egypt; for they obviated my covenant and I became a baal, says YHWH: But this [shall be] the covenant that I will make with the house of Israel; After those days, says YHWH, I will put my law in their inward parts, and write it in their hearts; and will be their God, and they shall be my people. And they shall teach no more every man his neighbour, and every man his brother, saying, know YHWH: for they shall all know me (כי כולם ידעו אותי), from the least of them unto the greatest of them, says YHWH: for I will forgive their iniquity, and I will remember their sin no more. (Jer 31:31–34)

The Deuteronomic passage fully realizes the import of Jer 31:31–34. The דבר, Deut 30:14 tells us, is very near (כי קרוב אליך הדבר מאוד), so near that it is not only in the individual's heart but, as with the Mosaic prophets under the old covenant, it is in each individual's *mouth* (בפיך). This is a functional corollary to Jer 31:32, which tells us that when the new covenant takes effect there will be no more hierarchy; all the people will have covenantal knowledge of YHWH (כי כולם ידעו אותי). We see here an intrinsic relationship established between the Jeremianic and exilic editions of the Deuteronomic Torah. The new covenant of Jeremiah and the Deuteronomic concept of Mosaic authority (Deut 18:15–22, especially v. 18) are harmonized in Deut 30:11–14, with one ratifying the other. Of note as well is the influence of Jeremianic diction. The standard Deuteronomic notion of turning one's heart to YHWH and being ready to adhere to the דבר (i.e., Deut 6:5; 2 Kgs 23:25) is here replaced by the notion of the דבר itself being in one's heart (ובלבבך). This closely parallels Jeremiah's statement in Jer 31:33 that YHWH's Torah will be written on the heart, and suggests that the meditation/exegesis of Torah and the prophetic word form a binary pair capable of sustaining the covenant.[27] But the connection between the Deuteronomic Torah and the prophetic word in these verses, coupled with the echoes of Jeremiah's oracle, implies that while the Levites may have been empowered to interpret and adjudicate in exile, the parameters defining the character of their activities were set by the Deuteronomistic–Jeremianic tradition.

SUBSEQUENT SCRIBAL ADDITIONS AND EMENDATIONS

Later scribes working with the Jeremianic material drew methodological and stylistic inspiration from the manner in which the prophet and the author of the Supplement composed and edited their work. Many of these additions and editorial emendations emerge during the late-sixth-century BCE Restoration that followed the fall of Babylon and the rise of Cyrus. A particularly striking use of this method may be found in Jeremiah 33, which breaks with the older vilification of Jerusalem and offers a more hopeful prognosis for that city's future. The chapter's secondary status is suggested by the superscription in v. 1: "And the word of YHWH came to Jeremiah a second time (שנית)." This message is syntactically distinct from that of Jeremiah 32 by virtue of the term שנית,[28] but it is nonetheless situated in circumstances that are narrated in the Supplement – in particular, Jeremiah's imprisonment (depicted in Jer 37:12) as he goes to make good on the purchase narrated in Jer 32:6–15.[29] Furthermore, this addition follows the form of Jer 1:13, which also employs the term שנית to connote a distinct but legitimate divine declaration. The scribe behind Jer 33:1 therefore draws from both the prophet's work and the Supplement in equal measure, reinforcing their association as a single literary corpus. The dynamics of these references point to the period when this scribal addition was incorporated into the corpus: the fall of Babylon and thus the end of exilic imprisonment. The text that follows (vv. 2–3) has much in common with the prophet's earliest oracles in Jeremiah 30–31 and may likewise date from the Josianic period:[30] it incorporates both a propagandistic use of the P concept of YHWH as creator (ה' יוצר אותה in v. 2) and an appeal to the Shiloh tradition and the narratives concerning Moses and Samuel (קרא אלי ואענך in v. 3).[31] The use of this text evidences the ongoing availability of the Jeremianic archive, where this fragment would have remained until its use by the editor of Jer 33:1–13.

Some scribal additions and emendations arise from editorial choices. This seems to be the case in Jeremiah 21, a passage drawn from several sources within the corpus.[32] While the narrative dimensions of Jeremiah 21 are apparently based upon Jer 37:3–10, a number of changes take place. The scribe behind Jeremiah 21 has replaced the name "Jehuchal b. Shelemaiah" (Jer 37:3) with "Pashhur b. Malchiah," which creates a connection with the Pashhur b. Immer of Jer 20:1, but this connection is more than just a matter of linguistic semantics. The scribe behind Jeremiah 21 already knew Jeremiah 20 in its final form, including the dramatic closing verses (vv. 14–18) that had once served as Jeremiah's reaction to the failure of the Deuteronomic reform and that were later reused to signify the doom secured against the nation by Jehoiakim in the post–604 BCE development of the book.[33] The appearance of the name Pashhur in Jer 21:1 serves to extend the earlier purpose of Jer 20:14–18 to a later period, namely, the last desperate days of Zedekiah's reign.[34]

The subsequent verses depict just how Jer 20:14–18 now applies to the new circumstance under Zedekiah. The officers who petition Jeremiah for an oracle in Jer 37:3 ask the prophet to "pray (התפלל) unto YHWH our God for us"; in Jer 21:2, the request is for Jeremiah to "inquire (דרש) of YHWH for us." Though the דרש terminology appears in a different context in the DH with respect to the Josianic narrative (2 Kgs 23:14), the shift here from the source text in Jeremiah 37 presupposes the eventual exilic redaction of that narrative, which is one of inescapable calamity. The scribe behind Jeremiah 21 makes it clear that Jeremiah's earlier ability to intercede for the good of the nation is no longer operative via the prophet's own rebuking of his role as intercessor in Jer 20:14–18. While the original point of these verses was to mourn the passing of Josiah and to question the purpose of Jeremiah's Josianic-era mission, the subsequent expansions to the call narrative had made Jeremiah a Mosaic prophet (Jer 1:9) and a foreteller of Babylon's dominance (Jer 1:13–19). The reuse of Jer 20:14–18 applies to these issues, signaling that Jeremiah's role as Mosaic intercessor had come to an end because the Babylonians had indeed arrived.[35] For this reason, the scribe behind Jeremiah 21 has the officers ask Jeremiah to "inquire" rather than to "pray," as intercessory acts of prayer on behalf of the post-597 BCE Judean community could no longer be employed to any good effect.[36] Further, whereas Jer 37:3 includes the phrase "YHWH our God," Jer 21:2 omits "our God" and has the officers simply ask for an oracle of YHWH. The scribal emendations in the account of Jeremiah 21 presuppose not only the specific narrative of Jeremiah 37 but also the broader implications of the Supplement: not only are these officers and their community cut off from Mosaic intercession and prayer, but YHWH is apparently no longer their God (Jer 44:26).

Jer 20:14–18 is therefore applied to the Judeans under Zedekiah through the scribe's construction of Jeremiah 21; the prophet cannot, indeed, pray for the Judeans in Judah. The question then becomes whether or not the cessation of prophetic intercession voiced by Jer 20:14–18 applies to those Judeans taken to Babylon in 587 BCE: could the new covenant (Jer 31:31–34) geared for the 597 community really function for the 587 deportees if the cessation of Jeremiah's Mosaic authority had already cut them off from the covenant? To this end, the scribe adds Jer 21:8–10, which continues the theme of the preceding verses in levying divine judgment upon Jerusalem. Captivity under Babylon, however, is no longer considered a curse along with the sword, famine, and pestilence, as in Jer 15:2.[37] Rather, it is a blessing: those who endure exile will have their lives as a prize (לשלל in v. 10). This draws from the blessing given to Ebed-Melech (Jer 39:18) and to Baruch (Jer 45:5), and demonstrates that subsequent exilic generations are exempt from the implications of Jer 20:14–18. They are able to participate in the ongoing covenantal existence secured by Jer 31:31–34.

THE INFLUENCE OF THE JEREMIANIC CORPUS ON THE BOOKS OF ISAIAH AND CHRONICLES

The purpose of the Supplement, in the end, was apparently successful. Though normative postexilic religion was Zadokite/Temple-based, the literature characterizing this period consistently appeals to the Jeremiah tradition inclusive of the Supplement. This confirms the position it obtained among the exiles; the postexilic writers had to contend with the popularity of the Jeremiah/Deuteronomistic tradition as the exile came to an end. Rather than reject it, they embraced it and used it as the foundation for new adjustments. The dependence of Deutero-Isaiah and Trito-Isaiah upon Jeremianic thought and language has been aptly demonstrated in a number of studies,[38] yet it is important to note that these works employ the scribal methodology evidenced in the book of Jeremiah. There is little to indicate that Deutero- or Trito-Isaiah stood and engaged in public oral proclamation and that their words were recorded and later worked into the extant Isaianic corpus. Rather, while inspired by historical circumstances, the text is their proving ground and their oracles are derived from extant materials.[39] Trito-Isaiah states this overtly in Isaiah 66:2: "On this [one] I will look . . . he who is poor and of a contrite spirit, who trembles at my word (דברי)." Piety is a matter of recognizing the authority of the דבר, but the דבר is no longer an external factor discerned by the prophetic mind and later translated into literary form; Trito-Isaiah's work is based on extant sacred text, and for him, divine favor is given to those who defer to it.

Text, in fact, becomes the fundamental characteristic of prophetic qualification during the period of the Restoration, as claims to prophetic authority among those active within the community were based exclusively upon their administration and manipulation of written material.[40] It is ultimately the scribal enterprise, however, that sustains the classical prophetic impulse: anonymous poets and historians generate texts that seek to merge variant older prophetic traditions within each other through the transformation of earlier prophetic words.[41] Thus, Jeremiah's oracles are incorporated into the Isaianic corpus through reapplication, facilitating a sense of continuity between the Isaianic and Jeremianic literature and infusing the earlier prophetic missions with renewed vitality and immediacy.[42]

The Chronicler's work presupposes the unity of the previously mentioned literary collections.[43] The last few chapters of Chronicles draw from the DH narrative, the Jeremianic corpus, and independent archival traditions preserved by Jeremianic tradents (and others, no doubt).[44] As noted earlier, the Chronicler appeared to view Jeremiah and the DH as some sort of a united corpus.[45] It is thus notable that the Chronicler names Jeremiah (2 Chr 36:22) as the prophet whose word gives rise to the reality of the Restoration rather than Isaiah, whose literary corpus had by that time accrued the words of comfort and the Restoration ideology of the prophet-scribes who wrote in his name. Some scholars see 2 Chr 36:22 as a reference to Jeremiah's 70-year prophecies in Jer 29:10 and Jer 25:11–12 applying to the 70-year gap from the death of Josiah (609 BCE) to the rise of Cyrus (539).[46] The Chronicler, however, would have already had the prophecies of Haggai before him as he wrote his narrative, and the attribution of 2 Chr 36:22 to Jeremiah's 70-year prophecies would negate Haggai's own understanding of that time period's having come to a conclusion roughly 20–25 years *after* the rise of Cyrus.[47]

Considering the overt reference to Cyrus in 2 Chr 36:22–23, one would expect the prophetic reference to relate to a prophetic text that speaks of Cyrus personally; such a text exists in Deutero-Isaiah (Isa 45:1), and one would imagine that the Chronicler could have just as easily invoked the name of Isaiah rather than Jeremiah.[48] Jeremiah's oracles were not more suited to the circumstance of Restoration under Persia than Isaiah. Though Jer 33:14–26 does relate to general sympathies for the Davidic and Levite circles,[49] the pro-Persian elements of Deutero-Isaiah are closer to the Chronicler's work in support of the Zadokite establishment sustained by the Persian political universe. The centrality of Jeremiah in 2 Chr 36:22 is therefore likely based upon a hermeneutical principle rather than a reference to a specific Jeremianic prophecy.

To this end, the particular terminology in 2 Chr 36:22 demands attention, and a comparison with 2 Chr 36:12 is instructive. 2 Chr 36:12 speaks of Zedekiah's refusal to "submit before Jeremiah, from the mouth of YHWH" (מפי ה׳). In 2 Chr 36:12, which likely refers to the complex of narratives and the collection of oracles preserved in the Jeremianic corpus concerning Zedekiah, there is no mention of the דבר, simply a shorthand reference to the narratives of the Supplement and the belief that Jeremiah served as the mouthpiece of YHWH. The phrase מפי ה׳ is found elsewhere in the Chronicler's work regarding prophetic messages (2 Chr 35:22), which also tends to characterize prophecy in terms of the "spirit" (רוח).[50] This makes the phrase דבר ה׳ בפי ירמיהו of 2 Chr 36:22 all the more significant. The דבר in question does not refer to a specific Jeremianic oracle but rather to an understanding of the *phenomenological* dimensions of the prophetic word of the Mosaic prophet in Deuteronomy (Deut 18:18), carried forward by Jeremiah in his own mission (Jer 1:9) and preserved by the scribes behind the Supplement (Jer 36:17–18; 45:1). The shape of the Jeremianic corpus makes it clear that while Mosaic prophecy has returned asunder to Egypt,[51] the prophetic authority still characterized by the prophetic דבר reemerges as a text borne by scribes like Baruch who were divinely charged with its application.[52]

This understanding, employed by both Deutero- and Trito-Isaiah in the construction of their literary oracles from Jeremianic prototypes,[53] was not lost on the Chronicler. Though 2 Chr 36:22 addresses the rise of Cyrus as depicted by Deutero-Isaiah (Isa 45:1), the Chronicler viewed this Isaianic verse as an extension of the דבר placed in Jeremiah's mouth as a Mosaic prophet and later entrusted to the scribes who developed his book, which in turn was taken up by Deutero- and Trito-Isaiah. Thus, the work of prophet-scribes during the postexilic period became, in effect, the continuation of the דבר ה׳ בפי ירמיהו, which now spoke to a far more expansive body of literature than just the Jeremianic corpus itself and which was "fulfilled" (לכלות) in the Chronicler's day.[54]

IMPLICATIONS FOR RABBINIC THOUGHT

One last subject worth examining is the degree to which the scribal standards and mandates within the Jeremiah tradition (or, perhaps more accurately, the Deuteronomistic–Jeremianic tradition) may be sensed in later postbiblical Jewish tradition. Recent studies on the dimensions of rabbinic mythic thought demonstrate strong continuity of ancient Near Eastern myths discernible in biblical materials and from extrabiblical Canaanite and Mesopotamian epic texts;[55] it is not beyond the horizon of possibility to posit similar continuity with respect to scribal hermeneutics and methods from the biblical period to that of the rabbinic writers.[56] We must be cautious in attempting to identify biblical antecedents with the hermeneutical models that obtain in rabbinic texts, since the authors of those texts make certain assumptions regarding the origin and function of their sources that modern scholars cannot accept uncritically. Still, we may cautiously provide some brief observations regarding notable resonances from the Deuteronomistic–Jeremianic tradition regarding the scribal-Levitical methods as discussed in the present study that survived into that later time.

We will consider here one significant text: the famous Mishnaic passage in *Avot* 1.1, often viewed as the "foundation myth" of the Rabbinic exegetical tradition:[57]

> Moses received *Torah* from Sinai and transmitted it Joshua. Joshua transmitted it to the elders, the elders to the prophets, and the prophets transmitted it to the men of the Great Assembly . . .

This passage is clearly etiological in origin, attempting to establish an unbroken connection between the theophany at Sinai and the beginnings of the exegetical tradition current among the early rabbis. Many scholars correctly question the historical veracity of such an epic statement, and indeed, one would be hard pressed to categorize the sequence of institutions/figures detailed in *Avot* 1.1 according to an objective chronology.[58] Of course, it is the specific figures and institutions mentioned in the passage that strongly suggest that the author of *Avot* 1.1 is not interested in objective chronology, and the rhetoric of the passage is as much influenced by what is not mentioned as by what is. Thus, while we find Moses, Joshua, and the elders, we find no mention of the judges, the kings or, most importantly, the Zadokite priests in the transmission of Torah.[59] Rather, the process of Torah transmission moves directly from the elders to the prophets and from the prophets to the Great Assembly.

Some of these features lend themselves to fairly easy explanation. Moses/Joshua/the elders are all tightly bound to the Pentateuchal traditions regarding the Sinai theophany, Moses and Joshua are a binary pair in the schemata of Deuteronomy–Joshua, and the institution of the elders as communal leaders would have doubtless left an impression upon the memory of the author of *Avot* 1.1 as well as that of his audience.[60] That the chronology provided by the passage ends with the Great Assembly, an institution understood in rabbinic tradition as founded by Ezra in the mid-fifth century BCE,[61] further supports the incorporation of the elders into the picture, since anthropological examinations of literature subsequent to that period support the ongoing importance of elders in a lineage-based society among the Jewish population of the Persian period.[62] Yet, from an historical perspective, the nonmention of the Zadokite priests is perplexing, as it was the Zadokites who served as the preeminent religious leaders at the time when this Great Assembly would have existed.[63] One might view the absence of the Zadokites from the list as a result of a hostile attitude toward the Zadokites inherited from the Pharisaic movement. Yet, in other instances, the rabbinic literature bears witness to the authority of the priesthood in the teaching and safeguarding of Pentateuchal law.[64] Indeed, the Great Assembly invoked in *Avot* 1.1 was understood as founded by a Zadokite (Ezra),[65] and the period to which tradition ascribes the establishment of this institution was characterized by a rapprochement between Zadokite and Levite-scribal groups.[66]

The reason for the omission of the Zadokites in *Avot* 1.1 is suggested by two features of the passage. First, while the passage goes on to instruct one to build a fence around the Torah, the passage opens by telling us that Moses received not "the Torah" but simply "Torah" (lacking the definite article) at Sinai, that is, oral instruction.[67] This characterization of what began at Sinai has led some to view the passage as a reaction against written tradition,[68] but this is problematic when the second part of the passage appears to have a written text in mind (the Torah) and one that is worthy of safeguarding. The author of the passage, then, does not polemicize against written law but wishes to emphasize the significance and auspicious origins of oral Torah, namely, the exegetical tradition that must accompany the written tradition.[69] From the rabbinic perspective, the Zadokites could hardly be included in this paradigm, as classical sources reveal that oral teachings beyond the written text were not viewed by the priesthood as divine in origin or inspiration.[70] The second feature of the passage to suggest why Zadokites are not of concern may be inferred from the last link in the chain of transmission, that is, the Great Assembly. This group is extrapolated from the teachers and community leaders Ezra brought together during his tenure in Jerusalem, and the outstanding figures we may identify with the foundation of this group are those individuals named in Nehemiah 8.[71] The single predominant quality shared by these figures is that they are Levites, acting as administrative agents and scribes who, like Ezra himself, were skilled in the science of interpreting the written tradition (Neh 8:7–9).[72]

What concerns us is that *Avot* 1.1 ends the transmission of the exegetical tradition with the Great Assembly and specifies that the Great Assembly received this tradition *directly* from the prophets; the intervening institutions of later periods that controlled the formation of the canon and the political fortunes of Second Temple Judaism are of no concern. This points to a belief that the revelation communicated by the prophets themselves was manifestly exegetical in nature;[73] while prophecy eventually disappeared, the exegetical method did not, and the later rabbis noted in *Avot* keep the voice of these inspired scribes alive by adopting their methods. In the foregoing examination of the Jeremianic–Deuteronomistic tradition, we find this same dynamic moved back one step in the chain of transmission: the Shaphanide–Levite scribal group(s) during the exile kept the prophetic voice alive. As per our earlier observations regarding both Jer 36:17–18 and 2 Chr 36:22, this should be understood as a phenomenological matter, empowering scribal exegesis to take on authentic, divinely based revelatory dimensions.[74] This, we have seen, began as early as the Josianic period, with the regional judges/scribal magistrates empowered to interpret and apply national Deuteronomic law, indeed paralleling the prophetic qualification of that same law at the central sanctuary.[75] We have also seen that these exegetical qualifications were eventually absorbed into the evolving tradition of written covenantal ideology, and both the former and the latter characterize the compositional methods and purpose of the Supplement, the larger Jeremianic corpus, and ultimately the Jeremianic–Deuteronomistic written tradition.[76] At every step, the Levite scribes (Shaphanide or otherwise) are intimately involved in this process.

For the author of *Avot* 1.1, the scribes of the Great Assembly founded by Ezra bear the exegetical mantle of prophetic authority as well, and it is no coincidence that the genotype of this institution was Levitical (according to the biblical sources).[77] It is also no coincidence that the teachings of scribes are understood as more binding than the canonical scriptures themselves[78] or that the figure of Jeremiah factored significantly in the shaping of narrative traditions regarding important rabbinic figures from the last decades of the Second Temple period.[79] It is this paradigm that is still used by those who would place themselves in line as the successors to the Great Assembly, keeping their exegetical authority alive through rabbinic *midrash* the same way that the Shaphanide scribes of the exilic period preserved the voices of the preexilic prophets, or how the regional Levitical judges/scribal magistrates were to keep the final exhortation of Moses alive within Deuteronomy's concept of national existence.[80]

THE CONCLUSIONS OFFERED HERE CANNOT HOPE TO ACCOUNT FOR ALL the elements of the Jeremianic text that speak to subsequent accretions, editing, preservation, and influence on subsequent minds. Rather, this study attempts to discern running themes and an extended discourse in the Supplement that carries forward earlier ideas that may have been challenged by competing systems of ideology. To safeguard what the author believed to be the fundamental features of Israelite belief, the construction of a more complex and comprehensive literary collection was begun, one that prompted later writers to offer their own significant textual contributions over time. The various versions of the Jeremianic corpus that resulted from this endeavor all share a common heritage: they emerge from a culture that placed immeasurable importance not only on the divine word but also on the manner of its written transmission. Biblical Israel, as it emerged into Judaism during the exilic and postexilic periods, became a most *literate* culture, with competing ideologies championed by competing literary works. The words of Ecclesiastes 12:12, reflecting a later culture, are nonetheless appropriate: "of the making of books, there is no end."

Notes

INTRODUCTION

1. For the classical source critical paradigms, see B. Duhm, *Das Buch Jeremia* (Tubingen: Mohr, 1901); S. Mowinckel, *Zur Komposition des Buches Jeremia* (Kristiania: [Oslo], Norway: Jacob Dybwad, 1914). A detailed overview of Jeremiah scholarship is provided by C. J. Sharp, *Prophecy and Ideology in Jeremiah: Struggles for Authority in the Deutero-Jeremianic Prose* (New York/London: T. & T. Clark, 2003), 1–39.
2. See the collected essays in the volume *Troubling Jeremiah* (ed. A. R. P. Diamond et al., JSOTSup 260; Sheffield, UK: Sheffield Academic Press, 1999). For a discussion of the merits and limitations of these approaches, see M. Leuchter, *Josiah's Reform and Jeremiah's Scroll: Historical Calamity and Prophetic Response* (Sheffield, UK: Sheffield Phoenix Press, 2006), 2–6.
3. See, among others, E. W. Nicholson, *Preaching to the Exiles: A Study of the Prose Tradition in the Book of Jeremiah* (Oxford: Basic Blackwell/New York: Schocken, 1970).
4. R. P. Carroll, in fact, believes that it is impossible to recover authentic Jeremianic sentiments, as "the prophet is lost to the scribe" through the redactional process ("Something Rich and Strange: Imagining a Future for Jeremiah Studies," *Troubling Jeremiah*, 432). See also id., *From Chaos to Covenant* (New York: Crossroads, 1981); *Jeremiah: A Commentary* (OTL; Philadelphia: Westminster Press, 1986).
5. See, comprehensively, M. Weinfeld, *Deuteronomy and the Deuteronomic School* (Oxford: Clarendon Press, 1972), 27–32, 138–146.
6. W. Thiel, *Die deuteronomistische Redaktion von Jeremia 1–25* (Neukirchen-Vluyn, Germany: Neukirchener Verlag, 1973); *Die deuteronomistische Redaktion von Jeremia 26–45* (Neukirchen-Vluyn, Germany: Neukirchener Verlag, 1981).
7. T. C. Römer, "How Did Jeremiah Become a Convert to Deuteronomistic Ideology?" in *Those Elusive Deuteronomists: The Phenomenon of Pan-Deuteronomism* (ed. L. S. Shearing and S. L. McKenzie, JSOTSup; Sheffield, UK: Sheffield Academic Press, 1999), 189–199.
8. B. Gosse, "Trois Etages de la Redaction du Livre de Jeremie: La Venue du Malheur Contre ce Lieu (Jerusalem) puis Contre tout Chair (Judah et les Nations) et Enfin de Noveau Contre ce Lieu, Mais Identifie Cette Fois en Babylon," *ZAW* 111 (1999), 508–529.

9. R. Albertz, *Israel in Exile: The History and Literature of the Sixth Century B.C.E.* (Atlanta: SBL, 2003), 312–345. Immediately problematic here, however, are the linguistic features of the narratives within the book of Jeremiah that Albertz dates to the Persian period. The syntactical style of these narratives possesses features that place them within the historical nexus of the late seventh through mid-sixth centuries BCE, as they lack the frequency of embedded clauses and noun strings of narrative passages that can be dated to the Persian period. See the later discussion.
10. Leuchter, *JRJS*, 75–81.
11. Leuchter, *JRJS*, 116–131 (re: the Temple Sermon), 172–175 (re: Jeremiah 11).
12. Leuchter, *JRJS*, 116–131, 170–175.
13. W. M. Schniedewind, *How the Bible Became a Book: The Textualization of Ancient Israel.* (Cambridge: Cambridge University Press, 2004), 154–157. See "The Supplement in Literary and Historical Context" for a discussion of scholarly theories concerning the priority and development of the LXX and MT versions.
14. B. D. Sommer, *A Prophet Reads Scripture: Allusion in Isaiah 40–66* (Stanford, CA: Stanford University Press, 1998), 32–72; "New Light on the Composition of Jeremiah," *CBQ* 61 (1999), 646–666.
15. Several scholars view Isaiah 40–55 as evidencing significant redactional activity that persisted for an extended period of time, but the work contains a unified method of allusion (especially to Jeremiah) throughout its chapters, suggesting largely common authorship (Sommer, *A Prophet Reads Scripture*, 32–72). Furthermore, P. Machinist points to passages within the work that identify a composition during the later periods of the exile, reacting to political trends of the time ("Mesopotamian Imperialism and Israelite Religion: A Case Study from the Second Isaiah," *Symbiosis, Symbolism and the Power of the Past: Canaan, Ancient Israel, and Their Neighbors from the Late Bronze Age through Roman Palaestina* [ed. W. G. Dever and S. Gitin; Winona Lake, IN: Eisenbrauns, 2003], 237–258).
16. B. Halpern, "Why Manasseh Is Blamed for the Babylonian Exile: The Evolution of a Biblical Tradition," *VT* 48 (1998), 473–513.
17. Halpern, "Why Manasseh," 511. See the Conclusion to the present study for additional discussion of this phenomenon.
18. D. M. Carr, *Writing on the Tablet of the Heart: Origins of Scripture and Literature* (New York/Oxford University Press, 2005), 134–142. This does not preclude the possibility that the prophet's parenetic prose was later shaped and augmented by those who supported him (like the Shaphanides; see Carr, *Tablet of the Heart*, 146–149), but given the high frequency of Deuteronomic influence in the prophet's poetry, it seems unlikely that this subsequent reshaping would vary much from the prophet's *ipssisima verba.*
19. Carr, *Tablet of the Heart*, 146–149.
20. W. M. McKane, *A Critical and Exegetical Commentary on Jeremiah*, Vols. 1, 2 (ICC; Edinburgh: T. & T. Clark, 1986/1996), l–lxxxiii.
21. G. Parke-Taylor, *The Formation of the Book of Jeremiah: Doublets and Recurring Phrases* (SBLM 51; Atlanta: SBL, 2000).
22. Parke-Taylor, *Formation*, 298.
23. Sharp, *Prophecy and Ideology in Jeremiah*, passim.

24. F. Pohlmann: *Studien zum Jeremiabuches* (Göttingen: Vandenhoeck & Ruprecht, 1978). C. R. Seitz: "The Crisis of Interpretation Over the Meaning and Purpose of the Exile," *VT* 35 (1985), 78–97; id., *Theology in Conflict* (BZAW, 176; Berlin: De Gruyter, 1989). Pohlmann's position that much of this material dates from the Persian period, however, is problematic; see the later discussion.
25. R. P. Carroll, "Exile! What Exile? Deportation and the Discourses of the Diaspora," *Leading Captivity Captive: "The Exile" as History and Ideology* (ed. L. L. Grabbe, JSOTSup 278; Sheffield, UK: Sheffield Academic Press, 1998), 62–79. See also H. Barstad, *The Myth of the Empty Land: A Study of the History and Archaeology of Judah during the Exilic Period* (SOFS 28; Oslo: Scandinavian University Press, 1996), 42–45. O. Lipschits, however, estimates that roughly 65–70% of the Judean population was removed or fled from Judah during the period of the exile, and most of the settlements in Judah proper suffered significantly from the Babylonian military campaigns ("Demographic Changes in Judah Between the Seventh and Fifth Centuries B.C.E.," *Judah and the Judeans in the Neo-Babylonian Period* [ed. O. Lipschits and J. Blenkinsopp; Winona Lake, IN: Eisenbrauns, 2003], 323–376; id., *The Fall and Rise of Jerusalem* [Winona Lake, IN: Eisenbrauns, 2005], 261–262). See also E. Stern, "The Babylonian Gap: The Archaeological Reality," *JSOT* 28.3 (2004), 273–277, who notes that significant destruction throughout Judah that would have led invariably to massive displacement and social catastrophe, regardless of whether the majority of the population was deported or simply relocated to the northern frontier.
26. See especially P. R. Bedford, "Diaspora: Homeland Relations in Ezra-Nehemiah," *VT* 52 (2002), 147–165.
27. Y. Levin, "From Lists to History: Chronological Aspects of the Chronicler's Genealogies," *JBL* 123 (2004), 601–636.
28. On these adjustments within Jeremiah 7:1–15 (a text that Sharp views as evidencing redaction from opposing groups [*Jeremiah*, 44–54]), see M. Leuchter, "The Temple Sermon and the Term מקום in the Jeremianic Corpus," *JSOT* 30.1 (2005), 93–109. For the Deuteronomic origin of this method, see B. M. Levinson, *Deuteronomy and the Hermeneutics of Legal Innovation* (New York/Oxford: Oxford University Press, 1997).
29. Sharp, for example, views Jer 29:10 as part of the "pro-*golah*" argument for an estimated 70-year period of residence in Babylon, arising during the exile as a response to earlier pro-homeland sentiments (*Jeremiah*, 91). This passage, however, is better understood as a rhetorical device referring to an earlier neo-Assyrian inscription that was certainly known to the prophet's audience and initially circulated as part of an independent literary unit spanning Jeremiah 27–29; see M. Leuchter, "Jeremiah's 70-Year Prophecy and the ששך\לב קמי *Atbash* Codes," *Bib* 85 (2004), 503–522. That Jer 25:11–12 refers to this passage points to its composition between 597 and 587 BCE, as these verses were part of the chapter by the beginning of the exilic period in 587 (see M. Fishbane, *Biblical Interpretation in Ancient Israel* [Oxford: Oxford University Press, 1985], 479–480). The reference points to a conscious awareness of Jeremiah 27–29 on the part of the compiler of Jeremiah 1–25, who redacted the final chapter to refer to Jeremiah 27–29 as a companion piece to the primary active corpus.

30. The specific matter of the construction of these units will be discussed later ("Jeremiah 26–45: An Exilic Supplement to the Jeremianic Corpus").
31. See Leuchter, "Jeremiah's 70-Year Prophecy," 506.
32. H. J. Stipp, "Zedekiah in the Book of Jeremiah: On the Formation of a Biblical Character," *CBQ* 58 (1996), 627–648; J. Pakkala, "Zedekiah's Fate and the Dynastic Succession," *JBL* 125 (2006), 443–452.
33. Schniedewind, *How the Bible Became a Book*, 141–146. See also E. Ben Zvi, "Introduction: Writing, Speeches, and the Prophetic Books – Setting an Agenda," *Writings and Speech in Israelite and Ancient Near Eastern Prophecy* (ed. E. Ben Zvi and M. H. Floyd; Symposium 10; Atlanta: SBL, 2000), 6–16; Carr, *Tablet of the Heart*, 168. I do not wish to suggest, however, that the population remaining in the land did not generate significant narrative or liturgical works; see the later disscussion for references to examinations of these materials. The point I wish to make is that the style, form, and function of the Jeremiah material (especially the narrative units) demonstrate the work of a cohesive school of trained scribes rather than popular composers or other unrelated literary figures, possessing the same features as the Deuteronomistic narratives in the book(s) of Kings that employ subtle rhetorical techniques in the presentation of historical events to advance ideological agendas. B. Halpern's comment on this scribal methodology in the Josianic narrative applies to the composition of the Jeremiah narratives: "This disparity between rhetoric and reality again confirms the authenticity of the account and its contemporaneity with that king [i.e., Josiah]: were the account later, it would not employ mere ambiguity to deceive the reader. These are the tools, the linguistic technologies, of royal inscriptions" ("Late Israelite Astronomies and the Early Greeks," *Symbiosis, Symbolism, and the Power of the Past*, 336).
34. For the identification of the deportees of 597 BCE, see N. Lohfink, "Die Gattung der 'Historischen Kurzgeschichte' in den letzten Jahren von Juda und in der Zeit des Babylonischen Exils," *ZAW* 90 (1978), 319–347. Though literate figures surely were counted among Gedaliah's community at Mizpah following the destruction of Jerusalem, I shall discuss later why they are unlikely candidates for constructing an extensive literary work (though it is possible that some collation of earlier literature was carried out during this period).
35. Lipschits, "Demographic Changes"; Schniedewind, *How the Bible Became a Book*, 146; M. Z. Brettler, "Judaism in the Hebrew Bible? The Transition from Ancient Israelite Religion to Judaism," *CBQ* 61 (1999), 434.
36. Lipschits, *Jerusalem*, 104.
37. J. Middlemas, *The Troubles of Templeless Judah* (Oxford: Oxford University Press, 2005), 145–170, 174–226. For the refugee status of the majority of the Judean population that migrated to the territory of Benjamin during the Babylonian incursions in the early sixth century BCE, see Lipschits, *Jerusalem*, 105–106.
38. See Leuchter, "Jeremiah's 70-Year Prophecy," 516–520. A key passage in establishing the prophet's allegiance to this community is the oracle of the "bad figs" in Jeremiah 24, an oracle that presents itself as originating before the fall of Jerusalem in 587 BCE. Stipp views the entire passage as inauthentic since Jer 24:8 makes reference to the Egyptian remnant community ("Zedekiah in the Book of Jeremiah," 642) but this view

is precipitous. The reference to the Egyptian remnant in v. 8 is an independent clause that can easily be attributed to a redaction of the original oracle once the bad figs in Judah ultimately settle in Egypt. The rhetoric of the oracle supports this position, since the oracle speaks of these people eventually being "driven out" of their land (vv. 9–10); this threat could hardly apply to a people already settled in Egypt and thus already driven out of their homeland.

39. Pace Thiel (*Jeremia 1–25*; *Jeremia 26–45*), who argues that the Deuteronomistic redaction of the Jeremianic literature took place in Judah during the exile.
40. Some scholars view an initial exilic redaction of the DH as taking place among this community; see D. N. Freedman, *Divine Commitment and Human Obligation* (Grand Rapids, MI: Eerdmans, 1997), 344–345; S. L. McKenzie, "The Trouble with Kingship," *Israel Constructs Its History* (ed. A. de Pury et al., JSOTSup 306; Sheffield, UK: Sheffield Academic Press, 2000), 312–314. The biblical accounts in Kings and Jeremiah present Gedaliah's tenure as lasting to roughly 582 BCE, but Lipschits has demonstrated that this is a literary construct. According to Lipschits, Gedaliah was in power for little more than two months before his assassination (*Jerusalem*, 98–102).
41. Middlemas, *Templeless Judah*, 67–70.
42. Both the DH and the Jeremianic corpus present the post–582 BCE land of Judah as devoid of Shaphanide scribes; all evidence indicates that they were either carried off to Babylon (as per Lohfink, "Historichen Kurzgeschichte") or forcibly brought to Egypt. Had any remained in the land, we should expect some textual indication of this akin to the discourse in Jeremiah 43–44, where the presence of Baruch (and, in all likelihood, others like him) is reported in some detail.
43. By "Deuteronomistic tradition," I refer to the books of Deuteronomy–Kings. As demonstrated in the recent papers presented in the Deuteronomistic History section at the 2005 annual metting of the Society of Biblical Literature in Philadelphia, there is wide disagreement on whether or not these texts may be viewed as a unity. Many scholars do see a corpus emerging during Josiah's reign corresponding to F. M. Cross's model of a Josianic DH narrative spanning Joshua–Kings (*Canaanite Myth and Hebrew Epic* [Cambridge, MA: Harvard University Press, 1973], 278–289); see R. D. Nelson, "The Double Redaction of the Deuteronomistic History: The Case Is Still Compelling," *JSOT* 29 (2005), 319–337; Carr, *Tablet of the Heart*, 140; M. A. Sweeney, *King Josiah of Judah: The Lost Messiah of Israel* (New York: Oxford University Press, 2001), 170–177; R. E. Friedman, "From Egypt to Egypt: Dtr1 and Dtr2," *Traditions in Transformation: Turning Points in Biblical Faith* (ed. B. Halpern and J. D. Levenson; Winona Lake, IN: Eisenbrauns, 1981), 167–192; J. D. Levenson, "Who Inserted the Book of the Torah in the Deuteronomistic History?" *HTR* 68 (1975), 301–333. Others still see a relationship between Deuteronomy and Joshua–Kings, though they point to some thematic or ideological variations. See G. N. Knoppers, "Rethinking the Relationship between Deuteronomy and the Deuteronomistic History: The Case of Kings," *CBQ* 63 (2001), 393–415; (Knoppers, though, still supports the basic model advanced by Cross; see his *Two Nations Under God: The Deuteronomistic History of Solomon and the Dual Monarchies*, Vols. 1 and 2 [*HSM*, 52/53; Atlanta: Scholars Press, 1993/1994]); B. M. Levinson, "The Reconceptualization of Kingship in Deuteronomy and the Deuteronomistic History's Transformation of Torah," *VT* 51 (2001),

511–534. Alternately, some view the Josianic historiography as spanning only Samuel–Kings developed into a more comprehensive narrative in subsequent periods via the joining of the Exodus–Joshua narrative to Samuel–Kings by the formation of the book of Judges; see R. G. Kratz, *The Composition of the Narrative Books of the Old Testament* (London: T. & T. Clark, 2005), 153–209. Others still see the material as arising from a postexilic context; see P. Sacchi, *The History of the Second Temple Period* (JSOTsup 285; Sheffield, UK: Sheffield Academic Press, 2000), 90–111; J. R. Linville, "Rethinking the 'Exilic' Book of Kings," *JSOT* 75 (1997), 21–42. Nevertheless, good evidence has been adduced by J. C. Geoghegan for a systematic preexilic redaction throughout Deuteronomy–Kings, pointing at least to a late seventh-century BCE collection of independent texts that were later brought together as a single literary tradition ("'Until This Day' and the Preexilic Redaction of the Deuteronomistic History," *JBL* 122 [2003], 201–227). In the present study, I shall refer to the redaction of this literature as the Josianic or preexilic DH, leaving open the discussion as to whether or not these texts were worked into a *single* document during the Josianic period.

44. Leuchter, *JRJS*, passim. Friedman: "The Deuteronomistic School," *Fortunate the Eyes That See* (Fs. D. N. Freedman; ed. A. B. Beck et al.; Grand Rapids, MI: Eerdmans, 1995), 70–80; Sweeney, *King Josiah*, 218–233; J. A. Dearman, "My Servants the Scribes: Composition and Context in Jeremiah 36," *JBL* 109 (1990), 403–421; J. R. Lundbom, *Jeremiah 1–20* (AB; New York: Doubleday, 1999), 92 and passim. See also id., *Jeremiah 21–36* (AB; New York: Doubleday, 2004), and *Jeremiah 37–52* (AB; New York: Doubleday, 2004).

45. For a general discussion of the scribal tradition in Jerusalem, see E. Lipinski, "Royal and State Scribes in Ancient Jerusalem," *Congress Volume 1986* (VTSup 40; Leiden: Brill, 1988), 157–164. For Jeremiah's connection to and membership in the Shaphanide scribal school, see Lundbom, "Baruch, Seraiah, and Expanded Colophons in the Book of Jeremiah," *JSOT* 36 (1986), 107–108; H. M. I. Gevaryahu, "Baruch ben Neriah the Scribe" [Heb.], *Zer L'gvurot* (Fs. Z. Shazar, ed. N. Avigad; Jerusalem: Israel Exploration Society, 1971), 235–238. The stumbling block here is usually Jer 8:8, which most scholars view as the prophet's critique of scribes (and, for many, his critique of the Deuteronomic reform). However, I have argued elsewhere that this verse is far better seen as the prophet quoting his own adversaries, who identify him with the scribes (*JRJS*, 129–132). Upon viewing "the lying pen of scribes" passage in Jer 8:8 as a quotation of the prophet's detractors, we encounter no impediment in any way throughout the entire Jeremianic corpus in associating the prophet with a scribal background and close allegiance with the Shaphanide scribes behind the Deuteronomistic literature.

46. J. R. Lundbom, *Jeremiah: A Study in Ancient Hebrew Rhetoric* (Winona Lake, IN: Eisenbrauns, 1997 [reprinted from the 1975 edition]); *Jeremiah 1–20*, passim.

47. Leuchter, *JRJS*, chapter 8.

48. A brief but significant example from the book of Kings reinforces this position. Z. Talshir notes that the report of Josiah's death at Megiddo in 2 Kgs 23:29 employs language that portrays the king as a vassal answering the call of his suzerain, Necho ("The Three Deaths of Josiah and the Strata of Biblical Historiography (2 Kings xxiii 29–30; 2 Chronicles xxxv 20–5; 1 Esdras i 23–31)," *VT* 46 [1996], 217–218). Though Talshir concludes that

this notice argues against a military conflict between Josiah and Necho, the language she notes is inconsistent with the wealth of literature associated with Josiah's reign that persistently resists vassalage to any other suzerain but YHWH and safeguards against any external imperial influence on Judah. See R. H. Lowery, *The Reforming Kings: Cults and Society in First Temple Judah* (JSOTsup, 120; Sheffield, UK: Sheffield Academic Press, 1991), 154–156, for a discussion of the anti-imperial theme in the Deuteronomistic legislation regarding the king (Lowery dates this material to the Hezekian period, but even if it originated then, it was preserved in the Josianic-era Deuteronomic corpus and resonates with the language therein that limits suzerainty to YHWH alone). As such, the notice of Josiah's death probably dates from Jehoiakim's reign, when that king was indeed Necho's vassal, and would have been written by scribes closely associated with Jehoiakim rather than those associated with Josiah who stood behind the majority of Deuteronomistic literature. This would have been done to imply continuity between the reigns of Josiah and Jehoiakim, and demonstrated the degree to which the political sentiments of Jehoiakim's court affected the lexical decisions of his scribes. Certainly, the linguistic differences found between the Deuteronomistic and priestly works, roughly contemporaneous in origin, attest to the dramatic difference in style that we might expect from groups so diametrically opposed to each other as the *golah* and homeland groups discussed by Sharp, Seitz, and Pohlmann.

49. A potential argument against this view may be made with respect to the oracles of Ezekiel, which often deploy Deuteronomistic-type language. But Ezekiel's use of Deuteronomistic terms is strategically subordinated to Zadokite ideas and language; see Chapter 5 of the present study for a full discussion.
50. See, for example, R. F. Person, *The Deuteronomistic School: History, Social Setting, and Literature* (Atlanta: SBL, 2002); Linville, "Rethinking the 'Exilic' Book of Kings," 38–42.
51. L. S. Fried comes to this conclusion on archaeological grounds; see her "The High Places (Bamôt) and the Reforms of Hezekiah and Josiah: An Archaeological Investigation," *JAOS* 122 (2002), 460. See also several of the essays in the volume *Good Kings and Bad Kings* (ed. L. L. Grabbe; London: T. & T. Clark, 2005), which posit that the literature depicting Josiah significantly postdates the period in which he lived.
52. F. H. Polak, "the Oral and the Written: Syntax, Stylistics and the Development of Biblical Prose Narrative," *JANES* 26 (1998), 59–105; id., "Style Is More Than the Person: Socio-Linguistics, Literary Culture, and the Distinction Between Written and Oral Narrative," *Biblical Hebrew: Studies in Chronology and Typology* (ed. I. Young, JSOTsup 369; London/New York: T. & T. Clark, 2003), 38–103.
53. Polak, "Style," 40–42, 63–65.
54. Polak, "Style," 43–45; "The Oral and the Written," 101–105.
55. Polak, "Style," 63–65.
56. Polak, "Style," 50–55, 89–98.
57. Polak, "Style," 85–103. Also highly significant here is that there is a paucity of Persian loanwords in the literary complex of Samuel–Kings, whereas the influence of Persian language is frequently present in Ezra–Nehemiah and Chronicles. This corresponds with the chronological model proposed by Polak and conflicts with the compositional proposals of Person, Linville, and Sacchi, which argue for significant development of

Samuel–Kings in the Persian period. See also Polak's article "Sociolinguistics and the Judean Speech Community in the Achaemenid Empire," *Judah and the Judeans in the Persia Period* (ed. O. Lipschits and M. Oeming; Winona Lake, IN: Eisenbrauns, 2006), 598–628. The seventh through mid-sixth centuries BCE emerge as the most likely background for the redaction of older materials and the composition of narratives set in this same historical period, especially concerning the more textual role of prophecy. For the increased significance of literacy in the concept of prophecy during this period, see H. Najman, "The Symbolic Significance of Writing in Ancient Judaism," *The Idea of Biblical Interpretation: Essays in Honor of James L. Kugel* (ed. H. Najman and J. H. Newman; Boston/Leiden: Brill, 2003), 139–173; J. Schaper, "Exilic and Post-Exilic Prophecy and the Orality/Literacy Problem," *VT* 55 (2005), 324–342.

58. For the persistence of a Jeremiah "archive," see Leuchter, *JRJS*, 171–172.
59. The brevity of Gedaliah's tenure, as noted previously, strongly decreases the likelihood that much composition or redaction occurred under his watch. The primary exilic redaction of the DH is better understood as taking place later during the course of the exile, subsequent to the composition of the Supplement; see the Conclusion to the present study for a discussion.
60. Pace G. Wanke, *Untersuchungen zur sogennante Baruchschrift* (BZAW, 146 ; Berlin: De Gruyter, 1971), 146. The narratives dealing with the post-Gedaliah period, as we have seen, do not likely derive from a homeland group that remained after the flight to Egypt following Gedaliah's death. More significantly, the passages that might otherwise point to a pro-homeland perspective in these chapters are actually part of a polemical crescendo leading to a final rejection of the Judeans who descend to Egypt, but for symbolic purposes relating to sociological developments among the Judeans in Babylon (see the further discussion later in this Introduction, in Chapter 4, and in the Conclusion to the present study).
61. Lundbom, *Jeremiah 1–20*, 92; Lohfink, "Historische Kurzgeschichte," 333–342.
62. Leuchter, "Jeremiah's 70-Year Prophecy"; Sommer, "New Light," 661–662.
63. R. C. Steiner, "The Two Sons of Neriah and the Two Editions of Jeremiah in Light of the Two *Atbash* Code Words for Babylon," *VT* 46 (1996), 74–84. See also Friedman, "The Deuteronomistic School," 79–80.
64. Steiner, "The Two Sons of Neriah," 83–84. See also Lundbom, "Baruch, Seraiah," 108–109.
65. Steiner, "The Two Sons of Neriah"; Lundbom, "Baruch, Seraiah," 108–109. In the case of Seraiah, Steiner adduces additional evidence with respect to the *atbash* ciphers for Babylon (Jer 51:1, 41, though the *atbash* codes should, rather, be attributed to Jeremiah himself at the point of authorship of the anti-Babylon oracle. See Leuchter, "Jeremiah's 70-Year Prophecy," 518).
66. Leuchter, *JRJS*, 172–175.
67. W. L. Holladay, for example, views a good amount of shaping in Jeremiah 26–52 as emerging from the Persian period (*Jeremiah 2: A Commentary on the Book of the Prophet Jeremiah Chapters 26–52* [Hermeneia; Philadelphia: Fortress Press, 1989], passim).
68. Polak, "The Oral and the Written," 101–105; "Style," 54.

69. A. Van Selms, "Telescoped Discussion as a Literary Device in the Book of Jeremiah," *VT* 26 (1976), 99–112.
70. Van Selms, "Telescoped Discussion," 111–112. Van Selms concludes that this strengthens the likelihood that a single author like Baruch is responsible for shaping the material that eventually became the MT from an earlier collection that is represented by the LXX. This conclusion is too simple with regard to authorship or text-critical considerations, but it does support the view that the telescopic features of the MT derive from a limited circle of authorship rather than decades or even centuries of redactional accretions.
71. Lipschits, *Jerusalem*, 302–350.
72. See the convenient chart in Lipschits, *Jerusalem*, 350.
73. M. Roncace, *Jeremiah, Zedekiah and the Fall of Jerusalem* (New York/London: T. & T. Clark, 2005), 4. Roncace and Lipschits follow other scholars in suggesting that this narrative was originally on a scroll separate from Jeremiah 36 (so also Parke-Taylor, who sees ch. 36 as the final block in a distinct collection [*Formation*, 303]). Though this is possible, the matter is likely more complex and will be addressed in Chapter 4 of the present study.
74. Geoghegan, "Until This Day," 226; see also M. Weinfeld, "The Emergence of the Deuteronomic Movement: The Historical Antecedents," *Das Deuteronomium: Entstehung, Gestalt und Botschaft* (ed. N. Lohfink, BETL; Leuven, Brussels: Leuven University Press, 1985), 77–83. Parke-Taylor notes a paucity of Deuteronomistic phrases in these chapters (*Formation*, 303), but the organization and function of these chapters match those of literature widely recognized as Deuteronomistic. Furthermore, as will be discussed later, these chapters do possess significant Deuteronomistic language that has largely gone unnoticed by commentators.
75. See especially the discussion in Chapter 3 regarding the relationship of Jeremiah 27–31 to Jer 32:1–15.
76. For the deportation of 582 BCE, see Albertz, *Israel in Exile*, 74, 81, 95–96 (though Albertz views the deportation of 582 as a result of Gedaliah's assassination, an event that, we have seen, took place much earlier [Lipschits, *Jerusalem*, 100–101]).
77. See, for example, Lipschits's discussion of Jeremiah 37–38 (*Jerusalem*, 316–325).
78. This is in fact anticipated within the network of Jeremiah 34–36; see Chapter 3.
79. For the references to Jeremiah 7 in ch. 44, see Parke-Taylor, *Formation*, 303 (the relationship between chs. 7 and 26 is well known).
80. As most scholars recognize, Jer 45:1 dates the chapter to 605 BCE, the same year as the events in Jeremiah 36 and thus in connection to the reference to foreign nations in Jer 36:2. This is reinforced in Jer 45:5, where Baruch is told that he will find himself in many places beyond Judah.
81. Van Selms ("Telescoped Discussion," 112), Lundbom (*Jeremiah 21–36*, 254 [though Lundbom makes room for the possibility that another companion of the prophet like Baruch could be responsible]), J. Muilenberg ("Baruch the Scribe," *Proclamation and Presence: Old Testament Essays in Honour of Gwynne Henton Davies* [ed. J. Durham and J. R. Porter; Macon, GA: Mercer University Press, 1983 (reprint of the 1970 edition)], 215–238) and others look to Baruch b. Neriah, specifically, as the figure responsible for a

majority of this material. Though we should not rule out the possibility that Baruch had a hand in contributing to the Supplement, Chapter 5 of this study will suggest that the nature of Baruch's contributions and his relationship to the Shaphanides in Babylon are very complex matters and require a reevaluation of materials associated with Baruch in these chapters.

82. See Chapters 1 and 3 for further discussion of the influence of the preexilic DH on pivotal narrative units within the Supplement.
83. For example, the ambiguities created by the differing traditions create a meta-narrative using the same techniques identified by Halpern in relation to the Josianic literature ("Late Israelite Astronomies," 336).
84. For these devices in Deuteronomy, see Levinson, *Deuteronomy*, 4–6, 18–20, 107–137. The use of these techniques will be discussed throughout the present study.
85. The constituent parts of the Supplement draw from historical episodes, authentic proclamations, and copies of earlier texts attributable to Jeremiah himself. For the Jeremianic archive, see Leuchter, *JRJS*, 178–179.
86. See the Conclusion to the present study.
87. Y. Hoffman, "History and Ideology: The Case of Jeremiah 44," *JANES* 28 (2000), 43–51. Hoffman deals only with Jeremiah 44 and suggests that it was either written or edited around 570 BCE (47–50). However, as I will argue in this study, Jeremiah 44 is woven from the same fabric as the rest of the Supplement, and the year 570 is in fact an appropriate background to its composition. This will be discussed in detail in Chapter 5 with respect to Judean political/religious developments in Mesopotamia that may have prompted the composition of the Supplement. But dating its composition to roughly 570 also supports some observations presented earlier and others that will be discussed in the Conclusion to this study that the Exilic DH (redacted ca. 560) appears to know and rely on the Supplement. See Friedman, "The Deuteronomistic School," 79–80, for a brief discussion of the sequence of composition between these works.
88. See F. M. Cross, "The Evolution of a Theory of Local Texts," 1972, *Proceedings. IOSCS Pseudepigrapha* (ed. R. Kraft; Septuagint and Cognate Studies 2; SBL, 1972), 108–126; G. Janzen, *Studies in the Text of Jeremiah* (*HSM*, 6; Cambridge, MA: Harvard University Press, 1973); Parke-Taylor, *Formation*, 304. There is, however, little consensus about when the two traditions parted ways. While Lundbom and Steiner view the division as occurring at a fairly early period (sixth century BCE), others (Cross, Janzen, Parke-Taylor) see it as occurring much later. On this perspective, see also A. Aejmelaeus, "Jeremiah at the Turning-Point of History: The Function of Jer. xxv 1–14 in the Book of Jeremiah," *VT* 52 (2002), 460; J. Hill, "Review of J. Edward Wright, *Baruch ben Neriah: From Biblical Scribe to Apocalyptic Seer*," *Review of Biblical Literature* (2004) [http://www.bookreviews.org].
89. "Some Aspects of the Textual and Literary History of the Book of Jeremiah," *Le Livre de Jérémie* (ed. P. M. Bogaert, BETL; Leuven, Brussels: Leuven University Press, 1981), 145–167. See also his subsequent study, "The Literary History of the Book of Jeremiah in the Light of Its Textual History," *Empirical Models for Biblical Criticism* (ed. J. H. Tigay; Philadelphia: University of Pennsylvania Press, 1985), 211–237.

90. C. J. Sharp, "Take Another Scroll and Write: A Study of the LXX and the MT of Jeremiah's Oracles Against Egypt and Babylon," *VT* 47 (1997), 508–509 (see the further discussion later on).
91. A. Rofé, "The Arrangement of the Book of Jeremiah," *ZAW* 101 (1989), 396–397.
92. So also Parke-Taylor, who identifies Jeremiah 25–36 as a unit based on similar dates in the superscription (*Formation*, 299–302).
93. Many scholars view the call narrative as a late redactional addition to the book because of its concern with foreign nations, pointing ahead to the OAN. However, if Jeremiah was a Josianic agent sent to address the mixed populations of the north, his characterization as a "prophet to the nations" is wholly appropriate, and major portions of the call narrative may therefore date from Jeremiah's early career. For Jer 1:2 as original to the early call narrative, see Leuchter, *JRJS*, 75–79.
94. Holladay, *Jeremiah* 2, 118–119; Leuchter, "Jeremiah's 70-Year Prophecy," 516–520.
95. Sommer, *A Prophet Reads Scripture*, 32–72.
96. Sharp, "Take Another Scroll and Write," 508–509.
97. The sizable community remaining in the land would also have preserved a number of Jeremianic texts, though as discussed earlier, it seems unlikely that this community would have engaged in a systematic redaction of these materials.
98. The polemic against the Egyptian remnant community in both the LXX and MT of Jeremiah points to Egypt as a major competitive community with Babylon, wherein a number of these variant traditions would have been preserved. The widespread agreement among scholars that the LXX emerged from Egypt and that the MT had its roots in Babylon is very likely the correct view, though I would suggest that we may also view these communities as epicenters where many varieties of smaller text traditions were eventually collated and preserved during the sixth century BCE. The pro-Babylonian position that dominates in both the LXX and MT, however, attests to the influence of the MT sequence on the curators of what would become the LXX tradition. See Chapter 5 of the present study for a full discussion.
99. Carr, *Tablet of the Heart*, 168 and passim.
100. Steiner, "The Two Sons of Neriah," 83–84; Lundbom, "Baruch, Seraiah," 108–109. See also D. N. Freedman and B. Kelly, "Who Redacted the Primary History?" in *Sefer Moshe: The Moshe Weinfeld Jubilee Volume* (ed. C. Cohen et al.; Winona Lake, IN: Eisenbrauns, 2004), 43–45.
101. C. W. Seitz, "The Prophet Moses and the Canonical Shape of Jeremiah," *ZAW* 101 (1989), 18–27.
102. See Chapter 4.
103. Such, for example, is the assertion of W. L. Holladay, "A Fresh Look at 'Source B' and 'Source C' Sources in Jeremiah," *A Prophet to the Nations* (ed. L. G. Perdue and B. W. Kovacs; Winona Lake, IN: Eisenbrauns, 1984), 219.
104. This is most pronounced in the Temple Sermon (Jer 7:1–15), which is perhaps why the author of the Supplement begins his work with this episode in the prophet's career.
105. I have discussed this in greater detail in *JRJS*, 97–100. Lipschits also recognizes the significance of the Jeremiah tradition as an historical resource (*Jerusalem*, passim) in contradistinction to those who discount its credibility.

106. Most scholars do not question the usefulness of the Josiah narrative in the book of Kings, viewing it as emerging from or at least reflecting the events of that king's reign to one degree or another. Still, the Josiah narrative is heavily informed by rhetorical agenda. The difference between the Kings and Chronicles accounts already demonstrates disagreement concerning the sequence and significance of events. For an analysis of the Kings account, see Weinfeld, *Deuteronomy 1–11*, 69–74, though I disagree with Weinfeld's view that a book was actually "discovered" in the Temple. Rather, the narrative metaphorically and symbolically associates the Deuteronomic Torah with the ancient Jerusalem Temple for propagandistic purposes via the discovery narrative. For a discussion of the propagandistic strategy behind the composition of Deuteronomy and, ultimately, its place in the Josianic literature, see M. Leuchter, "Why Is the Song of Moses in the Book of Deuteronomy?" (*VT*, forthcoming). See also T. C. Römer, "Transformations in Deuteronomistic and Biblical Historiography: On 'Book Finding' and Other Literary Strategies," *ZAW* 109 (1997), 1–11. I do not share Römer's skepticism regarding the appearance of Deuteronomy in a substantial form in the year 622 BCE among the royal and Temple elite in Jerusalem (or that 2 Kings 22–23 dates in large part from the Josianic period), but it seems reasonable that if we cannot accept the account of its discovery at face value, we may adopt the view that ancient symbolic narrative conventions were used for rhetorical purposes regarding the emergence of these literary works and the unfolding of related historical events.
107. Z. Kallai, "Biblical Historiography and Literary History: A Programmatic Survey," *VT* 49 (1999), 345.
108. Fishbane, *Biblical Interpretation in Ancient Israel*, passim.
109. For the former perspective, see Lundbom, *Jeremiah 21–36*, 284. For the latter, see E. K. Holt, "Jeremiah's Temple Sermon and the Deuteronomists: An Investigation of the Redactional Relationship between Jeremiah 7 and 26," *JSOT* 36 (1986), 73–87.
110. Leuchter, "Jeremiah's 70-Year Prophecy," 516–522.
111. Lundbom, "Baruch, Seraiah," 97–98.
112. Stipp correctly notes stylistic similarities in Jer 32:1–5 and 34:1–7 ("Zedekiah in the Book of Jeremiah," 634–638) that facilitate the transition, though Stipp's view that Jeremiah 32 is dependent on Jer 34:1–7 will be critiqued later. See also Parke-Taylor, *Formation*, 206, who notes a deliberate lexical inversion shared by these passages.

1. THE HERMENEUTICS OF CITATION: JEREMIAH 26

1. J. Bright, *Jeremiah* (AB; Garden City, NY: Doubleday, 1965), 165–172; W. Breuggemann, *To Build and to Plant* (ITC; Grand Rapids, MI: Eerdmans, 1991), 5–6; McKane, *Jeremiah* 2, 681.
2. This possibility has been explored by K. M. O'Connor, "Do Not Trim a Word: The Contribution of Chapter 26 to the Book of Jeremiah," *CBQ* 51 (1989), 618. O'Connor's contention that the author of Jeremiah 26:4–6 is "radically abridging" (620) the original Temple Sermon does not, however, sufficiently address the scope and purpose of the author's citation of the earlier prophetic passage.

3. Holladay (*Jeremiah* 2, 104) and McKane (*Jeremiah* 2, 667) view v. 5 as an interruption of an older compositional stratum in vv. 4–6; a similar argument is made by F. L. Hossfelt and I. Meyer, "Der Prophet vor dem Tribunal: Auslegungsversuch von Jer. 26," *ZAW* 86 (1974), 48–49. This perspective rests on the too-narrow view of vv. 4–6 as a summary of the Temple Sermon rather than a hermeneutical reflex addressing the prophet's broader message (see later).
4. So also O'Connor, "Do Not Trim a Word," 620.
5. E. Tov views this verse as a secondary expansion based on the parallel in Jeremiah 26 ("Some Aspects," 152). This is unlikely, however, as Jer 26:2 adjusts Jer 7:2 in light of what is to come in both Jeremiah 26 and Jeremiah 36; see the later discussion. Jer 7:2 should be viewed as original to the author's source and not, as Tov maintains, as a subsequent accretion.
6. The etymology of דבר suggests something primordial and unformed in nature, lying behind what eventually takes shape; see G. J. Botterweck and H. Ringgren, *Theological Dictionary of the Old Testament*, vol. 4 (Grand Rapids, MI: Eerdmans, 1978), 94; op. cit. 98–99 for the distinction between דבר and terms relating to specific delineated speech. See also T. E. Fretheim, "Word of God," *ABD* 6, 962, for the inherent multivalence associated with the term.
7. Scribal methodology and ideology permit fluidity with respect to the דבר. See R. F. Person, Jr., "The Ancient Israelite Scribe as Performer," *JBL* 117 (1998), 601–609.
8. O'Connor identifies this apparent inconsistency as evidence that "the sermon is not the point of interest here" ("Do Not Trim a Word," 620). The Sermon is, however, of interest insofar as the phrase אל תגרע דבר calls attention to the differences between the citation and its source and the understanding of the term דבר itself.
9. O'Connor, "Do Not Trim a Word," 620.
10. The closest parallel and most immediate antecedent is that of Huldah in 2 Kgs 22:15–20. See Holladay, *Jeremiah* 2, 64; Leuchter, "The Temple Sermon and the Term מקום in the Jeremianic Corpus," 96.
11. For Jeremiah 7:25 as Jeremianic in origin, see the discussion by W. L. Holladay, *Jeremiah 1: A Commentary on the Book of the Prophet Jeremiah Chapters* 1–25 (Hermeneia; Philadelphia: Fortress Press, 1986), 258–263 (pace Thiel, *Jeremia 1–25*, 122).
12. Jeremiah 1:6 qualifies the prophet as one who, like Moses, cannot speak (Exod 3:11). The reason for this is that the prophet is a youth (נער), akin to Samuel's age/status (I Sam 2:11,18; 3:1,8). It is debatable, though, that this should be the basis for assuming that the prophet experienced a calling as a boy, as the term carries an implication of official status as much as age; see Leuchter, *JRJS*, 2–73.
13. A near-identical reference occurs in Jer 29:19 (עבדי הנבאים), which is part of an independent collection of authentic Jeremianic material dating from the period between 597 and 587 BCE. See Sommer, "New Light," 661–662; Holladay, *Jeremiah* 2, 137–39. For the *Zophim* as a prophetic group, see Leuchter, *JRJS*, 19–34. See also L. S. Tiemeyer, "The Watchman Metaphor in Isaiah lvi–lxvi," *VT* 55 (2005), 378–400.
14. See the discussion in the Introduction to the present study that argues for this verse as a citation of the prophet's adversaries and not as a reflection of Jeremiah's own regard for the scribes.

15. This constitutes a method identical in function to the telescoping noted by Van Selms in other contexts ("Telescoped Discussion"), though the content being telescoped is an extant literary collection rather than a dialogue. Nevertheless, this collection preserves dialogues between Jeremiah and his adversaries and may thus be similarly classified.
16. We may trace a development in Jeremianic discourse through the successive adjustment of the terminology. In Jer 25:4–5, YHWH's sending of his prophets and his words are communicated separately, in distinct verses. In Jer 29:19, they are more closely associated in one verse (אשר שלחתי אליהם את עבדי הנבאים לא שמאו את דברי...). Finally, they are fused into a single idiom in Jer 26:5 (דברי עבדי הנבאים).
17. Lundbom, *Jeremiah 21–36*, 294; Brueggemann, *To Build and to Plant*, 8–10; Holladay, *Jeremiah 2*, 107–108.
18. O'Connor, "Do Not Trim a Word," 622–623; McKane, *Jeremiah 2*, 667–672, 675, 682; Hossfelt and Meyer, "Der Prophet vor dem Tribunal," 48–50.
19. Holt, "Jeremiah's Temple Sermon and the Deuteronomist," 83; H. G. Reventlow, "Gattung und Uberlieferung in der 'Templerede Jeremias,'" *ZAW* 81 (1969), 350; Nicholson, *Preaching*, 53.
20. None of the aforementioned authors support the chapter's historicity. As argued earlier, however, the chapter draws from events and presents figures represented throughout Jeremiah 1–25, and thus likely possesses some historical basis (however it may have been shaped for rhetorical purposes).
21. See most recently the comments by W. Holladay, "Elusive Deuteronomists, Jeremiah and Proto-Deuteronomy," *CBQ* 66 (2004), 66–69. For the relationship between Jer 11:18–23 and Deut 13:7–10, see Leuchter, *JRJS*, chapter 5.
22. On Deut 18:15–18 as depicting a succession of prophets, see the discussion by R. R. Wilson, *Prophecy and Society in Ancient Israel* (Philadelphia: Fortress Press, 1980), 162 (n. 52); Seitz, "The Prophet Moses," 5.
23. J. Tigay also notes this semantic difficulty (*Deuteronomy: The JPS Torah Commentary* [New York: Jewish Publication Society, 1989], 177–178).
24. Cross, *CMHE* 274–289; Sweeney, *King Josiah*, 170–177; Geoghegan, "Until This Day," 225–227.
25. A dramatic parallel between the Deuteronomic legislation (especially that of Deut 17:8–13) and the DH obtains in the account of 2 Kings 22–23; see Leuchter, *JRJS*, chapter 2, for a discussion.
26. It is noteworthy, too, that the author gives prominence to the elders (v. 17), alluding to the role afforded them by the Deuteronomic legislation in matters of jurisprudence (Deuteronomy 21:2); see Lundbom, *Jeremiah 21–36*, 294; J. Stackert, "Why Does Deuteronomy Legislate Cities of Refuge? Asylum in the Covenant Collection (Exodus 21:12–14) and Deuteronomy (19:1–13)," *JBL* 125 (2006), 23–49. Stackert is correct to view the elders as important components in the execution of regional justice, but the elders function as witnesses in Deuteronomy 21:2, following the Deuteronomic marginalization of the elders from regional jurisprudence (Deut 16:18); more generally, Deuteronomy bestows upon the elders an executive position rather than a juridical one, which is reserved for administrative officers. On this, see Levinson, *Deuteronomy*, 125–126.

27. This alteration is recognized by Carroll, *Jeremiah*, 518. Lundbom, Holladay, and McKane do not note this shift in their respective commentaries. Holladay, in fact, points to the change from עיין in Mic 3:12 to עיים in Jer 26:18 as the only variant between the two texts (*Jeremiah* 2, 108).
28. Van Selms, "Telescoped Discussion."
29. For the connections between chs. 26 and 36, see Parke-Taylor, *Formation*, 204–205. See also Dearman, "My Servants the Scribes," 409–410; O'Connor, "Do Not Trim a Word," 625–627.
30. See Dearman, "My Servants the Scribes," 411–412.
31. Carr, *Tablet of the Heart*, 159–160.
32. The *Urrolle* is ostensibly "all the words" that Jeremiah has spoken to Judah from 609 to 605 BCE: a rather sizable collection of oracles. That it is presented a year after its compilation begins (Jer 36:9) is also suggestive of the extensive nature of its contents and the work required to arrange them into a cohesive form. For a discussion of the proposed contents of this scroll, see Leuchter, *JRJS*, chapter 8.
33. See Person, "The Israelite Scribe as Performer," 608–609. Carr (*Tablet of the Heart*, passim) demonstrates that memorization of texts was an inherent part of the scribal process, and Jeremiah 36 does attest to scribal internalization of the *Urrolle*. Nevertheless, the chapter focuses on the written scroll itself, and the narrative paints a picture of events that does not leave the scribes much time to memorize the lengthy scroll.
34. See among others Holladay, *Jeremiah* 2, 258; Hoffman, "Aetiology, Redaction and Historicity," 184–185; Carr, *Tablet of the Heart*, 146.
35. Holladay notes that the scribes here draw attention to Jeremiah's Deuteronomic qualifications via the word in his mouth (*Jeremiah* 2, 258) but does not note the emphasis on the transference of that word to Baruch's pen and its infusion into the scroll he has produced. Holladay opts for deleting the term מפיו from v. 17, viewing it as a later gloss that is not present in the LXX. As such, he states that these verses simply present Baruch as mocking those who question him or playing dumb concerning the ramifications of his role in producing the scroll; such readings are at cross-purposes to the chapter, which aims to emulate the scribes and which explicitly identifies them as Baruch's allies. Hoffman's understanding of the passage is closer to that proposed herein, though he too misses the Deuteronomic valence intimated by the language of the passage ("Aetiology, Redaction and Historicity," 184–185).
36. Deuteronomy emphasizes the writing of the law and presents Moses as a scribe as well as a prophet (e.g., Deut 31:19, 22, 24; cf. Deut 1:5). Furthermore, the שפטים \ שוטרים of Deut 16:18 carry scribal duties. See A. Rofé, "The Organization of the Judiciary in Deuteronomy," *The World of the Arameans, Vol. 1* (Fs. P. E. Dion, ed. P. M. M. Daviau; JSOTSup 324, 2001), 96–98; M. Weinfeld, "Judge and Officer in Ancient Israel and the Ancient Near East," *IOS* 7 (1977), 65–88. They are therefore charged with implementing the Mosaic law on the regional level.
37. The characters and events within the text certainly describe the features of the culture that generated it, as the prominence of prophecy as a written enterprise was a hallmark of the seventh through sixth centuries BCE throughout the ancient Near East. See Schaper, "Exilic and Post-Exilic Prophecy," 330–331.

38. See Lundbom, "Baruch, Seraiah," 96–106. We should also note the lemmatic transformation of Deuteronomic law in Jer 29:5–7 typical of the scribal methodology behind the Deuteronomic composition itself (discussed by Levinson, *Deuteronomy*, passim); see A. Berlin, "Jeremiah 29:5–7: A Deuteronomic Allusion?" *HAR* 8 (1984), 3–11.
39. For a range of translations, see McKane, *Jeremiah* 2, 663.
40. Very telling of the city's already-existing cultic function is the declaration by the men of Bet Shemesh that a group of people is needed to "stand before" YHWH's Ark; the phrase is decidedly priestly/sacral in character (see the discussion in Chapter 3 concerning this phrase as it relates to the Rechabites). Furthermore, we should note the priestly designation of the family that is charged with guarding the Ark. Abinadab "sanctifies" his son Elazar in 1 Sam 7:1, a term typical of priests initiating other priests into specific sacral roles; see Exod 19:6, 10; Lev 10:3; 19:2. In comparison, see Judg 17:5,12, where the presiding figure is not himself a priest. Other references to the city's cultic heritage can be found in Ps 132:6 (see Cross, *CMHE*, 94–95) and Judg 18:12, where the Josianic editor has suggested the site's cultic dimensions by the phrase "until this day" (Geoghegan, "Until This Day," 225–227). For Kiriath Yearim as an active cult center, see B. Rosen, "Early Israelite Cultic Centres in the Hill Country," *VT* 38 (1988), 115–117.
41. See N. Na'aman, "'The House-of-No-Shade Shall Take Away Its Tax from You' (Micah i 11)," *VT* 45 (1995), 527, for dating the city double entendres to 701 BCE.
42. For Hezekiah's depopulation strategy and its effect on the rural cult, see B. Halpern, "Jerusalem and the Lineages in the Seventh Century BCE: Kinship and the Rise of Individual Moral Liability," *Law and Ideology in Monarchic Israel* (ed. B. Halpern and D. W. Hobson, JSOTsup 124; Sheffield, UK: Sheffield Academic Press, 1991), 41–59, 68–75.
43. For this perspective, see Carroll, *Jeremiah*, 517–519; McKane, *Jeremiah* 2, 665, 669, 675; Brueggemann, *To Build and to Plant*, 11–12. None of these examinations consider במות יער as a reference to Kiriat Yearim and thus do not note the organic connection between vv. 17–19 and vv. 20–23(24). O'Connor notes the connection between vv. 17–19 and 20–23 but views them both as secondary accretions ("Do Not Trim a Word," 623).
44. The cumulative evidence discussed earlier regarding the use of these citations suggests that vv. 17–24 were not secondarily added to the chapter but were part of a single unified composition (pace O'Connor, "Do Not Trim a Word," 622–623; McKane, *Jeremiah* 2, 667–672, 675, 682; Hossfelt and Meyer, "Der Prophet vor dem Tribunal," 48–50).
45. See Levinson, *Deuteronomy*, 144–152.
46. O'Connor, "Do Not Trim a Word," 624.
47. Jer 7:3–7 reveals that the Temple is legitimate but subordinate to carrying out the spirit of the Deuteronomic law; the same idea is applied to kingship via the evaluation of Josiah in Jer 22:15–16. The criticisms of Jer 7:8–11 and throughout Jeremiah 22 arise from neglecting the law and replacing it with less worthy interests or reducing it to an empty gesture. A similar critique underlies the episode of Jer 34:8–22, which castigates Zedekiah and the Jerusalem aristocracy for fetishizing the Deuteronomic law of slave release (Deut 15:12–15; see Chapter 3 for a full discussion). See B. Halpern, "Brisker Pipes Than Poetry: The Development of Israelite Monotheism," *Judaic Perspectives on*

Ancient Israel (ed. J. Neusner et al.; Philadelphia: Fortress Press, 1987), 98–99, 102. See also idem., "Why Manasseh," 505, for the external prophetic validation of Deuteronomic law.

2. THE IDENTIFICATION OF LEGITIMATE ISRAEL: JEREMIAH 27–32:15

1. See Sommer, "New Light," 661–662; Holladay, *Jeremiah* 2, 137–139. On the Josianic origination of Jeremiah 30–31, see Sweeney, *King Josiah*, 231–232. Despite their early origins, the current form of these chapters contains a careful and cohesive discourse on theological transformation that was no doubt essential to the developing theology of the exilic community. For a detailed examination, see B. Becking, *Between Fear and Freedom: Essays on the Interpretation of Jeremiah 30–31* (Boston/Leiden: Brill, 2004).
2. See Excursus 1 for a detailed discussion. See also Lundbom, "Baruch, Seriah," 101–104, 107–109.
3. Sweeney, *King Josiah*, 225–233; Leuchter, *JRJS*, 177–178.
4. McKane's suggestion (*Jeremiah* 2, 685) that the superscription in Jer 27:1 is based on 26:1 and should be deleted must be questioned, as should the view that the king's name therein is erroneous (Rofé, "Arrangement," 393 n. 16). Holladay (*Jeremiah* 2, 22–23, 114–119) suggests that Jeremiah 27–29 relate specifically to political developments of 594 BCE, and the texts may be seen as originating in this period along with the prophet's poetic materials dealing with the exiles of 597. However, we must pause before accepting Holladay's replacement of the date formula in Jer 27:1 with that of 28:1 (p. 112), as it is based on grounds of chapter-to-chapter literary consistency and overlooks the possibility that the Jehoiakim reference in 27:1 serves a hermeneutical purpose as the beginning of an (originally) independent literary cycle.
5. See the Introduction.
6. The question is left open, though, as to how early this superscription would have found its way into the chapter before the chapter was worked into the Supplement. It is possible that Jeremiah himself, following a scribal convention in which he was well versed, is responsible for this superscription. As I have discussed elsewhere, the earliest collections of Jeremiah's Josianic-era oracles were consciously shaped to emulate extant and older prophetic collections replete with their superscription formulae (Leuchter, *JRJS*, 70–74). It is also possible, though, that the formation of materials entrusted to Seraiah in his mission to the Babylonian Judeans ca. 594/593 BCE saw the collation and organization of these oracles as a unique corpus of Jeremianic literature began to form among those already taken captive in 597. In either case, the superscription would have originated long before the construction of the Supplement.
7. See the later discussion of Jer 32:6–15.
8. See the discussion in Chapter 1 ("The Prophetic Word and the Scribal Word").
9. The hermeneutical function of literary sequences was already established in the pre-exilic stratum of Deuteronomy; see Levinson, *Deuteronomy*, 107–137; Leuchter, "Song of Moses."

10. See Jer 27:6–8. The reference to Nebuchadnezzar's son and grandson seems to preface the 70-year prophecy in Jer 29:10 and, indeed, matches well with that figure in terms of the time it would take for the third generation (grandchildren) to mature. Holladay's assertion (*Jeremiah 2*, 121) that it is a secondary expansion due to the absence of the verse in the LXX from a later period must be questioned, as McKane (*Jeremiah 2*, 689) calls attention to the essential agreement between Jer 27:7 and 29:10. The verse may have been omitted by the scribes behind the LXX *Vorlage* who felt that it was not applicable to their Egyptian Jewish audience.
11. The very clearly pro-Davidic sentiments in Jer 33:14–26 are the result of a postexilic addition to the Supplement, at a time in the late sixth century BCE when Davidic royalists and Zadokite priestly groups were both granted a degree of administrative authority under Persian rule. For a detailed discussion of the stages of composition in Jer 33:14–26, see Excursus 2.
12. The issue is left to no uncertainty in v. 8b, which repeats specifically that it is Nebuchadnezzar who must be served after bringing up the issue of service in the first part of the verse. Holladay (*Jeremiah 2*, 112) argues for a conflated text here, but this overlooks the force of the statement. An earlier example of this literary device may be found in YHWH's command for Abraham to sacrifice Isaac in Gen 22:2, where numerous clauses appear in succession for the purpose of intensification. The additional reference to Nebuchadnezzar reveals not only Jeremiah's perspective but also the resistance to this perspective among his audience, necessitating the forceful repetition.
13. The phrase "that nation" in Jer 27:8 plainly applies to those already mentioned in v. 3, and the monolithic tone of the phrase seems to marginalize any feeble attempts on the part of the nation(s) in question to assert an independent identity. Holladay (*Jeremiah 2*, 120) points out that there is no mention of the Philistines because they were already under Babylonian control. Jeremiah must have discerned this reality as a foreshadowing of what could be expected with the other nations in v. 3; it is fitting that this matter is presented to the community already taken to Babylon, since they too would have by then tasted what was to come in Judah. In any event, Jeremiah's words here represent continuity with his earlier proclamations based on an analysis of history and the programmatic/ideological declarations that result (i.e., Jer 7:1–15; 11:1–17).
14. We should note that Jer 32:21 contains the more familiar Deuteronomic formula when dealing with a return to the land (i.e., the purchasing of the field in Anatoth in vv. 6–15), which is, of course, a major theme of Deuteronomy. See Weinfeld, *Deuteronomy 1–11*, 57–60.
15. A. R. P. Diamond ("Portraying Prophecy: Of Doubts, Variants, and Analogics in the Narrative Representatives of Jeremiah's Oracles – Reconstructing the Hermeneutics of Prophecy," *JSOT* 57 [1993], 111–115) notes the similarities between Jeremiah's position and that of the Rabshakeh in the Hezekiah narrative. Diamond discusses this issue with regard to Jeremiah 37–38, though the same issue applies here, without the narrative stylization of the later chapters that draw upon 2 Kgs 18–19 ("Portraying Prophecy," 112). These later chapters deliberately set up a reverse scenario of the Hezekiah account (where a pious king and prophetic intercession lead to salvation) to support the larger aims of the Supplement. The presence of the same ideology in the once-independent

texts of Jeremiah 27–29 supports the view that the narrative (however stylized) is not a rhetorical invention of the Supplement but is rooted in the prophet's own historical experience and point of view.

16. See D. Rudman, "Is the Rabshakeh Also among the Prophets? A Rhetorical Study of 2 Kings xviii 17–35," *VT* 50 (2000), 100–110.
17. The repudiation in Jer 27:9 of alternate forms of intermediaries invokes figures depicted in Deut 18:9–14. However, the pairing of these figures with שקר of v. 10 suggests that the reference is polemical rather than a depiction of the actual prophetic opponents, who were in all likelihood more akin to Jeremiah in their behavior (as suggested by the figure of Hananiah in Jeremiah 28).
18. Leuchter, "The Temple Sermon," 105.
19. The ordering of Jeremiah 27 prior to Jeremiah 28 may have provided the impetus for the secondary insertion in Jer 27:16–20 in the MT version of this material, establishing further thematic connections and continuity between the two chapters. The LXX version would therefore appear to derive from an older copy of what would become MT Jeremiah 27, prior to the redaction of the chapter into the Supplement.
20. This is reinforced by the appending of the title "the prophet" to both figures, a title that does not occur in the LXX. A number of scholars have ascribed this to later expansion in the MT (Holladay, *Jeremiah 2*, 124–125; Janzen, *Studies*, 48, 69–76; McKane, *Jeremiah 2*, 714–716). However, a later redactor would not be inclined to lend Hananiah a title that equated him with Jeremiah once the former's message had proved to be fallacious and Jeremiah's corpus had been validated. Rather, it seems more likely that the prophet titles are original to the account for the purpose of pointing out to the reader that Jeremiah and Hananiah were similar in every way except in the content of their respective messages. The LXX counterpart narrative may reflect a later copy or retelling of the original tale where the scribe did not feel it necessary to deploy the term "prophet" in either case.
21. This is a central motif in Jeremiah's Judean career and is drawn from long-standing traditions (see 1 Sam 1:1; 1:23; 15:13). It is emphasized in phenomenological terms in Jer 32:6–9, where Hanamel's actions are presented as the divine דבר (cf. 1 Sam 1:23).
22. For the typological antecedents to prophets as analysts of history, see Leuchter, *JRJS*, 30–34.
23. Sharp notes the difficulties in viewing Jeremiah 28 as arising simply as a Deuteronomistic addition to the Jeremianic corpus on the basis of style and content (*Jeremiah*, 152–153). The author of the Hananiah episode may have been connected with the Supplement's authorship given the stylistic similarities with other narratives therein, but the narrative's content and placement within the once-independent unit of chs. 27–29 demonstrate that it originates at a time prior to the fall of Jerusalem and, therefore, prior to the Supplement's construction. Sharp's conclusion, then, that Jeremiah 28 may have influenced the development of Deuteronomy's concept of prophecy is reasonable (*Jeremiah*, 153).
24. Hananiah's Gibeonite roots may also relate to a tradition tied to the Ark and to David (see B. Halpern, *David's Secret Demons: Messiah, Murderer, Traitor, King* [Grand Rapids, MI: Eerdmans, 2001], 292–293, 332), which would account for his allegiance to the Temple vessels and Jerusalem-centric ideology in Jer 28:3. The showdown between Hananiah and Jeremiah may therefore also reflect the pro-Davidic faction's attempt to match

Jeremiah's own claims to Mosaic heritage with that of a contender who also comes from a background connected to the Ark.

25. A polemical interest governs this association, as Hananiah's position, though different from that of Jeremiah, might have been considered Deuteronomistically sound. Hananiah's argument is consistent with the anti-imperialism agenda in Deuteronomy; see Lowery, *The Reforming Kings*, 153–155.
26. This is implied through the oblique references to Deut 18:20–22 found in Jer 28:6–9.
27. This strategy is already present, in a much earlier form, in the prophet's Temple Sermon. See Leuchter, "The Temple Sermon," 105–109.
28. M. White, *The Elijah Legends and Jehu's Coup* (BJS 311; Atlanta: Scholars Press, 1997), 36–43, 47.
29. This may have influenced the similar wording in Jer 26:7–8, connecting Jeremiah 26 to both the oracles in chs. 1–25 and the subsequent material in chs. 27–29.
30. Holladay (*Jeremiah* 2, 136–137, 145–147) and McKane (*Jeremiah* 2, 740–748) both discuss the nature of Jer 29:24–32 as a secondary addition to the core of the chapter (though they disagree on what constitutes that core). The addition of the Shemaiah material may therefore be based on the structure of Jeremiah 28 and the role played therein by Hananiah, providing typological balance. For the authenticity of the letter in Jeremiah 29, see M. Dijkstra, "Prophecy by Letter (Jeremiah xxxix 24–32)," *VT* 33 (1983), 419–422.
31. In the case of Shemaiah, though, this is a matter of contextual inference, as the letter itself mentions nothing concerning the fall of Babylon or the return of the Temple vessels. The reference in v. 28 to Jeremiah's original letter to the exiles of 597 BCE (29:1–23), though, creates this connection, as does the lodging of the שקר accusation in v. 31.
32. See Berlin, "Jer 29:5–7," 3–11, who identifies Deut 20:5–10 as the specific passage that Jeremiah employs in formulating his letter to the exiles of 597 BCE. This provides the audience with an opportunity to sustain the covenant by following the law, in marked distinction to the community remaining in Judah under Zedekiah (especially in Jeremiah 34). Jer 29:5–7 is a parade example of Fishbane's "qualifying exegesis" (*Biblical Interpretation*, 252), as the *traditio* incrementally adds new features to the *traditum*, facilitating the continuity from one state to the next.
33. For an overview of scholarship on this passage, see Leuchter, "Jeremiah's 70-Year Prophecy," 503–505. Lundbom's position that "70 years" was a stereotyped phrase in ancient discourse and in Jer 29:10 is merely a "round number and no more" (*Jeremiah 21–36*, 249, 353) is too limited a view. The phrase does not appear in other Akkadian texts, and most of the biblical verses he cites that employ the phrase appear to be readings of Jeremiah's prophecy. The sole exception to this is Isa 23:17, but this verse is likely part of a Josianic-era redaction; see Sweeney, *King Josiah*, 247 (though Sweeney views the number 70 in Isaiah 23 as a strictly chronological device). Jeremiah's 70-year prophecy in Jer 29:10 was directed in no small part to the same circles responsible for the Josianic redaction of Isaiah, and therefore Isa 23:17 constitutes a reference to the same Esarhaddon inscription alluded to by Jeremiah in our current passage (see later). For a discussion of the Isaiah passage, see M. Leuchter, "Tyre's 70 Years in Isaiah 23,15–18," *Bib* 87 (2006), 412–417.
34. Leuchter, "Jeremiah's 70-Year Prophecy," 509–511.

35. Leuchter, "Jeremiah's 70-Year Prophecy," 515–519.
36. The cuneiform character for 70, when inverted, is the character for 11, and it was 11 years after Sennacherib's devastation of Babylon that Esarhaddon began to rebuild the city. See Leuchter, "Jeremiah's 70-Year Prophecy," 509–510.
37. Leuchter, "Jeremiah's 70-Year Prophecy," 518–519.
38. Holladay's proposal (*Jeremiah 2*, 139–140) that the letter addresses anti-Babylonian foment ca. 594/593 BCE seems a logical background to the mention of these prophetic figures without further elaboration in the original letter.
39. The superscription "in the same year" (Jer 28:1) reflects this editorial strategy; McKane's suggestion that Jer 28:1 has no link to Jeremiah 27 (*Jeremiah 2*, 710) seems too dramatic given the shared themes of competing prophetic voices and the common accusation of שקר present in both Chapters (27:10, 14, 16; 28:15). A "corrected" reading of Jer 28:1 ignores the editorial strategy in locating it after 27 and before 29. The base material of Jeremiah 28 is homogenized with the message of Jeremiah 27 and the named figures of Jeremiah 29, equating the competing prophetic voices in Babylon with those in Jerusalem and tying them both to the failed Davidic circles.
40. That Shemaiah's letter was preserved by the Judean supporters of Jeremiah rather than the Babylonian community leaders is evidenced by the standard spelling of Jeremiah's name (Jer 29:27), and its secondary status as an appendage to 29:1–23 is reflected in the standard name form's reappearance in the narration of 29:29–30. Holladay (*Jeremiah 2*, 114) does not point out that the standard name form appears in Shemaiah's letter, only that it resumes in the narration of 29:29.
41. The addition of Jer 27:16–22, then, may be credited to the author of the Supplement, since (as discussed earlier) these verses facilitate the connection between that chapter and the content of the debate detailed in Jeremiah 28.
42. The addition of the prophet title in Jer 29:29 should not therefore be understood as serving the same purpose as the appearance of the title throughout Jeremiah 28. Its position in a passage that obtains only during a later editorial period would no longer relate to any attempt to convince the audience that Jeremiah was a particular type of prophet. Rather, it would derive from an editorial attempt to harmonize the secondary material with the older collection (27–29:1–23) and, specifically, provide a balanced typological structure between Shemaiah and Hananiah in the previous chapter. This leaves open the question of why Jer 29:30 does not include the prophet title with Jeremiah's name. This may be an error in the transmission of the text, but it also may represent a deliberate attempt to massage the once-independent texts of Jeremiah 27–29 into a larger corpus through a metered linguistic transition (from ירמיה הנביא to ירמיהו הנביא to, finally, ירמיהו as it appears throughout the rest of the book).
43. This is most prominent in the language of Jer 29:5–7, thereby subtly implying continuity with the Deuteronomic law it cites (Deut 20:5–10) and the prophet's corpus as Deuteronomically legitimate.
44. See Seitz (*Theology in Conflict*, 226). It is likely that Jeremiah 24 was composed after Jeremiah 29, as the latter appears to be making a case that is already apparently accepted by the 597 BCE community blessing in Jer 24:5–7. See Parke-Taylor, *Formation*, 297, for a similar argument in dating Jeremiah 24 relative to Jeremiah 27.

45. As Seitz has demonstrated (*Theology in Conflict*, 226), Jeremiah 21 attempts to present pre-Zedekian materials in Jeremiah 22–23 within the context of a 587-centric perspective, though as McKane has demonstrated ("The Construction of Jeremiah Chapter xxi," *VT* 32[1982], 59–73), Jeremiah 21 is a late composition dependent upon Jeremiah 37 and the materials in Jeremiah 22, and should be viewed as subsequent to the Supplement. See the Conclusion to the present study for additional observations concerning the composition of this chapter.
46. For an overview, see Leuchter, *JRJS*, 81–89, 178.
47. B. Gosse, "La Nouvelle Alliance de Jérémie 31,31–34: Du Livre d'Ezéchiel au Livre de Jérémie," *ZAW* 116 (2004), 568–580; Sweeney, *King Josiah*, 229, 231; Seitz, *Theology in Conflict*, 211–214; McKane, *Jeremiah 2*, 815; Holladay, *Jeremiah 2*, 163. The observations by Sweeney and McKane that the sour grapes aphorism suggests influence by the Ezekiel traditions neglect the political purpose of the "new covenant" in the following verses introduced by invocation of the aphorism. Furthermore, Sweeney does not discuss the political circumstances addressed by these verses and bases his suggestion strictly upon the terminological similarities with the Ezekiel passages, which could be either contemporary with or subsequent to the Jeremianic material. Holladay's reading of Jer 31:28–29 as the finale of the "recension to the south" automatically suspends consideration of the aphorism as part of the same unit, and McKane's understanding of these chapters as late compositions assumes that the Ezekiel material was written earlier ands thus eliminates an important dynamic between the Josianic and post–597 BCE layers of composition (one of submersion akin to Jer 3:6–11 and the surrounding texts).
48. See especially D. Rom-Shiloni, "Facing Destruction and Exile: Inner-Biblical Exegesis in Jeremiah and Ezekiel," *ZAW* 117 (2005), 194–202.
49. The passage takes up familiar Deuteronomic language (e.g., לב, תורה, כתב) but reassigns the relationship between them. For example, Deut 6:5–9 makes reference to YHWH's commandments being on the heart of the individual (meditation) but being written on doorposts and village gates. In the Jeremiah passage, the commandments (YHWH's Torah) will be written on the individual's heart. This signifies a dramatic paradigm shift, on which see the later discussion.
50. M. Weinfeld, "Jeremiah and the Spiritual Metamorphosis of Israel," *ZAW* 88 (1976), 31–32.
51. Leuchter, *JRJS*, 84–86. Subsequent oracles, however, show a marked decrease in the reliance upon P traditions, as the prophet appears to have viewed them as obsolete following the death of Josiah.
52. Weinfeld, "Spiritual Metamorphosis," 32–33. The chapter is a prime example of Ezekiel's connection to the Zadokite Holiness School. See I. Knohl, *The Sanctuary of Silence* (Minneapolis: Fortress Press, 1995), 103, 200–203, and Chapter 5 of the present study for additional discussion.
53. See the additional later discussion of this important point. Contrast this scenario to the preexilic presupposition preserved in Jer 18:18 that Torah is under the jurisdiction of the Jerusalem (Zadokite) priesthood, a view against which Jeremiah argued. This is also the view of Jeremiah's critics quoted in Jer 8:8, who condemned Jeremiah and his scribal peers for attempting to pervert the concept of Torah.

54. For an overview, see Lundbom, *Jeremiah 21–36*, 459–463. See also S. M. Olyan, "The Search for the Elusive Self in the Texts of the Hebrew Bible," *Religion and the Self in Antiquity* (ed. D. Brakke; Bloomington/Indianapolis: Indiana University Press, 2005), 45; Carroll, *Jeremiah*, 569.
55. Leuchter, "Jeremiah's 70-Year Prophecy," 518–519.
56. For additional evidence within Jeremiah 24 that chs. 27–29 and 30–31 were once understood as part of a single independent collection, see Leuchter, "Jeremiah's 70-Year Prophecy," 519 n. 57.
57. This view simply carries forward the ideology of Jer 27:7 and 29:10, and follows the logic that if Babylon's rise saw their exile, Babylon's fall would see their return, but both events attest to an international theology whereby the people have been and will be subject to political forces acting on YHWH's behalf. This same idea surfaces in the word against Babylon in the OAN (Jer 51:48).
58. The text's current position makes this message speak to the exiles of 587 BCE (Sweeney, *King Josiah*, 228; Holladay, *Jeremiah* 2, 161).
59. The reference to the fathers corresponds to the mention of the fathers in the Temple Sermon and its own basis in the Deuteronomic concept of a covenant with the fathers (see Deut 6:10, 8:1, 9:5, 27).
60. Following Becking's translation (*Between Fear and Freedom*, 228–229).
61. The use of שקר here further suggests that Jeremiah 30–31 were redacted in relation to Jeremiah 27–29 by virtue of the שקר reference in Jer 27:10, employing the same type of wordplay found in Jer 1:11–12 in relation to the שקר terminology emerging in the ensuing oracles (Leuchter, *JRJS*, 151).
62. For this reason, Holladay's contention (*Jeremiah* 2, 162–163) that vv. 27–28 provide the closing frame to the "recension for the south" of Jeremiah 30–31 must be questioned. The verses cannot rightly address the southern community in Judah, since there is no indication that this community was considered to be legitimate by the prophet; the recension applies more readily to the good figs awaiting Jeremiah's word in Babylon. We should thus not view vv. 29–34 as arising from a subsequent period of composition.
63. Contrast this to Jer 31:38–40, where devastation is presupposed. See the additional later discussion.
64. See Berlin, "A Deuteronomic Allusion"; Fishbane, *Biblical Interpretation*, 252. This is further suggestive of a proximate date of compositional origin with Jer 29:5–7 (penned by Jeremiah himself; see earlier), as the hermeneutical/exegetical function of the two passages are identical.
65. McKane (*Jeremiah* 2, 815–817) points out that the invocation of the aphorism reflects "low political fortunes" (816). While McKane's view that this also draws from Ezekiel may be questioned, he is right to point out that vv. 29–30 do address issues of individual theodicy as distinct from corporate retribution and that this sets out new parameters for the definition of the community in question.
66. See Leuchter, "The Temple Sermon," 105–109. See also Lowery, *The Reforming Kings*, 155, who notes that the Deuteronomic law mandates against foreign imperialistic influence in Israelite royal affairs. Those in Judah advocating monarchic independence from Babylon would have relied upon this aspect of the Deuteronomic legislation to legitimize their

political interests on theological grounds, but Jeremiah's earlier dissociation of sacral concepts from Jerusalem and its royal/cultic institutions would allow those adopting the prophet's "submit to Babylon" position to avoid charges of treason and heresy.

67. For the northern Israelite emphasis of these oracles, see Leuchter, *JRJS*, chapter 4.
68. McKane recognizes the similar diction here (*Jeremiah* 2, 816) but does not offer a specific context for compositional origins or political/ideological purpose.
69. Most commentators take the phrase to be a marital reference, i.e., "though I was their husband." The wording possesses the qualities of a double entendre, though, especially considering the prophet's persistent charge of Baalism in the pre–597 BCE period (see Leuchter, *JRJS*, 91–102, 145–46; see additional discussion later). For additional discussion, see M. Fishbane, "Accusations of Adultery: A Study of Law and Scribal Practice in Numbers 5:11–31," *HUCA* 45 (1974), 43. Both meanings are possible and even intended; see Carr, *Tablet of the Heart*, 148. D. Novak, however, suggests a different reading: that the term בעלתי means "I compelled," i.e., YHWH forced Israel to accept older concepts of covenant in contradistinction to the new covenant that will be voluntarily accepted (*The Jewish Social Contract: An Essay in Political Theology* [Princeton, NJ: Princeton University Press, 2000], 65–66).
70. McKane's rejection of this common element shared by vv. 29–30 and 31–34 is founded upon his view that Jeremiah 30–31 never addressed Josiah's agenda or endeavors (*Jeremiah* 2, 816–817). If vv. 29–34 are meant to qualify and correct older (and now outdated) modes of piety that were born in the Josianic period, then vv. 29–30 and 31–34 are not contradictory, and McKane's reading of these verses as discordant must be abandoned.
71. The anti-Egypt sentiment in Deuteronomy is developed strongly at all levels of the Jeremiah tradition, culminating in the material currently found in Jeremiah 42–44; see Chapter 4 for a full discussion.
72. Halpern, "Brisker Pipes Than Poetry," 98–99, 102.
73. See the concise discussion by H. D. Potter, "The New Covenant in Jeremiah xxxi 31–34," *VT* 33 (1983), 349–350.
74. Holladay, *Jeremiah* 2, 198; Potter, "The New Covenant," 351; J. Swetnam, "Why Was Jeremiah's New Covenant New?" VTsup 26 (Leiden: Brill, 1974), 111–115; Lundbom, *Jeremiah 21–36*, 467–469; Weinfeld, "Spiritual Metamorphosis," 29–32; Becking, *Between Fear and Freedom*, 240–241.
75. Potter, "The New Covenant," 351–352; Lundbom, *Jeremiah 21–36*, 469.
76. Carr, *Tablet of the Heart*, passim.
77. Lundbom notes the ancient practice of inscribing animal organs with oracles (*Jeremiah 21–36*, 469), but the interaction between "law" and "heart" in Deuteronomistic discourse seems the more likely background for the shift in terminology encountered here, especially given the education-enculturation emphasis in Deuteronomy and the DH. See H. Weippert, "Das Wort von neuen Bund in Jeremia xxxi 31–34," *VT* 29 (1979), 336–351.
78. Carr, *Tablet of the Heart*, 126–142.
79. Levinson has demonstrated this thoroughly with regard to both the Deuteronomistic tradition (*Deuteronomy*, passim) and the Zadokite tradition ("The Birth of the Lemma:

The Restrictive Re-Interpretation of the Covenant Code's Manumission Law in the Holiness Code [Leviticus 25:44–46]," *JBL* 124 [2005], 617–639).

80. This had already been anticipated to a certain degree in the preexilic Deuteronomic legislation, where regional judges/scribal magistrates were empowered to interpret and implement the written law according to national standards (Deut 16:18–20), though these administrators were still subordinate to the legislative and executive figures bound to the Temple in Jerusalem (Deut 17:8–13). See Chapter 6 for a more detailed discussion of this legislation as understood during the exile.
81. Leuchter, *JRJS*, 168–169, 173.
82. Berlin, "A Deuteronomic Allusion."
83. Pace Sweeney, *King Josiah*, 229–230. Carr suggests that the oracle is founded upon a Jeremianic teaching but shaped through the vernacular of the Shaphanide scribes in exile in their reconstruction of older traditions (*Tablet of the Heart*, 148–149). This may well be possible, but the fundamental dynamic of this oracle is so dramatically different from the Deuteronomic model of an external written Torah to which one should devote one's attention and upon which one should meditate (Deut 6:5–9) that we cannot view the specifics of the language in Jer 31:33 as resulting simply from the use of Deuteronomistic discourse in reconstructing an older oracle. Even if subsequent scribes did develop the prophet's original oracle, the oracle must have introduced the shift from an external written text to internal modes of exegesis based on established ideas, and this indeed would characterize the prophet's methods in the other texts we have seen as directed to the deportees of 597 BCE (e.g., Jer 29:5–7). Lohfink's observation that many of the Shaphanides had been part of this audience suggests the appropriateness of the oracle's language and purpose ("Historichen Kurzgeschichte," 336–342).
84. For the current passages as emblematic of such a shift, see Becking, *Between Fear and Freedom*, 262–263.
85. Carr, *Tablet of the Heart*, 134–142. Jeremiah's own exegetical accretions pick up on his Levitical responsibility as a teacher of Torah; see Leuchter, *JRJS*, 168, 172–174. See also Chapter 3 for similar reflexes in the work of the author of the Supplement.
86. Potter comes very close to this view in discussing how the new covenant eliminates the concept of a sacral elite but places scribes alongside this now-nullified elite ("The New Covenant," 353). Potter does not recognize the significance of the "heart" as an allusion to the scribal imagination in this passage, instead viewing the oracle as part of a critique of scribes alongside Jer 8:8, another verse that we have seen is commonly and incorrectly understood as the prophet's invective against scribal circles. The purpose of the oracle in Jer 31:31–34, by contrast, frees scribal imperatives from the agendas of the Jerusalem establishment (royal or Zadokite) that otherwise claimed dominion over the Torah.
87. The single sin (חטאתם) speaks to the annulment of broad corporate culpability. The passage therefore does not refer to a sinless Utopia but a paradigm shift concerning liability.
88. Pace Holladay, *Jeremiah* 2, 198.
89. Holladay (*Jeremiah* 2, 206–211) discusses the problems concerning the redaction history of 32:16–44, which evidence a confluence of authentic Jeremianic sayings and much later expansion. These elements are secondary to the function of vv. 1–15. See also

D. Rom-Shiloni, "The Prophecy for 'Everlasting Covenant' (Jeremiah xxxii 36–41): An Exilic Addition or a Deuteronomistic Redaction?" *VT* 53 (2003), 201–223, for an analysis of the redactional strategy in 32:16–44 and a likely date for its compilation/composition.

90. See Lundbom, "Baruch, Seraiah," 97–98, for Jer 32:6–15 as a once-independent unit.
91. Holladay suggests a fifth-century BCE context (*Jeremiah 2*, 199), but Lundbom ascribes it to Jeremiah and dates it to the prophet's tenure at Mizpah from 586 to 582 (*Jeremiah 21–36*, 489, 494). As Lipschits has discussed, the Mizpah community was extremely short-lived following the destruction of Jerusalem (*Jerusalem*, 98–102), and it was unlikely that much literature was redacted during this very brief period for this community, especially Jeremiah 30–31, that were earlier directed to the deportees of 597 residing in Babylon. Lundbom is certainly correct, though, to view the passage as a link to Jeremiah 32; the best setting for the composition of these verses is during the exile, addressing a largely Jerusalemite population in a way that would prepare them for the themes of Jer 32:6–15.
92. Thiel (*Jeremia 26–45*, 30) highlights the continuity between Jer 31:31–34 and 32:6–15 but discounts 32:1–5 as part of the same compositional layer. Though he is correct to see the relationship between Jer 31:31–34 and 32:6–15 in terms of addressing exilic circumstances, his view that this is strictly the result of a broad Deuteronomistic redaction obscures the force of the author's editorial strategy in following a text meant for the 597 BCE Babylonian community with one geared to a post-587 audience, to which end Jer 32:1–15 plays an important role in the transition between direct prophetic address and scribal presentation. And while Jer 32:6–15 originated independently of vv. 1–5, both passages were bound together and placed in the Supplement at the same time as a single unit; vv. 1–5 may thus be secondary in relation to the origins of vv. 6–15, but are not secondary to the place of ch. 32 in the Supplement; see the later discussion.
93. Leuchter, *JRJS*, 185–186.
94. Holladay (*Jeremiah 2*, 210) concludes that vv. 2–5 are not from the same author as v. 1 due to the peculiarities of form, but this does not take into account the function of these peculiarities as an editorial device bringing the tradition of Jer 32:6–15 in line with the extant active corpus as part of a larger redaction.
95. Zedekiah is indeed eclipsed by Nebuchadrezzar in the superscription both in terms of the situation depicted in the ensuing verses and in the years of their respective reigns (Nebuchadrezzar holds seniority). The statement is not secondary. The inclusion of Nebuchadrezzar in the superscription more readily fits the event of an author writing to a Judean community in early mid-sixth-century BCE Babylon than Thiel's proposed post-Deuteronomistic author of vv. 1–5 (*Jeremia 26–45*, 30).
96. These verses may therefore constitute a response to the hopes once ascribed to the figure of Jehoiachin as a Davidic scion by the exilic community; see Seitz, *Theology in Conflict*, 209. By the time the author engaged in his work, those hopes were still in force (though the material in Jer 27–31 suggests that they had temporarily subsided by ca. 593 BCE) and likely constituted a threat to Jeremiah's message concerning submission to Babylon.
97. T. Overholt ("Jeremiah," *The HarperCollins Bible Commentary* [New York: HarperCollins, 2000], 569) points out that vv. 1–5 preface and summarize Jer 34:8–22, Zedekiah's corrupt covenant rituals. The distinction between legitimate scribe and illegitimate king would therefore be reinforced by this prolepsis.

98. We should also note the very similar proclamation in Jer 34:3 that specifies that Zedekiah's eyes will behold the Babylonian king; both ironically anticipate Jer 39:7; see the later discussion.
99. As per Lundbom, "Baruch, Seraiah,"98.
100. McKane's observation (*Jeremiah* 2, 840–841) that the event is given symbolic significance is correct, particularly his view that regular activities of common citizenship are the stuff of restoration, not political/royal grandiloquence (841). However, the emphasis on the דבר as history itself recalls the old Shilonite tradition that viewed the דבר in the same way; see Leuchter, *JRJS*, 30–34. The current context is entirely suited for a reference to this tradition, as the land Jeremiah is to redeem from his uncle is to be found in Anatoth, the home of the Shilonite priesthood since the days of Solomon (1 Kgs 2:26).
101. Diamond points to this understanding of the prophetic דבר already at work in the dialogues between Zedekiah and Jeremiah ("Portraying Prophecy," 106).
102. Lundbom, "Baruch, Seraiah," 97–98.
103. It is ultimately this dynamic that provides the thematic core of the unit, not Jeremiah's allegiance to the remnant community (contra Seitz, *Theology in Conflict*, 243). The promise of a return to the land pertains more to the Babylonian community based on the new covenant first given to the exiles of 597 BCE and, through the author's editing of the chapters, now extended to those of 587 as well. The exilic circumstance, not the remnant circumstance, informs the discourse. The concern is with the communication of the prophet's voice to an exilic Babylonian community, not strictly with regard to Jer 32:[1–5] 6–15 but as part of a broader polemical work. Seitz does recognize the meaning of the event for the exilic community (243–244) but presumes that Jer 32:6–15 prefaced the narrative of Jeremiah 38 and initially pertained to the "submit-and-live" idea that the prophet wished to convey to the remnant community under Zedekiah. The colophonic nature of vv. 6–15 supports the greater likelihood that the passage was originally an independent document worked into its current context specifically for an exilic audience. Verses 1–5 tie it to the narratives of chs. 37–38 (and more immediately to Jeremiah 34, as per Overholt, "Jeremiah," 569) not out of any sympathetic association with the remnant community but to highlight the reasons why the figures in those later narratives bring about ruin: they prohibit Jeremiah from realizing a divine directive (the purchase of the field already depicted in 32:6–15) and, worse, punish him for it. The reader is thus prepared in Jer 32:1–15 for what occurs in Jeremiah 38, and understands that the theo-dynamics among those loyal to Jerusalem and Davidic interests are topsy-turvy: fidelity to YHWH's command equals treason in their eyes.
104. So Diamond, "Portraying Prophecy," 107.
105. Baruch's role in the communication of Jeremiah's prophecy is made paramount, since it is within the scribal colophon itself that the prophetic message is contained.
106. See Excursus 1.
107. See especially the Conclusion to the present study, which discusses this matter in greater detail. We should again note that appending Jer 32:1–15 to Jeremiah 27–31 establishes a rhetorical connection to Jeremiah 26 but also looks directly ahead to Jer 34:1–7 (see Chapter 3). In this sense, Stipp may be correct in his view that Jeremiah 32 was composed with an eye to Jer 34:1–7 ("Zedekiah in the Book of Jeremiah," 634–635). However, the

patterning he adduces should not be so stringently maintained, as he identifies Jer 32:6–7 as part of the secondary derivative composition, and Lundbom has demonstrated that these verses are part of the once-independent colophonic unit of 32:6–15 ("Baruch, Seraiah," 97–98). Furthermore, the differences in the characterization of Zedekiah that Stipp identifies are not as stark as he supposes, as Jer 34:1–7 is no gentle address to that king (see the ensuing discussion in Chapter 3).

EXCURSUS 1

1. Jer 24:7 presupposes that the 597 BCE community accepted the message of Jeremiah 27–29 but does not necessarily require a period of composition subsequent to the prophet's redaction of Jeremiah 30–31. The composition of Jeremiah 24 subsequent to Jeremiah 29 is further supported by the apparent reference to Jer 29:17 in Jer 24:8. See also Parke-Taylor, *Formation*, 297.
2. Parke-Taylor, *Formation*, 296–297. This pertains, of course, only to the early form of Jeremiah 1–24, as several passages currently found therein date from later periods (e.g., Jer 21; see the Conclusion to the present study).
3. See Lundbom, "Baruch, Seraiah," 101–104.
4. This position recognizes, however, that Jeremiah 50–51 went through significant secondary expansion over time.
5. The *atbash* codes for Babylon in Jeremiah 51 provide a rhetorical answer to the 70-year prophecy in Jer 29:10, following the prototype of Esarhaddon's Black Stone inscription regarding the rebuilding of Babylon. In this text, a decree by Marduk originally stating that Babylon would remain desolate for 70 years is nullified by the physical inversion of the cuneiform characters for the number 70. This Assyrian text was likely well known to Jeremiah's audience, and the prophet's allusion to it would help situate the deportation of 597 BCE within a broader historical/political context. See Leuchter, "Jeremiah's 70-Year Prophecy," 509–511, 516–521.
6. Those scholars who view the call narrative and ch. 25 as originating at the same time by a later exilic redactor do not pay enough attention to the clearly secondary nature of Jer 1:3, which adjusts the superscription to address the various kings dealt with throughout chs. 1–25. Had the superscription originated in the exilic period, we would not encounter the secondary accretion in Jer 1:3; instead, the range of kings would be more integrated into a single statement akin to the superscriptions of other prophetic books (e.g., Amos 1:1; Hos 1:1; Isa 1:1; Mic 1:1). The call narrative also deploys careful rhetorical strategies consonant with an early address to the north in Josiah's day; see Leuchter, *JRJS*, 72–78.
7. It is thus noteworthy that Jer 25:3 deploys the phrase עד היום הזה, a hallmark of the Deuteronomistic literature that existed in Josiah's day (Geoghegan, "Until This Day," 225–227) and that was used in relation to Josiah both in the closing exhortation of the prophet's *Urrolle* and in the narrative depiction of its composition (Jer 36:2). See Leuchter, *JRJS*, chapter 8, for additional discussion. The conspicuous use of the phrase in Jer 25:3 points to a general period of composition falling shortly after the Josianic period, when the phrase was still in vogue and would have carried significant rhetorical

implications. Scholarly arguments concerning a late date for Jeremiah 25 must account for the appearance of the phrase, which fell into disuse after the mid-sixth-century BCE (see the Conclusion to the present study for further discussion).

8. The MT reading of Jer 25:9 is to be preferred over the LXX reading on rhetorical grounds. The recurring language in the verse creates a very neat *inclusio* with MT Jer 1:15. MT Jer 1:15 refers to both families *and* kingdoms (its LXX counterpart mentions only kingdoms but is otherwise very close in form), which is semantically paralleled in the MT of Jer 25:9 via the mention of both the families of the north and an example of the outstanding king representing them, Nebuchadrezzar. By contrast, the LXX version of Jer 25:9 mentions *only* families, creating a weak parallel to MT Jer 1:15 and an even weaker parallel to LXX Jer 1:15, which omits references to families. Many of the other pluses involving "Nebuchadrezzar" in the MT, however, should be credited to subsequent expansion following the lead of Jer 25:9 (see Parke-Taylor, *Formation*, 102–104).
9. See Leuchter, *JRJS*, 179–182.
10. See Lundbom, *Jeremiah 21–36*, 251.
11. For a discussion of colophons in the book of Jeremiah, see Lundbom, "Baruch, Seraiah," 89–95. For colophons in the Bible and the ancient Near East more generally, see Fishbane, *Biblical Interpretation*, 27–32; H. M. I. Gevaryahu, "Biblical Colophons: A Source for the 'Biography' of Authors, Texts and Books," *Congress Volume, 1974* (VTSup 28; Leiden: Brill, 1975), 42–59; E. Leichty, "The Colophon," *Studies Presented to A. Leo Oppenheim* (Chicago: Oriental Institute of the University of Chicago, 1964), 147–154.
12. Lundbom is critical of the view that this phrase looks back on a collection and argues strenuously that it is simply there to anticipate the Babylonian oracle currently in chs. 50–51 (*Jeremiah 21–36*, 238–239). This view is certainly reinforced by the reappearance of the phrase in the colophon attached to the Babylonian oracle (Jer 51:63). However, Jer 25:13 may function as a bridge, looking forward to the Babylonian oracle *as well as* back to a larger collection. Lundbom has posited that Jer 36:1–8 was originally a colophon ("Baruch, Seraiah," 104–106), yet in its current state it also serves as an introduction to the subsequent material in Jer 36:9–32.
13. A similar type of location marker is found in Jer 11:6, 12–13 which identify the streets of Jerusalem and the cities of Judah as the place where the prophet's words are to be declared, preserved, and applied.
14. As suggested earlier, the chapter's date should therefore be viewed as hermeneutical in function. This challenges the view that Jeremiah 25 originated as part of the actual *Urrolle* (see, e.g., M. Haran, "The Place of the Prophecies Against the Nations in the Book of Jeremiah," *Emanuel: Studies in Hebrew Bible, Septuagint, and Dead Sea Scrolls in Honor of Emanuel Tov* [ed. S. M. Paul et al.; Leiden/Boston: Brill, 2003], 705–706).
15. Holladay's theory concerning Jeremiah's pronouncements as coinciding with the septennial readings of Deuteronomy complements the features of Jeremiah 1–25:13+OAN as a standard theological curriculum for the deportees of 597 BCE (*Jeremiah 2*, 27; id., "Had Ezekiel Known Jeremiah Personally?" *CBQ* 63 [2001], 34).
16. Fishbane's observations regarding this unit as preexilic in origin support this proposed background to its composition (*Biblical Interpretation*, 479–480). However, his

conclusion that Jer 29:10 is a subsequent accretion dependent on 25:11 is challenged by the previous discussion.

17. Following the standards of scribal practice, Seraiah would have composed a copy of the Babylonian oracle before throwing it into the Euphrates (Lundbom, "Baruch, Seraiah," 107). This copy would have provided the textual basis for the oracle's introduction into the developing OAN. Many of these oracles would have been drawn from the archive of Jeremianic oracles that had existed as early as the last decade of the seventh century BCE; see Leuchter, *JRJS*, 178–179.
18. See Chapter 4 for a discussion of these chapters.
19. This ideological precedent, here already made part of the prophet's preexilic oracles, will become profoundly significant for the author of the Supplement and will indeed provide the impetus for the cumulative purpose of his work; see Chapter 4.
20. The reference to the 70-year prophecy in Jer 29:10 points to the application of Jeremiah 25 to the literature preserved only by the 597 BCE community in Babylon. The flurry of diplomatic exchanges between Babylon and Judah between 597 and 592 would have provided ample opportunity for the transmission of the prophet's work to his peers in Mesopotamia (see Holladay, *Jeremiah* 2, 118–119, 434–435).
21. See Haran, "The Prophecies Against the Nations."
22. Sharp, "Take Another Scroll and Write," 508–509.

EXCURSUS 2

1. Jer 33:1–13 is discussed in the Conclusion to the present study.
2. For the omission as deliberate, see P. Volz, *Der Prophet Jeremia* (KZAT, 1922), 310–312. For the omission as a result of haplography, see Lundbom, *Jeremiah 21–36*, 538.
3. See McKane, *Jeremiah* 2, 862, for commentary. See also Holladay, *Jeremiah* 2, 230.
4. Duhm, *Das Buch Jeremia*, 276.
5. See M. Stern, "The Period of the Second Temple," in *A History of the Jewish People* (ed. H. H. Ben-Sasson; Cambridge, MA: Harvard University Press, 1976), 229–230. Stern notes that with the exception of Alexander Jannaeus (r. 103–76 BCE), the Hasmoneans were reluctant to adopt the traditional qualifications of the Davidic-type monarchy, emphasizing instead their positions as high priests and ethnarchs. See also J. C. Vanderkam, *An Introduction to Early Judaism* (Grand Rapids, MI: Eerdmans, 2001), 24–32; J. Bright, *A History of Israel*, 3rd ed. (Louisville, KY/Philadelphia: Westminster/John Knox Press, 1981), 425–427.
6. E. M. Roberts notes that "the fate of the Davidic line after Shelomith [who represents the generation after Zerubbabel] is difficult to recover" (*Ancient Israelite Religion* [Fs. F. M. Cross, ed. P. D. Miller et al.; Philadelphia: Fortress Press, 1987], 510) but argues that the note in 1 Chr 3:17–24 points to its persistence through the fifth century BCE. Even if the Davidic line did persist for this duration, however, the lack of Davidide leadership in the mid-fifth century (neither Ezra nor Nehemiah is bound to the Davidic line) demonstrates the marginalization of Davidic heritage from political discourse by this time.
7. G. Boccaccini, *Roots of Rabbinic Judaism: An Intellectual History, from Ezekiel to Daniel* (Grand Rapids, MI: Eerdmans, 2002), 56–60.

8. Other scholars adopting this position include Bocaccini, *Roots of Rabbinic Judaism*, 52; K. E. Pomykala, *The Davidic Dynasty Tradition in Early Judaism: Its History and Significance for Messianism* (SBLD; Atlanta: Scholars Press, 1995), 42–45.
9. Among these scholars, see E. Tov, "Some Aspects of the Textual and Literary History of the Book of Jeremiah," in Bogaert (1981), 154; Lundbom, *Jeremiah 21–36*, 537–546; Cross, *CMHE*, 259.
10. Lundbom identifies four units in Jer 33:14–26 (*Jeremiah 21–36*, 537–546), but the syntactical divisions in the text only point to three.
11. See Sweeney, *King Josiah*, 226–230.
12. The origins of Zadok are notoriously difficult to determine. Cross has suggested that he is indeed an Aaronide from Judah installed alongside the Mushite Abiathar (*CMHE*, 213–215), though others have suggested that this conclusion rests on too speculative an analysis (see L. L. Grabbe, *Priests, Prophets, Diviners, Sages: A Socio-Historical Study of Religious Specialists in Ancient Israel* [Valley Forge, PA: Trinity Press, 1995], 62). S. M. Olyan, however, convincingly argues for a Judean/Aaronide origin for Zadok; see his "Zadok's Origins and the Tribal Politics of David," *JBL* 101 (1982), 177–193. Whatever position one takes on Zadok's origins, the Jerusalem priesthood descending from him viewed themselves as Aaronides. Boccaccini notes the Pentateuchal genealogy that provided the basis for Zadok's lineage, though he views this as a postexilic composition (*Roots of Rabbinic Judaism*, 67–68).
13. Compare v. 22 to Gen 15:5; 22:17; 32:13; the patriarchal reference in v. 26 is overt.
14. This discussion of the proper place of the Davidide and Zadokite family lines in the cosmos draws from a firmly entrenched understanding of the Israelite family as a cosmic expression; see D. L. Petersen, "Genesis and Family Values," *JBL* 124 (2005), 5–23. In noting the *toledoth* formulae in Genesis, Petersen writes: "there is a familial relationship between the broader created universe and that of humanity . . . for the Priestly writer, the human family is embedded in the very structure of the universe" (10).
15. Sommer, *A Prophet Reads Scripture*, 32–72 (the analysis also covers the material often attributed to Trito-Isaiah, who Sommer feels is not to be distinguished from Deutero-Isaiah). On Haggai's dependence upon Jeremiah, see B. Peckham, *History and Prophecy* (New York: Doubleday, 1993), 750–755. Zechariah takes up the issue of Jeremiah's 70-year prophecy in Zech 1:4,12; 7:5.
16. Such is the position adopted by Lundbom, who argues that the oracle is a post–587/586 BCE composition by the prophet (*Jeremiah 21–36*, 541).
17. See the later discussion.
18. Leuchter, *JRJS*, 82–83.
19. Jeremiah's reliance on P is evident here and elsewhere, and supports the position that some form of P material had obtained an authoritative position by the time of Josiah's reforms. For P as a pre-Deuteronomistic tradition, see Knohl, *The Sanctuary of Silence*, passim. See also B. Halpern and D. S. Vanderhooft, "The Editions of Kings in the 7th–6th Centuries BCE," *HUCA* 62 (1991), 223–227 (Huldah's oracle presupposes P terminology); Weinfeld, *Deuteronomy and the Deuteronomic School*, 179–189.
20. See Gen 1:14–19. We should also note the term חק/חקים, typical of P legal terminology, and the term ישבתו in v. 34, an allusion to the centrality of the Sabbath (שבת) to the P concept

of covenant and cosmos. For the Sabbath liturgy as an essential Jerusalemite-priestly concept, see N. Sarna, "Psalm 92: A Song for the Sabbath Day," *JBL* 81 (1962), 155–168; Schniedewind, *How the Bible Became a Book*, 132. Jeremiah engages in wordplay on the P Sabbath ideology in Jer 4:23–26, a reversal of the creation account. See M. Fishbane, "Jeremiah iv 23–26 and Job iii 3–13: A Recovered Use of the Creation Pattern," *VT* 21 (1971), 151–153.

21. See Boccaccini, *Roots of Rabbinic Judaism*, 49–60, for a discussion of the political sentiments of the Restoration community in the late sixth century BCE.
22. For example, the Josianic redaction of the Hezekiah narrative presents Sennacherib's death as the result of his siege on sacred Jerusalem.
23. Jeremiah 22 relates the prophet's positive evaluation of Josiah, but this is a retrospective account. Jeremiah also speaks favorably of Jehoiachin, but only in terms of his submission to Babylon, not as a leader possessing any real political power. Insofar as priestly figures are concerned, nothing beyond the early layers of Jeremiah 30–31 identifies any positive attitude toward priesthood. Already by Jer 2:8, the priests are accused of not knowing YHWH, and this negative critique of priesthood persists throughout the bulk of the Jeremianic corpus. Even the priests of Anatoth are presented as adversaries and incur the prophet's wrath (Jer 11:18–23). For Jer 2:8 as Josianic in origin but subsequent to Jer 30–31 (and presupposing the audience's rejection of these initial oracles), see Sweeney, *King Josiah*, 233.
24. For *setumot* as syntactical indicators in the ancient versions, see Lundbom, *Jeremiah 1–20*, 74.
25. For a discussion of Seidel's Law, see Levinson, *Deuteronomy*, 18–20.
26. The relationship between this passage and the more standard הכהנים הלוים in v. 18 will be discussed later.
27. Here we should note that the שרת terminology does not specify cultic activity, in contradistinction to the language of v. 18 (discussed later). For Levites as juridical administrators of Deuteronomic law, see Leuchter, *JRJS*, 41–42.
28. See Boccaccini, *Roots of Rabbinic Judaism*, 49–72, for a discussion of the tensions between the Zadokites and Levites as well as the lack of Levitical participation in the Restoration community. It would not be until significantly later that Levites and Zadokites would mend fences, as evidenced by the presentation of Levites in Chronicles; see Boccaccini, *Roots of Rabbinic Judaism*, 71–72; P. D. Hanson, "1 Chronicles 15–16 and the Chronicler's View of the Levites," *Sha'arei Talmon* (Fs. Shemaryahu Talmon, ed. M. Fishbane and E. Tov with W. W. Fields; Winona Lake, IN: Eisenbrauns, 1992), 74–77.
29. For a detailed discussion of this theme on Jeremiah's early oracles, see Leuchter, *JRJS*, chapters 4, 5.
30. Leuchter, "Jeremiah's 70-Year Prophecy," 519–520.
31. Pomykara, *Davidic Dynasty Tradition*, 43–45.
32. We find here no recurrence of Seidel's Law, but the author/compiler of this oracle may no longer have felt the need to engage in such referencing, as this was already accomplished through the binding of v. 18 and v. 21. Moreover, the author incorporates new terminology from the P creation account (חקות שמים וארץ; see Gen 1:1; 2:4a), exegetically deferring to the base tradition that originally informed the older material in vv. 19–22.

33. The allusion to the patriarchs follows the same exegetical impulse that included the חקות שמים וארץ of v. 25. Here as well, a reference to older tradition in the older Jeremianic fragment (the patriarchal promise alluded to in v. 22; see Gen 15:5; 22:17; 32:13) has inspired the author to highlight the source more overtly by naming the patriarchs.
34. For the fifth-century BCE separation of the Pentateuch from a larger historiographic work, see T. C. Eskenazi, "Implications for and from EzraNehemiah," "In Conversation with W. M. Schneidewind, *How the Bible Became a Book: The Textualization of Ancient Israel* (Cambridge, 2003), ed. G. N. Knoppers, *JHS* 5 (2005), 18.

3. THE STANDARDS OF FAITH AND INTERMEDIATION: JEREMIAH 34–36

1. See, for example, Dearman, "My Servants the Scribes," 408–409.
2. See Excursus 2.
3. Römer sees Jeremiah 35 as the closing chapter of an early redactional edition of the Jeremianic corpus ("Convert," 193) only to be expanded later, and thus does not see a close structural relationship at work with the sequence of Jeremiah 34–36.
4. McKane (*Jeremiah* 2, 868–869) argues for the independence of vv. 2–3 from vv. 4–5, claiming that they are unrelated oracles (877). Thiel (*Jeremia 26–45*, 38) also reaches this conclusion, arguing against the historicity of the content. However, historicity in its pure sense is not the issue or even the intention of vv. 2–5. Rather, there is present in vv. 2–5 the same principle of transmission found in Jer 32:1–5: a scribe is repeating or summarizing Jeremiah's word to Zedekiah, and writing from an *ex eventu* perspective that begs for a certain dramatic license in the presentation of Jeremiah's words. The "but hear the word of YHWH, Zedekiah king of Judah" that begins v. 4 should not be viewed as a secondary intrusion or the corruption of an earlier version of the text; it functions as an emphatic aside to the exilic reader, who would have been fully aware of the double entendres of the ensuing proclamations, already having been familiar with Zedekiah's fate.
5. That Jeremiah 34 begins with an oracle to Zedekiah suggests that it initially followed Jer 32:1–15 when the Supplement was constructed, creating a keyword and a topical bridge between one unit and the next. Jeremiah 33 constitutes a later accretion and is itself composed of different redactional strata. See the Conclusion to the present study for additional discussion.
6. Z. B. Begin, "Does Lachish Letter 4 Contradict Jeremiah xxxiv 7?" *VT* 52 (2002), 166–174.
7. See McKane, *Jeremiah* 2, 868–869, 875; id., "The Construction of Jeremiah Chapter xxi," 61–62.
8. Stipp, "Zedekiah in the Book of Jeremiah," 646; Pakkala, "Zedekiah's Fate," 447–448. As discussed in the Introduction to the present study, the Jeremiah text most likely responds to such alternate traditions concerning Zedekiah's fate rather than incorporating them directly into the narrative.
9. Pace McKane, *Jeremiah* 2, 869; Holladay, *Jeremiah* 2, 23. Both associate the שרף term strictly with funerary rites rather than viewing it as an anticipatory and ironic device in relation to Jer 39:8 (so also Overholt, "Jeremiah," 569). It is worth noting that the DH does not mention fire as part of any royal funerary rites.

10. See especially the earlier discussion of Jer 32:1–5. A similar observation is made by Overholt, "Jeremiah," 569.
11. For a detailed discussion of the different texts regarding Josiah's death and the material in Jeremiah that sheds additional light on the event, see Leuchter, *JRJS*, chapter 5.
12. Beyond Huldah's oracle to Josiah in 2 Kgs 22:15–20, the context of שלום statements elsewhere in the book of Jeremiah (Jer 6:14; 12:5) is decidedly negative. The likelihood, then, is that a negative meaning is implied here in Jeremiah 34, and the similarity to 2 Kgs 22:20 suggests conscious awareness of Huldah's oracle. This likelihood is strongly reinforced by what immediately follows in Jer 34:8–22, i.e., a covenant ceremony based on Deuteronomic law that attempts to emulate Josianic norms but that, according to the prophetic critique therein, fails (see later). The construction of Jeremiah 34 en masse, then, further attests to a degree of historicity in the narratives regarding Josiah and his reform, as the entire chapter is structured to contrast Zedekiah with his father, Josiah.
13. Nicholson, *Preaching*, 63–65; Thiel, *Jeremia 26–45*, 42–43; McKane, *Jeremiah 2*, 880.
14. H. Weippert, *Die Prosareden des Jeremiabuches* (BZAW, 132; Berlin: De Gruyter, 1973), 86–106.
15. Pace McKane, *Jeremiah 2*, 880, who too quickly opts to excise vv. 13–14 from the passage as secondary.
16. In this context, I translate the term as "peer" because of the gender-neutral application of the term to both males and females in the verse. At the same time, it is precisely this concept that dominates the Deuteronomic concept of society, where a king is chosen from the peer-based community (Deut 17:15) and the rural Levites administered the Josianic Passover among their peers (2 Kgs 23:9).
17. The very important introduction to this verse will be discussed later in a separate section.
18. See, among others, S. Chavel, "Let My People Go! Emancipation, Revelation and Scribal Activity in Jeremiah 34:8–14," *JSOT* 76 (1997), 78. For a critique of this perspective, see B. M. Levinson, " The Manumission of Hermeneutics: The Slave Laws of the Pentateuch as Challange to Contemporary Pentateuctual Theory," *Congress Volume 2004* (ed. A. Lemaire; Leiden: Brill 2006), 302 n. 61.
19. Carr, *Tablet of the Heart*, 160. See also Person, "The Ancient Israelite Scribe," 603–608.
20. As discussed previously, and with many other scholars, I take the position that Jeremiah was active in Josiah's time, though I argue that he was quite active from the outset of the king's reign. See Leuchter, *JRJS*, 72–78.
21. See Leuchter, "The Temple Sermon," 99, 103.
22. For the conciliatory dimensions of the Josianic literature with respect to northern tradition, see Leuchter, *JRJS*, 56–51; id., "Jeremiah's 70-Year Prophecy," 511 (n. 29), 512–513.
23. For a discussion of Seidel's Law, see Levinson, *Deuteronomy*, 18–20.
24. Leuchter, *JRJS*, 122–124.
25. It is significant to note that Jer 34:13 contains a short *Heilsgeschichte*, a hallmark of Levitical expression in Deuteronomistic discourse if Levites are to be identified as the redactors of the Josianic DH (Geoghegan, "Until This Day," 225–227). The tradition of the *Heilsgeschichte* may have very ancient roots, as Psalm 78, a Solomonic-era composition,

takes up the tradition for Jerusalem-centric purposes. See the closing comments by M. Leuchter, "The Reference to Shiloh in Psalm 78," *HUCA* (forthcoming).

26. The MT of this passage should be given priority over the LXX version, which reads, "I will render them as the calf which they have made." The matter has been discussed by C. D. Crawford, "Cutting the Calf or Making the Calf? On the Preferred Reading of Jeremiah 34:18–20," read at the annual meeting of the Society of Biblical Literature, Philadelphia, 2005. See also Stipp, "Zedekiah in the Book of Jeremiah," 641; Lundbom, *Jeremiah 21–36*, 564–566.
27. For a discussion, see Leuchter, *JRJS*, 112–113.
28. This lexical trope can be found elsewhere in the preexilic materials (Jer 7:33 and 19:7). Jeremiah 16 is the likely source due to similar language in Jer 34:16 (ותחללו) and Jer 16:18 (חללם).
29. The use of חללם as opposed to the טמא terminology may be attributed to the same memorization process that resulted in the minute changes in Jer 34:14; see the earlier discussion. The allusion is otherwise identical in terms and function to the Deuteronomic source text, and even the terminological variant is consistent in theme and purpose.
30. For Jeremiah 2–4 as originating as part of Jeremiah's mission to the north as a Josianic agent, see Sweeney, *King Josiah*, 215–225, 233; Weinfeld, *Deuteronomy 1–11*, 67; Leuchter, *JRJS*, 87–97.
31. The marital imagery we encounter earlier in the chapter (Jer 16:2, 9) suggests a connection between the covenantal union with the deity and the sanctity of Israelite marital unions, an idea found elsewhere in Jeremiah (especially in Jeremiah 2–3), undoubtedly influenced by the Hosea tradition. For further discussion concerning the sacral dimensions of human marriage in Israelite religion and its persistence into later Judaism, see M. Weinfeld, "Feminine Features in the Imagery of God and Israel: The Sacred Marriage and the Sacred Tree," *VT* 46 (1996), 516–528.
32. Parke-Taylor notes other significant doublets connected to Jeremiah 16 (*Formation*, 113–114), including parallels in other parenetic prose passages (195–197). He does not, however, discuss the doublet we have identified here. Though we may disagree with Parke-Taylor's view that the doublets in these prose passages may largely be attributed to later redactors, his discussion concerning the editorial commentary and intertextual relationship they signify may be applied to the function of the doublet in Jer 34:20.
33. Verse 20b is derived from Jeremiah's oracles as well but, as we have seen, is secondarily applied to this context.
34. Rofé, "Arrangement"; Lundbom, *Jeremiah 1–20*, 92.
35. For the significance of literary sequences (such as those involving the various oracles and citations in Jeremiah 34) in conveying meaning, see Leuchter, "Song of Moses"; Levinson, *Deuteronomy*, 107–137.
36. This idea conforms to a long history of Mushite/Levitical polemical works. One immediately thinks of the critique of the Bethel and Jerusalem cults found in Exodus 32, as well as the brief narrative of the death of Nadab and Abihu in Lev 10:1–7; see Cross, *CMHE*, 198–206; B. Halpern, "Levitic Participation, in the Reform Cult of Jeroboam I," *JBL* 95 (1976), 33–35; Leuchter, "Jeroboam the Ephratite," *JBL* 125 (2006), 70–71. See also G. N. Knoppers, "Aaron's Calf and Jeroboam's Calves," *Fortunate the Eyes That*

See: *Essays in Honor of Noel Freedman in Celebration of His Seventieth Birthday* (ed. A. Beck et al.; Grand Rapids, MI: Gerdmans, 1995), 92–104; Knoppers demonstrates how the retelling of Exodus 32 by the Deuteronomist lessens the critique of the Solomonic cult that was more prominent in his source text. Jeremiah's critique is Deuteronomistic in character due to the prevailing ideological curriculum of the time and the nature of Zedekiah's covenant proceedings, but the dynamics of his criticism fall into a well-entrenched Levitical pattern.

37. See, among others, N. Sarna, "Zedekiah's Emancipation of Slaves and the Sabbatical Year," *Studies in Biblical Interpretation* (Philadelphia: JPS, 2000 [reprinted from the original 1973 article]), 295–304; N. P. Lemche, "The Manumission of Slaves – The Fallow Year – The Sabbatical Year – The Jobel Year," *VT* 26 (1976), 51–53; Lundbom, *Jeremiah 21–36*, 560–563; McKane, *Jeremiah 2*, 870, 880; Chavel, "Let My People Go!," 83; Carroll, *Jeremiah*, 648.
38. See especially Sarna, "Zedekiah's Emancipation," 301.
39. Lundbom argues for flexibility in the temporal meaning of the phrase מקץ שבע שנים with relation to the sixth/seventh year (*Jeremiah 21–36*, 563) in an attempt to make sense of the phrase's grafting onto the manumission law from Deut 15:12. But there is no additional evidence to support this view, and such an explanation is not necessary; see the later discussion.
40. The author of the LXX *Vorlage* or his later translator clearly understood Jer 34:14 as mistaken, correcting the phrase to read "after six years" pursuant to the Deuteronomic source.
41. Reckoning from 622 BCE, the emergence of Deuteronomy during Josiah's reign, we find the following scheme: 622/615/608/601/594/587. Holladay's theory of Jeremiah's parenetic proclamations coinciding with these septennial readings may be justified in this case (*Jeremiah* 2, 27), though it is difficult to establish that all the prose oracles attributable to Jeremiah (e.g., Jer 3:6–11) conform to this dating scheme.
42. Chavel is correct to see intertextual resonances shared by Jeremiah 34 and the Holiness Code manumission law in Leviticus 25 ("Let My People Go!" 89–92), which he argues results from a scribe's reliance upon the Holiness Code in shaping Jeremiah 34. However, the episode's critique of Zadokite ritual (vv. 18–20) and the pervasive influence of Deuteronomic law and ideology (especially with an eye to contrasting Zedekiah to Josiah in vv. 1–7; see the earlier discussion) suggest a different compositional sequence. If the מקץ שבע שנים formula is indeed drawn from Deut 31:10, then the difficulties that lead commentators to consider the Holiness Code legislation as an influence on the text disappear. The intertexual elements Chavel cites would therefore run in the opposite direction, i.e., the Holiness Code would appear to be aware of Jeremiah 34 and rely upon it as a source. A reaction to a prophetic text such as Jeremiah 34 is consistent with Knohl's model of the Holiness school's general modus operandi as a response to prophetic critiques (*Sanctuary of Silence*, 214–216). Though I agree with Knohl's general argument that the Holiness Code derives significantly from the late eighth century BCE, Levinson has made a strong case for its subsequent development ("Manumission of Hermeneutics," 316–324). The dependence on Jeremiah 34 suggests that the development of the Holiness Code should be dated to the exilic period or the early postexilic

period, subsequent to the emergence of the Supplement and in relation to the redaction of the Pentateuch (Knohl, *Sanctuary of Silence*, 100–103; see the further discussion in Chapter 5).

43. The reference to a text from an external source of a different genre/form (a legal stipulation has been worked into a prophetic narrative) for thematic emphasis finds precedent in the preexilic period with the citation of Mic 1:2 in the narrative of 1 Kgs 22:28. See K. Bodner, "The Locution of 1 Kgs 22:28: A New Proposal," *JBL* 122 (2003), 543.
44. The exegetical process here exemplifies Fishbane's observation about the secondary accretions to texts generated by their scribal redactors: "... the received divine teachings are supplemented and focused by human comments grafted upon it ... though they appear to derive from different sources, the two are complementary and – so their conjoint preservation attests – ultimately one" (*Biblical Interpretation*, 61–62).
45. Precedent for grafting the formula onto Jeremiah 34:14 as an address to the exilic community may be found in the aforementioned suggestion that Jeremiah's new covenant (Jer 31:31–34) and the redaction of Jeremiah 1–25:13+OAN took place in the context of the septennial reading of Deuteronomy in 594 BCE (see Excursus 1).
46. So also Holladay, *Jeremiah* 2, 247.
47. The appearance of the phrase "my servants the prophets" in Jer 35:15 suggests that those gathered in the office of Hanan b. Igdaliah were counted among this circle. The term איש אלהים is typically associated with Shilonite or Deuteronomic prophetic interests. It applies to both the anonymous prophet of 1 Sam 2:27–36 and then to Samuel in 1 Sam 9:6–7, 10; Shemaiah in 1 Kgs 12:24 provides ratification for Ahijah's earlier designation of Jeroboam; the anonymous prophet of 1 Kgs 13:1–10 inveighs against the use of Bethel and non-Levite priests. The term does not occur as often in later periods, however. A Temple office and prophetic guild begun by an איש אלהים must have possessed significant antiquity if it was still operative in Jeremiah's day.
48. White, *The Elijah Legends*, 36–43.
49. White, *The Elijah Legends*, 1–43.
50. White, *The Elijah Legends*, 47.
51. See Cross, *CMHE*, 200–201; B. Mazar, "The Sanctuary of Arad and the Family of Hobab the Kenite," *JNES* 24 (1965), 299–303; Lundbom, *Jeremiah 21–36*, 572–574; M. Weinfeld, "The Tribal League at Sinai," *Ancient Israelite History: Essays in Honor of Frank Moore Cross* (ed. P. D. Miller et al.; Philadelphia: Fortress Press, 1987), 304.
52. See R. J. Hess, "The Divine Name in Late Bronze Age Sources?" *UF* 23 (1991), 180–182; M. Weippert, "Semitiche Nomaden des zweiten Jahrtausends: Über die *š3św* der ägyptischen Quellen," *Bib* 55 (1974), 265–280, 427–433 (though Weippert identifies the Yahwistic name with a clan or region rather than with a deity); Weinfeld, "Tribal League," 304.
53. Cross, *CMHE*, 100–103. See also Weinfeld's discussion of the connections to the Kenite–Midianite YHWH tradition in Habbakuk 3, Psalm 68, and Deut 33:2–3 ("Tribal League," 305–308).
54. Levin, "From Lists to History," 633.
55. Weinfeld, "Tribal League," 304. See also Chapter 6 for additional discussion.
56. Weinfeld, "Tribal League," 310–311.

57. Compare the fulfillment of Jeremiah's word in Jer 28:16 with the presentation of the Mosaic prophet in Deut 18:19–20. Sharp is correct that this alone should not be the basis for identifying Jeremiah with the Deuteronomic image of prophecy (*Jeremiah*, 152; see also her discussion of other fairly superficial commonalities), but it does contribute to an extant and profound association between Jeremiah and the Deuteronomistic literature.
58. McKane (*Jeremiah* 2, 895–898) claims that the plethora of details points to a deliberate attempt to infuse a nonhistorical narrative with historical authenticity, but this logic is very questionable. The details point to genuine historicity and are recounted in such an elaborate manner for rhetorical purposes, i.e., bringing the exilic reader into the story. Furthermore, the details concerning the Temple attempt to prove the author's familiarity with that institution rather than simply serve as a description for stylistic purposes; see the later discussion.
59. See Halpern, "Jerusalem and the Lineages," 41–59, for a discussion of Hezekiah's urbanization policies in anticipation of Sennacherib's campaign in 701 BCE.
60. Contra McKane (*Jeremiah* 2, 891), who states that if the account is indeed historical, it would have transpired ca. 600 BCE. Overholt ("Jeremiah," 570) suggests 598–597, during the last period of Jehoiakim's reign (following Jer 35:1). That the event transpires in the days of Jehoiakim is unlikely, however. If Jer 36:5 is any indication, Jeremiah had been prohibited from entering the Temple during Jehoiakim's reign, presumably because of his Temple Sermon and the (implicit) royal reaction to it (Jer 26:20–24). Yet, in Jer 35:3–4, Jeremiah takes the Rechabites into the Temple to hear their story and to pronounce YHWH's blessing upon them. This suggests that while Jeremiah may have been prohibited from entering the Temple in the days of Jehoiakim, the prohibition was either lifted or otherwise came to an end at a later time. This is certainly suggested by Shemaiah's letter to Zephaniah the priest (Jer 29:25–28), insofar as it depicts Jeremiah as having some influence within the priestly circles during Zedekiah's reign, which is confirmed by Zephaniah's visit to Jeremiah after reading the letter (Jer 29:29). The episode with the Rechabites must therefore have taken place after the time of Jehoiakim, likely during the brief period when Jehoiachin held power before his deportation.
61. See 2 Kgs 17:13, 23; Jer 26:5, 25:4. The wording of Jeremiah's condemnation of the faithless people in v. 14 mirrors that of Jer 25:3, suggesting that the passage in Jeremiah 35 is dependent upon this verse and that the fleeing of the Rechabites from the Babylonian army is presented as a witness to the realization of Jer 25:1–11.
62. Pace Römer, "Convert," 193, though Römer's observations on the pervasiveness of Deuteronomistic language in these chapters do reveal that the disparate authors were equally influenced by the Deuteronomistic stream of education-enculturation. See Carr, *Tablet of the Heart*, 134–142, 146–149.
63. Jer 29:5–7, we must recall, suggests (among other things) that YHWH's blessings can be secured through the adjustment of legal tradition and its implementation in a new dwelling environment such as Babylon; see Chapter 2.
64. McKane (*Jeremiah* 2, 897) points out that the refusal to take wine need not have involved the lengthy statement of their traditions currently found in vv. 7–10. These and v. 11 point to a desperate apologetic argument, though, not necessarily a later (unauthentic) composition.

65. For the sacral nature of the phrase, see G. N. Knoppers, "Hierodules, Priests or Janitors? The Levites in Chronicles and the History of the Israelite Priesthood," *JBL* 118 (1999), 58; J. D. Levenson, "On the Promise to the Rechabites," *CBQ* 38 (1976), 513; P. J. Leithart, "Attendants of YHWH's House: Priesthood in the Old Testament," *JSOT* 85 (1999), 15–18. Leithart notes that the עמד terminology applies in other contexts beyond the priesthood, especially with respect to kings, but we must bear in mind that throughout most of the preexilic period, kings headed their cults and possessed sacral characteristics; standing before such a figure may not have been strictly "priestly," but it was certainly sacral. In any event, the term is very much at home in the priestly milieu. Lundbom argues that anybody could "stand before" YHWH by citing Jer 7:10, which is addressed in part to the laity (*Jeremiah 21–36*, 573). Jer 7:10, however, occurs within the context of a harsh criticism of improper cultic ideology and should not be seen as a comment on legitimate practice among the ordinary Judean population. In most other contexts, the phrase is tied to sacral intercessory behavior. See Chapter 4 for a discussion of this same terminology in Jer 40:10.
66. Lundbom makes a similar observation (*Jeremiah 21–36*, 581) but concludes that the chapter addresses Israel's disobedience to YHWH. This reading is possible but is not integrated as well into the rhetorical logic of the surrounding chapters.
67. Holladay (*Jeremiah* 2, 248) points out that "keeper of the threshold" (Jer 35:4) refers to specific priestly duties relating to various gates in the Temple; Jer 36:10 specifies that Gemariah's chamber is above one such gate. The description closely matches that of Jer 35:4, as the chamber of the officers is also on the second floor of the Temple, overlooking a gate/threshold. Holladay's observation should not be brushed aside despite his own contention that the specific location of the chamber of Hanan b. Igdaliah is of "little help to the modern reader" (!).
68. This corresponding information suggests that the inclusion of the detail of the Rechabite meeting's location may be deliberate, but it is not historically unfounded (pace McKane, *Jeremiah* 2, 897).
69. The presence of a prophetic guild that supported Mosaic traditions need not have challenged Jeremiah's role as the Mosaic prophet of the period. Huldah holds the office of Mosaic prophet during the activity of Zephaniah and Jeremiah (and probably others such as Uriah; cf. Jer 26:20), who must have functioned under the guidelines of Deuteronomic orthodoxy. The chapter's concern with Mosaic tradition in Deuteronomy is in good keeping with the antiquarian Deuteronomistic ideology of the time (Halpern, "Jerusalem and the Lineages," 86–87; B. M. Levinson, "The Hermeneutics of Tradition in Deuteronomy: A Response to J. G. McGonville," *JBL* 119 [2000], 283–284).
70. It may be that the shift in terminology from Jer 35:4 ("the chamber of the officers") to Jer 36:10 ("the chamber of Gemariah b. Shaphan, the scribe") reflects the shift in historical circumstance. The events of Jeremiah 35 take place seven to eight years after the events of Jeremiah 36 and, indeed, during a major paradigm shift in the governmental infrastructure with the first Babylonian conquest. See Lohfink, "Historischen Kurzgeschichte," 333–342, for a discussion of the deportation of specific Shaphanide scribal officers in 597 BCE. The shift from a personal name to a general title associated with the same chamber may reflect the subsequent readjustment after the deportation.

71. McKane (*Jeremiah* 2, 914–915) questions the veracity of royal scribes possessing an official chamber in the Temple and criticizes Lohfink's view that this would have stemmed from Josiah's piety. It is not unlikely, though, that Josianic scribes would have assumed a liturgical position, since it is they who were responsible for the emergence of the Mosaic law code that formed the theological basis of Josiah's Temple-centered covenantal ideology (see Levinson, *Deuteronomy*, passim). See also Geoghegan, "Until This Day," 225–227, who posits that these scribes were Levites; their position in the Temple would therefore be quite appropriate. This matter will be discussed extensively in Chapters 5 and 6. Josiah need not have been "pious" so much as committed to the political program that would result from the application of the Deuteronomic Torah; the scribes thus obtain an important position in generating religious dogma. Furthermore, the scribal craft becomes far more intertwined with religious politics in the period of the seventh century BCE and beyond; see Schaper, "Exilic and Post-Exilic Prophecy," 336–342.
72. There is little scholarly consensus concerning the historicity of this chapter. Opinions range from that of Muilenberg ("Baruch the Scribe," 245), who affirms its reliability as an historical source, to that of C. Rietzschel (*Das problem der Urrolle: Ein Beitrag Ziir Redatitionsgeschichte des Jeremiahbuches* [Guterslöh: Gutserslöher (Mohn)], 1966, 105–108) and C. D. Isbell ("II Kings 22:3–23:24 and Jeremiah 36: A Stylistic Comparison," *JSOT* 8 [1978], 33–45), who point to its formalism. O'Connor ("Do Not Trim a Word," 625–627) and Dearman ("My Servants the Scribes," 409) also discuss its formal parallels to Jeremiah 26, suggesting its deliberate nature. Dearman, however, points to the wealth of information that verifies the historical veracity of elements within the narrative; this must inform any reading of the chapter and be taken into account before one may disregard its historical reliability. Nicholson's view (*Preaching*, 43 n. 2) that it possesses a limited historical core that was shaped by later Deuteronomistic editors should not be adopted for two reasons: the chapter possesses unique Jeremianic language (see Weippert, *Prosareden*, 140–148), and the attribution of the chapter to a Deuteronomistic editor automatically assumes that a secondary agenda has obscured original information. McKane (*Jeremiah* 2, 911) points to the difficulty in Nicholson's study in defining the relationship between his two proposed strata and offers the criticism that Nicholson's study renders Jeremiah 36 as simply a parasite on 2 Kings 22. McKane's term "parasitic" with regard to Jeremiah 36's dependence on 2 Kings 22 goes too far and marginalizes the rhetorical significance of these similarities. McKane does, however, note with Wanke (*Baruchschrift*, 74) the difficulty in determining where history ends and drama begins. To make this determination, though, is to nullify the purpose of the chapter, which is to account for the sacred dimensions of history using an exegetical approach. The chapter is best understood as based on an historical event or events (Leuchter, *JRJS*, chapters 8, 9; so also Dearman, "My Servants the Scribes," 403–404 n. 2, 417–418) but utilized as a platform to advance the author's agenda, as I shall argue later.
73. Sharp, "Take Another Scroll," 508–509.
74. See Lundbom, "Baruch, Seriah," 104–106. Lundbom identifies standard colophonic features in Jer 36:1–8 but concludes that Jeremiah 45 was the original colophon to Baruch's scroll read in the Temple (105). It is more likely, though, that Jer 36:4–8 was the colophon

to this work (or at least was based on that colophon), as it comes after the report of the composition of the first scroll and before the tense events that result from its public reading.

75. The likelihood that Jeremiah simply dictated from memory the intricately structured materials comprising the *Urrolle* is unlikely, particularly since these materials had already obtained some written form by 605 BCE. It is possible that the redaction of his 609–605 oracles may have involved Baruch's schooled scribal hand, but it may be that v. 2 hermeneutically summarizes Jeremiah's written materials from this period and attempts to present them not as the result of any ongoing debates with the Jerusalem establishment but as a single and consistent issuance. McKane (*Jeremiah* 2, 914) points to the past-tense construct of the term דברתי in v. 2, which hints at the compositional prehistory that goes unmentioned in the opening to this chapter. Though he goes on to support Thiel's view (*Jeremia 26–52*, 49 n. 1) that the phrase ודברתי . . . ועד היום הזה must be deleted to obtain a coherent reading of vv. 2 and 4, such a deletion obscures the emphatic nature of the phrase in relation to the chapter's introduction, which connects Baruch's scribal role to Jeremiah's prophetic work and establishes important connections to the literature of the Josianic period (Geoghegan, "Until This Day," 225–227).

76. See E. Leichty, "The Colophon," 147–154. Leichty provides a list of standard features of scribal colophons throughout the ancient Near East from the old Babylonian period down to the Seleucid period. Jer 36:4–8 and 36:32 both possess a number of these features, indicating their positions either as former colophons (36:4–8) or as current colophons (36:32). The subject is discussed extensively by Lundbom, who suggests that Jer 36:1–8 was a colophon to an earlier collection whereas Jeremiah 45 was the actual colophon to the prophet's *Urrolle* ("Baruch, Seraiah"). I take Jeremiah 45 to be an exilic composition (perhaps based on or inspired by an earlier colophon); if we wish to identify Baruch's colophon to the *Urrolle* as a passage now embedded within the Supplement, Jer 36:4–8 seems to me the more likely candidate. M. Fishbane has observed that colophons contain allusions to their contents ("Biblical Colophons, Textual Criticism and Legal Analogies," *CBQ* 42 [1980], 438–449; see also id., "Accusations of Adultery," 35). Following this principle, Jer 36:4–8 seems to reflect upon a more limited collection of oracles from an earlier time than Jeremiah 45. The latter, by contrast, contains allusions to episodes found elsewhere in the Supplement. See also Fishbane, *Biblical Interpretation*, 27–31 for examples of colophonic passages throughout a wide variety of biblical genres. The common view that the repeated מפיו phrase throughout the chapter refers to Jeremiah dictating the oracles misunderstands the phenomenological dimensions implied in the process as discussed in Chapter 1 ("The Prophetic Word and the Scribal Word").

77. Dearman is certainly correct to note the centrality of this scribal family to the chapter and the affiliation of the various named scribes therein to that family ("My Servants the Scribes," 406 n. 8).

78. See Leuchter, *JRJS*, 175.

79. Most scholars view Deut 1:1 as part of an exilic opening frame and not as part of the Josianic stratum of text. Lundbom, however, views Deuteronomy 1 as part of the preexilic corpus ("The Inclusio and Other Framing Devices in Deuteronomy,

i–xxvii," *VT* 46 [1996], 312–314). Regardless of its compositional origins, Deut 1:1 employs language identical to that of Deut 5:18 in describing the Mosaic Torah.

80. So Dearman, "My Servants the Scribes," 403–407. McKane (*Jeremiah* 2, 916–918) discounts the role of the officers as interested allies of Jeremiah, claiming that their reaction had to do more with political unrest caused by the public reading of the *Urrolle* than with actual concern for its message (917). Part of this, McKane argues, is that the officers had never paid much attention to Jeremiah before and were only secondarily transformed into pious figures at a later stage in the chapter's development (918). This view cannot be accepted, though, if some of the officers of the chapter are to be seen as scribes (Dearman, "My Servants the Scribes," 417–421; Lundbom also points out that many of the officers in this chapter may have functioned as scribes and had scribal training even if they did not bear the official title of scribe ["Baruch, Seriah," 102–103]). If Jer 8:8 associates these scribes *with* Jeremiah, as I have argued elsewhere (*JRJS*, 135–136; see also the Introduction to the present study), then their behavior in Jeremiah 36 (if stylized) is entirely consistent with a group that had always regarded his word as legitimate.
81. The repeated function of scribes in this capacity further indicates common authorship behind these chapters. See the discussion in Chapter 2 with respect to Jer 32:6–15.
82. Holladay (*Jeremiah* 2, 258) points out that the scribes show no signs of doubt as to Jeremiah's being a true Mosaic prophet; the concern throughout the chapter is with the scroll itself. In these verses, though, the author makes it absolutely clear how scribal methods are directly connected to the prophetic דבר. See the discussion in Chapter 1 ("The Prophetic Word and the Scribal Word").
83. I have discussed this issue in greater detail in Chapter 1 in the section "The Prophetic Word and the Scribal Word." See also Leuchter, *JRJS*, 165–166.
84. Holladay (*Jeremiah* 2, 254–255, 261–262) suggests that the second scroll is to be viewed in light of Moses crafting a second set of tablets at Sinai (Exod 34:1). The circumstances are different, though, since Moses himself destroys the first set of tablets, and the second set contains the same material.
85. This is consistent with similar strategies discussed earlier in the author's shaping of Jeremiah 34.
86. So also Schaper, "Exilic and Post-Exilic Prophecy," 338–339; Najman, "Symbolic Significance," 161–165, 173.
87. For an overview, see Carr, *Tablet of the Heart*, 114–142; Schniedewind, *Book*, 91–106.
88. Halpern, "Brisker Pipes Than Poetry," 98–99, 102.
89. Leuchter, *JRJS*, 49–52.
90. So Halpern, "Why Manasseh," 505.
91. See McKane, *Jeremiah* 2, 919–920, for the possible superstitious dimensions to this act.
92. This reading of the event would eliminate much of the difficulty discussed by Holladay (*Jeremiah* 2, 259–260) in relation to the reasons behind the burning of the scroll.
93. Nicholson (*Preaching*, 43 n. 2) and Rietzschel (*Urrolle*, 106–108) both discuss the terminological distinctions with respect to the servants and officers in this section of Jeremiah 36, though they do not attempt to associate these figures with factions discussed in the *Urrolle*.

94. See the discussion by Sharp regarding the quotation of Jer 2:5 in 2 Kgs 17:15 (*Jeremiah*, 144–145; see also Weippert, *Prosareden*, 218). The author of 2 Kgs 17:15 attempts to provide an example to the reader of how a prophetic servant of YHWH actually speaks. Though Sharp views this as a post-Jeremianic accretion, it may also be the result of an update to an earlier version of 2 Kings 17 that was written during the period of Jeremiah's preexilic activity.
95. The phrase "all his servants" in v. 24 need not be taken literally but hermeneutically as part of the telescopic rhetoric of the narrative, but the naming of the three servants in v. 26 (Jerahmeel, Seraiah, and Shelemiah) grounds the phrase within historical terms. The structure here is again deliberate, as the three servants parallel the three officers of v. 25.
96. Holladay (*Jeremiah 2*, 257) notes that Micaiah's "going down" to the scribal office in the royal palace is a reflex to the "going up" from the king's house in Jer 26:10.
97. Scholars are divided on the provenance of what we encounter in Deuteronomy 27. The current form may be the result of seventh-century BCE shaping, but good arguments can be made for its origins in an ancient Levitical context. See Weinfeld, "Emergence," 79–83; Richter, "The Place of the Name."
98. Leuchter, *JRJS*, 173–174.
99. This would certainly reinforce the understanding of Jeremiah as a prophet like Moses, since Moses charges the Levites with the very responsibilities that Jeremiah gives to Baruch and his scribal peers.
100. Lundbom, *Jeremiah 1–20*, 92; Geoghegan, "Until This Day," 226.
101. Carr, *Tablet of the Heart*, 116–120.
102. Pace McKane, *Jeremiah 2*, 914–918, who does not consider the sacral dimensions of scribal practice. See D. W. Baker, "Scribes as Transmitters of Tradition," *Faith, Tradition and History: Old Testament Historiography in Its Near Eastern Context* (ed. A. R. Millard, J. K. Hoffmeier, and D. W. Baker; Winona Lake, IN: Eisenbrauns, 1994), 65–78.
103. See also Dearman, "My Servants the Scribes," 409 n. 16, who observes a connection to Deut 31:11.
104. Dearman, "My Servants the Scribes," 415 n. 30; McKane, *Jeremiah 2*, 904. Lundbom considers the patronymic information to be intentional (*Jeremiah 21–36*, 601) and views it as an important connection to Jehudi's Ethiopian background via his ancestor's name, Cushi. I agree with Lundbom that the patronymic list is intentionally extended in relation to the name Cushi, though the matter is more complex than a determination of Ethiopian ethnicity. See Chapter 6 for a full discussion.
105. D. A. Glatt-Gilad, "The Personal Names in Jeremiah as a Source for the History of the Period," *Hebrew Studies* 41 (2000), 31–45.
106. See the overview by Dearman, "My Servants the Scribes," 414–418.
107. As Carr has discussed, scribal convention would have included the memorization of texts (*Tablet of the Heart*, 159–160), but the narrative of Jeremiah 36 does not allow for the time it would have taken for the text to be memorized, at least within the time frame of the narrative. The summary/interpretation offered by the scribes, however, is also in keeping with Israelite scribal convention. See Person, "Israelite Scribe," 603–608. For

a general discussion of the oral-written culture of ancient Israel, see S. Niditch, *Oral World and Written Word: Ancient Israelite Literature* (Louisville, KY: Westminster/John Knox Press, 1996).

108. See also Deut 32:45, which characterizes the preceding Mosaic exhortation with the same terminology. I have argued elsewhere that this formula refers to the entire preexilic book of Deuteronomy ending with the Song of Moses, a work of northern Levitical origin (Leuchter, "Song of Moses"). The appearance of the formula throughout Jeremiah 36 may consciously echo its appearance throughout Deuteronomy (the formula also notably appears in Jer 11:6) or simply attest to a common mode of Levitical-scribal discourse prevalent in the author's day. See Chapter 4 for the reuse of this terminology with overt reference to the Song of Moses in Jer 43:1.
109. Person, "Israelite Scribe," 603–608.
110. Dearman notes that interpretation is fundamental to the scribes' activity in the chapter ("My Servants the Scribes," 411), which certainly constitutes a didactic method.
111. The Josianic stratum in Deuteronomy already conceives of the regional judges/scribal magistrates in Deut 16:18 as empowered to interpret and teach text; see Leuchter, *JRJS*, 41–42, for the likelihood that these figures were imagined by Deuteronomy to be the local Levites divested of cultic responsibility. See also Chapter 5.
112. Uriah's body is not reported to have been left exposed to the elements, but it is not deposited in his ancestral tomb; this certainly must have been an issue given the fact that Uriah's father and his hometown, Kiriath Yearim, are both identified. He had a known lineage and an ancestral location. Halpern ("Jerusalem and the Lineages," 72–75) discusses the norms of burial at the ancestral tomb as a fundamental feature of preexilic society, which highlights the severity of Jehoiakim's act against Uriah. Though Jeremiah's proclamation in 36:30 is not identical to the fate of Uriah, it addresses the same issue. For a detailed discussion of gradations of burial praxes from desirable to abhorrent, see S. M. Olyan, "Some Neglected Aspects of Israelite Interment Ideology," *JBL* 124 (2005), 601–616.
113. Halpern,"Jerusalem and the Lineages," 72–75.
114. Halpern, "Jerusalem and the Lineages," 56–59.
115. It is, in fact, the ritualistic function of text that was current at the time that is being critiqued in this passage. See J. W. Watts, "Ritual Legitimacy and Scriptural Authority," *JBL* 124 (2005), 401–417. The progression of text from functioning in a ritual context to obtaining a broader social significance that Watts discusses may result in part from this critique.
116. That Jer 34:20 alludes to Jeremiah 16 is significant in this regard, as the latter comes to an end with a meditation on the foibles of idolatry (vv. 19–20; cf. Jer 7:8, which addresses the same problems). See Halpern, "Brisker Pipes," 98–99, 102.
117. See Parke-Taylor, *Formation*, 196–197, for a discussion of the burial motif throughout Jeremiah's oracles.
118. We will recall that Jeremiah 11:3, 6, 8 refer to their surrounding corpus as הברית הזאת; cf. also 2 Kgs 23:3, where the law book discovered in 2 Kings 22 is referred to as a ספר ברית.
119. Jehoiakim remained partial to Egypt even after the Babylonian victory at Carchemish in 605 BCE. Zedekiah's nonenforcement of the manumission ritual/law is presented in

Jeremiah 34 as a result of Babylonian forces withdrawing in the face of Egyptian military pressure. See Lundbom, *Jeremiah 21–36*, 566. Egypt is overtly mentioned in Jer 34:13, but only in the context of the short *Heilsgeschichte.* Egyptian forces are not cited as the reason for the Babylonian withdrawal, which suggests that this chapter was written for an audience that possessed a fresh memory of the military/political circumstances surrounding Jerusalem's last days (pace Chavel, "Let My People Go!," 93–95).

120. Weinfeld, "Emergence"; Levinson, "Hermeneutics of Tradition," 283–284.
121. The typological relationship between the Rechabites in Jeremiah 35 and the scribes in Jeremiah 36 further suggests a reevaluation of Römer's view that initial redaction of the book of Jeremiah ended in ch. 35 ("Convert," 197–199).
122. Lundbom suggests that Jer 36:30 testifies to a more accurate account of Jehoiakim's fate, with 2 Kgs 24:6 muting the facts (*Jeremiah 21–36*, 144–145). But the book of Kings does not pull punches regarding its criticism of the post-Josianic rulers in Jerusalem, and it seems unlikely that a violent death of a king would be suppressed if that king received condemnation. Such is clearly not the case with Zedekiah, as the authors of 2 Kings 24–25 recount his fate in gruesome detail.
123. So, too, the telescopic elements in Jer 34:1–7 discussed earlier.
124. Rietzschel, *Urrolle*, 105–108; McKane, *Jeremiah 2*, 911; Carroll, *Jeremiah*, 662–668.
125. The foregoing examination of Jeremiah 34–36 thus challenges redactional theories that see a separate background to the composition of Jeremiah 37–44 (Wanke, *Baruchschrift*, 146–147; see Chapter 4) or random editing/compositional accretion throughout (McKane, *Jeremiah 2*, passim).

4. THE FALL OF JUDAH, THE DESCENT INTO EGYPT, AND BARUCH BEN NERIAH: JEREMIAH 37–45

1. For example, Wanke, *Baruchschrift*, 146; Lipschits, *Jerusalem*, 312 n. 166; Parke-Taylor, *Formation*, 303.
2. For example, the invective against the kings, cultic prophets, and priests in chs. 22–23; the personal suffering of the prophet in the "laments" in chs. 11–20; the division of the Judean community in Jeremiah 24; and the devastation of the land in isolated units throughout chs. 1–25.
3. On the murder of Sennacherib as a theological response to his devastation of Babylon (and its relationship to the biblical account of his death and the succession of Esarhaddon in 2 Kgs 19:37, which follows the form in which the death and succession of Israelite kings is typically reported), see W. W. Hallo, "The Death of Kings: Traditional Historiography in Contextual Perspective," *Ah, Assyria... Studies in Assyrian History and Ancient Near Eastern Historiography Presented to Hayim Tadmor* (ed. M. Cogan and I. Eph'al; Jerusalem: Magnes, 1991), 148–165, esp. 162–163; M. Cogan and H. Tadmor, *II Kings* (AB, 11; Garden City, NY: Doubleday, 1988), 244. The fragmentary text known as "The Sin of Sargon" further implies that Sennacherib's devastation of Babylon led to his violent demise; see H. Tadmor, "The Sin of Sargon," *EI* 5 (1958), 93, 150–163.

4. See Leuchter, "Jeremiah's 70-Year Prophecy," 512.
5. This idea also underlies 2 Kgs 24:19, which reports that Zedekiah carried on in the manner of Jehoiakim before him.
6. This dovetails with the linguistic features of the narrative as discussed by Polak, "Style," 53, who identifies these narratives as characteristic of late-seventh through mid-sixth-century BCE composition.
7. For the connection between 2 Kings 22 and Jeremiah 36, see Chapter 3. See also McKane, *Jeremiah* 2, 911–916.
8. Lundbom, *Jeremiah 37–52*, 60.
9. These anticipatory connections between earlier chapters and Jeremiah 39 call into question the conclusion by Lipschits that much of the chapter results from a temporally removed secondary redaction (*Jerusalem*, 336–338). This is based on Lipschits's view that the historical events depicted in Jeremiah 39 draw directly from Jeremiah 52, which he views as entering the Jeremiah tradition after the "biography" (Lipschits's term) of Jeremiah 37–44 had been constructed. Lipschits's view that Jer 39:4–13 (especially vv. 4–10) is based largely on the details *found* in Jeremiah 52 seems sound, but the anticipatory references in earlier chapters to what is depicted in Jer 39:4–10 make it unlikely that this occurred well after the majority of the biography had been composed. One might argue that the references look forward not to Jeremiah 39 but, rather, to Jeremiah 52, where similar details are provided regarding the blinding of Zedekiah and the burning of Jerusalem. However, Jeremiah 52 is almost universally regarded as a separate appendix to the book of Jeremiah and stands apart from the narrative materials in both the MT and LXX versions of the book, and this still does not account for their presence according to Lipschits's view, which has Jeremiah 52 entering the tradition after the biography. In terms of literary logic, the anticipatory references to Zedekiah's blinding and the burning of Jerusalem require a fulfillment *within* the parameters of the Supplement, and this is accomplished by Jer 39:4–10. As such, the view of Cogan and Tadmor that Jer 39:4–10, Jeremiah 52, and 2 Kings 25 are all based on a common annalistic source appears to be the best explanation for the information shared by all three literary complexes (*II Kings*, 326; see Chapter 5 for additional discussion). This would also explain the lack of vv. 4–12 in the LXX parallel to MT Jeremiah 39: the LXX parallel was based on an earlier tradition originating from a time before the construction of the Supplement and the interpolation of information into that tradition from the annalistic source behind Jeremiah 52/2 Kings 25. One may also argue that the LXX suffers from haplography; see Lundbom, *Jeremiah 37–52*, 81; Parke-Taylor, *Formation*, 210. Nevertheless, Lipschits makes a strong case for historical information secondarily worked into a shorter independent account, though I view the process as occurring concurrently with the development of the Supplement as opposed to the secondary interpolation he suggests.
10. See the discussion in Chapter 3.
11. The paralleling of the Jehoiakim and Zedekiah *inclusios* (Jer 26/36; 37–44, respectively) suggests that the Zedekiah *inclusio* is indeed an integral part of the narrative design and thus that Jer 44:30 should not be viewed as a secondary accretion (pace Hoffman, "History and Ideology," 47–48). This carries significant implications for the dating of the Supplement to 570 BCE or shortly thereafter (see Chapter 5).

12. See the later discussion; Zedekiah is characterized differently from Jehoiaikim, but this only amplifies the polemical perspective that Jerusalemite kingship, as an office, is invalid, regardless of each king's personal qualities. The same idea is taken up by the exilic redactors of the DH, who categorically deny legitimacy to all the post-Josianic kings.
13. See also the discussion in the Introduction to the present study.
14. Also telling is the mention of Nebuchadrezzar in the archival-style introduction in Jer 37:1.
15. This also suggests the temporal proximity of the narrative's composition to the deportations themselves.
16. See the discussion of Diamond, "Portraying Prophecy," 104–111; Stipp, "Zedekiah in the Book of Jeremiah" (though here I offer an alternate reading of the character's presentation and development).
17. Holladay, *Jeremiah 2*, 19; Leuchter, *JRJS*, 181.
18. Diamond, "Portraying Prophecy," 104–106.
19. See Chapter 3. See also Leuchter, "Jeremiah's 70-Year Prophecy," 506.
20. Seitz correctly points to the rhetorical rather than historical emphasis in these passages (*Theology in Conflict*, 241–245), though his identification of multiple redactions is questionable, as discussed previously.
21. As Lipschits observes, many Judeans had already fled to Benjamin, and thus Jeremiah's similar act would have been in keeping with popular practice at the time; the detaining of the prophet by the royal officers likely had more to do with the propagandistic repercussions of an important figure like Jeremiah joining this migration to the north (*Jerusalem*, 366).
22. See the discussion by Lundbom, *Jeremiah 37–52*, 61. It may be that this particular tale regarding the redemption of Jeremiah's ancestral land was inspired by the episode in Jer 32:6–15. The author's creation of the account in 37:11–21 establishes thematic connections between 32:6–15 and the later narratives of the Supplement, reinforcing their collective rhetorical function.
23. Lipschits makes a similar observation with regard to Judean officers in later chapters as wicked and Babylonian officers as good (*Jerusalem*, 327 n. 214).
24. Lipschits, *Jerusalem*, 77.
25. The use of the term "officers" in these chapters stands in stark contrast to the use of the term in Jeremiah 36. It is clear that there has been a regime change of the order suggested by Lohfink ("Historischen Kurzgeschichte," 341), but this regime does not possess the meritorious factions that were part of the Jerusalem establishment prior to Zedekiah; these, as Lohfink has argued, have gone to Babylon.
26. Two elements should be noted in the discussion of Gedaliah's tenure at Mizpah. First, Gedaliah's administrative post appears to have commenced even before the destruction of Jerusalem. Second, the author of the Supplement has gone to some length to anticipate the army officers as perpetrators of impiety in the ensuing narrative through their lexical presentation in Jeremiah 40. On both matters, see Lipschits, *Jerusalem*, 92–97, 327 n. 214. Concerning the presentation of the army officers, I concur with Lipschits's approach to reconstructing an original annalistic source that has been developed by

the author of the Supplement, though Lipschits does not consider the MT of Jer 40:7 to be original to this author's redactional/compositional design and thereby misses an important rhetorical feature of the episode. See the fuller discussion later on in this chapter.

27. The antecedents to a Babylon-sympathetic party among the elite of Judah date back at least to the Josianic court; see J. A. Wilcoxen, "The Political Background of Jeremiah's Temple Sermon," *Scripture in History and Theology: Essays in Honor of J. Coert Rylaarsdam* (ed. A. L. Merill and T. W. Overholt; Pittsburgh: Pickwick Press, 1977), 151–165.
28. For example, Seitz, "Crisis," 92–97; id., *Theology in Conflict*, 274, 290.
29. The connection here is strengthened by Lipschits's observation that the summer fruit in question would have indeed been figs (*Jerusalem*, 99 n. 224).
30. The references almost uniformly refer to the complex of literature directed to the deportees of 597 BCE. For a discussion, see Leuchter, "Jeremiah's 70-Year Prophecy."
31. Lipschits notes the intercessory dimensions of this phrase as well (*Jerusalem*, 89) but does not discuss its sacral implications. See the discussion in Chapter 3.
32. Lipschits, for example, dates the passage to the postexilic period, reflecting the interests of the Restoration community over against those who had remained in the land during the period of Babylonian domination (*Jerusalem*, 358).
33. The LXX parallel also lacks the mention of "children" (וטף in MT Jer 40:7); in this case, the copyist appears to have jumped from the final letter in the word "women" (נשים, which would not have possessed a final *mem* form in paleo-Hebrew script) in his source text to the first *mem* in the word מאשר, which resumes the verse (so also Lundbom, *Jeremiah 37–52*, 110).
34. That is, Gedaliah's decree that implements Jeremiah's oracles. The Deuteronomic parallel here contradicts Parke-Taylor's contention that Jeremiah 40 is part of a narrative unit (chs. 37–43) that has no Deuteronomic/Deuteronomistic valences (*Formation*, 303). Additional examples are enumerated later with respect to Jeremiah 42–43.
35. As discussed earlier, Jeremiah 1–25 was already a well-known corpus among the exiles as of 587 BCE and would have been familiar to anybody who suffered the very calamity predicted therein. Jeremiah's pre-597 oracles had already been presented as genetically connected to the Deuteronomic Torah (Leuchter, *JRJS*, 168), and the prophet's letter to the exiles of 597 possesses similar features (Berlin, "A Deuteronomic Allusion," 8–11). The well-known parallel between Jeremiah's *Urrolle* in Jeremiah 36 and the Torah scroll in 2 Kings 22 further solidifies this connection within the world of the Supplement narrative. That the author wrote for an audience that would catch the reference to Deut 31:10–13 supports those who view the primary development of the Jeremianic tradition among the exiles in Babylon rather than among those who remained in the homeland, the latter of whom were largely from the rural classes, possessed limited literacy, and were not likely well versed in the careful rhetoric of Deuteronomy. See Lipschits, *Jerusalem*, 258–271 for a discussion of the socioeconomic background of the population in Judah during the period of Babylonian hegemony. As regards the parallel between Jer 40:7 and Deut 31:12, the reference may have been detected among the larger audience, but

it certainly would have resonated with the Levites living in exile; see Chapter 6 for a detailed discussion.

36. Compare this to Deut 29:5–7, which seeks to accomplish the same with respect to the exiles of 597 in Babylon (see Chapter 2).
37. Specifically, the Shaphanides may have possessed northern Levitical heritage. Both Dearman ("My Servants the Scribes," 410–411) and Lundbom (*Jeremiah 21–36*, 299) have provided genealogical overviews of the Shaphanides. The biblical record provides information only as far back as the Hezekian period, though many scholars view this as a time when a large number of northern refugees settled in Judah and made inroads into the Jerusalem scribal and administrative establishment, influencing Jerusalemite literature with a distinctively Ephraimite voice (Schniedewind, *Book*, 69–90; H. L. Ginsburg, *The Israelian Heritage of Judaism* [New York: JTS, 1982], passim). The northern and Levitical foci of literature associated with the Shaphanides (Geoghegan, "Until This Day," 225–227) dovetail very well with the possibility that their ancestor, Meshullam, who would have lived in Hezekiah's day and who is invoked in 2 Kgs 22:3, was a northern official who also possessed a Levitical heritage. Though the DH informs us that the northern cult was composed of non-Levites, this polemical statement is very likely inaccurate; see B. Halpern, "Levitic Participation." See also Amos 7:10–17; Amos takes aim at the inadequacies of the Bethel cult but does not offer any condemnation of the priesthood as non-Levitic and illegitimate, and there is no comment regarding Amaziah holding an inappropriate office. Considering Amaziah's statement that the cult center is "the king's sanctuary and a royal house" (v. 13), we should expect that important cultic personnel would have had some connection to the royal administration and would have been quite literate. Indeed, Carr draws attention to the close relationship among priests, scribes, and royal establishments in the ancient Near East (*Tablet of the Heart*, 115–122, 152); See also I. M. Young, "Israelite Literacy: Interpreting the Evidence," *VT* 48 (1998), 408–422. Meshullam may have been a member of this type of northern elite, which would explain the interests of his descendants. The discussion here regarding Gedaliah as a Levitical figure attempts to reinforce these observations.
38. Geoghegan, "Until This Day," 226; Leuchter, "Song of Moses." However, this should not be viewed as support for Von Rad's theory of Deuteronomistic parenesis as deriving from a tradition of "Levitical sermons." The parenetic discourses in Deuteronomy do not themselves derive directly from an oral/sermonic background but from careful literary transformation of older written traditions. See Levinson, *Deuteronomy*, passim; Stackert, "Cities of Refuge," 48–49.
39. The elders are addressed in this passage as well, but the focus appears to be on the Levites, who are singled out as bearing the Ark where the law will eventually be kept. Furthermore, it is the Levites who are repeatedly characterized as curators of the law in Deuteronomy; the mention of the elders typically presents them as carrying out executive duties under the administrative auspices of the Levites. Such is the case in Deut 31:25–28, where Moses commands *the Levites* to gather the elders and entrusts them with the Torah he has written.
40. Leuchter, *JRJS*, 41–42.

41. That this same terminology is applied to the faithful Rechabites (Jer 35:19) suggests that Gedaliah's role as a Babylonian governor has the same degree of piety as that of the Rechabites.
42. Pace McKane, *Jeremiah* 2, 914–915.
43. For Hosea's Levitical lineage roots, see S. L. Cook, *The Social Roots of Biblical Yahwism* (Atlanta: SBL, 2004), 231–266. For an overview of Hosea's influence upon Deuteronomic discourse, see Weinfeld, *Deuteronomy 1–11*, 44–50; id., "Emergence," 83–89.
44. S. L. Richter, "The Place of the Name in Deuteronomy," *VT* (forthcoming); Cook, *Social Roots*, 259–266; Weinfeld, "Emergence," 76–83.
45. This, too, suggests another parallel between Gedaliah and Jeremiah, who had already identified himself as standing in the tradition of Samuel (Jer 15:1). The view of Lipschits that Mizpah obtained prominence only during the period of Babylonian domination and that the narratives about the location are late (*Jerusalem*, 109–110) is problematic, especially since these narratives possess linguistic and sociolinguistic features that significantly predate seventh- to sixth-century BCE styles of composition (Polak, "Style," 40–41; see also 60–66, 80–84; id., "'Now There Was One Man': The Character of the Book of Samuel and Its Place in Ancient Israelite Historiography" *Shnaton – An Annual for Biblical and Ancient Near Eastern Studies* 12 [2000], 13–47 [Hebrew, with English summary]).
46. See Lundbom, *Jeremiah 37–52*, 114–115.
47. Lipschits, *Jerusalem*, 112–117. See also the discussion regarding northern liturgies preserved in subsequent Judean compositions by G. A. Rendsburg, "The Northern Origins of Nehemiah 9," *Bib* 72 (1991), 348–366.
48. See the discussion in Leuchter, *JRJS*, 53–72, for the scope of Josiah's agenda in the north. The cities mentioned in Jeremiah 41 would have fit Josiah's interests in annexing the north, and thus the event possesses some historical resonance.
49. For an overview of the Shechem tradition taken up by the Deuteronomists, see Weinfeld, "Emergence," 76–82; Cook, *Social Roots*, 258–260. For the Shiloh tradition, see Leuchter, *JRJS*, 18–49. Samaria, as the capital of the north, is also taken up by the Deuteronomists at a number of points in the book of Kings and is the subject of the extended discourse in 2 Kings 17.
50. Though the account is polemical in its purpose, it reflects what must have been actual practice among those in the land who engaged in pilgrimage to the ruins of the Temple (Lipschits, *Jerusalem*, 115).
51. The first instance of rebellion against Nebuchadnezzar, it will be recalled, is that of Jehoiakim in 598 BCE, who died before Babylon overtook Jerusalem. For an historical discussion, see Bright, *A History of Israel*, 326–327.
52. Descent into Egypt during the same historical period is attested within the Lachish Letters; see D. Pardee, *Handbook of Ancient Hebrew Letters* (Chico, CA: Scholars Press, 1982), 84–85. As Lipschits notes, however, the Babylonian deportation of roughly 582 BCE was independent of Gedaliah's assassination, which occurred very shortly after the destruction of Jerusalem years earlier (*Jerusalem*, 100–102). The association between Ishmael's massacre and the Babylonian deportation years later is constructed along the

lines of the presentation of Sennacherib's assassination in 2 Kgs 19:36–37 (discussed earlier in relation to the transition from Jeremiah 36 to Jeremiah 37).

53. Sharp views Jeremiah 42 as evidence of a pro-*golah* agenda (*Jeremiah*, 90), but the issue is not one of homeland vs. the Diaspora in Babylon. The ultimate purpose of the text is to validate the Babylonian political superstructure irrespective of locale. As regards potential leadership under Baruch, the protests of Johanan in Jer 43:2–3 suggest the possibility of such a political scenario; see the later discussion.
54. Jeremiah had indeed relocated Jerusalem's sacral terminology to Babylon (even if for only a transitory period) via the application of the term מקום to that city in Jer 51:62, part of Seraiah's colophon accompanying the Babylonian oracle. See Leuchter, "The Temple Sermon," 108–109.
55. See Van Selms, "Telescoped Discussion."
56. Van Selms, "Telescoped Discussion." Even if the wording of the oracle in Jeremiah 42 is not directly attributed to the prophet, the prophet's original oracle would have sounded very similar. As we have already seen, the prophet's own parenetic prose is highly Deuteronomistic in character. Part of this is due to the prophet's direct allusion to Deuteronomic passages (Berlin, "A Deuteronomic Allusion"; Holladay, *Jeremiah 2*, 27), as well as his own training as a scribe and enculturation with Deuteronomistic tradition (Lundbom, *Jeremiah 1–20*, 92; Carr, *Tablet of the Heart*, 148–149). Furthermore, since the author of the Supplement had in his possession an early version of Jeremiah 1–25, the prophet's own parenetic prose in that collection would have served as a guide in his reconstruction of Jeremiah's oracles.
57. So also Lundbom, *Jeremiah 37–52*, 130, 134. On the prohibitions in Deuteronomy 28 concerning Egypt and its influence in Jeremiah 42, see the later discussion.
58. Pace Parke-Taylor, *Formation*, 303, who sees no Deuteronomistic elements within Jeremiah 37–44.
59. P. Sanders has demonstrated conclusively that the Song of Moses is preexilic in origin (*The Provenance of Deuteronomy 32* [Boston/Leiden: Brill, 1996]), and M. Thiessen's observations concerning its liturgical quality suggest that the presence of both early and standard Hebrew forms resulted from generations of liturgical recitation, with later forms pushing aside some of the older forms from the poem's origin as it was repeatedly performed ("The Form and Function of the Song of Moses [Deuteronomy 32:1–43]," *JBL* 123 [2004], 401–424). Alternately, D. A. Robertson (*Linguistic Evidence in Dating Early Hebrew Poetry* [SBLD 3; Missoula, MT: SBL, 1972], 155) and S. A. Nigosian ("Linguistic Patterns of Deuteronomy 32," *Bib* 78 [1997], 206–224) suggest a period of linguistic transition, where both archaic and standard forms were in use, for the background to the poem's composition. In either case, the poem was early in origin and a fixture of Israel's liturgical consciousness. For the poem as a source for First Isaiah, see R. Bergey, "The Song of Moses (Deuteronomy 32.1–43) and Isaianic Prophecies: A Case of Early Intertextuality?" *JSOT* 28 (2003), 33–54. For the inclusion of the poem in Deuteronomy during the preexilic (and probably Josianic) period, see B. Halpern and D. S. Vanderhooft, "The Editions of Kings," 237; Holladay, "Elusive Deuteronomists," 73–74; Leuchter, "Song of Moses." See Chapter 6 for additional discussion of Jer 43:1.

60. Implicit here is a meta-literary comment on the formation of the book of Jeremiah before the author's day. Jeremiah had himself invoked the lexemes of the Song of Moses in his criticism of the north in Josiah's reign and, specifically, in his castigation of the Shilonites of Anatoth who refused to accept Josianic hegemony (most references occur in Jeremiah 2–3, which originated during the reign of Josiah; see Leuchter, *JRJS*, 91–102; id., "Song of Moses"). Jeremiah would later view his own northern brethren as illegitimate, cutting them off from the covenant community via the call for vengeance in Jer 11:18–23, pursuant to the legislation in Deut 13:7–10. A similar threat underlies the reference to the Song of Moses in Jer 43:1, with the fate of the Shilonites and other northerners (who are excluded from any direct address in Jeremiah's discourse beyond the Josianic-era texts) serving as the prototype for what will happen to the remnant community should they ignore Jeremiah's words. The comment would not have escaped the literati of the Judean Babylonian community, who no doubt would have remembered Josiah's difficulties with the north that ultimately cost him his life and the nation its security.
61. For the Exodus as a mythic motif in Ephraimite tradition, see Y. Hoffman, "A North Israelite Typological Myth and a Judaean Historical Tradition: The Exodus in Hosea and Amos," *VT* 39 (1989), 169–182. Jeremiah's anti-Egypt position is also concurrent with traditional Levitical thought; see Chapter 6.
62. Leuchter, *JRJS*, 53–90.
63. For a summary of scholarly discussion on this brief passage, see Nelson, *Deuteronomy*, 306–310.
64. For ethnic diversity as part of Josiah's concept of a "greater Israel," see Leuchter, *JRJS*, 64–69.
65. Johanan's naming of Baruch as a conspirator preserves what was likely an actual political/social tension of the time. Baruch is clearly a figure of significance in order to be named a traitor by Johanan; he must have led or represented the pro-Babylonian faction still remaining in the land. The allegation was not included in the narrative to formulate a defense against this charge, for no defense is given, which supports the authenticity of Johanan's statement.
66. McKane (*Jeremiah* 2, 1032–1033), Seitz (*Theology in Conflict*, 277), and Holladay (*Jeremiah* 2, 299–300) all recognize that Jer 42:10 employs language similar to that of the call narrative in Jer 1:10, though this should not be viewed as a parallel to the use of the same language in Jer 31:27, meant for the 597 BCE community in Babylon. As McKane notes, the wording is not the same, and Holladay makes the crucial observation that the conditional promise recalls the message of Jer 18:7–8 (see the immediately following discussion).
67. So also Holladay, *Jeremiah* 2, 299–300.
68. See Chapter 1 for a discussion of this feature at work in Jer 26:17–19.
69. For the purpose of the chapter as a defense of the Deuteronomic reform, see Hoffman, "Jeremiah 44." The conspicuous appearance of עד היום הזה in Jer 44:10 alludes to the literature associated with Josiah's reign (Geoghegan, "Until This Day," 225–227), extending the standards of that period to Jeremiah's oracle (as in Jer 36:2; see Chapter 3). For further discussion, see "The Redactional and Hermeneutical Purpose of Jeremiah 45."

70. For a discussion of "the Queen of Heaven," see M. S. Smith, *The Early History of God: YHWH and the Other Deities in Ancient Israel* (2nd ed.; Grand Rapids, MI/Cambridge, MA: Eerdmans, 2002), 127, 182, 197; S. Ackerman, "At Home with the Goddess," *Symbiosis, Symbolism and the Power of the Past*, 461–63; Middlemas, *Templeless Judah*, 85–90. See also Halpern, "Brisker Pipes," 101–103, for the qualification of the traditional cult as foreign.
71. See the discussion in Chapter 2 of this study regarding this translation.
72. See the discussion by E. Ben Zvi, "Who Wrote the Speech of the Rabshakeh and When?" *JBL* 109 (1990), 79–92. See also Rudman, "Is the Rabshakeh Also Among the Prophets?" Rudman notes that the Rabshakeh communicates in a prophetic vein but is revealed to be a false prophet. Sharp points to thematic commonalities between the Rabshakeh's address and Jeremiah 29 and suggests that this speaks to an exilic shaping of the Rabshakeh episode (*Jeremiah*, 165–166). If any literary influence is to be felt between Jeremiah 29 and the speech of the Rabshakeh, however, it would be in the opposite direction: the Rabshakeh's speech is a perfect example of the type of false prophetic rhetoric that the faithful Israelite must resist in Deut 13:2–6, a passage that is decidedly preexilic in origin (Levinson, *Deuteronomy*, 107–127). Placing this false rhetoric in the mouth of an Assyrian officer constitutes effective polemical logic. The dramatization of Deut 13:2–6 in a narrative dealing with the survival of Jerusalem against Assyrian temptation credits the city's survival to the faithfulness of the king and the people's resistance to the Rabshakeh's taunting (2 Kgs 18:36 = Isa 36:21). This best fits a Josianic environment, invoking history as a witness at a time when Assyria, though weakened, was still a viable option for political allegiance. Assyria would only fall in 612 BCE, a full decade after the emergence of the Deuteronomic law code (2 Kgs 22:8). For the looming specter of Assyria as a political alternative to Josiah's Deuteronomic program, see Leuchter, *JRJS*, 91–107. By contrast, Jeremiah's message to the exiles of 597 perfectly fits his desire to preserve Deuteronomic law in an entirely new sociological and geographic environment (Berlin, "A Deuteronomic Allusion?," 8–11).
73. The connection between the protest in Jer 44:15–19 and the detailed rhetoric of the Rabshakeh's threats rings with increased poignancy if the position of Cogan and Tadmor is adopted that the Rabshakeh was once a northern Israelite who scaled the ranks of the Assyrian military and was sent back by Sennacherib to address his Judean kin (*II Kings*, 230; the likelihood of this decision is supported by Josiah's decision to use Jeremiah to address his own northern kin, one of many Josianic policies that were influenced by Assyrian praxes). From the Deuteronomistic perspective, though, the Rabshakeh is no Israelite, as ethnicity was defined by the very ideology that the Rabshakeh's speech rejects; see Halpern, "Jerusalem and the Lineages," 71–75. The same forces are at play in Jer 44:15–19, the details of the protest serving to condemn the protestors to the same foreign ethnic status that characterizes the Rabshakeh, regardless of his actual genealogical heritage.
74. For the historical basis underlying the account, see the discussion by Cogan and Tadmor, *II Kings*, 223–250; Ben Zvi, "The Speech of the Rabshakeh," 91–92. See also J. S. Holladay, "Assyrian Statecraft and the Prophets of Israel," *HTR* 63 (1970), 29–51.

75. Lundbom is certainly correct to note that the chapter is purposely explosive in its content and intensity as the finale of the extended narrative of chs. 37–44 (*Jeremiah 37–52*, 155).
76. The eventual movement of the remnant of this community into Egypt realizes the oracle concerning incomplete burial in Jer 34:20; separation from the homeland precludes them from burial in their ancestral tombs (see Halpern, "Jerusalem and the Lineages," 49–59), and separation from Babylon provides them with no means of adapting covenantal norms for life beyond the land (Jer 29:5–7).
77. See also G. E. Yates, "Narrative Parallelism and the 'Jehoiakim Frame': A Reading Strategy for Jeremiah 26–45," *JETS* 48 (2005), 268–270.
78. McKane (*Jeremiah* 2, 1082) suggests that the prediction concerning the defeat of Hophra by Nebuchadrezzar is an *ex eventu* statement from 570 BCE or later (in relation to the usurpation of Hophra in that year). See also Hoffman, "Jeremiah 44," 49–51, who views the Hophra reference as a post-570 addition to the chapter, though we have already seen that the *inclusio* formed by the Zedekiah reference at the beginning of Jeremiah 37 makes unlikely the secondary nature of Jer 44:30.
79. Lipschits's observations on the "poorest of the land" trope are relevant here (*Jerusalem*, 358), though as discussed previously, the appearance of this trope is not always used to discredit the post–582 BCE homeland community.
80. Pace Seitz, *Theology in Conflict*, 278; Wanke, *Baruchschrift*, 127–129; Sharp, *Jeremiah*, 157–159.
81. Again, those who remained in Judah during the period of exile are not the focus of the discussion in the Supplement; all emphasis is placed on those who fled from Judah to Egypt. It is no accident that the narrative presents the flight from the land and the consequent repudiation of the Deuteronomic covenant law (Jeremiah 44) as the direct result of Gedaliah's murder. The implication here is consistent with the rest of the Supplement: that Shaphanides like Gedaliah hold the key to properly preserving and implementing prophetic/scriptural tradition, while other forms of leadership are illegitimate. We should note that once again, the author has "skipped over" the historical chronology for the sake of rhetorical force, as with the transition from Jeremiah 36 to 37, and following the precedent set in the DH regarding Sennacherib's death at the end of 2 Kings 19.
82. So noted also by Lundbom (*Jeremiah 37–52*, 181), though only in relation to Egypt as a setting at the end of Jeremiah 44 and as the opening setting of Jeremiah 46. Whether the position of the Egypt oracle reflects the original structuring of the OAN or not is difficult to determine. Within the MT, the sequence of Jeremiah 44 as a lead-in to the OAN (following the brief Jeremiah 45; see later) makes rhetorical sense, though this may have been the result of a scribal reworking of an earlier and different OAN sequence to amplify the Supplement's argument concerning the foreign status of the Egyptian diaspora. Sharp's study of the OAN traditions in the LXX and MT strongly suggests that different versions of the OAN existed from an early point in time ("Take Another Scroll and Write," 508–509), which may have emboldened an editor to rearrange the sequence he had before him and create another version that suited the purpose of the MT sequence.
83. See Excursus 1. See also the succinct overview by Schniedewind, *Book*, 154–157.

84. See Lundbom, "Baruch, Seriah," 101–104, 107.
85. For a discussion of this interruption, see Aejmelaeus, "Turning-Point," 476–478, though one need not conclude that the chapter is a very late composition. The MT of Jeremiah 25 makes reference to texts that were directed to the 597 BCE community in Babylon and may therefore have been redacted specifically for that community. Earlier versions of the chapter would have been preserved by other communities, and one such version stands behind the LXX tradition. Furthermore, in noting similarities between the call narrative and Jeremiah 25, Aejmelaeus does not consider that the reference to foreign nations in the call narrative may relate to Jeremiah addressing the mixed ethnicities of the north in Josiah's day (see Leuchter, *JRJS*, 75–79) and thus assumes that the call narrative and Jeremiah 25 are late redactional additions to the book reflecting a significantly later era when foreign nations factored into the consciousness of the redactor/s (Aejmelaeus, "Turning-Point," 481). The role of foreign nations, in fact, is prevalent in Jeremiah's early oracles (e.g., the references to Assyria and Egypt in Jeremiah 2), and the oracles datable to the reign of Jehoiakim very often presuppose the rise of Babylon. Aejmelaeus is correct to view Jer 25:1–13 as an introduction to the OAN, but this need not arise from a post-Josianic-era redaction. The prophet was deeply concerned with the shifting political tides facing his audience (Berlin, "A Deuteronomic Allusion," 8–11; Leuchter, "Jeremiah's 70-Year Prophecy," 516–521), and Jer 25:1–13 reflects the prophet's desire to preserve the applicability of his earlier work in the face of changing international circumstances. Aejmelaeus is correct, however, to note that the disruption between Jer 25:13 and 25:14 (the latter of which is not present in the LXX) marks the point where the OAN was dislodged. The "cup of wrath" motif that was originally found in the closing portions of the OAN (Jer 51:7) and the discussion of various foreign nations in Jer 25:15–28 constitute an attempt to provide a redactional surrogate for the dislodging of the OAN from its familiar position in the text. That Jer 25:14 is absent from the LXX simply demonstrates that the curators of the LXX constructed their tradition from a textual collection that predated the composition of the Supplement and its inclusion in the Jeremianic corpus; see Chapter 5.
86. Jer 25:18 – part of the secondary composition to compensate for the incorporation of the Supplement – begins its castigation of foreign nations with a rebuking of Judah and Jerusalem. The castigation points ahead to the Supplement, which is concerned primarily with the reasons Judah and Jerusalem should receive such criticism.
87. Seitz notes that Jeremiah 45 looks forward to the OAN by virtue of its connection to כל הגוים in Jer 36:2 ("The Prophet Moses," 22) but argues that the inclusion of the OAN in the Jeremianic tradition was only secondarily facilitated by the addition of Jeremiah 45 ("The Prophet Moses," 22–25). See also Brueggemann, *To Build and to Plant,* 207, 210; Brueggemann views the phrase כל הארץ in Jer 45:5 as a bridge to the OAN. But in addition to looking ahead to the OAN, the chapter looks back to Jeremiah's call narrative. Parke-Taylor notes that Jer 45:4 refers back to Jer 1:10, where Jeremiah is commissioned as a prophet to the nations (*Formation,* 101); Lundbom (*Jeremiah 37–52*, 173) and Wanke (*Baruchschrift,* 134) both identify Jer 45:4, 5 as looking back to Jer 1:15, 18. While this may be viewed as evidence of rhetorical closure, creating an *inclusio* to delimit the extent of an initial collection ending with the word to Baruch (i.e., the LXX

sequence), it may simply reflect the desire to establish a phenomenological or pseudo-typological parallel between Baruch and Jeremiah, not necessarily for the purpose of ending a comprehensive collection. See the later discussion.

88. For Jeremiah 45 as a colophon, see Lundbom, "Baruch, Seraiah," 99–100; id., *Jeremiah 37–52*, 171–179.
89. The chapter's styling as a colophon continues the trajectory of presenting scribes as the preservers of authentic prophecy, and its placement thus colors the entire Supplement as the work of one such scribe.
90. Jer 36:16–17.
91. Seitz, "The Prophet Moses," 22.
92. Geoghegan, "Until This Day," 225–227.
93. Some scholars have viewed Jeremiah 45 as having once played a different role in earlier forms of the Jeremianic corpus. Lundbom ("Baruch, Seraiah," 100), Rietzschel (*Urrolle*, 127), and Bright (*Jeremiah*, 184–186) all suggest that Jeremiah 45 was once located after Jeremiah 20; for Lundbom, the colophonic features of the chapter pertain to its position as the actual colophon for Jeremiah's *Urrolle*, which he believes spanned Jeremiah 1–20. Sharp also views Jeremiah 45 as having originated with earlier literature subjected to a later redaction (*Jeremiah*, 89). Seitz suggests that the composition is exilic ("The Prophet Moses," 18–27); this suits its current purpose as the closing frame to the Supplement, as it creates hermeneutical connections between the various levels of tradition (i.e., the corpus inherited by the author and the Supplement created by that author). Nevertheless, Lundbom's identification of the colophonic elements in the chapter points to its foundation upon some earlier text tradition associated with Baruch and emerging from the orchestration of the prophet's *Urrolle*, even if the current text derives from an exilic hand.
94. The superscription also establishes a keyword redactional connection to the OAN, since both Jeremiah 45 and Jeremiah 46 are dated to the same year ("the fourth year of Jehoiakim").
95. See Jer 5:5. See also Lundbom, "Baruch, Seraiah," 101. Lundbom takes this sentiment to be at the heart of Jer 45:3.
96. The date of Jeremiah 25:1 should be viewed as a symbolic note marking the extension of the rewritten *Urrolle* to include the collection of oracles spanning Jeremiah 1–25 (as discussed in Excursus 1). While several scholars group Jeremiah 25 together with other chapters possessing the same date (Lundbom, *Jeremiah 21–36*, 253–254; Rofé, "Arrangement," 393–395), it seems to me that these other chapters are in fact inspired by the earlier symbolic use of "the fourth year of Jehoiakim" in Jer 25:1, especially considering the literary and temporal separation between Jeremiah 1–25 (a version of which existed by 587 BCE) and subsequent units of tradition. The date in Jer 25:1 is, as I have suggested, part of the prophet's own conclusion to the collection of his oracles in Jer 25:1–13 that came together sometime between 597 and 587. In this case, the subsequent chapters in the Supplement employing this trope are hermeneutically connected to the earlier and authoritative Jeremianic corpus. The author of the Supplement likely had Jeremiah 1–25 in mind as the literary work symbolically represented in Jeremiah 36. See R. L. Hicks, "*Delet* and *Mᵉgillāh*: A Fresh Approach to Jeremiah xxxvi," *VT* 33 (1983),

66. Hicks discusses the likely length of the scroll depicted in Jeremiah 36 as containing "between 18 and 24 chapters of our Masoretic book of Jeremiah," very closely approximating the corpus of oracles known to the exiles. Though the historical *Urrolle* would have been shorter, Jeremiah 36 is not strictly concerned with history, as we have seen. If the narrative seeks to establish Jeremiah 1–25 as the basic work of the prophet, then the "many more similar words" added to it (Jer 36:32) would certainly apply to the Supplement. Closing the Supplement with a colophonic unit like Jeremiah 45 dated to the same time as Jer 25:1 would help facilitate the connection between the author's work and his received tradition in Jeremiah 1–25.

97. For Jer 25:1–13 as a colophon, see Excursus 1.

98. Thiel (*Jeremia 26–45*, 82–90) argues that Jeremiah 45 is currently the result of Deuteronomistic relocation of the passage from its original position, and considers the שלל of 45:5 as the older composition, inspiring the appearance of the term in the Ebed-Melech episode. The redactor, for Thiel, sought to arrange the text so that Baruch is an anti-type to Jehoiakim on par with Ebed-Melech. This is certainly the effect of the current textual sequence, but it need not be attributed to secondary redaction.

99. For a discussion of how the Baruch/Ebed-Melech blessings contribute to the presentation of Jeremiah as a Mosaic prophet, see Seitz, "The Prophet Moses," 16–18.

100. See Wanke, *Baruchschrift*, 150.

101. Hoffman ("Jeremiah 44") notes that the chapter's very composition provides strong evidence not only of the historicity of Josiah's religious reform but also of a subsequent backlash against it. Thus, the religious behavior of the Judeans in Egypt is not strictly a rhetorical device but is rooted in a real social context of the author's day.

102. Here, I follow Carr's model that trained scribes like Baruch would have memorized vast amounts of standard literature (*Tablet of the Heart*, passim), though there is no reason to doubt that Baruch and others like him taken to Egypt would not have preserved some important texts in an archival fashion.

103. Dearman, "My Servants the Scribes," 418–420; Lundbom, *Jeremiah 21–36*, 590; Avigad, *Hebrew Bullae*, passim.

104. Lipschits makes a similar observation but assumes that this is reflected by the position of Baruch's colophon in the LXX (*Jerusalem*, 314).

105. Lundbom notes that a Babylonian incursion into Egypt resulting in a deportation of Judeans is recorded by Josephus and dated to shortly after 582 BCE (*Jeremiah 37–52*, 208, 215). See also Van Selms, "Telescoped Discussion," 112.

106. Even if Baruch did not go to Babylon, interchange between Babylon and Egypt in 582 BCE would have provided the opportunity for his notes, transcriptions, and annalistic materials to reach the Shaphanides. The stylistic similarity between the narratives in the Supplement and those of the DH suggests that the Supplement's narratives are based upon earlier materials much like those in the DH. In some cases, the DH involves a rewriting of annalistic sources from an earlier period. Such appears to be the case in Judges 18, which originated as propaganda for Jeroboam's cult (see Halpern, "Levitic Participation," 36–37) but, in its current state, bears the linguistic features of a later period (F. H. Polak, in conversation; Polak suggests a mid-eighth-century date for the current form of Judges 18. Space limits preclude a full treatment here, but in light of

Polak's observation, I suggest that the background to this rewriting might thus have occurred in the reign of Jeroboam II, when the legitimacy of the northern cult was indeed called into question by prophets such as Amos, with some significant public reaction [Amos 7:10]. For a summary of Polak's approach to the linguistic analysis of biblical narrative, see his "The Oral and the Written," 101–105). On the rewriting of annalistic sources in the DH, see M. Haran, "The Books of the Chronicles 'of the Kings of Judah' and 'of the Kings of Israel': What Sort of Books Were They?" *VT* 49 (1999), 156–164; see also N. Na'aman, "The Temple Library of Jerusalem and the Composition of the Book of Kings," *Congress Volume 2004* ([ed. A. Lemaire], Leiden: Brill, 2006): 129–152.

107. On a Jeremianic archive, see Leuchter, *JRJS*, 178–179.
108. Lipschits, *Jerusalem*, 314; Hoffman, "Aetiology, Redaction and Historicity in Jeremiah xxxvi," *VT* 46 (1996), 189; W. Brueggemann, "The Baruch Connection: Reflections on Jeremiah 43:1–7," *JBL* 113 (1994), 405–420.
109. The ferocity of Johanan's rebuke of Baruch in Jer 43:1–7 suggests that this was indeed the case for groups supporting ideologies that Johanan rejected. Hoffman's analysis of Jeremiah 36 points to the likelihood that Baruch was a major figure ("Aetiology," 189), as do the various seals found with his name (Dearman, "My Servants the Scribes," 412). Brueggemann notes that the historical Baruch became an emblematic character to those who developed the narratives regarding his descent into Egypt ("The Baruch Connection").
110. Pace Carroll (*Jeremiah*, 44–45), who gives little significance to Baruch (even symbolically, considering him little more than a secretary) in the formation of Jeremiah's book.
111. The uniform superscriptions should be viewed as Josianic in origin (M. A. Sweeney, *Zephaniah* [Minneapolis: Fortress Press, 2003], 46–47); thus, the recurrence of the terminology in relation to Baruch is yet another indication that he is shaded in Jeremianic colors, as Jeremiah very clearly is presented as the voice of the Deuteronomic movement surviving from Josiah's time.
112. See the earlier discussion regarding Lundbom and Wanke's comments on Jer 45:4,5 and Jer 1:15, 18. See also Brueggemann, *To Build and to Plant*, 28–29, regarding the "but you" passages in Jeremiah 1/Jeremiah 45.
113. So also O'Connor, "Do Not Trim a Word," 630.
114. To recap: the citation of prophecy in ch. 26, the addition of Jer 32:15 to the older material to the 597 BCE community, the exegetical formulae interpolated into ch. 34 and the scribes as stand-ins for Jeremiah in ch. 36, and Gedaliah's sacral leadership in ch. 40.

EXCURSUS 3

1. See Lundbom, *Jeremiah 37–52*, 501–510, for an overview of scholarship.
2. So also Lundbom, *Jeremiah 1–20/Jeremiah 21–36/Jeremiah 37–52*, passim.
3. That Seraiah's colophon (minus the "words of Jeremiah" notice) is still appended to the oracle against Babylon in the LXX tradition attests to its early connection to this oracle.

4. Dearman, "My Servants the Scribes," 421.
5. See Leuchter, "Jeremiah's 70-Year Prophecy," 521, for a discussion. See also Lundbom, *Jeremiah 37–52*, 511–538; Holladay, *Jeremiah 2*, 439–444.
6. Pace Lundbom, *Jeremiah 37–52*, 504.
7. Lundbom, *Jeremiah 1–20*, 92. See also id., "Baruch, Seraiah."
8. Gevaryahu discusses such dislodgement as resulting in the current position of the "30th year" notice in Ezekiel 1:1 ("Biblical Colophons," 530). As discussed earlier, Ezek 1:1 is best viewed as originating in its current position in relation to Ezek 1:2, but Gevaryahu's position on this scribal methodology is sound, as an early version of Jeremiah's call narrative was once connected to the early layers of Jeremiah 30–31. See Leuchter, *JRJS*, 75–81.
9. See D. W. Baker, "Biblical Colophons: Gevaryahu and Beyond," *OTWSA 27 (1984)* and *OTWSA 28 (1985)* (Pretoria, South Africa, 1986), 51. Baker notes that extraneous or anomalous material attached to colophons could be readily deleted by later editors.

5. THE POLEMICS OF EXILE

1. It is important that the text notes that there was no water (אין מים) in the pit. See D. Rudman, "The Use of Water Imagery in Descriptions of Sheol," *ZAW* 113 (2001), 240–244, for the connection between the underworld and primordial water imagery. Rudman points out that an individual's engulfment in water often indicates death and the full descent into the underworld (244). In our passage, the imagery keeps Jeremiah in a temporary though painful limbo rather than relegating him to death; his rescue by Ebed-Melech (38:11–13) symbolically parallels Jeremiah's own earlier proclamations to the 597 BCE community in Babylon that they will eventually be restored to life in the land (27:7, 22; 29:10, 14) and signifies that their residence in Babylon, like his time in the pit, will not consign them to death. This was apparently a serious concern within the exilic community; see S. M. Olyan, "'We Are Utterly Cut Off': Some Possible Nuances of נגזרנו לנו in Ezekiel 37:11," *CBQ* 65 (2003), 43–51; id., "Some Neglected Aspects," 607–608.
2. Holladay (*Jeremiah 2*, 290) notes that the dirge is a play on Zedekiah's fear that he will be mocked by the 597 BCE Babylonian community (38:19), for the women of the royal circles mock him in the dirge. This mockery, though, is a reflex to his own mistreatment of Jeremiah, and the reciprocity that characterized the proclamation against Jehoiakim in 36:30 surfaces here as well with the image of Zedekiah being stuck in the mud after having forced Jeremiah to suffer the same fate.
3. McKane (*Jeremiah 2*, 1089–1090) argues that 44:11–14 do not fit the paganistic concerns of the surrounding material in the chapter and should be considered late secondary accretions. But these verses function similarly to Huldah's oracle in announcing potential judgment (so Halpern, "Why Manasseh," 497–501) as well as the closing section of the Temple Sermon (Jer 7:12–15). Both of these are conditional upon an impious response from the audience. Jer 44:11–14 should thus be seen as original to the narrative, as the response in 44:15–19 is formally contingent upon the threat of judgment in vv. 11–14. The resulting presentation is of a community wholly separate from the foundational ideology of both the Deuteronomic and Jeremianic traditions.

4. Lundbom, however, consistently notes that the MT often does possess coherent and sometimes superior readings (*Jeremiah 21–36*, passim; id., *Jeremiah 37–52*, passim; id., "Haplography in the Hebrew Vorlage of LXX Jeremiah," *Hebrew Studies* 46 [2005], 301–320). The central question of the present study, though, concerns the overall structure of the MT vs. LXX sequences of the larger text rather than the matter of smaller-scale accretions.
5. Tov, "Some Aspects"; Janzen, *Studies in the Text of Jeremiah*; Parke-Taylor, *Formation*, 304–305. See also Aejmelaeus, "Turning-Point," 459–462, 479–481.
6. Steiner, "The Two Sons of Neriah," 83–84; Lundbom, "Baruch, Seraiah," 108–109; Freedman and Kelly, "Who Redacted the Primary History?," 43–45.
7. So also Seitz ("The Prophet Moses," 24–26), though his view of the redactional process is different from that advanced here.
8. See especially Levinson, *Deuteronomy*, 144–151, for Deuteronomy as a carefully constructed scribal work pseudepigraphically attributed to Moses. Similar anonymous scribal redaction in the service of prophetic figures characterizes the redaction of various other prophetic texts during the Josianic period. See Sweeney, *King Josiah*, 311–313.
9. So also J. E. Wright, *Baruch ben Neriah: From Biblical Scribe to Apocalyptic Seer* (Columbia: University of South Carolina Press, 2003), 36–37.
10. For these scribes as associated with the Deuteronomistic group, see Dearman, "My Servants the Scribes," 419. Hoffman has challenged the possibility that a narrative such as Jeremiah 36 could have been written by a scribe mentioned within its verses for the same reason that scholars do not attribute narratives about Jeremiah to the prophet's own hand ("Aetiology, Redaction and Historicity in Jeremiah xxxvi," 181), but if this material was meant to be subsumed within the "words of Jeremiah," then authorship of the narratives is hermeneutically connected to the prophet.
11. Leuchter, *JRJS*, 169.
12. Bedford, "Diaspora: Homeland Relations."
13. See the discussion in Excursus 2.
14. The appeal to Jeremianic prophecy is uniformly evidenced in texts associated with Judeans in Babylon or restored from there to the homeland. For the centrality of Jeremiah to Deutero-Isaiah, see Sommer, *A Prophet Reads Scripture*, 32–72. See also Hag 1:2 (implicitly), Zech 1:12, Ezra 1:1, and 2 Chr 36:22, all of which are concerned with Jeremianic prophecy regarding residence in Babylon and eventual restoration.
15. See the discussion in the Introduction to this study.
16. On the Supplement's recognition of variant collections, see Sharp, "Take Another Scroll and Write," 508–509.
17. The commonalities between the MT and LXX demonstrate that the LXX curators relied heavily on the Supplement in its MT form, but in many places, significant variants occur that attest to parallel sources used by these scribes to replace that which had obtained in the earlier version emanating from Babylon. See the additional later discussion.
18. The subsequent appearance of the Supplement in the developing LXX tradition accounts for the lack of certain material currently found in MT Jer 25:13b–38; much of this secondary unit eventually reached the scribes who shaped the LXX, as it was secondarily worked into that text following the OAN (MT 25:13b = LXX 32:13; MT 25:15–26 = LXX

32:1–12). The scribes preserving the developing LXX material had no need to provide a surrogate for the OAN following Jer 25:13 and therefore left this material out of their already fixed version of Jeremiah 25. It is clear, however, that the OAN in the MT has undergone significant subsequent editing and expansion, as it does not correspond closely with the material in Jer 25:15–26; see Parke-Taylor, *Formation*, 111–112. Moreover, different forms of the OAN collection appear to have circulated at various times (Sharp, "Take Another Scroll and Write," 508–509). It is best simply to say that the editors of the MT and the LXX versions recognized the need for *some* OAN collection tied to the Jeremianic tradition to factor into the respective text sequences they produced; the present study proposes that the collection in the MT finds its roots in a fairly early version of the OAN already bound to the preexilic corpus. This same period may, however, be the best background to view the interpolation of Jeremiah 21 into the LXX sequence of Jeremiah 1–25, anticipating as it does the eventual narratives in the Supplement at the end of the corpus.

19. See Seitz, "The Prophet Moses," 24; W. E. Lemke, "The Near and Distant God: A Study of Jeremiah 23:23–24 in Its Biblical Theological Context," *JBL* 100 (1981), 554–555; Parke-Taylor, *Formation*, 101.

20. Indeed, the formation of the LXX tradition in this manner attests to the relative fluidity of Jewish scripture in the Second Temple period, a fluidity witnessed as late as the composition of the Temple Scroll at Qumran, which rewrites various Pentateuchal laws into a systematic and unified collection with minor but important changes in terminology. Carr suggests that it is only with the Hasmoneans that Jewish scripture obtains a "fixed" form (*Tablet of the Heart*, 253–272), though the Temple Scroll demonstrates that even this fixed canon was not accepted by all Second Temple Jewish factions. For the gradual fixing of scripture, see Watts, "Scriptural Authority," 412–417.

21. Wright, *Baruch ben Neriah*, 36–37. Though Wright's proposed relative dating of the LXX and the MT differs from the scenario proposed herein, his insight into the function of Baruch's colophon in both traditions is applicable to the present discussion.

22. It is noteworthy that in Neh 8:9, the people weep at the words of the Torah only *after* Ezra's Levite officers offer exegesis, suggesting that the "Torah" in question is inclusive of their exegesis. The process of scribal exegesis thus replaces prophecy as the facilitator of YHWH's instruction. For Levites as scribal officers during this period, see note 23. For connections between the Deuteronomistic tradition and the period of Ezra, see T. Veijola, "The Deuteronomistic Origins of Judaism," *Sefer Moshe: The Mose Weinfeld Jubilee Volume* (ed. C. Cohen et al.; Winona Lake, IN: Eisenbrauns, 2004), 459–478.

23. See D. L. Petersen, *Late Israelite Prophecy: Studies in Deutero-Prophetic Literature and in Chronicles* (SBLM 23; Missoula, MT: Scholars Press, 1977), 45, 97–102 (though we adopt the majority view that this literature emerges from the fourth century BCE; see G. N. Knoppers, *I Chronicles 1–9* [AB 12; New York: Doubleday, 2003], 111–117; Boccaccini, *Roots of Rabbinic Judaism*, 72); M. S. Smith, "The Levitical Compilation of the Psalter," *ZAW* 103 (1991), 258–263. See also Schaper, "Exilic and Post-Exilic Prophecy," 334–342, for the prophetic antecedents to this phenomenon.

24. See J. M. Lindenberger (ed.), *Ancient Aramaic and Hebrew Letters* (2nd ed.; Atlanta: SBL, 2003), 63–64, 72–79.

25. Lundbom notes that there is some significant damage to the text in the LXX parallel of MT Jeremiah 44, which led the scribe to piece together as best he could a coherent reading (*Jeremiah 37–52*, 160–161). The scribe's sources were probably fairly old and damaged by time and handling in some places, and may reflect the long process of transmission of the sources of the LXX curators.
26. While many LXX cases reflect a reading that may be closer to an original version of a given unit (i.e., LXX Jer 25:1–13), the MT often preserves versions of texts that are closer to original readings and consistent with ancient Near Eastern culture in Israel's preexilic period. See B. M. Levinson, "Textual Criticism, Assyriology, and the History of Interpretation: Deuteronomy 13:7a as a Test Case in Method," *JBL* 120 (2001), 211–243. See also the careful analysis of B. Becking, "Jeremiah's Book of Consolation: A Textual Comparison: Notes on the Masoretic and the Old Greek Version of Jeremiah xxx–xxxi," *VT* 44 (1994), 145–169, which identifies pluses in the MT that constitute better readings than the LXX. For a general critique of text-critical problems with the LXX, see Lundbom, "Haplography." See also the later discussion.
27. Cogan and Tadmor, *II Kings*, 320–321. It is difficult to evaluate which version – Jeremiah 52 or 2 Kings 25 – more accurately reflects the events of the deportations of 587–582 BCE. Though Lipschits views Jeremiah 52 as directly derived from 2 Kings 25 (*Jerusalem*, 337), Albertz discusses some significant differences (*Israel in Exile*, 81–90). It does seem, though, that Jeremiah 39 is more closely related to Jeremiah 52, as Lipschits has demonstrated (*Jerusalem*, 336–338), though his view that Jer 39:4–10 was the result of a later redaction after Jeremiah 52 was appended to a larger narrative work is not conclusive. See the immediately following discussion.
28. The details in Jer 39:4–10 may have been drawn from the same source as those we currently encounter in Jeremiah 52, and this need not have occurred after the development of the larger narrative in Jeremiah 37–44 (or, indeed, the orchestration of material beginning in Jeremiah 26). As we have seen, multiple allusions within the Supplement anticipate the burning of Jerusalem, which suggests that the author composed these allusions with the details in Jer 39:4–10 already available to him. The view of Cogan and Tadmor that a common annalistic source (or sources) underlies this passage and those of 2 Kings 25/Jeremiah 52 is still quite tenable. In support of this is the discussion by G. Fischer, "Jeremia 52 – ein Schlüssel zum Jeremiabuch," *Bib* 79 (1998), 333–358. Fischer notes the secondary dependence of Jeremiah 39 on the details in Jeremiah 52 (353–355) but also points out that Jeremiah 52 was shaped with an eye to a much larger literary collection. This suggests that Jeremiah 52 incorporated the same details that lay behind Jer 39:4–10, but the redactor built around them materials that relate to the corpus well beyond the parameters of the Supplement.
29. As observed in Excursus 3, the LXX tradents did not feel compelled to include textual units that they considered unnecessary, and Lundbom has noted deletions in the LXX where the scribe in question considered his source to be redundant or verbose (*Jeremiah 21–36*, 242).
30. All evidence would suggest, in fact, that the community in Babylon behind the MT would have been able to preserve better copies of original Jeremianic texts even if some of those texts underwent subsequent revisions. The population deported in 597 BCE

constituted much of Jerusalem's literary elite, who would have been able to carry important texts with them into captivity or obtain copies over the years of interaction with the home community before Jerusalem's destruction (pace Carr, *Tablet of the Heart*, 167–168). In fact, the status that sacred scripture had obtained by the late seventh century would increase the likelihood that these texts were taken to Babylon according to the Babylonian practice of deporting the sacred icons of conquered people. The deportation of 587, though, would probably have matched more closely the circumstance that Carr reconstructs. By contrast, those retreating later into Egypt would have had less access to intact source texts and would have partially reproduced many text traditions from memory (Carr, *Tablet of the Heart*, 168). This would account for many of the text-critical variants in a number of LXX passages.

31. See Steiner, "The Two Sons of Neriah," 84.
32. So also Seitz, "The Prophet Moses," 22.
33. The appearance of Seraiah's colophon after the oracle against Babylon in the LXX identifies that oracle, in an early form, as the text initially closed by that colophon, and as observed earlier, a form of Jeremiah 1–25 was also connected to it via a redaction shortly after its composition (see Excursus 1). Thus, Seraiah's colophon would have originated well before we can speak of MT/LXX versions in any form. Lundbom is probably correct that the "book" referred to in Jer 25:13 related initially to the oracle against Babylon before additional foreign nation oracles were added (*Jeremiah 21–36*, 238–239, 251), though as discussed in Excursus 1, this reference both looks ahead to this oracle and back as a colophon to the preceding text in Jeremiah 1–24. The ability to summarize and anticipate is a feature of verses within the chapter; see D. Grossberg, "Pivotal Polysemy in Jeremiah xxv 10–11 a," *VT* 36 (1986), 481–485.
34. See Excursus 1. See also Holladay, *Jeremiah 2*, 434.
35. As discussed earlier, it is clear that Baruch's colophon is eventually used to close the LXX corpus, but as per the foregoing discussion, this is not because Baruch himself is responsible for editing the LXX.
36. On the cessation of classical prophecy, see R. J. Tournay, *Seeing and Hearing God in the Psalms* (JSOTsup 118; Sheffield, UK: Sheffield Academic Press, 1991), 46–56; Petersen, *Late Israelite Prophecy*, 97–100. The period seeing the end of this phenomenon, however, should be placed after the late sixth century BCE.
37. See the discussion by Peckham, *History and Prophecy*, 741, 750–755. For prophecy as still dominant during the late sixth century BCE, see B. D. Sommer, "Did Prophecy Cease? Evaluating a Re-Evaluation," *JBL* 115 (1996), 31–47. For classical prophetic works as a cornerstone of the Deuteronomistic tradition, see Sweeney, *King Josiah*, 311–313.
38. Pace Janzen, *Studies*, 116, who views the "words of Jeremiah" notice as a late gloss. See Excursus 3 for a discussion of the LXX version of Seraiah's colophon, which lacks the "words of Jeremiah" notice.
39. Pace Hoffman, "Aetiology," 181, who does not note that Jeremiah remains the author of the book, including the narrative material subsumed within its pages. Hoffman is probably quite correct, however, to be cautious about attributing these narratives solely to Baruch, as discussed in Chapter 4.

40. The counterargument, of course, is that while the Judeans in Babylon were taken captive, the Judeans in Egypt chose residency therein, and one might imagine that social conditions would differ significantly between the two locations. Nevertheless, both groups were resident aliens, separated from their national territory, cult, and political leadership, and both faced significant questions concerning how any continuity of life could be preserved. Indeed, we might suggest that the Judeans of Babylon had an advantage insofar as Judeans had been living in Mesopotamia since the eighth century BCE in distinct communities still able to stay in contact with the homeland until Jerusalem's destruction. Judah's position as an Assyrian vassal would have facilitated contact with Judeans living in Assyria proper; see J. Pečírková, "The Administrative Methods of Assyrian Imperialism," *Archív Orientální* 55 (1987), 162–175. Pečírková notes the close correspondence maintained between the governments of vassal states and the central administration in the Assyrian capitals. Only in the final decade of the seventh century would the kingdom of Judah be part of a different diplomatic/political sphere, which would hardly provide enough time for expatriate Judeans to lose touch with those who would eventually join them in Mesopotamia.
41. For the anti-Egyptian position, see Chapter 4 (re: Deuteronomic references to Egypt); Hoffman, "The Exodus in Hosea and Amos," Separation from Egypt as an elemental aspect of Israelite identity is felt in early narrative traditions as well, e.g., 1 Samuel 2:28; for the antiquity of this verse, see M. Leuchter, "Something Old, Something Older: Reconsidering 1 Sam 2:27–36," *JHS* 4 (2003), Article 6.1.1–3.1. See also S. D. Sperling, *The Original Torah: The Political Intent of the Bible's Writers* (New York/London: New York University Press, 1998), 41–60, 144–151. The presupposition of Egyptian illegitimacy underlies Ezekiel's diatribe against Egypt in Ezek 30:13–26 and his rebuking of the elders who consider idolatry in Ezek 20:1–38 (esp. vv. 5–10). See M. Greenberg, *Ezekiel 1–20* (AB 22; Garden City, NY: Doubleday, 1983), 376–388 (see also the additional later discussion on Ezek 20:1–38).
42. On the centrality of the scribal process in Deuteronomistic literature, see Levinson, *Deuteronomy*, passim; Weinfeld, *Deuteronomy and the Deuteronomic School*, 177–178.
43. See Leuchter, *JRJS*, 132–152.
44. Leuchter, "Jeremiah's 70-Year Prophecy," 515.
45. Leuchter, "The Temple Sermon," 105.
46. This may well have been prompted by a brief period of Babylonian political instability in the early years of the sixth century BCE. See Bright, *A History of Israel*, 329.
47. S. W. Hahn and J. S. Bergsma, "What Laws Were 'Not Good'? A Canonical Approach to the Theological Problem of Ezekiel 20:25–26," *JBL* 123 (2004), 217–218.
48. For a reconstruction of the forces leading to an exilic priestly redaction of the Pentateuch, see D. Rooke, *Zadok's Heirs* (Oxford: Oxford University Press, 2000), 12–13, though Rooke dates this P orchestration toward the end of the exile (ca. 550–540 BCE). The traditions and texts themselves must have predated this period of redaction. On the preexilic origin of the Holiness Code and other P traditions, see Knohl, *The Sanctuary of Silence*, 199–218; J. Milgrom, *Leviticus 1–16* (AB; Garden City, NY: Doubleday, 1991), 13–35; M. Haran, "Behind the Scenes of History: Determining the Date of the Priestly Source," *JBL* 100 (1981), 321–333; A. Hurvitz, "Once Again: The Linguistic Profile of the Priestly Material

in the Pentateuch and Its Historical Age: A Response to J. Blenkinsopp," *ZAW* 112 (2000), 180–191. See Leuchter, *JRJS*, 88–90, for a discussion of Jeremiah's preexilic reliance on P as a well-established tradition by the early Josianic period. Nevertheless, the Holiness Code appears to have received an update subsequent to the Deuteronomic law code as a reaction against it, and the exile would appear to have been an ideal environment to engender such a response. See Levinson, "Manumission of Hermeneutics"; id., B. A. Levine, "The Epilogue to the Holiness Code: A Priestly Statement on the Destiny of Israel," *Judaic Perspectives on Ancient Israel*, 29–31.

49. Geoghegan notes that the phrase עד היום הזה, which characterized the preexilic (possibly Josianic era) redaction of the DH ("Until This Day," 225–227), serves a very similar redactional purpose in the Tetrateuch ("Additional Evidence for a Deuteronomistic Redaction of the 'Tetrateuch,'" *CBQ* 67 [2005], 405–421). Geoghegan suggests that the Tetrateuch was redacted by the same scribe or scribes responsible for the preexilic DH (416–421), though Levinson has demonstrated that the Josianic scribes responsible for Deuteronomy composed their work to push aside other traditions, including the laws currently found in the Tetrateuch (*Deuteronomy*, 152–154). Geoghegan's argument is compelling with regard to an initial redaction of narrative traditions now found in the Pentateuch; the Josianic-era focus on the Deuteronomistic literature need not have obviated the significance of other narrative or liturgical compositions. One may view a Josianic redaction in Psalm 78, for example, a decidedly pre-Josianic composition having much in common with the epic Pentateuchal traditions. For a discussion; see also A. F. Campbell, "Psalm 78: A Contribution to the Theology of Tenth Century Israel," *CBQ* 41 (1979), 51–79; J. Day, "Pre-Deuteronomistic Allusions to the Covenant in Hosea and Psalm lxxviii," *VT* 36 (1986), 3–11; for a more recent evaluation of scholarship on this psalm and a proposal for a Solomonic date, see Leuchter, "Psalm 78." Still, whatever Josianic-era redactional flourishes we may identify in the Pentateuchal narratives were subordinated to exilic Zadokite redactional interests, which may also have included the appropriation of the lexical formulae originating at an earlier point (e.g., the appearance of עד היום הזה in Ezek 20:29). For a recent discussion of the Zadokite polemics in the redaction of the Tetrateuch, see G. Hepner, "The Begettings of Terah and the Structure of Genesis and the Tetrateuch: A Zadokite Polemic," *RB* 111 (2004), 31–60. For the Zadokite redaction of the Pentateuch, see Knohl, *The Sanctuary of Silence*, 95, 103, 200–203.

50. Rooke, *Zadok's Heirs*, 12. See also D. Rom-Shiloni, "Facing Destruction and Exile" (with respect to similar ideas emerging in Ezekiel; see the later discussion).

51. Hahn and Bergsma, "What Laws Were 'Not Good'?" 217–218.

52. Ezek 1:1 dates the first vision to "the 30th year" of the exile. Ezekiel was among those deported to Babylon in 597 BCE, and therefore many scholars view this notice as a late redactional accretion dating the book's principal shaping to the year 568/567; see Gevaryahu, "Biblical Colophons," 52–53; Freedman, *Divine Commitment and Human Obligation*, 346–347. However, in light of the date provided by Ezek 1:2 (592) and the prophet's antagonism to the Deuteronomic reform (reported in 2 Kgs 22:3 to have begun in 622, 30 years earlier than Ezek 1:2), the date in Ezekiel 1:1 would seem a very appropriate polemical statement against the Deuteronomistic movement.

53. For a recent analysis of Ezekiel's visions and their ideological function, see D. Launderville, "Ezekiel's Throne-Chariot Vision: Spritualizing the Model of Divine Royal Rule," *CBQ* 66 (2004), 361–377.
54. For the exclusivity of the Zadokite interpretation of events and visions, see M. A. Sweeney, "Ezekiel: Zadokite Priest and Visionary Prophet of the Exile," *SBL 2000 Seminar Papers* (Atlanta: SBL, 2000), 735–739. See also M. Haran, "The Law Code of Ezekiel xl–xlviii and Its Relation to the Priestly School," *HUCA* 50 (1979), 45–46.
55. On the Deuteronomic "mistake," see Hahn and Bergsma, "What Laws Were 'Not Good'?" 217–218. For a detailed examination of the restoration program in Ezekiel 40–48, see J. D. Levenson, *Theology of the Program of Restoration in Ezekiel 40–48* (*HSM* 10; Missoula, MT: Scholars Press, 1976).
56. See R. Levitt Kohn, "A Prophet Like Moses? Rethinking Ezekiel's Relationship to the Torah," *ZAW* 114 (2002), 236–254.
57. In "'The Levite in Your Gates': The Deuteronomic Redefinition of Levitical Authority," (forthcoming in *JBL*), I argue that the rural Levites of the Josianic period who were charged with supporting the central Deuteronomic laws of Jerusalem (by taking on the roles of judges and scribes/magistrates as per Deut 16:18) maintained a similar role during the exilic period as local custodians and interpreters of law and other written traditions. For a summary discussion of the scribal/administrative role of the Levites according to the Josianic-era legislation, see Leuchter, *JRJS*, 36, 41–42; id., "Jeremiah's 70-Year Prophecy," 512 n. 31. Both the local Levites and the Shaphanides stood to lose considerable influence due to the rhetoric of Ezekiel (e.g., Ezek 44:10–13) and the Zadokite agenda. The implicit role of rural Levites as scribes and local administrators in the preexilic period and the overt identification of Levites as scribes in the literature of the postexilic period suggest a close relationship forged between the Shaphanide scribes and the Levites as an exilic coalition opposing the Zadokites. See the further discussion later.
58. Though Lipschits argues convincingly that many Judean refugees fled to Benjamin and the northern frontier of Judah, the archaeological evidence he cites reveals that Jerusalem and the nearby regions suffered deportation; other urban centers and royal fortresses that held out against Babylon would have suffered the same fate (*Jerusalem*, 258). See further Albertz, *Israel in Exile*, 106–107; B. Oded, "Judah and the Exile," *Israelite and Judaen History* (ed. J. H. Hayes and J. M. Miller; London: SCM, 1977), 470, 479. J. Weinberg points to an intermediate system emulating the structure of the preexilic patrilineal lines but expanding their scope to suit the features of the communities forged through resettlement during the postexilic period (*The Citizen-Temple Community* [trans. D. L. Smith-Christopher; JSOTSup 151; Sheffield, UK: Sheffield Academic Press, 1992], 49–61). Given the dominance of the exilic experience to these communities, we may imagine some exilic antecedent to this postexilic model (Bedford, "Homeland: Diaspora Relations").
59. The scribal duties of the Levites are evidenced not only by the written character of the law code they are charged to administer and interpret (interpretation of the law is presupposed in Deut 17:8), but also by the etymology of the title שוטרים in Deut 16:18. The root שטר denotes writing in other biblical contexts as well as with its Akkadian cognate *šṭr*. See M. Fishbane, "*Min haššāmayim dibbartî*: 'I spoke from heaven' (Exod 20:22),"

Sefer Moshe, 36–37, for a brief discussion. The term שוטרים is therefore polyvalent, as it implies that administration/governance is firmly rooted in the interpretation and development of written materials. This matches well with the presentation of Gedaliah, a Shaphanide (scribe) who is presented as translating Jeremiah's written oracles into an administrative program in Jer 40:10.

60. The implicit role of rural Levites as scribes and local administrators in the preexilic period and the overt identification of Levites as scribes in the literature of the postexilic period suggest a close relationship forged between the Shaphanide scribes and the Levites as an exilic coalition opposing the Zadokites. See Chapter 6 for a full discussion of the relationship between the Shaphanides and the Levites during the exile.
61. Sweeney suggests that Ezekiel's active ministry corresponds to the time in which a Jerusalem priest was to carry out his active service in the Temple ("Ezekiel," 734–735).
62. Sweeney, "Ezekiel," 734–735.
63. Schniedewind notes that Ezekiel's actual career appears to have ended ca. 585 BCE (*Book*, 157). Zimmerli, however, considers the oracle in Ezek 29:17–21 – which is dated to 572/571 – to be authentic and historically reliable (*Ezekiel 2* [Minneapolis: Fortress Press, 1983], 118).
64. Sweeney, "Ezekiel," 734–735. Ezekiel 20 in particular contains an especially large number of Deuteronomistic terms, but they are all set within a distinctively Zadokite terminological/ideological matrix. See Greenberg, *Ezekiel 1–20*, 363–388; D. I. Block, *The Book of Ezekiel, Chapters 1–24* (Grand Rapids, MI: Cambridge, MA: Eerdmans, 1997), 641–645; T. Krüger, *Geschichtskonzepte im Ezechielbuch* (*BZAW*, 180; Berlin: de Gruyter, 1989), 210–212; see also Weinfeld, "Spiritual Metamorphosis," 31–33. For Ezekiel's use of Deuteronomistic language more generally, see Levitt Kohn, "A Prophet Like Moses?"
65. For Ezekiel as a Mosaic figure, see Levitt Kohn, "A Prophet like Moses?," 252–254. For the typological distinctions between Mosaic prophets and Jerusalem priests, see Sweeney, *King Josiah*, 163.
66. The Zophim constituted an old prophetic group associated first with the Shiloh sanctuary and whose tradition persists through subsequent northern prophetic discourses. See Leuchter, *JRJS*, 27–28, 30–31. See further L. S. Tiemeyer, "The Watchman Metaphor."
67. See Fishbane, "Accusations of Adultery," 42.
68. Boccaccini, *Roots of Rabbinic Judaism*, 44–48.
69. The early Babylonian chronicles do not present Jehoiachin as an imprisoned king; Albertz plausibly suggests that the murder of Gedaliah prompted Jehoiachin's imprisonment (*Israel in Exile*, 103–104).
70. Friedman and Kelly, "Who Redacted the Primary History?" 40–41.
71. See J. D. Levenson, "The Last Four Verses in Kings," *JBL* 103 (1984), 353–361. Lipschits notes that the presence of these verses, which constitute a supplemental accretion to the initial exilic redaction of the DH, emphasizes compliance with Babylonian rule (*Jerusalem*, 356–357).
72. Zimmerli, *Ezekiel 2*, 118.
73. See Leuchter, "Tyre's 70 Years."
74. Assyria's protological position had been in place for some time; see P. Machinist, "The Rāb Šāqēh at the Wall of Jerusalem: Israelite Identity in the Face of the Assyrian

'Other,'" *Hebrew Studies* 41 (2000), 166–168. The expiration of Isa 23:15–18 in one breath and its renewal under Babylon in the next must have extended this protological analogy.

75. For the attempted restoration of Hophra, see Albertz, *Israel in Exile*, 56–57. The restoration of Hophra was not successful, but the imperialistic efforts of Nebuchadrezzar in this regard undoubtedly would have had major implications for the scope of Babylon's geopolitical intentions.
76. See Boccaccini, *Roots of Rabbinic Judaism*, 44–48. The oracle in Ezekiel 37 may derive from a considerably earlier period, at a time when total capitulation to Babylonian imperialism had not yet become a matter of exilic Judean royal policy. We may tentatively date this oracle, in some form, to sometime after 593 BCE, as it appears to draw from the themes of north–south reconciliation in the oracles of Jeremiah 30–31 sent to the deportees at around that time (see Chapter 2) and develops the idea of a restoration of the old Zion tradition with the Davidic king depicted in Messianic language (Ezek 37:11).
77. Boccaccini, *Roots of Rabbinic Judaism*, 48; Schniedewind, *Book*, 153–157. The antecedents to the division of the royal literati into camps affiliated with specific descendants of Josiah (to the exclusion of others) emerge in Josiah's own time. See Wilcoxen, "Jeremiah's Temple Sermon."
78. Leuchter, "The Temple Sermon."
79. The chapter thus again anticipates Jeremiah 36, where this issue is further developed (Dearman, "My Servants the Scribes," 411–412).
80. For the important sociopolitical position of the elders and patrilineal structures during the exile, see Weinberg, *The Citizen-Temple Community*, 49–61. The influence of the elders no doubt informs both Ezekiel's appeals and the role of the elders in Jer 26:17–19.
81. As noted earlier, the view that the reference to Jehoiakim in Jer 27:1 is a textual corruption and that the subsequent scholarly attempts to "restore" the text are precipitous (e.g., McKane, *Jeremiah* 2, 685). They reflect a too narrow view of the text's meaning and purpose.
82. We might also see the exacting detail concerning the interior of the Temple in Jeremiah 35–36 as an attempt to demonstrate that the scribes have as much of a claim to intimate association with the Temple cult as the Zadokites, and that their views on its illegitimacy are thus the views of knowledgeable insiders.
83. In this respect, the Supplement's author follows an earlier and similar episode in Jer 11:18–23, where the prophet calls down vengeance upon his own Shilonite kin for transgressing Deuteronomic law and in keeping with the legislation of Deut 13:7–10. See Leuchter, *JRJS*, 97–100. For additional discussion of how transgression against Deuteronomistic tradition trumps matters of kinship or lineage, see B. M. Levinson, "Recovering the Lost Original Meaning of ולא תכסה עליו (Deuteronomy 13:9)," *JBL* 115 (1996), 601–620; L. Stulman, "Encroachment in Deuteronomy: An Analysis of the Social World of the D Code," *JBL* 109 (1990), 613–632.
84. Hoffman, "Jeremiah 44," 47–50. Such is also implied by the position of the Babylonian Judeans who approach Ezekiel in Ezekiel 20:32. See Rom-Shiloni, "Facing Destruction and Exile," 194–198.

85. Wright, *Baruch ben Neriah*, 32.
86. See the discussion in Chapter 4.
87. This would also account for the adaptation of Jer 27:1 by the author of the Supplement in Jer 26:1, who omits the phrase "unto Jeremiah" as a way of proclaiming his scribal work as subordinate to Jeremiah's ongoing prophetic authority (see Chapter 2).
88. The parallel between the Moses/Joshua and Jeremiah/Baruch dynamic has already been identified by Seitz ("The Prophet Moses," 17–18), though Seitz does not go beyond formalistic observations and consider the rhetoric purpose of such a parallel. Jeremiah identified himself as a Deuteronomic prophet like Moses as early as 609 BCE with the delivery of the Temple Sermon and reinforced this typological position with the creation of the *Urrolle* (Leuchter, *JRJS*, 116–117, 156–158).
89. Jer 18:18 presupposes the prevailing role of the priesthood in Torah instruction.
90. See the earlier discussion regarding the scribal dimensions of the שפטים ושוטרים addressed in this verse.
91. Jeremiah 45 also implies that these blessings are to be found in places other than Jerusalem and are not contingent upon strict devotion to the Temple. See Leuchter, "The Temple Sermon," 108–109.
92. The force of this particular point rings with an irony that would not have gone unnoticed by the exilic audience, as the book of Ezekiel reports that Ezekiel himself used the Exodus tradition to legitimize his politico-religious rhetoric against alternative cultic practices (Ezek 20:1–38). See Rom-Shiloni, "Facing Destruction and Exile," 194–202.
93. Here we must draw a distinction between Ezekiel's activity and the formation of the book of Ezekiel. Levitt Kohn discusses the similarities between the Zadokite redactor of the Pentateuch and the content of Ezekiel's prophecies ("A Prophet Like Moses," 250–254), and Knohl also assigns Ezekiel to the Zadokite group responsible for giving rise to the Pentateuch (*Sanctuary of Silence*, 101–102). While the prophet himself likely stands very closely behind the contents of the book, it seems reasonable to envision subsequent editorial activity involving his disciples, most likely Zadokite priests, and it is probably they who preserved his teachings after the final period of his activity and shaped Ezekiel's oracles into the closing section of the book (Ezek 40–48) and elsewhere. In any case, the book of Ezekiel contains a consistent theological and sociological position that faithfully represents the thought of the prophet.
94. As discussed in the Introduction to the present study, 570 BCE seems to be a likely approximate date for the Supplement's emergence. Despite Hoffman's suggestion that the reference in Jer 44:30 to Hophra's dethronement may be a secondary addition to the chapter ("History and Ideology," 47–48), we have already seen that there is good reason to date it as original to the chapter and indeed as an integral part of the entire Supplement (see Chapter 4). The entire enterprise, then, cannot much postdate Hophra's deposition in 570. It is unlikely that Jer 44:30 refers to Hophra's death during Nebuchadrezzar's attempt to restore him to power in 567; a pro-Babylonian writer would hardly depict YHWH delivering Hophra "into the hand of his enemies" if YHWH's chosen agent, Nebuchadrezzar, had been trying to support him. Furthermore, 570 is the year when Nebuchadrezzar himself appears to have publicly affirmed the preeminent position of Babylon via initiation of important religious and secular building projects (Albertz,

Israel in Exile, 58), a cue that would have likely influenced Shaphanide political perceptions. The *terminus ad quem* for the construction of the Supplement should therefore be placed between 570 and 567 (Nebuchadrezzar's attempt to restore Hophra to the throne).

6. THE EXILIC COALITION BETWEEN THE SHAPHANIDES AND LEVITES

1. Carr, *Tablet of the Heart*, 168–169; Schniedewind, *Book*, 156–157; see also Polak, "Style," 53 (though Polak does not restrict the redactional activity to an exilic context); S. B. Parker, "Did the Authors of the Book of Kings Make Use of Royal Inscriptions?" *VT* 50 (2000), 357–378, who notes that the redactional language of the book of Kings is highly conversant with the norms of ancient Near Eastern royal court discourse (373–374).
2. For example, Deuteronomy 4; 1 Kgs 9:8–9; 2 Kgs 17:19; 21:12–15 (see the Conclusion to the present study for an analysis of this passage); 23:26–27.
3. Weinfeld, *Deuteronomy and the Deuteronomic School*, 178–179.
4. Geoghegan, "Until This Day"; Leuchter, "Song of Moses"; Schniedewind, *Book*, 110–114.
5. 2 Kgs 23:9 is periodically understood as a fly in the ointment, with many scholars viewing the phrase כי אם as revealing a refusal of certain Levites to join in the Deuteronomic program. The occurrence of the phrase כי אם elsewhere, however, implies conditionality (i.e., "until"); see W. Boyd Barrick, *The King and the Cemeteries: Toward a New Understanding of Josiah's Reform* (Leiden/Boston/Köln: Brill, 2003), 189–193, for a full discussion. Consequently, 2 Kings 23:9 specifies that the rural Judean Levites did not come to minister at the Temple *until* they administered the Josianic Passover among their local communities, which suggests an effective application of the reform program among the Levites of Judah.
6. Leuchter, *JRJS*, 41–42; id., "The Levite in Your Gates."
7. These regional rulings were likely recorded in written form; see Weingreen, *From Bible to Mishna: The Continuity of Tradition* (Manchester, UK: Manchester University Press, 1976), 95–97.
8. Lipschits, *Jerusalem*, 271, who also notes significant deportation in the Shephelah.
9. Considering Jeremiah's own Levitical status, a methodological precedent may be found in Jeremiah 29:5–7 (see Chapter 2).
10. See especially E. Assis, "Why Edom? On the Hostility Towards Jacob's Brother in Prophetic Sources," *VT* 56 (2006), 14–19.
11. Weinfeld, *Deuteronomy 1–11*, 78–81; Weingreen, *From Bible to Mishna*, 115–128 (though Weinfeld and Weingreen both discuss preexilic activity that they see as carrying over into the exilic circumstance). See also Nicholson, *Preaching to the Exiles*, 134–135. Nicholson's proposal that the prose tradition in the book of Jeremiah directly reflects a tradition of synagogue-type sermons/preaching does not stand up to scrutiny, since as we have seen in the present study, these materials reveal very careful and deliberate literary subtleties uncharacteristic of oral discourse. See Polak, "Style," 54; id., "The Oral and the Written," 101–105. See also M. Z. Brettler, "A 'Literary Sermon' in Deuteronomy 4," *A Wise and Discerning Mind: Essays in Honor of Burke O. Long* (ed. S. M. Olyan and R. C. Culley; *BJS*, 325; Providence, RI: Brown University, 2000), 33–50. With respect to the common

redactional style and methods of the DH and the Supplement discussed herein, see Haran, "What Sort of Books," 163. Yet, though the current form of the Supplement and a variety of passages in the Deuteronomistic works reveal meticulous scribal design, we may accept the view that the origins of these compositions arose from a culture influenced by Levitical teachings and meditation; see the later discussion.

12. Brettler, "A 'Literary Sermon,'" 39; L. I. Levine, *The Ancient Synagogue: The First Thousand Years* (New Haven, CT/London: Yale University Press, 2000), 26–41; id., "The Nature and Origin of the Palestinian Synagogue Reconsidered," *JBL* 115 (1996), 425–448 (esp. 432–436).
13. Rom-Shiloni, "Facing Destruction and Exile," 203–204. Both the Jeremiah and Ezekiel traditions attest to the pervasive uncertainties regarding older traditions among the exiles.
14. For an example of this discourse as it appears in a different prophetic book, see S. L. Cook, "Micah's Deuteronomistic Redaction and the Deuteronomists' Identity," *Those Elusive Deuteronomists*, 228–231.
15. See the earlier discussion (re: "The Ezekiel Tradition").
16. See Lipschits, *Jerusalem*, 322–324. Lipschits notes the differences between the "folkloristic" passages and those that appear to be more formalistically constructed, replete with what he terms "Akkadianisms" that point to diplomatic/administrative training by the author(s). See also Polak, "Style," 51–55, who discusses the background to such modes of composition. The precedent for translating folkloristic sentiments or popular teachings into a programmatic exhortation or propagandistic narrative was already set within Jeremianic tradition via the "sour grapes" aphorism in Jer 31:27–30 and the Hananiah narrative of Jeremiah 28 (which dramatizes the conflict between Jeremiah and the prophets mentioned by name in Jeremiah 29). Earlier antecedents, however, may be found in Ephraimite traditions regarding Elijah and early narratives concerning Saul. For the former, see White, *The Elijah Legends*, 3–43; for the latter, see M. Leuchter, "Samuel, Saul, and the Deuteronomistic Categories of History," *From Babel to Babylon* (Fs. for Brian Peckham, ed. J. Rilett Wood et al.; New York/London: T. & T. Clark, 2006, 101–110); id., "Now There Was a (Certain) Man: Compositional Chronology in Judges–1 Samuel," *CBQ* (forthcoming).
17. See especially Geoghegan, "Until This Day," 226.
18. Leuchter, "Song of Moses."
19. Pace Haran, "The Law-Code of Ezekiel," 45–46, who states that the book of Jeremiah only emphasizes his prophetic status in contradistinction to that of Ezekiel, which repeatedly focuses attention on that prophet's Zadokite heritage. See the comments by M. A. Sweeney, "Review of Marti Nissinen and C. L. Seow and Robert K. Ritner, *Prophets and Prophecy in the Ancient Near East*," *Review of Biblical Literature* (2005), [www.bookreviews.org]. Jeremiah overtly places himself in line with Levitical archetypes such as Samuel and Moses (Jer 15:1), and the call narrative obviously introduces him as a Levite from Anatoth (Jer 1:1). But the call narrative also establishes parallels to the northern Levitical tradition in more subtle ways, additional connections may be seen between Jeremiah 11 and the Levitical ceremony in Deuteronomy 27 (Leuchter, *JRJS*, 160, 173), and Jer 7:2 situates the prophet "in the gate," precisely where Deuteronomy

repeatedly locates Levites. We have also seen that the historical elements in Jeremiah 34 involve Jeremiah acting as a Levite, and Jer 29:5–7 contains a brief but effective example of Levitical teaching/interpretation of Deuteronomic law as applicable to the exilic circumstance (Berlin, "A Deuteronomic Allusion," 8–11).

20. We may here see why the information in the Supplement was not simply redacted into an expanded version of the preexilic DH. Attaching this information to an historiographic work whose integrity was certainly in question by 587 BCE would not have served the interests of the Shaphanides in reinforcing their authority among the public. By contrast, placing the Supplement into an already-revered Jeremianic corpus would have provided a far better forum for the Shaphanide agenda to reach their Levite peers and, eventually, the exilic population. The subsequent exilic redaction of the DH would thus have had to account for this more fully developed Jeremianic corpus and the ideology it now espoused. See the Conclusion to the present study for examples of this process.
21. We should recall that the blessing given to the Rechabites in Jer 35:19 invokes the priestly/sacral phrase עמד לפני (cf. Gedaliah's decree in Jer 40: 10); the means by which Jeremiah is saved from the pit in Jer 38:11 constitutes a pun on the word "Levi" (בלוי הסחבות ובלוי מלחים); and of course, Jeremiah's recitation of the Deuteronomic manumission law to Zedekiah in Jer 34:14 puts into action the mandate for Levitical reading/teaching of the Torah in Deuteronomy. Finally, Jer 40:5 suggests that the Babylonian officer who supervised Jeremiah's transfer to Mizpah actually provided him with a Levitical tithe.
22. We should recall that in the unit of Jeremiah 34–36, the scribes' reading of Jeremiah's scroll to Jehoiakim in Jer 36:20–21 is paralleled/anticipated by Jeremiah's citation of Deuteronomy in Jer 34:14.
23. See Chapter 4. Following this pattern, we might also view the presentation of Baruch as a second Jeremiah in Jeremiah 45 as an indication that his activity should also be viewed under a Levitical rubric, though it is difficult to say for certain if he himself was a Levite.
24. See among others Hoffman, "Aetiology," 186–189; Dearman, "My Servants the Scribes," 419–420.
25. Pace Glatt-Gilad, "Personal Names," 33 n. 7, who remarks that Jehudi's role in Jeremiah 36 "consists of no more than fetching Baruch's scroll and reading it before the king." Glatt-Gilad does not consider the weighty implications of this role and its implicit connection to Deut 17:18–20, and also does not take note of Jehudi's allegiance to the scribes who support Jeremiah's words.
26. Glatt-Gilad is certainly correct to view the abundance of personal names as an indication of the author's firsthand familiarity with the detailed history he recounts and records (see "Personal Names").
27. For the Deuteronomistic presentation of Hezekiah's reign as a prototype or antecedent to that of Josiah, see Sweeney, *King Josiah*, 73–74.
28. Glatt-Gilad, "Personal Names," 33 n. 10.
29. See Weinfeld, "Emergence," 83–97; Sweeney, *King Josiah*, 73–74.
30. Lineage ties are ostensibly leveled in Deuteronomy (Deut 5:2-3; 13:7-12), but the presentation of various prophets in the book of Jeremiah suggests strongly that the connections

between these prophets and various regional priestly lines survived Deuteronomy's attempt to homogenize all regional priesthoods as "Levites." As demonstrated elsewhere, Jeremiah is selected to be a Josianic agent to his own Shilonite priestly line. This can hardly be an anomaly at a time when the Josianic scribes sought to unite various kinship groups, both northern and southern, under the banner of Deuteronomy and could not do so without the support of regional priesthoods. See Leuchter, *JRJS*, 50–86; idem, "Song of Moses." See also idem, "'The Prophets' and 'the Levites' in Josiah's Covenant Ceremony" (presented at the Chronicles/Ezra–Nehemiah section of the 2007 annual meeting of the Society of Biblical Literature, San Diego, CA); Lundbom, *Jeremiah 21–36*, 366. Although Zephaniah's oracles may be seen as serving the interests of Josiah's court (see Sweeney, *Zephaniah*, passim), he too may have been selected as a prophetic propagandist to a particular priestly group with a specific lineage affiliation.

31. The foregoing discussion reduces the patronymic name scheme of both Zephaniah and Jehudi, but we may still view the patronymic list for each pointing back to the Hezekian period. Zephaniah appears active early in Josiah's reign, and his grandfather Amariah would have thus lived during Hezekiah's reign (further suggested, as discussed earlier, by his title as a "servant of Hezekiah"). Jehudi appears to be a trusted member of the Shaphanide circle and possessed some significant standing in Jehoiakim's royal court. This would suggest that he was no youngster in 604 BCE and may be counted among those active in Josiah's own court (Dearman, "My Servants the Scribes," 418–419); his grandfather, Shelemaiah, would thus also have lived during Hezekiah's reign.

32. We should also note that according to Gen 10:8, Cush was the father of Nimrod. It is problematic to view this Cush as the same eponymous ancestor of the Ethiopian/Nubian group, because Nimrod is very clearly depicted as a Mesopotamian. Y. Levin notes that Cush in Gen 10:8 should be associated with the Mesopotamian city of Kish and derives from a much older Mesopotamian royal epic ("Nimrod The Mighty, King of Kish, King of Sumer and Akkad," *VT* 52 [2002], 350–366).

33. R. W. Anderson, Jr., provides a very detailed examination of the name Cushi in Zeph 1:1 and in relation to Jehudi in Jeremiah 36; see his "Zephaniah ben Cushi and Cush of Benjamin: Traces of Cushite Presence in Syria-Palestine," *The Pitcher Is Broken* (Fs. G. W Ahlström, ed. S. W. Holloway and L. K. Handy, JSOTsup 190; Sheffield, UK: Sheffield Academic Press, 1995), 45–70, and offers the view that these names reflect a sub-Saharan African ethnic presence in Israel. It is quite likely that this accurately describes the historical situation based on the evidence that Anderson discusses, though the term "Cush" associated with Jehudi and Zephaniah probably relates to a different geographic origin and ethnic group. See the following discussion.

34. See the discussion by Cross, *CMHE*, 200–201, 205–206; Mazar, "Sanctuary of Arad"; Sweeney, *Zephaniah*, 49; Weinfeld, "Tribal League," 304–311. The Aaron/Miriam complaint in Numbers 12 may reflect on an interpriestly struggle in Israel between variant forms of Yahwism and the Mushite priestly house, though the episode does not go on to address the disparaging remark concerning Moses's Cushite wife. As Anderson notes, this suggests that Cushites were accepted and well integrated into Israelite society ("Cushite Presence," 59). If the Cushite of Num 12:1 alludes to Zipporah's Kenite origins and to the Kenite priestly line to which she was connected, the criticism voiced by Miriam

and Aaron makes sense in the context of an inter-Israelite cultic debate. S. D. Sperling suggests that this debate should be seen as part of a larger discussion regarding earlier modes of prophecy versus written tradition set during the Persian Period ("Miriam, Aaron and Moses: Sibling Rivalry," *HUCA* 70 [1999], 39–55), but the linguistic features of the texts he identifies as deriving from the Persian period do not conform to the syntactical criteria discussed by Polak ("The Oral and the Written," 101–105). Furthermore, Numbers 12 in specific is far more concerned with oracular/revelatory phenomenology characteristic of early priestly groups (esp. Num 12:6–8) than with written texts, a hallmark of discourse from the late eighth century onward.

35. Halpern, "Jerusalem and the Lineages," 86–87; Schniedewind, *Book*, 74.
36. On the antiquity of Kenite Yahwism, see chapter 3.
37. An antecedent to this may also be found in 1 Sam 1:1, where the בן צוף in Elkanah's lineage identifies him as a member of a social caste and does not function as a reference to a personal name. See Leuchter, *JRJS*, 22–24.
38. This would especially be the case if Jehudi's patronymic information identifies him with a southern Kenite priestly line (Mazar, "The Sanctuary at Arad"), as he is allied with the Shaphanide group in Jeremiah 36, the latter of which appear to possess northern Levitical heritage, as we have seen. See also J. Weinberg, "The Babylonian Conquest of Judah: Some Additional Remarks to a Scientific Consensus," *ZAW* 118 (2006), 604. The implication of this pairing is that deportees – especially those of various priestly affiliations – should overlook differences once bound to geographic location, as all were now subject to the conditions of exile.
39. Halpern, "Why Manasseh," 505 (though Halpern's evaluation of Jer 8:8 as Jeremiah's critique of written tradition should be reconsidered in light of the discussion concerning this verse in the Introduction to the present study).
40. B. Halpern, "The Uneasy Compromise: Israel Between League and Monarchy," *Traditions in Transformation: Turning Points in Biblical Faith* (ed. B. Halpern and J. D. Levenson; Winona Lake, IN: Eisenbrauns, 1981), 76–87 (Halpern views substantial portions of Deut 17–18 as deriving from the early monarchy [84]; this is highly debatable, as Levinson has demonstrated that this material engages in careful scribal revision of earlier Israelite law [*Deuteronomy*, 98–143]. But it is reasonable to assume that the Deuteronomic passages in question evolved from an early tradition dealing with similar issues of Levitical/priestly jurisdiction in the transition to a monarchic state); id., "Levitic Participation," 41; Z. Ben-Barak, "The Mizpah Covenant (I Sam 10,25): The Source of the Israelite Monarchic Covenant," *ZAW* 91 (1979), 30–43; Cook, *Social Roots*, 249–259, 265–266.
41. Lipschits discusses the thematic commonalities in the stories regarding Jeremiah's imprisonment in chs. 37–38 (*Jerusalem*, 320–325), though he does note that the "folkloristic" material amplifies the culpability of the officers and demoralizes the king further than the more official-type records. This would be consistent with a Levitical critique of royal leadership and administration.
42. The existence of additional influential Jeremianic traditions is evident in the *Vorlage* to 2 Chronicles 35/1 Esdras 1; see H. G. M. Williamson, "The Death of Josiah," and the Continuing Development of the Deuteronomic History," *VT* 32 (1982), 247–248. That

the Jeremiah material discussed by Williamson was incorporated in Chronicles, a work that is extremely interested in the position of Levites, suggests that this material was preserved by Levites before its inclusion in the Chronicler's historiography.

43. One might view this as a result of his foreign status, but several Babylonian foreigners are mentioned by both title *and* name. See especially Jer 39:3, 10, 13; 40:1.
44. See N. Avigad, *Hebrew Bullae from the Time of Jeremiah* (Jerusalem: Israel Exploration Society, 1986), 24–25, 66, 158–160; id., "Hebrew Seals and Sealings and Their Significance for Biblical Research," *Congress Volume 1986* (VTSup 40; Leiden: Brill, 1988), 7–16.
45. Jeremiah 36:10, 20–21, and 40:7, 10 as informed by Deut 17:18–20, 31:9–13.
46. The political influence of Egypt during the reigns of both Jehoiakim and Zedekiah would certainly have facilitated the presence of Ethiopian/Nubian political figures. See Anderson, "Cushite Presence"; R. D. Haak, "'Cush' in Zephaniah," *The Pitcher Is Broken*, 238–251 (though Haak considers the "Cushi" in the superscription of the book to refer to Ethiopia [250–251]).
47. Lipschits views the repetitive resumption of terms (*Wiederaufnahme*) in the material surrounding the Ebed-Melech story in Jeremiah 38 as an attempt to blur the redactional lines and incorporate it smoothly into the larger narrative (*Jerusalem*, 322). This, however, is questionable. The *Wiederaufnahme* noted by Lipschits may indeed facilitate inclusion of the Ebed-Melech tale in the larger story, but this places it in the center of the chapter; its mediating position carries strong hermeneutical implications, as textual sequences convey meaning (we have already seen this at work in Jer 34–36; see also Levinson, *Deuteronomy*, 107–137; Leuchter, "Song of Moses"). Moreover, the editorial technique of *Wiederaufnahme* would indeed call attention to the redactional seams rather than blur them and would stress the tale's importance to the overall story while recognizing its independent origins. See B. Peckham, "Writing and Editing," *Fortunate the Eyes That See*, 368–369, 382. Peckham makes a strong case for editorial devices such as repetitive resumption as a way of guiding the reader to view the diachronic features of a text while recognizing the text's ultimate synchronic nature.
48. The entire historical episode behind Jer 34:8–22 may very well have been independently developed by Levites in exile as a didactic subject. The episode would have been highly useful for exilic Levites (who viewed Jeremiah as a symbol of their viability) to strike a chord with an exilic population desperate for religious and social leadership. The final form of Jer 34:8–22 derives from the Shaphanide author, but the otherwise pedestrian citation of Deut 31:10 suggests a reckoning with the more popular Levitical discussion regarding this historical incident.
49. See, among others, Levenson, "Who Inserted the Book of the Torah?" 221; Friedman, "From Egypt to Egypt," 187. For a detailed overview of scholarship, see Sanders, *Deuteronomy 32*, 1–98.
50. For the liturgical nature of the poem, see Thiessen, "Song of Moses." For the poem as a Levitical composition, see Leuchter, "Song of Moses."
51. That the Song of Moses was indeed current in exilic discourse is evidenced by its influence upon the oracles of Deutero-Isaiah; see T. A. Keiser, "The Song of Moses: A Basis for Isaiah's Prophecies," *VT* 55 (2005), 486–500.

52. The anti-Egyptian stance of the author is especially evident in Jeremiah 42–44 but can be found throughout the work, and the placement of the Supplement in the MT sequence intensifies the significance of the oracle against Egypt in Jeremiah 46.
53. Leuchter, "Something Old, Something Older," 2.1–3.1; id., "Psalm 78."
54. This is especially the case in the citation of Jeroboam's statement from 1 Kgs 12:28 found in Exodus 32:8. See Cross, *CMHE*, 198–199; Cook, *Social Roots*, 251–255.
55. Hoffman, "The Exodus in Amos and Hosea," 176–177. For the oldest traditions regarding Moses' Levitical status, see G. Widengren, "What Do We Know About Moses?", *Proclamation and Presence*, 37–45.
56. See the overview by Cook, *Social Roots*, 237–241 (though I take Psalm 78 as only secondarily associated with the Asaph psalms due to surface similarities rather than common composition).
57. For a similar understanding of the Levitical ideology common to Jeremiah and the DH, see J. C. Geoghegan, *The Time, Place and Purpose of the Deuteronomistic History: The Evidence of "Until This Day"* (BJS 347; Providence, RI: Brown University, 2006), 149–150, 159–164.
58. Cook's view that the exiled Levites and Judean elders were closely associated with each other would provide further reason for the appeal to Levitical families by the Shaphanides ("Micah's Deuteronomistic Redaction," 228–231).
59. This would constitute yet another chapter in the long-running literary polemics between Zadokites and Mushite-Levites. See Cross, *CMHE*, 198–205; Halpern, "Levitic Participation," 39; Leuchter, "Jeroboam the Ephratite," 70–71.
60. Boccaccini, *Roots of Rabbinic Judaism*, 68–71.
61. For a discussion of Malachi's pro-Levite and anti-Zadokite position, see Fishbane, *Biblical Interpretation*, 332–334; P. D. Hanson, "Israelite Religion in the Early Postexilic Period," *Ancient Israelite Religion*, 503.
62. So noted previously.
63. Geoghegan, "Until This Day," 225–227.
64. With respect to the association of Jeremiah-Deuteronomy/DH, see also Carr, *Tablet of the Heart*, 150; Geoghegan, *The Time, Place and Purpose*, 159–164. Though we may confidently identify a Deuteronomistic historiography beginning with Deuteronomy and ending with Kings, it is difficult to determine whether the Zadokites produced a Pentateuch or Hexateuch by the late sixth century BCE (though the Pentateuch is generally recognized as the ultimate product of their labors). See T. C. Römer and M. Z. Brettler, "Deuteronomy 34 and the Case for a Persian Hexateuch," *JBL* 119 (2000), 401–419. Knohl's observations concerning the redaction of the Pentateuch by the Zadokite Holiness School and its connection to the Ezekiel tradition (*The Sanctuary of Silence*, 103, 200–203) compromises Freedman and Kelly's suggestion that the earliest redaction of a narrative involving Genesis–Deuteronomy involved an editor sympathetic to both the DH and Jeremiah, whom they identify as Seraiah ("Who Redacted the Primary History?," 46–47). Freedman's earlier theory of a narrative spanning Genesis–Kings is still compelling (see later), but the animosity between the exilic Zadokites and the Shaphanide–Levite coalition would hinder the direct linear shift from a Deuteronomistic historiography to a Primary History. Rather, as suggested in the present study, the

Primary History would represent a reconciliation of Zadokite and Shaphanide–Levite positions. This best fits the early postexilic period when the Jeremianic tradition so closely associated with the Shaphanide–Levite Deuteronomistic tradition receives consistent attention from the postexilic writers concerned with the restoration of Jerusalem and its cult. See B. Halpern, "The New Names in Isaiah 62:4: Jeremiah's Reception in the Restoration and the Politics of 'Third Isaiah,'" *JBL* 117 (1998), 623–643; Peckham, *History and Prophecy*, 741, 750–755; S. Frolov, "The Prophecy of Jeremiah in Esr 1,1," *ZAW* 116 (2004), 595–601.

65. See Freedman, *Divine Commitment and Human Obligation*, 341–349. The merging of the disparate historiographic works during the same period as the formation of the book of Isaiah in its principal form suggests that this period also saw the beginnings of a standardized prophetic corpus inclusive of Isaiah, Jeremiah, Ezekiel, and probably some form of the Book of the Twelve. Against Freedman's proposed dating, however, we should view this as a late-exilic or postexilic process given the interexilic discordance between the DH and the Zadokite historiographic work. We must be cautious, however, in postulating the purpose of this collation of disparate historiographic and prophetic material. Though the emergence of a Primary History and an early prophetic corpus may have been a first step toward reconciliation, the fact that literature privileging Levites emerges only in the postexilic period points to sustained tensions between Zadokite and Levite groups.
66. See especially Halpern, "Why Manasseh," 511–512; C. Mitchell, "The Ironic Death of Josiah in 2 Chronicles," *CBQ* 68 (2006), 430–435, who discusses both the Levitical emphasis of the Chronistic account and the influence of the Jeremiah tradition (435). See also the Conclusion to the present study.

CONCLUSION

1. So also Sharp, *Jeremiah*, 155, though the discernment of the placement and function of these lexemes is useful in establishing the direction of influence from one corpus to the next. See Friedman, "The Deuteronomistic School," 78–80.
2. Friedman, "The Deuteronomistic School," 76–77; Leuchter, *JRJS*, 176 and passim.
3. This does not mean that subsequent editorial and redactional accretions did not take place; see the later discussion.
4. See Chapter 4.
5. For the rhetorical purpose of the ascription of Deuteronomy to Moses, see Levinson, "The Hermeneutics of Tradition," 279–282.
6. See Cogan and Tadmor, *II Kings*, 303–324, for a discussion of these notices. See also Friedman, "From Egypt to Egypt," 173–174.
7. Friedman, "From Egypt to Egypt," 173–174.
8. Such is the purpose of the related oracles in Jeremiah 24; 30–31. See Leuchter, "Jeremiah's 70-Year Prophecy," 518.
9. See Chapter 4 regarding the typological characteristics of Davidic kings established by the equation of Zedekiah and Jehoiakim.

10. Leuchter, "Jeremiah's 70-Year Prophecy," 520. The Chronicler apparently viewed the Jeremianic and Deuteronomistic works as composite, relying upon distinctively Jeremianic language (2 Chr 36:15) in his evaluation of the cause for Judah's demise otherwise drawn from the book of Kings. See Parke-Taylor, *Formation*, 107.
11. Dearman also notes that by excluding Jeremiah from the DH, the editors maintain an independent prophetic witness to the content of the Deuteronomistic works ("My Servants the Scribes," 421). This corresponds loosely to the preexilic strata of the DH, where prophets are characterized as independently bearing witness to the binding contents of Deuteronomy throughout Israel's history. The shift speaks to a later and more comprehensive collection of literature.
12. Lipschits, *Jerusalem*, 300.
13. Lipschits suggests that vv. 13–14 are postexilic interruptions of the Jehoiachin episode that serve just such a purpose (*Jerusalem*, 358–359). However, it is precisely their position within the Jehoiachin episode that suggests that the "poorest of the land" qualification pertains to those remaining in the land after 597 BCE who eventually flee to Egypt, as depicted in Jeremiah 40–44.
14. See the discussion in Chapter 4 on the absence of this "poorest of the land" in this verse as the result of haplography.
15. Leuchter, *JRJS*, 181–182.
16. Halpern argues for the Jeremianic influence on the exilic DH account of Manasseh ("Why Manasseh," 510–512) but does not distinguish the specifics of vv. 12–15 as intruding into the account and thus pointing to the other verses as original to the Josianic edition.
17. It is difficult to determine the date for this passage. Sharp suggests an exilic setting (*Jeremiah*, 145), which is supported in part by M. Z. Brettler's study of the redactional strata in the text of 2 Kings 17 (*The Creation of History in Ancient Israel* [London: Routledge, 1995], 115–128, 131–134). A preexilic origin, however, is likely. See Sweeney, *King Josiah*, 81–93.
18. This passage may be understood as a secondary accretion due to the syntactical break with the surrounding material (in v. 10, which initiates the unit) and its presupposition of the Babylonian conquest and exile.
19. See Halpern, "Why Manasseh," 511. Though the parallel to Jer 19:3 is drawn, he does not discuss the secondary (and deliberate) nature of the messenger formula of v. 12 and the allusion to the "uprooting" theme from Jeremiah's work.
20. The terminology in 2 Kgs 21:12 also echoes that of 1 Samuel 3:11, but the subsequent use of Jeremianic lexemes in v. 14 increases the likelihood that the source text is not Samuel but Jeremiah. For additional discussion, see Halpern, "Why Manasseh," 511–512, who argues that the blaming of Manasseh originates with the Jeremianic material and influenced the exilic redactor of the DH.
21. Geoghegan, *The Time, Place, and Purpose*, 159–164.
22. It is possible to view this accretion as inspired the preexilic DH, where it first appears, and it is reasonable to assume that the redactor utilized the phrase in our passage out of consistency with its preexilic occurrences. Yet, since it also appears in the Jeremiah material and our passage is heavily inspired by that corpus, it seems more likely that a connection to its Jeremianic occurrences is implied here.

23. So Halpern, "Why Manasseh," 507, 513–514.
24. R. E. Friedman (*The Exile and Biblical Narrative* [*HSM*, 22; Chico, CA: Scholars Press, 1981], 20) considers vv. 11–14 to be preexilic and argues for an original continuity with Deut 29:29. He does not, though, consider the great thematic and linguistic similarities shared by Deut 30:11–14 and Jer 31:31–34. It is worth noting that Deut 30:1–10 also evidences strong influence from the Jeremianic tradition; see M. Z. Brettler, "Predestination in Deuteronomy 30.1–10," *Those Elusive Deuteronomists: The Phenomenon of Pan-Deuteronomism* (ed. L. S. Schearing and S. L. McKenzie, JSOTSup 268; Sheffield, UK: Sheffield Academic Press, 1999), 171–188.
25. So also Lemke, "The Near and Distant God," 553–555.
26. We will recall that the "heart" is the scribe's own mind and memory, and as we have seen, the Supplement presents the scribal mind as an exegetical vehicle. See Chapter 3.
27. Deut 30:11–14 would appear to reciprocate the ideology of Jer 31:31–34 as a statement on the consistency between the Jeremianic and Deuteronomic teachings. The prophetic text tells us that the exegetical imagination will constitute תורה (Jer 31:33), whereas the Deuteronomic Torah text tells us that the exegetical imagination will constitute the prophetic דבר.
28. Jeremiah 32 possesses its own complex exilic redaction history in the material subsequent to v. 15. See Rom-Shiloni, "Everlasting Covenant," 201–223.
29. Holladay (*Jeremiah* 2, 222–223) sees Jer 33:1–13 as a "companion piece" to Jeremiah 32, though he discusses the difficulty in determining how much of the material is genuinely Jeremianic. He dates the proposed Jeremianic portions to roughly the same time as the final siege of Babylon against Jerusalem in 587 BCE and demonstrates the parallels to narrative portions of Jeremiah 37 and Jer 32:2 that take place during this period, though he allows that the secondary material may derive from a postexilic period (224). Holladay questions whether Jer 33:1 can be attributed to a secondary expansion. Thiel (*Jeremia 26–45*, 37) notes that Jer 33:1 has been drawn from the preexisting position of Jeremiah 32 within the extant corpus.
30. Pace Holladay (*Jeremiah* 2, 224) and McKane (*Jeremiah* 2, 855). McKane alludes to F. Giesebrecht's view that calls for the deletion of vv. 2–3 as a later gloss, composed subsequent to Deutero-Isaiah (*Das Buch Jeremia* [Göttingen: Handkommentar zum AT, 1907], 182–183). McKane disagrees with this proposed deletion but only on the grounds that Jeremiah 33:1, 4–13 are later than Deutero-Isaiah as well, intimating that vv. 2–3 rightly belong in the passage because they too are late.
31. For a discussion of this call/answer idiom as Shilonite in origin, see M. Leuchter, "The Literary Strata and Narrative Sources of Psalm xcix," *VT* 55 (2005), 30–36.
32. McKane ("The Construction of Jeremiah Chapter xxi") argues that the chapter is entirely redactional, but Weippert's study (*Prosareden*, 75–78) demonstrates that the language of 21:1–7 is Jeremianic, not independently superimposed. Moreover, the literary disjunctions within the chapter are not as haphazard as McKane suggests; see J. Applegate, "The Fate of Zedekiah: Redactional Debate in the Book of Jeremiah, Part I," *VT* 48 (1998), 146–149. The best way to understand the results of both McKane's and Weippert's studies is to view the later redactor/author of Jeremiah 21 as drawing from authentic Jeremianic traditions and writing within the linguistic parameters of the extant Jeremianic literary

corpus. That the LXX also possesses a parallel to Jeremiah 21 within the generally older complex of Jeremiah 1–25 indicates that the curators of that collection developed their corpus not simply after encountering the Supplement as an individual literary work but also in response to a more mature and comprehensive "book" of Jeremiah including, in a penultimate form, Jeremiah 1–25/the Supplement/the OAN.

33. For 20:14–18 as a Josianic-era lament, see Leuchter, *JRJS*, 113–114. For its reuse as the conclusion to a subsequent stage in the book's development, see Lundbom, *Jeremiah 1–20*, 864–874.

34. Seitz (*Theology in Conflict*, 252–253) observes that the inclusion of Jer 21:1–10 in its current position envelopes pre-597 BCE materials in Jeremiah 22 within a post-597 framework, pointing to the central role of the 597 theology that emerges as the basis for the growth of the MT tradition. The envelope effect here is similar to the function of the doublet in 11:20/20:12, i.e., the submersion of various compositional strata in each other (11:20 being several verses short of the finale of the *Urrolle* and 20:12 approaching the end of a later compilation of Jeremianic text [following Lundbom, *Jeremiah 1–20*, 865–874]). In this case, the narrative of chs. 37–44 (and the Supplement en masse) is anchored within the older literary levels of the material that predated these chapters.

35. Holladay (*Jeremiah 2*, 570) points to the function of דרש in Jer 10:21 as an inherent part of prophetic intercession. However, 10:21 is a post–604 BCE expansion of the *Urrolle* and presupposes an end to Jeremiah's intercessory role; the language of prayer is prohibited beyond Jer 7:16–20.

36. The implication is therefore that the speaker in Jer 37:3 presumes that prophetic prayer is still possible, a misguided notion from the vantage point of the author of 21:2. Prophetic prayer suggests an affective action that will change the course of history to the benefit of those asking the prophet to pray on their behalf. Prophetic inquiry is different – it is reflective rather than affective and allows the petitioner to know circumstances rather than change them.

37. See M. J. Boda, "From Complaint to Contrition: Peering through the Liturgical Window of Jer 14,1–15,4," *ZAW* 113 (2001), 186–197, which identifies the passage as part of a preexilic penitential prayer. It is altogether possible that Jer 15:1–4 is for the most part original to Jeremiah and datable to 587 BCE, with only later glosses (i.e., "captivity" in Jer 15:2).

38. See Sommer, *A Prophet Reads Scripture*, 32–72; Halpern, "The New Names," 623–643; Williamson provides a response to Halpern (H. G. M. Williamson, "Isaiah 62:4 and the Problem of Inner-Biblical Allusions," *JBL* 119 [2000], 734–739), citing alternative (Isaianic) sources for the language employed in this verse. Halpern's reading, though, is sound given the role Jeremiah plays in Deutero-Isaiah's work, which must have weighed heavily upon Trito-Isaiah's compositional predilections and his (possible) deliberate employment of Jeremianic terms that had Isaianic corollaries. Further, see D. Rudman, "Midrash in the Isaiah Apocalypse," *ZAW* 112 (2000), 404–408 for a particularly dramatic example of reliance upon Jeremiah in terms of both content and methodology.

39. So Peckham, *History and Prophecy*, 149.

40. See Petersen, *Late Israelite Prophecy*, 98–100 for a summation of the prophetic dimensions of the Second Temple period Levites as cultic prophets dependent upon written liturgy for prophetic designation.
41. So Petersen, *Late Israelite Prophecy*, 45. I must disagree, though, with Petersen's observation, which follows that of F. M. Cross ("New Directions in the Study of Apocalyptic," *Apocalypticism* [JTC 6, ed. R. Funk; New York: Herder & Herder, 1969], 161) that the Deutero-prophetic writers bore stronger continuity with the classical prophets than did the writers who addressed the Restoration such as Deutero- and Trito-Isaiah. Petersen's important study of the Deutero-prophetic writers (13–53) demonstrates that the work was characterized largely by looking to the future as a precursor to Apocalyptic texts. The classical prophets may incorporate certain futuristic concerns (one immediately thinks of Jer 31:31–34, for example), but their principal focus is on current events and the proper way for the people to react (i.e., the underlying purpose of Huldah's oracle, Jeremiah's Temple Sermon, or even Amos's clash with Amaziah). In this sense, greater continuity may be seen with the anonymous scribes who addressed these matters than with the Deutero-prophetic writers who set prophecy far in the future.
42. See Rudman, "Midrash in the Isaiah Apocalypse," 405–407 for a particularly lucid example of this process.
43. The Ezra tradition's mention of Jeremiah appears to be the result of secondary redaction dependent upon Chronicles; see Knoppers, *I Chronicles 1–9*, 96–97. All the same, Ezra carries forward the impulse begun in the Supplement concerning the role of scribes as mediators of tradition, as discussed in Chapter 5. Veijola has noted the resonances with Deuteronomistic tradition in Ezra-Nehemiah ("The Deuteronomistic Roots of Judaism"); the redactional association of 2 Chr 36:22 with the beginning of the book of Ezra may reflect the redactor's recognition of the consistency between Jeremiah and the Deuteronomistic ideology at work in the Ezra narratives.
44. So Williamson, "The Death of Josiah and the Continuing Development of the Deuteronomic History," 247.
45. 2 Chr 36:15 and conflation of language from the DH and Jeremiah are discussed by Parke-Taylor, *Formation*, 107.
46. For an overview, see Leuchter, "Jeremiah's 70-Year Prophecy," 503–504.
47. See H. Tadmor, "The Appointed Time Has Not Yet Come: The Historical Background of Haggai 1:2," *Ki Baruch Hu*, 401–408. Tadmor demonstrates that the 70-year prophecy was indeed a matter of serious public concern (402–403) in terms of remaining in force, but Haggai argues that it has run its course. The period could apply to a time no earlier than the deportation of 597 BCE (405), an event that would have still weighed heavily upon the consciousness of biblical writers in the Chronicler's day and whose *Sitz im Zeit* would not have been easily played down.
48. Such would have indeed been a natural choice, as the Isaiah tradition and Chronicles were closely associated. See D. N. Freedman, *The Unity of the Hebrew Bible* (Ann Arbor: University of Michigan Press, 1991), 45–51.
49. Pomykala, *The Davidic Dynasty Tradition*, 42–45; Boccaccini, *Roots of Rabbinic Judaism*, 52, 54–55.
50. 1 Chr 12:18, 28:12; 2 Chr 15:1, 18:21–23 ("lying spirit"), 20:14, 24:20.

51. So also Seitz, "The Prophet Moses," 18.
52. Ergo, the colophon of Jer 45:1–5. See also Fishbane, *Biblical Interpretation*, 276–277; the exegetical method is itself understood to be divinely mandated and thus part of the *traditum*.
53. Sommer, *A Prophet Reads Scripture*, 32–72; Halpern, "The New Names."
54. Pace Frolov's reading of the verse ("The Prophecy of Jeremiah," 598–601). Frolov translates the term לכלות as "to reverse," i.e., Ezra 1:1/2 Chr 36:22 suggest a negation of Jeremiah's prophecies. However, לכלות appears in the Jeremiah tradition in the sense of completion (e.g., Jer 43:1) and establishes hermeneutical associations with the same use of the term as it appears in Deut 32:45 in relation to the divine דבר entrusted to Moses (see Chapter 4). A phenomenological connection is thus implied with the use of the term לכלות in Jeremiah, and considering the paramount position of the Jeremianic corpus in the oracles of Deutero-Isaiah, a similar reading should be adopted for לכלות in the case of 2 Chr 36:22 and Ezra 1:1, as the author may well be arguing for continuity between the Jeremiah tradition and Isa 45:1.
55. For a full discussion of this phenomenon, see M. Fishbane, *Biblical Myth and Rabbinic Mythmaking* (New York/Oxford: Oxford University Press, 2004).
56. Weingreen, *From Bible to Mishna*, passim. See also W. W. Hallo, "Midrash as Mnemonic: A New Approach to Rabbinic Exegesis," *HUCA* 74 (2003), 157–173, where a number of organizational processes in the *midrashim* bear close similarity to the work of the Supplement's author discussed earlier, especially in Chapters 1, 3, and 4.
57. J. M. Baumgarten, "The Unwritten Law in the Pre-Rabbinic Period," *JSJ* 3 (1972), 7–29. See, however, B. Eruvin 54b, the other foundational text regarding oral traditions and methods, in which Aaron and his son Elazar factor significantly. For a discussion, see M. S. Jaffee, *Torah in the Mouth: Writing and Oral Tradition in Palestinian Judaism 200BCE–400CE* (New York/Oxford: Oxford University Press, 2001), 3–5.
58. Boccaccini, *Roots of Rabbinic Judaism*, 203–209; H. L. Strack and G. Stemberger, *Introduction to the Talmud and Midrash* (trans. M. Bockmuel; Minneapolis: Fortress Press, 1996), 63. For a full treatment of *Avot*, see A. Tropper, *Wisdom, Politics and Historiography: Tractate Avot in the Context of the Graeco-Roman Near East* (Oxford/New York: Oxford University Press, 2004).
59. Schniedewind, *Book*, 201.
60. Ezra 7 preserves the list of ancestral household leaders; the ancestral founder of the scribal academy in Ben Sira retains high significance (Sir 50:27); the Hasmoneans rally under the leadership of the patriarch Mattathias (1 Macc 2:1–14).
61. A. Cohen, *Everyman's Talmud: The Major Teachings of the Rabbinic Sages* (New York: Schocken, 1995), xxxvi.
62. Levin, "From Lists to History"; Weinberg, *Citizen-Temple Community*, 49–65.
63. Boccaccini, *Roots of Rabbinic Judaism*, 57–72; Schniedewind, *Book*, 172–174.
64. This is the case, in fact, within *Avot* itself, as the tractate goes on to include Simeon the Just as a member of the Great Assembly (1.2), who is elsewhere identified by the rabbis as a high priest. See Strack and Stemberger, *Introduction*, 63. A similar presentation of priesthood is found in *Sota* 33a, where the high priest Johanan (John Hyrcanus) is

understood to have communicated under the ideological rubric of prophetic thought; see Cohen, *Everyman's Talmud*, 46.

65. Zadokite heritage need not preclude one from engaging in the Levite-scribal exegetical tradition, as evidenced through Ezra's depiction, on the one hand, as a Zadokite priest and, on the other, as a ranking member of this group (Ezra 7:1–10). I. Knohl further discusses the Zadokite ideological roots of significant early rabbinic schools of thought (*The Divine Symphony: The Bible's Many Voices* [Philadelphia: JPS, 2003], 126–127, 141; id., *Sanctuary of Silence*, 224), though the hermeneutical methodology of these schools owes more to the Levite-scribal tradition (see the later discussion).
66. Boccaccini, *Roots of Rabbinic Judaism*, 71–72; Levin, "From Lists to History," 630–631; Hanson, "1 Chronicles 15–16," 76–77 (though Hanson views this as deriving from a late-sixth-century BCE context).
67. So also Schniedewind, *Book*, 205–206.
68. Schniedewind, *Book*, 201–202.
69. *B. Kiddushin* 49a characterizes Torah as "exegesis" (מאי תורה מדרש תורה). See the discussion by Weingreen, *From Bible to Mishna*, 140.
70. Flavius Josephus, *Antiquities of the Jews*, xiii 10.6.
71. Cohen, *Everyman's Talmud*, xxxiv. There is no shortage of Persian-era literature to support this characterization of the Levites in this capacity (Smith, "The Levitical Compilation of the Psalter").
72. Especially significant is Neh 8:9, which specifies that the people congregated in Jerusalem wept when they heard the "words of the Torah," but this takes place only *after* Ezra's scribal agents engage in an exposition of the written text that Ezra read. The implication is that the "words of Torah" is a process including both the written text and the exegesis/teaching of that text.
73. For the tradition of interpretation beginning with the prophets themselves, see B. D. Sommer, "Prophecy as Translation: Ancient Israelite Conceptions of the Human Factor in Prophecy," *Bringing the Hidden to Light: The Process of Interpretation. Studies in Honor of Stephen A. Geller* (ed. D. Sharon and K. Kravitz; New York: JTS and Winona Lake, IN: Eisenbrauns, forthcoming).
74. See Schniedewind's brief discussion of the "textualization" of the divine word (*Book*, 187–190). See also Jaffee, *Torah in the Mouth*, 17–19, who discusses later scribal praxes that are already in effect in several of the passages discussed in the foregoing analysis (e.g., Jer 26:4–6, 18; 34:14, 20; see Hallo, "Midrash as Mnemonic") as well as presupposed in the narrative of Nehemiah 8.
75. See Chapter 6; Leuchter, *JRJS*, 40–49. See also Halpern, "Why Manasseh," 504–505. The prophetic qualifications apply broadly, whereas the rulings of the judges/scribal magistrates apply regionally; only when the regional authorities are unable to adjudicate is the case brought to national attention (Deut 17:8–13).
76. The impulse for the incorporation of oral exegesis (whether preserved strictly on an oral level or written in unofficial records; see Strack and Stemberger, *Introduction*, 34–37; Weingreen, *From Bible to Mishna*, 76–99) into the canon of sacred text characterizes every significant epoch of Jewish intellectual tradition from the late preexilic period well into the post-Talmudic rabbinic period. See B. D. Sommer, "Unity and Plurality

in Jewish Canons: The Case of the Oral and Written Torahs," *One Scripture or Many? Canon from Biblical, Theological and Philosophical Perspectives* (ed. C. Helmer and C. Landmesser; New York: Oxford University Press, 2004), 108–150; Z. Talshir, "Several Canon-Related Concepts Originating in Chronicles," *ZAW* 113 (2001), 393–394.

77. The maintenance of this prophetic voice, even on a scribal/exegetical level, is viewed by the Chronicler as grounds for ascribing prophetic status to these Levites (Petersen, *Late Israelite Prophecy*, 87), which may function as a bridge to the rabbinic view of pseudo-prophetic status to figures in the postprophetic period (Cohen, *Everyman's Talmud*, 46). We must recall here the protest of Amos that his prophetic standing is not a matter of lineage but of individual compulsion, as well as the fact that this protest is voiced as part of a dispute with a powerful priesthood that was defined by lineage (Amos 7:10–17). The distancing of lineage-based institutions in favor of individual compulsion meshes well with the thrust of Jer 31:31–34 and the Supplement's general approach to scribalism over priesthood as the proper medium of tradition; the author of *Avot* 1.1 distances rabbinic authority from the lineage-based qualifications of priesthood for the same reasons. I am indebted to Elisha Russ Fishbane for sharing this insight with me.
78. See *B. Eruvin* 21b; *Yoma* 28b; *Sanhedrin* 10.5.
79. The figures in question are no less than Jesus of Nazareth and Johanan b. Zakkai. See A. Tropper, "Yohanan ben Zakkai, *Amicus Caesaris*: A Jewish Hero in Rabbinic Eyes," *JSIJ* 4 (2005), 133–149; M. F. Whitters, "Jesus in the Footsteps of Jeremiah," *CBQ* 68 (2005), 229–247.
80. We are reminded here of Veijola's observations concerning Ezra's scribal imperatives and their Deuteronomic antecedents ("The Deuteronomistic Roots of Judaism").

Bibliography

Ackerman, S. "At Home with the Goddess," in Dever and Gitin (2003): 455–468.

Aejmelaeus, A. "Jeremiah at the Turning-Point of History: The Function of Jer. xxv 1–14 in the Book of Jeremiah," *VT* 52 (2002): 459–482.

Ahlström, G. W. *The History of Ancient Palestine from the Palaeolithic Period to Alexander's Conquest.* JSOTSup, 146. Sheffield, UK: Sheffield Academic Press, 1993.

Albertz, R. *Israel in Exile: The History and Literature of the Sixth Century B.C.E.* Atlanta: SBL, 2003.

Anderson, R. W., Jr. "Zephaniah ben Cushi and Cush of Benjamin: Traces of Cushite Presence in Syria-Palestine," in Holloway and Handy (1995): 45–70.

Applegate, J. "The Fate of Zedekiah: Redactional Debate in the Book of Jeremiah, Part I," *VT* 48 (1998): 137–160.

"The Fate of Zedekiah: Redactional Debate in the Book of Jeremiah, Part II," *VT* 48 (1998): 301–308.

Assis, E. "Why Edom? On the Hostility Towards Jacob's Brother in Prophetic Sources," *VT* 56 (2006): 1–20.

Avigad, N. (ed.). *Zer L'gevurot.* Fs. Z. Shazar. Jerusalem: Israel Exploration Society, 1971.

Hebrew Bullae from the Time of Jeremiah. Jerusalem: Israel Exploration Society, 1986.

"Hebrew Seals and Sealings and Their Significance for Biblical Research," *Congress Volume 1986.* VTSup, 40. Leiden: Brill, 1988: 7–16.

Baker, D. W. "Biblical Colophons: Gevaryahu and Beyond," *OTWSA 27 (1984)* and *OTWSA 28 (1985)*. Pretoria, South Africa, 1986, 29–61.

"Scribes as Transmitters of Tradition," in Millard et al. (1994): 65–78.

Barrick, W. Boyd. *The King and the Cemeteries: Toward a New Understanding of Josiah's Reform.* Leiden/Boston/Köln: Brill, 2002.

Barstad, H. *The Myth of the Empty Land: A Study of the History and Archaeology of Judah during the Exilic Period.* SOFS 28. Oslo: Scandinavian University Press, 1996.

Baumgarten, J. M. "The Unwritten Law in the Pre-Rabbinic Period," *JSJ* 3 (1972): 7–29.

Beck, A. (ed., with A. H. Bartelt, P. R. Raabe, and C. A. Franke). *Fortunate the Eyes That See: Essays in Honor of David Noel Freedman in Celebration of His Seventieth Birthday.* Grand Rapids, MI: Eerdmans, 1995.

Becking, B. "Jeremiah's Book of Consolation: A Textual Comparison: Notes on the Masoretic and the Old Greek Version of Jeremiah xxx–xxxi," *VT* 44 (1994): 145–169.

Between Fear and Freedom: Essays on the Interpretation of Jeremiah 30–31. Boston/Leiden: Brill, 2004.

Bedford, P. R. "Diaspora: Homeland Relations in Ezra-Nehemiah," *VT* 52 (2002): 147–165.

Begin, Z. B. "Does Lachish Letter 4 Contradict Jeremiah xxxiv 7?" *VT* 52 (2002): 166–174.

Ben-Barak, Z. "The Mizpah Covenant (I Sam 10,25): The Source of the Israelite Monarchic Covenant," *ZAW* 91 (1979): 30–43.

Ben Zvi, E. "Who Wrote the Speech of the Rabshakeh and When?" *JBL* 109 (1990): 79–92.

"Introduction: Writing, Speeches, and the Prophetic Books – Setting an Agenda," in Ben Zvi and Floyd (2000): 6–16.

Bergey, R. "The Song of Moses (Deuteronomy 32. 1–43) and Isaianic Prophecies: A Case of Early Intertextuality?" *JSOT* 28 (2003): 33–54.

Berlin, A. "Jer. 29:5–7: A Deuteronomic Allusion?" *HAR* 8 (1984): 3–11.

Blenkinsopp, J. (ed., with O. Lipschits). *Judah and the Judeans in the Neo-Babylonian Period.* Winona Lake, IN: Eisenbrauns, 2003.

Block, D. I. *The Book of Ezekiel, Chapters 1–24.* Grand Rapids, MI/Cambridge, MA: Eerdmans, 1997.

Boccaccini, G. *Roots of Rabbinic Judaism: An Intellectual History, from Ezekiel to Daniel.* Grand Rapids, MI: Eerdmans, 2002.

Boda, M. J. "From Complaint to Contrition: Peering through the Liturgical Window of Jer 14,1–15,4," *ZAW* 113 (2001): 186–197.

Bodner, K. "The Locution of 1 Kgs 22:28: A New Proposal," *JBL* 122 (2003): 533–543.

Bogaert, P. M. (ed.). *Le Livre de Jérémie.* BETL. Leuven, Brussels: Leuven University Press, 1997 (reprinted from the 1981 edition).

Botterweck, G. J. (with H. Ringgren). *Theological Dictionary of the Old Testament,* vol. 4. Grand Rapids, MI: Eerdmans, 1978.

Brakke, D. *Religion and the Self in Antiquity.* Bloomington/Indianapolis: Indiana University Press, 2005.

Brettler, M. Z. *The Creation of History in Ancient Israel.* London: Routledge, 1995.

"Predestination in Deuteronomy 30.1–10," in Schearing and McKenzie (1999): 171–188.

"Judaism in the Hebrew Bible? The Transition from Ancient Israelite Religion to Judaism," *CBQ* 61 (1999): 429–447.

"A 'Literary Sermon' in Deuteronomy 4," in Olyan and Culley (2000): 33–50.

Bright, J. "The Date of the Prose Sermons of Jeremiah," *JBL* 70 (1951): 15–35.

Jeremiah. AB, 21. Garden City, NY: Doubleday, 1965.

A History of Israel (3rd ed.). Louisville, KY/Philadelphia: Westminster John Knox Press, 1981.

Brueggemann, W. *To Build and to Plant.* ITC: Grand Rapids, MI: Eerdmans, 1991.

"The Baruch Connection: Reflections on Jeremiah 43:1–7," *JBL* 113 (1994): 405–420.

Campbell, A. F. "Psalm 78: A Contribution to the Theology of Tenth Century Israel," *CBQ* 41 (1979): 51–79.

Carr, D. M. *Writing on the Tablet of the Heart: Origins of Scripture and Literature.* New York/Oxford: Oxford University Press, 2005.

Carroll, R. P. *From Chaos to Covenant.* New York: Crossroads, 1981.

Jeremiah: A Commentary. OTL. Philadelphia: Westminster Press, 1986.

"Exile! What Exile? Deportation and the Discourses of the Diaspora," in Grabbe (1998), 62–79.

"Something Rich and Strange: Imagining a Future for Jeremiah Studies," in Diamond et al. (1999): 423–443.

Chavel, S. "Let My People Go! Emancipation, Revelation and Scribal Activity in Jeremiah 34:8–14," *JSOT* 76 (1997): 71–95.

Chazan, R. (ed., with W. W. Hallo and L. Schiffman). *Ki Baruch Hu: Near Eastern, Biblical, and Judaic Studies in Honor of Baruch A. Levine.* Winona Lake, IN: Eisenbrauns, 1999.

Christensen, D. L. (ed.). *A Song of Power and the Power of Song: Essays on the Book of Deuteronomy.* Winona Lake, IN: Eisenbrauns, 1993.

Cogan, M. (with H. Tadmor). *II Kings.* AB, 11. Garden City, NY: Doubleday, 1988.
Cohen, A. *Everyman's Talmud: The Major Teachings of the Rabbinic Sages.* New York: Schocken, 1995.
Cohen, C. (ed., with A. Hurvitz and S. Paul). *Sefer Moshe: The Mose Weinfeld Jubilee Volume.* Winona Lake, IN: Eisenbrauns, 2004.
Cook, S. L. "The Lineage Roots of Hosea's Yahwism," *Semeia* 87 (1999): 145–162.
"Micah's Deuteronomistic Redaction and the Deuteronomists' Identity," in Schearing and McKenzie (1999): 216–231.
The Social Roots of Biblical Yahwism. Atlanta: SBL, 2004.
Crawford, C. D. "Cutting the Calf or Making the Calf? On the Preferred Reading of Jeremiah 34:18–20." Read at the annual meeting of the Society of Biblical Literature, Philadelphia, 2005.
Cross, F. M. "New Directions in the Study of Apocalyptic," in Funk (1969): 157–165.
"The Evolution of a Theory of Local Texts," in Kraft (1972): 108–126.
Canaanite Myth and Hebrew Epic. Cambridge, MA: Harvard University Press, 1973.
Daviau, P. M. M. (ed.). *The World of the Arameans, Vol. 1.* Fs. P. E. Dion. JSOTSup 324. Sheffield, UK. Sheffield Academic Press, 2001.
Day, J. "Pre-Deuteronomistic Allusions to the Covenant in Hosea and Psalm lxxviii," *VT* 36 (1986): 3–11.
Dearman, J. A. "My Servants the Scribes: Composition and Context in Jeremiah 36," *JBL* 109 (1990): 403–421.
Delamarter, S. "The Death of Josiah in Scripture and Tradition: Wrestling with the Problem of Evil?" *VT* 54 (2004): 29–60.
de Pury, A. *Israel Constructs Its History.* JSOTsup 306. Sheffield, UK: Sheffield Academic Press, 2000.
Dever, W. (with S. Gitin). *Symbiosis, Symbolism and the Power of the Past: Canaan, Ancient Israel, and Their Neighbors from the Late Bronze Age through Roman Palaestina.* Winona Lake, IN: Eisenbrauns, 2003.
Diamond, A. R. P. "Portraying Prophecy: Of Doublets, Variants and Analogies in the Narrative Representation of Jeremiah's Oracles – Reconstructing the Hermeneutics of Prophecy," *JSOT* 57 (1993): 99–119.
(ed., with K. M. O'Connor and L. Stulman). *Troubling Jeremiah.* JSOTSup 260, Sheffield, UK: Sheffield Academic Press, 1999.
"Introduction," in Diamond et al. (1999): 15–32.
Dijkstra, M. "Prophecy by Letter (Jeremiah xxxix 24–32)," *VT* 33 (1983): 419–422.
Duhm, B. *Das Buch Jeremia.* Tübingen: Mohr, 1901.

Durham, J. (ed., with J. R. Porter). *Proclamation and Presence: Old Testament Essays in Honour of Gwynne Henton Davies.* Macon, GA: Mercer University Press, 1983.

Eskenazi, T. C. "Implications for and from Ezra-Nehemiah," "In Conversation with W. M. Schniedewind, How the Bible Became a Book: The Textualization of Ancient Israel (Cambridge, 2003)" (ed. G. N. Knoppers), *JHS* 5 (2005), Article 18.

Finkelstein, I. (with N. A. Silberman). *The Bible Unearthed.* New York: Free Press, 2001.

Fischer, G. "Jeremia 52 – ein Schlüssel zum Jeremiabuch," *Bib* 79 (1998): 333–358.

Fishbane, M. "Jeremiah iv 23–26 and Job iii 3–13: A Recovered Use of the Creation Pattern," *VT* 21 (1971): 151–167.

"Accusations of Adultery: A Study of Law and Scribal Practice in Numbers 5:11–31," *HUCA* 45 (1974): 25–45.

"Biblical Colophons, Textual Criticism and Legal Analogies," *CBQ* 42 (1980): 438–449.

Biblical Interpretation in Ancient Israel. Oxford: Oxford University Press, 1985.

(ed., with E. Tov). *Sha'arei Talmon.* Winona Lake, IN: Eisenbrauns, 1992.

"*Min haššāmayim dibbartî*: 'I Spoke from Heaven' (Exod 20:22)," in Cohen et al. (2004): 33–38.

Biblical Myth and Rabbinic Mythmaking. New York/Oxford: Oxford University Press, 2004.

Fox, M. V. (ed., with V. A. Hurowitz, A. Hurtivz, M. L. Klein, B. J. Schwartz, and N. Shupak). *Texts, Temples and Traditions: A Tribute to Menachem Haran.* Winona Lake, IN: Eisenbrauns 1996.

Freedman, D. N. *The Unity of the Hebrew Bible.* Ann Arbor: University of Michigan Press, 1991.

Divine Commitment and Human Obligation. Grand Rapids, MI: Eerdmans, 1997.

(with B. Kelly). "Who Redacted the Primary History?" in *Sefer Moshe: The Moshe Weinfeld Jubilee Volume* (ed. C. Cohen et al.). Winona Lake, IN: Eisenbrauns, 2004): 43–45.

Fretheim, T. E. "Word of God," *ABD* 6, 962.

Fried, L. S. "The High Places (Bamôt) and the Reforms of Hezekiah and Josiah: An Archaeological Investigation," *JAOS* 122 (2002): 437–465.

Friedman, R. E. *The Exile and Biblical Narrative. HSM,* 22. Chico, CA: Scholars Press, 1981.

"From Egypt to Egypt: Dtr1 and Dtr2," in Halpern and Levenson (1981): 167–192.
"The Deuteronomistic School," in Beck et al. (1995): 70–80.
Frolov, S. "The Prophecy of Jeremiah in Esr 1,1," *ZAW* 116 (2004): 595–601.
Funk, R. (ed.). *Apocalypticism.* JTC 6. New York: Herder & Herder, 1969.
Geoghegan, J. C. "'Until This Day' and the Pre-Exilic Redaction of the Deuteronomistic History," *JBL* 122 (2003): 201–227.
"Additional Evidence for a Deuteronomistic Redaction of the 'Tetrateuch'," *CBQ* 67 (2005): 405–421.
The Time, Place, and Purpose of the Deuteronomistic History: The Evidence of "Until This Day." BJS 347. Providence, RI: Brown University, 2006.
Gevaryahu, H. M. I. "Baruch ben Neriah the Scribe" [Heb.], in Avigad (1971): 198–243.
"Biblical Colophons: A Source for the 'Biography' of Authors, Texts and Books," *Congress Volume, 1974.* VTSup 28. Leiden, Brill, 1975: 42–59.
Giesebrecht, F. *Das Buch Jeremia.* Göttingen: Handkommentar zum AT, 1907.
Ginseberg, H. L. *The Israelian Heritage of Judaism.* New York: JTS, 1982.
Glatt-Gilad, D. A. "The Personal Names in Jeremiah as a Source for the History of the Period," *Hebrew Studies* 41 (2000): 31–45.
Gosse, B. "Trois Etages de la Redaction du Livre de Jeremie: La Venue du Malheur Contre ce Lieu (Jerusalem) puis Contre tout Chair (Judah et Les Nations) et Enfin de Noveau Contre ce Lieu, mais Identifie Cette Fois en Babylon," *ZAW* 111 (1999): 508–529.
"La Nouvelle Alliance de Jérémie 31, 31–34: Du Livre d'Ezéchiel au Livre de Jérémie," *ZAW* 116 (2004): 568–580.
Grabbe, L. L. *Priests, Prophets, Diviners, Sages: A Socio-Historical Study of Religious Specialists in Ancient Israel.* Valley Forge, PA: Trinity Press, 1995.
(ed.). *Leading Captivity Captive: "The Exile" as History and Ideology.* JSOTsup 278. Sheffield, UK: Sheffield Academic Press, 1998.
(ed.). *Good Kings and Bad Kings.* London: T. & T. Clark, 2005.
Greenberg, M. *Ezekiel 1–20.* AB. Garden City, NY: Doubleday, 1983.
Grossberg, D. "Pivotal Polysemy in Jeremiah xxv 10–11 a," *VT* 36 (1986): 481–485.
Haak, R. D. "'Cush' in Zephaniah," in Holloway and Handy (1995): 238–251.
Hahn, S. W. (with J. S. Bergsma). "What Laws Were 'Not Good'? A Canonical Approach to the Theological Problem of Ezekiel 20:25–26," *JBL* 123 (2004): 201–218.
Hallo, W. W. "The Death of Kings: Traditional Historiography in Contextual Perspective," in Cogan and Eph'al (1991): 148–165.

"Midrash as Mnemonic: A New Approach to Rabbinic Exegesis," *HUCA* 74 (2003): 157–173.

Halpern, B. "Levitic Participation in the Reform Cult of Jeroboam I," *JBL* 95 (1976): 31–42.

(ed., with J. D. Levenson). *Traditions in Transformation: Turning Points in Biblical Faith.* Winona Lake, IN: Eisenbrauns, 1981.

"The Uneasy Compromise: Israel Between League and Monarchy," in Halpern and Levenson (1981): 59–96.

"Brisker Pipes Than Poetry: The Development of Israelite Monotheism," in Neusner et al. (1987): 77–115.

(ed., with D. Hobson). *Law and Ideology in Monarchic Israel.* JSOTSup 124. Sheffield, UK: Sheffield Academic Press, 1991.

"Jerusalem and the Lineages in the Seventh Century BCE: Kinship and the Rise of Individual Moral Liability," in Halpern and Hobson (1991): 11–107.

(with D. Vanderhooft). "The Editions of Kings in the 7th–6th Centuries BCE," *HUCA* 62 (1991): 179–244.

"The New Names in Isaiah 62:4: Jeremiah's Reception in the Restoration and the Politics of 'Third Isaiah,'" *JBL* 117 (1998): 623–643.

"Why Manasseh Is Blamed for the Babylonian Exile: The Evolution of a Biblical Tradition," *VT* 48 (1998): 473–513.

David's Secret Demons: Messiah, Murderer, Traitor, King. Grand Rapids, MI: Eerdmans, 2001.

"Late Israelite Astronomies and the Early Greeks," in Dever and Gitin (2003): 323–352.

Hanson, P. D. "Israelite Religion in the Early Post-Exilic Period," in Miller et al. (1987): 485–508.

"1 Chronicles 15–16 and the Chronicler's View on the Levites," in Fishbane and Tov (1992): 69–77.

Haran, M. "The Law-Code of Ezekiel xl-xlviii and Its Relation to the Priestly School," *HUCA* 50 (1979): 45–71.

"Behind the Scenes of History: Determining the Date of the Priestly Source," *JBL* 100 (1981): 321–333.

"The Books of the Chronicles 'of the Kings of Judah' and 'of the Kings of Israel': What Sort of Books Were They?" *VT* 49 (1999): 156–164.

"The Place of the Prophecies Against the Nations in the Book of Jeremiah," *Emanuel: Studies in Hebrew Bible, Septuagint, and Dead Sea Scrolls in*

Honor of Emanuel Tov (ed. S. M. Paul et al. Leiden/Boston: Brill, 2003): 694–706.

Hayes, J. H. (ed., with J. M. Miller). *Israelite and Judaen History*. Philadelphia: Westminster Press, 1977.

Helmer, C. (ed., with C. Landmesser). *One Scripture or Many? Canon from Biblical, Theological and Philosophical Perspectives*. New York: Oxford University Press, 2004.

Hepner, G. "The Begettings of Terah and the Structure of Genesis and the Tetrateuch: A Zadokite Polemic," *RB* 111 (2004): 31–60.

Hess, R. J. "The Divine Name in Late Bronze Age Sources?" *UF* 23 (1991): 180–182.

Hicks, R. L. "*Delet* and *M^{e}gillāh*: A Fresh Approach to Jeremiah xxxvi," *VT* 33 (1983): 46–66.

Hill, J. "Review of J. Edward Wright, *Baruch ben Neriah: From Biblical Scribe to Apocalyptic Seer*," *Review of Biblical Literature* (2004) [http://www.bookreviews.org].

Hoffman, Y. "A North Israelite Typological Myth and a Judaean Historical Tradition: The Exodus in Hosea and Amos," *VT* 39 (1989): 169–182.

"Aetiology, Redaction and Historicity in Jeremiah xxxvi," *VT* 46 (1996): 179–189.

"History and Ideology: The Case of Jeremiah 44," *JANES* 28 (2000): 43–51.

Holladay, W. L. "A Fresh Look at 'Source B' and 'Source C' Sources in Jeremiah," in Perdue and Kovacs (1984): 213–228.

Jeremiah 1: A Commentary on the Book of the Prophet Jeremiah Chapters 1–25 Hermeneia; Philadelphia: Fortress Press, 1986.

Jeremiah 2: A Commentary on the Book of the Prophet Jeremiah Chapters 26–52. Hermeneia; Philadelphia: Fortress Press, 1989.

"Had Ezekiel Known Jeremiah Personally?" *CBQ* 63 (2001): 31–34.

"Elusive Deuteronomists, Jeremiah, and Proto-Deuteronomy," *CBQ* 66 (2004): 55–77.

Holloway, S. W. (ed., with L. K. Handy). *The Pitcher Is Broken*. Fs. G. W. Ahlström, JSOTsup 190. Sheffield, UK: Sheffield Academic Press, 1995.

Holt, E. K. "Jeremiah's Temple Sermon and the Deuteronomists: An Investigation of the Redactional Relationship Between Jeremiah 7 and 26," *JSOT* 36 (1986): 73–87.

Hossfelt, F. L. (with I. Meyer). "Der Prophet vor dem Tribunal: Auslegungsversuch von Jer. 26," *ZAW* 86 (1974): 48–49.

Hurvitz, A. "Once Again: The Linguistic Profile of the Priestly Material in the Pentateuch and Its Historical Age: A Response to J. Blenkinsopp," *ZAW* 112 (2000): 180–191.

Isbell, C. D. "II Kings 22:3–23:24 and Jeremiah 36: A Stylistic Comparison," *JSOT* 8 (1978): 33–45.

Jaffee, M. S. *Torah in the Mouth: Writing and Oral Tradition in Palestinian Judaism 200 BCE–400 CE*. New York/Oxford: Oxford University Press, 2001.

Janzen, G. *Studies in the Text of Jeremiah. HSM*, 6. Cambridge, MA: Harvard University Press, 1973.

Kallai, Z. "Biblical Historiography and Literary History: A Programmatic Survey," *VT* 49 (1999): 338–350.

Keiser, T. A. "The Song of Moses: A Basis for Isaiah's Prophecies," *VT* 55 (2005): 486–500.

King, Phillip J. (with Lawrence E. Stager). *Life in Biblical Israel*. Louisville, KY/London: Westminster/John Knox Press, 2001.

Knohl, I. *The Sanctuary of Silence*. Philadelphia: Fortress Press, 1995.

The Divine Symphony: The Bible's Many Voices. Philadelphia: JPS, 2003.

Knoppers, G. *Two Nations Under God: The Deuteronomistic History of Solomon and the Dual Monarchies*, Vols. 1 and 2. *HSM*, 52/53. Atlanta: Scholars Press, 1993/1994.

"Aaron's Calf and Jeroboam's Calves," in Beck et al. (1995): 92–104.

"Hierodules, Priests or Janitors? The Levites in Chronicles and the History of the Israelite Priesthood," *JBL* 118 (1999): 49–72.

"Rethinking the Relationship between Deuteronomy and the Deuteronomistic History: The Case of Kings," *CBQ* 63 (2001): 393–415.

I Chronicles 1–9. AB, 12. New York: Doubleday, 2003.

Kraft, R. (ed.). *1972 Proceedings. IOSCS Pseudepigrapha*. Septuagint and Cognate Studies 2. SBL, 1972.

Kratz, R. G. *The Composition of the Narrative Books of the Old Testament*. London: T. & T. Clark, 2005.

Krüger, T. *Geschichtskonzepte im Ezechielbuch*. BZAW 180. Berlin: de Gruyter, 1989.

Launderville, D. "Ezekiel's Throne-Chariot Vision: Spritualizing the Model of Divine Royal Rule," *CBQ* 66 (2004): 361–377.

Leichty, E. "The Colophon," *Studies Presented to A. Leo Oppenheim*. Chicago: Oriental Institute of the University of Chicago, 1964: 147–154.

Leithart, P. J. "Attendants of YHWH's House: Priesthood in the Old Testament," *JSOT* 85 (1999): 3–24.

Lemaire, A. (ed.). *Congress Volume 2004*. VTsup 109. Leiden: Brill, 2006.

Lemche, N. P. "The Manumission of Slaves – The Fallow Year – The Sabbatical Year – The Jobel Year," *VT* 26 (1976): 38–59.

Lemke, W. E. "The Near and Distant God: A Study of Jer. 23:23–24 in Its Biblical Theological Context," *JBL* 100 (1981): 541–555.

Leuchter, M. "Something Old, Something Older: Reconsidering 1 Sam. 2:27–36," *JHS* 4 (2003), Article 6.

"Jeremiah's 70-Year Prophecy and the ששך/לב קמי *Atbash* Codes," *Bib* 85 (2004): 503–522.

"The Literary Strata and Narrative Sources of Psalm xcix," *VT* 55 (2005): 20–38.

"The Temple Sermon and the Term מקום in the Jeremianic Corpus," *JSOT* 30.1 (2005): 93–109.

"'The Levite in Your Gates': The Deuteronomic Redefinition of Levitical Authority," *JBL*, forthcoming.

"Jeroboam the Ephratite," *JBL* 125 (2006): 51–72.

Josiah's Reform and Jeremiah's Scroll: Historical Calamity and Prophetic Response. Sheffield, UK: Sheffield Phoenix Press, 2006.

"Tyre's 70 Years in Isaiah 23, 15–18," *Bib* 87 (2006): 412–417.

"'The Prophets' and 'The Levites' in Josiah's Covenant Ceremony" (presented at the Chronicles/Ezra–Nehemiah section of the 2007 annual meeting of the Society of Biblical Literature, San Diego, CA).

"Why Is the Song of Moses in the Book of Deuteronomy?" *VT* (forthcoming).

"The Reference to Shiloh in Psalm 78," *HUCA* (forthcoming).

"Now There Was a (Certain) Man: Compositional Chronology in Judges–Samuel," *CBQ* (forthcoming).

"Samuel, Saul, and the Deuteronomistic Categories of History," *From Babel to Babylon.* Fs. for Brian Peckham, ed. J. Rilett Wood et al., New York/London: T. & T. Clark, 2006, 101–110.

Levenson, J. D. "Who Inserted the Book of the Torah in the Deuteronomistic History?" *HTR* 68 (1975): 301–333.

Theology of the Program of Restoration in Ezekiel 40–48. HSM 10: Missoula, MT: Scholars Press, 1976).

"On the Promise to the Rechabites," *CBQ* 38 (1976): 508–514.

"The Last Four Verses in Kings," *JBL* 103 (1984): 353–361.

Levin, Y. "Nimrod the Mighty, King of Kish, King of Sumer and Akkad," *VT* 52 (2002): 350–366.

"From Lists to History: Chronological Aspects of the Chronicler's Genealogies," *JBL* 123 (2004): 601–636.

Levine, B. A. "The Epilogue to the Holiness Code: A Priestly Statement on the Destiny of Israel," in Neusner et al. (1987): 9–34.

Levine, L. I. "The Nature and Origin of the Palestinian Synagogue Reconsidered," *JBL* 115 (1996): 425–448.

The Ancient Synagogue: The First Thousand Years. New Haven, CT/London: Yale University Press, 2000.

Levinson, B. M. "Recovering the Lost Original Meaning of ולא תכסע עליו (Deuteronomy 13:9)," *JBL* 115 (1996): 601–620.

Deuteronomy and the Hermeneutics of Legal Innovation. New York/Oxford: Oxford University Press, 1997.

"The Hermeneutics of Tradition in Deuteronomy: A Response to J. G. McGonville," *JBL* 119 (2000): 269–286.

"The Reconceptualization of Kingship in Deuteronomy and the Deuteronomistic History's Transformation of Torah," *VT* 51 (2001): 511–534.

"Textual Criticism, Assyriology, and the History of Interpretation: Deuteronomy 13:7a as a Test Care in Method," *JBL* 120 (2001): 211–243.

"The Birth of the Lemma: The Restrictive Re-Interpretation of the Covenant Code's Manumission Law in the Holiness Code (Leviticus 25:44–46)," *JBL* 124 (2005): 617–639.

"The Manumission of Hermeneutics: The Slave Laws of the Pentateuch as Challenge to Contemporary Pentateuchal Theory," in Lemaire (2006): 281–324.

Levitt Kohn, R. "A Prophet Like Moses? Rethinking Ezekiel's Relationship to the Torah," *ZAW* 114 (2002): 236–254.

Lindenberger, J. M. (ed.). *Ancient Aramaic and Hebrew Letters* (2nd ed.). Atlanta: SBL, 2003.

Linville, J. R. "Rethinking the 'Exilic' Book of Kings," *JSOT* 75 (1997): 21–42.

Lipinski, E. "Royal and State Scribes in Ancient Jerusalem," *Congress Volume 1986.* VTSup. 40. Leiden: Brill, 1988: 157–164.

Lipschits, O. (ed., with J. Blenkinsopp). *Judah and the Judeans in the Babylonian Period.* Winona Lake, IN: Eisenbrauns, 2003.

"Demographic Changes in Judah Between the Seventh and Fifth Centuries B.C.E.," in Lipschits and Blenkinsopp (2003): 323–376.

The Fall and Rise of Jerusalem. Winona Lake, IN: Eisenbrauns, 2005.

(ed., with M. Oeming). *Judah and the Judeans in the Persia Period.* Winona Lake, IN: Eisenbrauns, 2006.

Lohfink, N. "Die Gattung der 'Historischen Kurzgeschichte' in den letzten Jahren von Juda und in der Zeit des Babylonischen Exils," *ZAW* 90 (1978): 319–347.

(ed.). *Das Deuteronomium: Entstehung, Gestalt und Botschaft.* BETL. Leuven, Brussels: Leuven University Press, 1985.

"The Cult Reform of Josiah of Judah: 2 Kings 22–23 as a Source for the History of Israelite Religion," in Miller et al. (1987): 459–479.

Lowery, R. H. *The Reforming Kings: Cults and Society in First Temple Judah.* JSOT-sup, 120. Sheffield, UK: Sheffield Academic Press, 1991.

Lundbom, J. R. "Baruch, Seraiah, and Expanded Colophons in the Book of Jeremiah," *JSOT* 36 (1986): 89–114.

"The Inclusio and Other Framing Devices in Deuteronomy i–xxviii," *VT* 46 (1996): 296–215.

Jeremiah: A Study in Ancient Hebrew Rhetoric. Winona Lake, IN: Eisenbrauns, 1997 (reprinted from the 1975 edition).

Jeremiah 1–20. AB, 21 A. Garden City, NY: Doubleday, 1999.

Jeremiah 21–36. AB, 21 B. Garden City, NY: Doubleday, 2004.

Jeremiah 37–52. AB, 21 C. Garden City, NY: Doubleday, 2004.

"Haplography in the Hebrew Vorlage of LXX Jeremiah," *Hebrew Studies* 46 (2005): 301–320.

Machinist, P. "The Rab Šāqēh at the Wall of Jerusalem: Israelite Identity in the Face of the Assyrian 'Other,'" *Hebrew Studies* 41 (2000): 151–168.

"Mesopotamian Imperialism and Israelite Religion: A Case Study from the Second Isaiah," in Dever and Gitin (2003): 237–258.

Mazar, B. "The Sanctuary of Arad and the Family of Hobab the Kenite," *JNES* 24 (1965): 297–303.

McKane, W. "The Construction of Jeremiah Chapter xxi," *VT* 32 (1982): 59–73.

A Critical and Exegetical Commentary on Jeremiah, Vols. 1 and 2. ICC: Edinburgh: T. & T. Clark, 1986/1996.

McKenzie, S. L. "The Trouble with Kingship," in de Pury (2000): 286–314.

Merill, A. L. (ed., with T. W. Overholt). *Scripture in History and Theology: Essays in Honor of J. Coert Rylaarsdam.* Pittsburgh: Pickwick Press, 1977.

Middlemas, J. *The Troubles of Templeless Judah.* Oxford: Oxford University Press, 2005.

Milgrom, J. *Leviticus 1–16.* AB 3, Garden City, NY: Doubleday, 1991.

Millard, A. R. (ed., with J. K. Hoffmeier and D. W. Baker). *Faith, Tradition, History: Old Testament Historiography in Its Near Eastern Context.* Winona Lake, IN: Eisenbrauns, 1994.

Miller, P. (ed., with P. D. Hanson and S. D. McBride). *Ancient Israelite Religion: Essays in Honor of Frank Moore Cross.* Philadelphia: Fortress Press, 1987.

Mitchell, C. "The Ironic Death of Josiah in 2 Chronicles," *CBQ* 68 (2006): 421–435.

Mowinckel, S. *Zur Komposition des Buches Jeremia.* Kristiania [Oslo], Norway: Jacob Dybwad, 1914.

Muilenberg, J. "Baruch the Scribe," in Durham and Porter (1983): 215–238.

Na'aman, N. "'The House-of-No-Shade Shall Take Away Its Tax from You' (Micah i 11)," *VT* 45 (1995): 516–527.

"The Temple Library of Jerusalem and the Composition of the Book of Kings," in Lemaire (2006): 129–152.

Najman, H. "The Symbolic Significance of Writing in Ancient Judaism," in Najman and Newman (2003): 139–173.

Nelson, R. D. *Deuteronomy.* OTL. Louisville, KY/London: Westminster/John Knox, 2002.

"The Double Redaction of the Deuteronomistic History: The Case Is Still Compelling," *JSOT* 29 (2005): 319–337.

Neusner, J. (ed., with E. Frerichs and B. Levine). *Judaic Perspectives on Ancient Israel.* Philadelphia: Fortress Press, 1987.

Nicholson, E. W. *Preaching to the Exiles: A Study of the Prose Tradition in the Book of Jeremiah.* Oxford: Basil Blackwell/New York: Schocken, 1970.

Niditch, S. *Oral World and Written Word: Ancient Israelite Literature.* Louisville, KY: Westminster/John Knox Press, 1996.

Nigosian, S. A. "Linguistic Patterns of Deuteronomy 32," *Bib* 78 (1997): 206–224.

Novak, D. *The Jewish Social Contract: An Essay in Political Theology.* Princeton, NJ: Princeton University Press, 2000.

O'Connor, K. M. "'Do Not Trim a Word': The Contribution of Chapter 26 to the Book of Jeremiah," *CBQ* 51 (1989): 617–630.

Oded, B. "Judah and the Exile," in Hayes and Miller (1977): 435–488.

Olyan, S. "Zadok's Origins and the Tribal Politics of David," *JBL* 101 (1982): 177–193.

(ed., with R. C. Culley). *A Wise and Discerning Mind: Essays in Honor of Burke O. Long. BJS*, 325. Providence, RI: Brown University, 2000.

"'We Are Utterly Cut Off': Some Possible Nuances of נגזרנו לנו in Ezekiel 37:11," *CBQ* 65 (2003): 43–51.

"The Search for the Elusive Self in the Texts of the Hebrew Bible," in Brakke (2005): 40–50.

"Some Neglected Aspects of Israelite Interment Ideology," *JBL* 124 (2005): 601–616.

Overholt, T. "Jeremiah," *The HarperCollins Bible Commentary*. New York: Harper Collins, 2000: 538–576.

Pakkala, J. "Zedekiah's Fate and the Dynastic Succession," *JBL* 125 (2006): 443–452.

Pardee, D. *Handbook of Ancient Hebrew Letters*. Chico, CA: Scholars Press, 1982.

Parke-Taylor, G. *The Formation of the Book of Jeremiah: Doublets and Recurring Phrases*. SBLM, 51. Atlanta: SBL, 2000.

Parker, S. B. "Did the Authors of the Book of Kings Make Use of Royal Inscriptions?" *VT* 50 (2000): 357–378.

Pečírková, J. "The Administrative Methods of Assyrian Imperialism," *Archív Orientální* 55 (1987): 162–175.

Peckham, J. B. *History and Prophecy*. New York: Doubleday, 1993.

"Writing and Editing," in Beck et al. (1995): 364–383.

Perdue, L. G. (ed., with B. W. Kovacs). *A Prophet to the Nations: Essays in Jeremiah Studies*. Winona Lake, IN: Eisenbrauns, 1984.

Person, R. F. "The Ancient Israelite Scribe as Performer," *JBL* 117 (1998): 601–609.

The Deuteronomistic School: History, Social Setting, and Literature. Atlanta: SBL, 2002.

Petersen, D. L. *Late Israelite Prophecy: Studies in Deutero-Prophetic Literature and in Chronicles*. SBLM, 23. Missoula, MT: Scholars Press, 1977.

"Genesis and Family Values," *JBL* 124 (2005): 5–23.

Pohlmann, K. F. *Studien zum Jeremiabuches*. Göttingen: Vandenhoeck & Ruprecht, 1978.

Polak, F. "The Oral and the Written: Syntax, Stylistics and the Development of Biblical Prose Narrative," *JANES* 26 (1998): 59–105.

"'Now There Was One Man:' The Character of the Book of Samuel and Its Place in Ancient Israelite Historiography," *Shnaton – An Annual for Biblical and Ancient Near Eastern Studies* 12 (2000): 13–47.

"Style Is More Than the Person: Sociolinguistics, Literary Culture, and the Distinction between Written and Oral Narrative," in Young (2003): 38–103.

"Sociolinguistics and the Judean Speech Community in the Achaemenid Empire," in Lipschits and Oeming (2006): 598–628.

Pomykala, K. *The Davidic Dynasty Tradition in Early Judaism: Its History and Significance for Messianism*. SBLD. Atlanta: Scholars Press, 1995.

Potter, H. D. "The New Covenant in Jeremiah xxxi 31–34," *VT* 33 (1983): 347–357.

Rendsburg, G. A. "The Northern Origins of Nehemiah 9," *Bib* 72 (1991): 348–366.

Reventlow, H. G. *Liturgie und prophetisches Ich bei Jeremia.* Guterslöh, Germany: Gerd Mohn, 1963.

"Gattung und Uberlieferung in der 'Tempelrede Jeremias,'" *ZAW* 81 (1969): 315–352.

Richter, S. L. "The Place of the Name in Deuteronomy," *VT* (forthcoming).

Rietzschel, C. *Das Problem der Urrolle: Ein Beitrag zür Redaktionsgeschichte des Jeremiahbuches.* Guterslöh, Germany: Guterslöher [Mohn], 1966.

Roberts, E. M. *Ancient Israelite Religions.* (Fs. F. M. Cross, ed. P. D. Miller et al.). Philadelphia: Fortress Press, 1987.

Robertson, D. A. *Linguistic Evidence in Dating Early Hebrew Poetry.* SBLD, 3, Missoula, MT: SBL, 1972.

Rofé, A. "The Arrangement of the Book of Jeremiah," *ZAW* 101 (1989): 398–407.

"The Organization of the Judiciary in Deuteronomy," in Daviau (2001): 92–112.

Rom-Shiloni, D. "The Prophecy for 'Everlasting Covenant' (Jeremiah xxxii 36–41): An Exilic Addition or a Deuteronomistic Redaction?" *VT* 53 (2003): 201–223.

"Facing Destruction and Exile: Inner-Biblical Exegesis in Jeremiah and Ezekiel," *ZAW* 117 (2005): 189–205.

Römer, T. C. "Transformations in Deuteronomistic and Biblical Historiography: On 'Book Finding' and Other Literary Strategies," *ZAW* 109 (1997): 1–11.

"How Did Jeremiah Become a Convert to Deuteronomistic Ideology?" in Schearing and McKenzie (1999): 189–199.

Römer, T. C. (with M. Z. Brettler). "Deuteronomy 34 and the Case for a Persian Hexateucle," *JBL* 119 2000): 401–419.

Roncance, M. *Jeremiah, Zedekiah and the Fall of Jerusalem.* New York/London: T. & T. Clark, 2005.

Rooke, D. *Zadok's Heirs.* Oxford: Oxford University Press, 2000.

Rosen, B. "Early Israelite Cultic Centres in the Hill Country," *VT* 38 (1988): 115–117.

Rudman, D. "Midrash in the Isaiah Apocalypse," *ZAW* 112 (2000): 404–408.

"Is the Rabshakeh Also among the Prophets? A Rhetorical Study of 2 Kings xviii 17–35," *VT* 50 (2000): 100–110.

"The Use of Water Imagery in Descriptions of Sheol," *ZAW* 113 (2001): 240–244.

Sacchi, P. *The History of the Second Temple Period.* JSOTsup, 285. Sheffield, UK: Sheffield Academic Press, 2000.

Sanders, P. *The Provenance of Deuteronomy 32.* Boston/Leiden: Brill, 1996.

Sarna, N. "Psalm 92: A Song for the Sabbath Day," *JBL* 81 (1962): 155–168.

Exodus: The JPS Commentary. New York: Jewish Publication Society, 1989.
"Zedekiah's Emancipation of Slaves and the Sabbatical Year," *Studies in Biblical Interpretation*. Philadelphia: JPS, 2000 (reprinted from the original 1973 article), 295–304.

Schaper, J. "Exilic and Post-Exilic Prophecy and the Orality/Literary Problem," *VT* 55 (2005): 324–342.

Schearing, L. S. (with S. L. McKenzie). *Those Elusive Deuteronomists: The Phenomenon of Pan-Deuteronomism* (JSOT sup, 268; Sheffield, UK: Sheffield Academic Press, 1999).

Schniedewind, W. M. *How the Bible Became a Book: The Textualization of Ancient Israel*. Cambridge: Cambridge University Press, 2004.

Seitz, C. R. "The Crisis of Interpretation Over the Meaning and Purpose of the Exile," *VT* 35 (1985): 78–97.
"The Prophet Moses and the Canonical Shape of Jeremiah," *ZAW* 101 (1989): 3–27.
Theology in Conflict (*BZAW*, 176; Berlin: De Gruyter, 1989).

Sharon, D. (ed., with K. Kravitz). *Bringing the Hidden to Light: The Process of Interpretation. Studies in Honor of Stephen A. Geller*. New York: JTS and Winona Lake, IN: Eisenbrauns, forthcoming.

Sharp, C. J. "Take Another Scroll and Write: A Study of the LXX and the MT of Jeremiah's Oracles Against Egypt and Babylon," *VT* 47 (1997): 487–516.
Prophecy and Ideology in Jeremiah: Struggles for Authority in the Deutero-Jeremianic Prose. New York/London: T. & T. Clark, 2003.

Smith, M. S. "The Levitical Compilation of the Psalter," *ZAW* 103 (1991): 258–263.
The Early History of God: YHWH and the Other Deities in Ancient Israel (2nd ed.). Grand Rapids, MI/Cambridge, MA: Eerdmans, 2002.

Sommer, B. D. "Did Prophecy Cease? Evaluating a Re-Evaluation," *JBL* 115 (1996): 31–47.
A Prophet Reads Scripture: Allusion in Isaiah 40–66. Stanford, CA: Stanford University Press, 1998.
"New Light on the Composition of Jeremiah," *CBQ* 61 (1999): 646–666.
"Unity and Plurality in Jewish Canons: The Case of the Oral and Written Torahs," in Helmer and Landmesser (2004): 108–150.
"Prophecy as Translation: Ancient Israelite Conceptions of the Human Factor in Prophecy," in Sharon and Kravitz (forthcoming).

Sperling, S. D. "Miriam, Aaron and Moses: Sibling Rivalry," *HUCA* 70 (1999): 39–55.

Stackert, J. "Why Does Deuteronomy Legislate Cities of Refuge? Asylum in the Covenant Collection (Exodus 21:12–14) and Deuteronomy (19:1–13)," *JBL* 125 (2006): 23–49.

Stager, L. E. (with P. J. King). *Life in Bibical Israel.* Louisville, KY/London: Westminster/John Knox, 2001.

Steiner, R. C. "The Two Sons of Neriah and the Two Editions of Jeremiah in Light of the Two *Atbash* Code-Words for Babylon," *VT* 46 (1996): 74–84.

Stern, M. "The Period of the Second Temple," in *A History of the Jewish People* (ed. H. H. Ben-Sasson). Cambridge, MA: Harvard University Press, 1976.

Stipp, H. J. "Zedekiah in the Book of Jeremiah: On the Formation of a Biblical Character," *CBQ* 58 (1996): 627–648.

Strack H. L. (with G. Stemberger). *Introduction to the Talmud and Midrash* (trans. M. Bockmuel). Minneapolis: Fortress Press, 1996.

Stulman, L. "Encroachment in Deuteronomy: An Analysis of the Social World of the D Code," *JBL* 109 (1990): 613–632.

Sweeney, M. A. "The Critique of Solomon in the Josianic Edition of the Deuteronomistic History," *JBL* 114 (1995): 607–622.

"Ezekiel: Zadokite Priest and Visionary Prophet of the Exile," *SBL 2000 Seminar Papers.* Atlanta: SBL, 2000: 728–751.

King Josiah of Judah: The Lost Messiah of Israel. New York: Oxford University Press, 2001.

Zephaniah. Hermeneia, Minneapolis: Fortress Press, 2003.

"Review of Martti Nissinen and C. L. Seow and Robert K. Ritner, *Prophets and Prophecy in the Ancient Near East,*" *Review of Biblical Literature* (2005) (www.bookreviews.org).

Swetnam, J. "Why Was Jeremiah's New Covenant New?" VT Sup, 26. Leiden: Brill, 1974: 111–115.

Tadmor, H. "The Sin of Sargon," *EI* 5 (1958): 93, 150–163.

"The Appointed Time Has Not Yet Come: The Historical Background of Haggai 1:2," in Chazan et al. (1999): 401–408.

Talshir, Z. "The Three Deaths of Josiah and the Strata of Biblical Historiography (2 Kings xxiii 29–30; 2 Chronicles xxxv 20–5; 1 Esdras i 23–31)," *VT* 46 (1996): 213–236.

"Several Canon-Related Concepts Originating in Chronicles," *ZAW* 113 (2001): 386–403.

Thiel, W. *Die deuteronomistische Redaktion von Jeremia 1–25.* Neukirchen-Vluyn, Germany: Neukirchener Verlag, 1973.

Die deuteronomistische Redaktion von Jeremia 26–45. Neukirchen-Vluyn, Germany: Neukirchener Verlag, 1981.

Thiessen, M. "The Form and Function of the Song of Moses (Deuteronomy 32:1–43)," *JBL* 123 (2004): 401–424.

Tiemeyer, L. S. "The Watchman Metaphor in Isaiah lvi–lxvi," *VT* 55 (2005): 378–400.

Tigay, J. (ed.). *Empirical Models for Biblical Criticism.* Philadelphia: University of Pennsylvania Press, 1985.

Deuteronomy: The JPS Torah Commentary. New York: Jewish Publication Society, 1989.

Tournay, R. J. *Seeing and Hearing God in the Psalms.* JSOTsup, 118. Sheffield, UK: Sheffield Academic Press, 1991.

Tov, E. "Some Aspects of the Textual and Literary History of the Book of Jeremiah," *Le Livre de Jérémie* (ed. P. M. Bogaert). Leuven, Brussels: Leuven University Press, 1981: 145–167.

"The Literary History of the Book of Jeremiah in the Light of Its Textual History," in Tigay (1985): 211–237.

Tropper, A. *Wisdom, Politics and Historiography: Tractate Avot in the Context of the Graeco–Roman Near East.* Oxford/New York: Oxford University Press, 2004.

"Yohanan ben Zakkai, *Amicus Caesaris**: A Jewish Hero in Rabbinic Eyes," *JSIJ* 4 (2005): 133–149.

Vanderkam, J. C. *An Introduction to Early Judaism.* Grand Rapids, MI: Eerdmans, 2001.

Van Selms, A. "Telescoped Discussion as a Literary Device in the Book of Jeremiah," *VT* 26 (1976): 99–112.

Veijola, T. "The Deuteronomistic Roots of Judaism," in Cohen et al. (2004): 459–478.

Volz, P. *Der prophet Jeremia* (KZAT, 1922).

Wanke, G. *Untersuchungen zur sogenannten Baruchschrift.* BZAW, 122. Berlin: De Gruyter, 1971.

Watts, J. W. "Ritual Legitimacy and Scriptural Authority," *JBL* 124 (2005): 401–417.

Weinberg, J. *The Citizen-Temple Community* (trans. D. L. Smith-Christopher). JSOTSup; 151. Sheffield, UK: Sheffield Academic Press, 1992.

Weinfeld, M. *Deuteronomy and the Deuteronomic School.* Oxford: Clarendon Press, 1972.

"Jeremiah and the Spiritual Metamorphosis of Israel," *ZAW* 88 (1976): 17–56.

"Judge and Officer in Ancient Israel and in the Ancient Near East," *IOS* 7 (1977): 65–88.

"The Emergence of the Deuteronomic Movement: The Historical Antecedents," in Lohfink (1985): 76–98.

"The Tribal League at Sinai," in Miller et al. (1987): 303–314.

Deuteronomy 1–11. AB, 5. New York: Doubleday, 1991.

"Feminine Features in the Imagery of God and Israel: The Sacred Marriage and the Sacred Tree," *VT* 46 (1996): 516–528.

Weingreen, J. *From Bible to Mishna: The Continuity of Tradition*. Manchester, UK: Manchester University Press, 1976.

Weippert, H. *Die Prosareden des Jeremiabuches*. BZAW, 132. Berlin: De Gruyter, 1973.

"Das Wort von neuen Bund in Jeremia xxxi 31–34," *VT* 29 (1979): 336–351.

Weippert, M. "Semitiche Nomaden des zweiten Jahrtausends: über die *š3św* der ägyptischen Quellen," *Bib* 55 (1974): 265–280, 427–433.

White, M. *The Elijah Legends and Jehu's Coup*. BJS, 311. Atlanta: Scholars Press, 1997.

Whitters, M. F. "Jesus in the Footsteps of Jeremiah," *CBQ* 68 (2005): 229–247.

Widengren, G. "What Do We Know About Moses?" in Durham and Porter (1983): 37–45.

Weinberg, J. "The Babylonian Conquest of Judah: Some Additional Remarks to a Scientific Consensus," *ZAW* 118 (2006): 597–610.

Wilcoxen, J. A. "The Political Background of Jeremiah's Temple Sermon," in Merill and Overholt (1977): 151–165.

Williamson, H. G. M. "The Death of Josiah and the Continuing Development of the Deuteronomic History," *VT* 32 (1982): 242–248.

"Isaiah 62:4 and the Problem of Inner-Biblical Allusions," *JBL* 119 (2000): 734–739.

Wilson, R. *Prophecy and Society in Ancient Israel*. Philadelphia: Fortress Press, 1980.

Wright, J. E. *Baruch ben Neriah: From Biblical Scribe to Apocalyptic Seer*. Columbia: University of South Carolina Press, 2003.

Yates, G. E. "Narrative Parallelism and the 'Jehoiakim Frame': A Reading Strategy for Jeremiah 26–45," *JETS* 48 (2005): 263–281.

Young, I. "Israelite Literacy: Interpreting the Evidence," *VT* 48 (1998), 239–253, 408–422.

(ed.). *Biblical Hebrew: Studies in Chronology and Typology*. JSOTsup, 369. London/New York: T. & T. Clark, 2003.

Zimmerli, W. *Ezekiel* 2. Hermeneia, Minneapolis: Fortress Press, 1983.

Author Index

Scriptural and Extra-Biblical Texts Index

Subject Index